...For Dummies™

BESTSELLING
BOOK SERIES

629.222
SCL

P9-CQZ-501

Cheat Sheet

How to Outsmart a Car Dealer

- **Leave your present vehicle down the street.** Walk into the dealership so salespeople won't add its trade-in value to the prices they quote.

- **Wear casual clothing and leave the jewelry at home.** If you look well-off you may be quoted higher prices.

- **Shop during daylight hours.** Floodlights make cars look more exotic and they can hide a lot of damage.

- **Take your time.** If you're in a hurry you may overlook defects, accept higher prices, and sign contracts without reading the fine print.

- **Be indefinite about exactly what you want.** If you show interest in a particular model, the asking price for it will rise.

- **Carry a notebook and take notes.** This really shows that you mean business.

- **Make sure they know you're shopping around.** Bring along sales material from other dealerships and compare features and prices.

- **Openly consult data sheets that show the *invoice* prices of the models and options you want.** You can get this information from the Internet and from car-pricing services.

- **Always bargain *up* from the invoice price, not *down* from the price on the windshield sticker.**

- **Use the inspection and test-drive checklists in this book to check each vehicle out thoroughly.** Dealers will be less prone to try to unload the losers on you.

- **Never negotiate until you've found exactly what you want.** Shop several places first, and then return to deal for your choice.

- **Refuse to talk about trade-ins until you've reached the lowest price.**

- **Always have a used vehicle checked by your mechanic *before* you buy.** If the seller refuses to allow this, head for the door.

- **Be sure the cost of a lease is based on the lowest sales price you've negotiated.** Unscrupulous dealers may base it on the MSRP!

- **Get everything in writing.** Oral promises by dealers are difficult — if not impossible — to enforce.

- **Read the purchase agreement slowly and carefully before you sign it.** If anything isn't clear or doesn't reflect what you agreed to, discuss it until you're satisfied.

- **Check the vehicle again before you sign the final papers and drive away.**

How to Foil Car Thieves and Carjackers

- **Keep an eye out for suspicious vehicles and dangerous situations.** If the car in front of you repeatedly slows down, maintain your distance, change lanes, or drive to a safe place.

- **Choose your routes carefully.** Don't turn down activities in remote locations, just get there by the safest route possible.

- **Don't pick up hitchhikers.** There are safer ways to make friends.

- **Drive with the doors locked and the windows raised.**

- **Drive in the center lane so you can't be forced off the road.**

- **Don't use automated self-service stations at night or in remote or risky areas.**

- **If someone at a mall lot says your brake lights are out or your car's been damaged lock your doors, say thanks through your closed window, and drive to a safe location to check it out.**

- **Keep your car in good shape to avoid breaking down in unsafe places.**

- **Keep your car keys on a separate or easily detachable ring.** Take other keys with you when you leave your car with someone else.

- **Never put your name and address on a key ring or leave anything with your address in your parked car.**

- **Park in well-lit, highly visible, well-populated areas where you can get safely to and from the car.**

- **At night, opt for a busy garage with 24-hour attendants or pay for valet parking.**

- **If possible, choose a "park and lock" garage or a lot that doesn't require you to leave your keys.**

- **Carry a copy of your registration on your person — not in your car — and leave the original at home.**

- **Place valuables out of sight *before* your park.** Lock them in the trunk or hide them under the seat before leaving your previous destination.

- **Take the time to sit and wait for a spot near the entrance to a mall; don't park at the back of the lot.**

- **To foil thieves with tow trucks, turn the wheels to the curb or sharply to one side and set the emergency brake.**

- **Be alert to those around you when walking to or from your car.** Walk confidently, keys in hand. If someone seems suspicious, walk away and return a little later.

- **Don't be a hero.** If you see someone trying to break into your vehicle, do not attempt to stop them. Head for the nearest phone and let the police handle it.

- **Always look under and into the car before you get in to make sure nobody's hiding inside.**

- **If you're accosted outside your car:** Hand over your keys, money, and jewelry immediately. They're worth a lot less than your life.

- **If an armed thief demands you open your door when your car is idling at a red light, the police advise you to hightail it out of there!** Average human reaction time is between .5 and 1.5 seconds and in most cases that's enough time to get away.

- **If you're in danger of being kidnapped, take drastic measures to avoid being forced into the car.** Fight back. If you can't run, then kick, scream, create as big a disturbance as you can.

- **Use a locking steering wheel cover, rather than a hook-type device to prevent thieves from stealing your air bag as well as your car.**

- **Etch your vehicle's VIN on its windshield and rear window, inside the rear bumper, and on the engine and other vital parts.**

Buying a Car For Dummies®

Cheat Sheet

BESTSELLING BOOK SERIES

How to Protect Yourself in an Accident or Breakdown

- **Call the Highway Patrol on your cellular phone,** if you have one.

- **Do not dial 911 unless someone is seriously injured or you feel you're in real danger.**

- **Draw attention to yourself.** If you have no cellular phone, place a "Call Police" sun visor or sign in your windshield, wedge a white rag or paper between your closed window and the door, and turn on emergency flashers to alert passing motorists.

- **Don't get out to accept help from strangers.** Lock your doors and let others come to you. Roll your window down a crack and gracefully refuse assistance. Ask them to phone the police, the highway patrol, or your auto club.

- **Don't walk along the highway alone.** Use a highway call box only if you can park directly in front of it and hop right back into your car.

- **If there's no phone in sight, and both cars in an accident are driveable, tell the other driver to follow you to the nearest police station.** Stop at a busy corner and ask someone for directions.

- **If there's no police station nearby, head for a well-lit, well-populated service station, hotel, hospital, or mall.** Drive right up to the entrance and locate a telephone or ask a security guard to call the police.

- **If you don't feel you can leave your car safely, park or double-park and lean on the horn.**

- **Get a police report, even if the damage is negligible.** This can deter inflated claims for bogus damage later on.

Used Vehicles to Avoid Buying

- **Police cars, fleet cars, and taxis.** They've probably been run into the ground.

- **Commercial trucks and vans.** The transmission and suspension may have deteriorated from hauling heavy loads.

- **Discontinued models.** You may have trouble getting parts.

- **Vehicles with modified engines.** "Souped-up" engines can strain the transmission and other parts, and operate poorly at low speeds.

- **Very new used vehicles.** Unless it's a previously leased vehicle, it may be a lemon or may have been wrecked.

- **Old vehicles with low mileage.** The odometer may have been set back.

- **Any car that's been in a wreck.** Even though you think it's as good as new, when *you're* ready to sell, other buyers may disagree.

- **Cars that have been recalled for defective parts.** Call the DOT Auto Safety Hotline (800-424-9393) to see whether a vehicle has been recalled.

- **Previously salvaged vehicles.** Insurance companies automatically deduct 40 percent from the value of a salvaged car, even if it's in good condition.

- **Foreign vehicles that don't meet emission and safety standards can be impounded or cause insurance problems.**

- **Possibly stolen vehicles.** It's your loss if the police repossess it. Have the DMV search for the title by owner and Vehicle Identification Number.

Signs That a Vehicle May be Stolen

- **The registration location** is far away from where it's being sold.

- **The Vehicle Identification Number (VIN)** on the title differs from the VIN on the vehicle.

- **The license plate** is brand new or has been mounted with very new looking bolts.

- **The license plate number** doesn't match the one on a recent registration.

- **The name on the title** is that of the dealer rather than a previous owner.

- **The ID numbers on the engine** have been removed.

- **The *original* keys** to the vehicle are missing.

- **The ignition switch** is loose or shows signs of tampering.

- **The price** is far below what it's worth.

If something looks suspicious, call the National Insurance Crime Bureau at 800-TEL-NICB.

The IDG Books Worldwide logo is a registered trademark under exclusive license to IDG Books Worldwide, Inc., from International Data Group, Inc. The ...For Dummies logo is a trademark, and For Dummies and ...For Dummies are registered trademarks of IDG Books Worldwide, Inc. All other trademarks are the property of their respective owners.

® Copyright © 1998 IDG Books Worldwide, Inc. All rights reserved.

Cheat Sheet $2.95 value. Item 5091-8.

For more information about IDG Books, call 1-800-762-2974.

IDG BOOKS WORLDWIDE

...For Dummies®: Bestselling Book Series for Beginners

TM

References for the Rest of Us!™

BESTSELLING BOOK SERIES

Do you find that traditional reference books are overloaded with technical details and advice you'll never use? Do you postpone important life decisions because you just don't want to deal with them? Then our *...For Dummies*® business and general reference book series is for you.

...For Dummies business and general reference books are written for those frustrated and hard-working souls who know they aren't dumb, but find that the myriad of personal and business issues and the accompanying horror stories make them feel helpless. *...For Dummies* books use a lighthearted approach, a down-to-earth style, and even cartoons and humorous icons to dispel fears and build confidence. Lighthearted but not lightweight, these books are perfect survival guides to solve your everyday personal and business problems.

> *"More than a publishing phenomenon, 'Dummies' is a sign of the times."*
>
> — The New York Times

> *"A world of detailed and authoritative information is packed into them..."*
>
> — U.S. News and World Report

> *"...you won't go wrong buying them."*
>
> — Walter Mossberg, Wall Street Journal, on IDG Books' ...For Dummies books

Already, millions of satisfied readers agree. They have made *...For Dummies* the #1 introductory level computer book series and a best-selling business book series. They have written asking for more. So, if you're looking for the best and easiest way to learn about business and other general reference topics, look to *...For Dummies* to give you a helping hand.

IDG BOOKS WORLDWIDE ®

1/99

Praise For Buying a Car For Dummies

"Car buyers often make terribly costly mistakes, but Deanna Sclar has empowered consumers with almost all the information necessary to get a fair deal. The advice is comprehensive, clear, and easy to follow, whether it involves avoiding the pitfalls of complex leasing contracts or dodging a lemon on the used car market. A little time spent with this book will make the next several thousand hours you spend inside your future car a lot more rewarding."

— Ralph Vartabedian, Author of "Your Wheels" in the *Los Angeles Times*

Praise For Auto Repair For Dummies

"If only a few titles are purchased for an automotive collection, this should be one of them."

— *Library Journal*

"Ms. Sclar stresses preventative medicine for the automotive patient . . . with a bedside manner that any physician would envy."

— *The Dallas Morning News*

"An auto repair manual for people who think they can't do it themselves."

— *The Times-Picayune,* New Orleans, LA

"An indispensable manual for any do-it-yourselfer."

— *Auto Advocate*

"Even car-owners who consider do-it-yourself car repair with the same trepidation as they would a self-performed tonsillectomy will find valuable material in this volume . . . valuable to anyone who drives."

— *The News Tribune,* Tacoma, WA

BUYING A CAR
FOR
DUMMIES®

by Deanna Sclar

IDG Books Worldwide, Inc.
An International Data Group Company

Foster City, CA ♦ Chicago, IL ♦ Indianapolis, IN ♦ New York, NY

Buying a Car For Dummies®

Published by
IDG Books Worldwide, Inc.
An International Data Group Company
919 E. Hillsdale Blvd.
Suite 400
Foster City, CA 94404
www.idgbooks.com (IDG Books Worldwide Web site)
www.dummies.com (Dummies Press Web site)

Prospect Public Library
17 Center St.
Prospect, CT 06712

Copyright © 1998 IDG Books Worldwide, Inc. All rights reserved. No part of this book, including interior design, cover design, and icons, may be reproduced or transmitted in any form, by any means (electronic, photocopying, recording, or otherwise) without the prior written permission of the publisher.

Library of Congress Catalog Card No.: 98-85835

ISBN: 0-7645-5091-8

Printed in the United States of America

10 9 8 7 6 5 4 3

1B/RV/RR/ZZ/IN

Distributed in the United States by IDG Books Worldwide, Inc.

Distributed by CDG Books Canada Inc. for Canada; by Transworld Publishers Limited in the United Kingdom; by IDG Norge Books for Norway; by IDG Sweden Books for Sweden; by IDG Books Australia Publishing Corporation Pty. Ltd. for Australia and New Zealand; by TransQuest Publishers Pte Ltd. for Singapore, Malaysia, Thailand, Indonesia, and Hong Kong; by Gotop Information Inc. for Taiwan; by ICG Muse, Inc. for Japan; by Intersoft for South Africa; by Eyrolles for France; by International Thomson Publishing for Germany, Austria and Switzerland; by Distribuidora Cuspide for Argentina; by LR International for Brazil; by Galileo Libros for Chile; by Ediciones ZETA S.C.R. Ltda. for Peru; by WS Computer Publishing Corporation, Inc., for the Philippines; by Contemporanea de Ediciones for Venezuela; by Express Computer Distributors for the Caribbean and West Indies; by Micronesia Media Distributor, Inc. for Micronesia; by Chips Computadoras S.A. de C.V. for Mexico; by Editorial Norma de Panama S.A. for Panama; by American Bookshops for Finland.

For general information on IDG Books Worldwide's books in the U.S., please call our Consumer Customer Service department at 800-762-2974. For reseller information, including discounts and premium sales, please call our Reseller Customer Service department at 800-434-3422.

For information on where to purchase IDG Books Worldwide's books outside the U.S., please contact our International Sales department at 317-596-5530 or fax 317-596-5692.

For consumer information on foreign language translations, please contact our Customer Service department at 1-800-434-3422, fax 317-596-5692, or e-mail rights@idgbooks.com.

For information on licensing foreign or domestic rights, please phone +1-650-655-3109.

For sales inquiries and special prices for bulk quantities, please contact our Sales department at 650-655-3200 or write to the address above.

For information on using IDG Books Worldwide's books in the classroom or for ordering examination copies, please contact our Educational Sales department at 800-434-2086 or fax 317-596-5499.

For press review copies, author interviews, or other publicity information, please contact our Public Relations department at 650-655-3000 or fax 650-655-3299.

For authorization to photocopy items for corporate, personal, or educational use, please contact Copyright Clearance Center, 222 Rosewood Drive, Danvers, MA 01923, or fax 978-750-4470.

LIMIT OF LIABILITY/DISCLAIMER OF WARRANTY: THE PUBLISHER AND AUTHOR HAVE USED THEIR BEST EFFORTS IN PREPARING THIS BOOK. THE PUBLISHER AND AUTHOR MAKE NO REPRESENTATIONS OR WARRANTIES WITH RESPECT TO THE ACCURACY OR COMPLETENESS OF THE CONTENTS OF THIS BOOK AND SPECIFICALLY DISCLAIM ANY IMPLIED WARRANTIES OF MERCHANTABILITY OR FITNESS FOR A PARTICULAR PURPOSE. THERE ARE NO WARRANTIES WHICH EXTEND BEYOND THE DESCRIPTIONS CONTAINED IN THIS PARAGRAPH. NO WARRANTY MAY BE CREATED OR EXTENDED BY SALES REPRESENTATIVES OR WRITTEN SALES MATERIALS. THE ACCURACY AND COMPLETENESS OF THE INFORMATION PROVIDED HEREIN AND THE OPINIONS STATED HEREIN ARE NOT GUARANTEED OR WARRANTED TO PRODUCE ANY PARTICULAR RESULTS, AND THE ADVICE AND STRATEGIES CONTAINED HEREIN MAY NOT BE SUITABLE FOR EVERY INDIVIDUAL. NEITHER THE PUBLISHER NOR AUTHOR SHALL BE LIABLE FOR ANY LOSS OF PROFIT OR ANY OTHER COMMERCIAL DAMAGES, INCLUDING BUT NOT LIMITED TO SPECIAL, INCIDENTAL, CONSEQUENTIAL, OR OTHER DAMAGES.

Trademarks: For Dummies, Dummies Man, A Reference for the Rest of Us!, The Dummies Way, Dummies Daily, and related trade dress are registered trademarks or trademarks of IDG Books Worldwide, Inc. in the United States and other countries, and may not be used without written permission. All other trademarks are the property of their respective owners. IDG Books Worldwide is not associated with any product or vendor mentioned in this book.

is a registered trademark under exclusive license to IDG Books Worldwide, Inc. from International Data Group, Inc.

About the Author

Deanna Sclar is the internationally bestselling author *of Auto Repair For Dummies,* a guide to car maintenance and troubleshooting, and *Driving For Dummies: The Glove Compartment Guide,* an on-the-road handbook. A former contributing editor to *Family Circle, Boys' Life,* and *Exploring,* her articles have also appeared in the *Los Angeles Times, Redbook, New Woman,* and other national magazines.

As an automotive expert and consumer spokesperson, Deanna has appeared on more than 700 radio and TV shows including *Good Morning America, Today, Sonya Live,* and the *The Gayle King Show.* Her "Auto Repair For Dummies" video was a National Home Video Awards finalist. She's co-hosted *Outrageous Women,* a weekly TV talk show; and has produced, written, hosted, and edited several documentaries.

The former "Thumbs Sclar" has restored two classic cars, a truck, and a house. An inveterate gypsy and blue-water sailor, she's crewed her way across the Pacific and Polynesia; sailed and dived the Great Barrier Reef; trekked alone for nine months through southeast Asia and five months through Brazil; and crossed the Atlantic in a small boat with a companion and a cat.

"My goal is to prove that we have control over our lives," she says. "Whether you are working on a car or making a life-long dream come true, it's a do-it-yourself world. Knowing this has turned my life into a great adventure and I want to pass the good news on to everybody else!"

ABOUT IDG BOOKS WORLDWIDE

Welcome to the world of IDG Books Worldwide.

IDG Books Worldwide, Inc., is a subsidiary of International Data Group, the world's largest publisher of computer-related information and the leading global provider of information services on information technology. IDG was founded more than 30 years ago by Patrick J. McGovern and now employs more than 9,000 people worldwide. IDG publishes more than 290 computer publications in over 75 countries. More than 90 million people read one or more IDG publications each month.

Launched in 1990, IDG Books Worldwide is today the #1 publisher of best-selling computer books in the United States. We are proud to have received eight awards from the Computer Press Association in recognition of editorial excellence and three from Computer Currents' First Annual Readers' Choice Awards. Our best-selling ...*For Dummies*® series has more than 50 million copies in print with translations in 31 languages. IDG Books Worldwide, through a joint venture with IDG's Hi-Tech Beijing, became the first U.S. publisher to publish a computer book in the People's Republic of China. In record time, IDG Books Worldwide has become the first choice for millions of readers around the world who want to learn how to better manage their businesses.

Our mission is simple: Every one of our books is designed to bring extra value and skill-building instructions to the reader. Our books are written by experts who understand and care about our readers. The knowledge base of our editorial staff comes from years of experience in publishing, education, and journalism — experience we use to produce books to carry us into the new millennium. In short, we care about books, so we attract the best people. We devote special attention to details such as audience, interior design, use of icons, and illustrations. And because we use an efficient process of authoring, editing, and desktop publishing our books electronically, we can spend more time ensuring superior content and less time on the technicalities of making books.

You can count on our commitment to deliver high-quality books at competitive prices on topics you want to read about. At IDG Books Worldwide, we continue in the IDG tradition of delivering quality for more than 30 years. You'll find no better book on a subject than one from IDG Books Worldwide.

IDG BOOKS WORLDWIDE

John Kilcullen
Chairman and CEO
IDG Books Worldwide, Inc.

Steven Berkowitz
President and Publisher
IDG Books Worldwide, Inc.

Eighth Annual
Computer Press
Awards ≥1992

Ninth Annual
Computer Press
Awards ≥1993

Tenth Annual
Computer Press
Awards ≥1994

Eleventh Annual
Computer Press
Awards ≥1995

IDG is the world's leading IT media, research and exposition company. Founded in 1964, IDG had 1997 revenues of $2.05 billion and has more than 9,000 employees worldwide. IDG offers the widest range of media options that reach IT buyers in 75 countries representing 95% of worldwide IT spending. IDG's diverse product and services portfolio spans six key areas including print publishing, online publishing, expositions and conferences, market research, education and training, and global marketing services. More than 90 million people read one or more of IDG's 290 magazines and newspapers, including IDG's leading global brands — Computerworld, PC World, Network World, Macworld and the Channel World family of publications. IDG Books Worldwide is one of the fastest-growing computer book publishers in the world, with more than 700 titles in 36 languages. The "...For Dummies®" series alone has more than 50 million copies in print. IDG offers online users the largest network of technology-specific Web sites around the world through IDG.net (http://www.idg.net), which comprises more than 225 targeted Web sites in 55 countries worldwide. International Data Corporation (IDC) is the world's largest provider of information technology data, analysis and consulting, with research centers in over 41 countries and more than 400 research analysts worldwide. IDG World Expo is a leading producer of more than 168 globally branded conferences and expositions in 35 countries including E3 (Electronic Entertainment Expo), Macworld Expo, ComNet, Windows World Expo, ICE (Internet Commerce Expo), Agenda, DEMO, and Spotlight. IDG's training subsidiary, ExecuTrain, is the world's largest computer training company, with more than 230 locations worldwide and 785 training courses. IDG Marketing Services helps industry-leading IT companies build international brand recognition by developing global integrated marketing programs via IDG's print, online and exposition products worldwide. Further information about the company can be found at www.idg.com.   1/24/99

Dedication

To the two people who've taught me the most about money:

PAUL R. HOOPER
My trusted friend
and financial advisor

and

MICHAEL GREENWALD
The best brother this only
child has ever had

Author's Acknowledgments

This book drew on material from hundreds of sources, and I'm especially grateful to the following automotive experts for unselfishly sharing their expertise and allowing me to incorporate valuable data and tips from their outstanding publications:

Rosemarie Kitchin, dear friend, mentor, and Executive Secretary of the Automotive Public Relations Council, MEMA, for her unflagging support and generosity. Thanks for reviewing the book and always coming up with the information, opportunities, and personal contacts I need.

David Steventon, the Canadian Automobile Association's Mgr. Technical & Travel Services and Editor of *CAA AutoPinion,* for his unfailing responsiveness and wide-ranging knowledge of the Canadian automotive scene. If he didn't know the answer, he always knew who did.

Cindy Miller, Head Librarian, and the wonderful staff at the Marina del Rey Library, for being the finest "one-stop shopping center" for any fact or source I needed.

Steve Mazer, Auto Club of Southern California, for patiently allowing his brain to be picked on numerous occasions, and always coming up with the right source or AAA publication.

Paul Dean, Automotive Editor, *Los Angeles Times,* for a superlative technical review of all the chapters that dealt with buying new and used cars.

Dixon Q. Dern, for negotiating the contract that enabled IDG to publish this book.

Eric Tyson, author *Personal Finance For Dummies,* for reviewing the chapters on financing, leasing, and warranties.

Maryann Keller, President of the Society of Automotive Analysts and expert on leasing, for reviewing the original financing chapter and providing her advice in an area where it's practically impossible to find an impartial and honest expert.

Jeanne Salvatore, Director of Public Relations and Consumer Affairs, Insurance Information Institute, for reviewing the insurance chapter and providing sources and illustrations for it.

Jon Hoch, Assistant Communications Manager, National Insurance Crime Bureau for conscientiously seeing to it that the illustrations they provided arrived in the best possible format.

David Dre Solomon of the *Nutz & Boltz* newsletter and *The Automotive Panic Button,* for sharing his data and expertise.

Al and Matt Ulmer of *Common Sense Car Care* newsletter and *The Woman's Guide to Finding an Honest Mechanic,* for sharing data and telling their readers about my books.

Fred Uhlig, Director of Service R&D, Service Tech. Group, General Motors, for never being too busy to supply good advice, information, and illustrations.

Sheena Dupree of the U.S. Environmental Protection Agency, for being the only one at her desk after I was shunted through nine voice mails at the EPA and for sending me updates of EPA publications.

Maria Ingra, Assistant of Public Affairs, California Highway Patrol; Officer Bill Longacre, carjacking specialist, Los Angeles Police Department; Lt. Ed Wilson, LAPD Combat Auto Theft Program (CAT); and Lt. Joe Lombardi, Executive Officer, Beverly Hills Police Department, for their valuable tips on auto security.

The National Highway Traffic Safety Administration (NHTSA) for illustrations, information, and its good work in keeping the automotive industry on its toes.

Mary Crystal of the Western Insurance Information Service for data and advice.

Mariah Bear, Production Manager, Ten-Speed Press, for rescuing the original version of this book and restoring it to excellence.

Donna Braunstein, who spent endless hours on hold to come up with crucial facts and figures so I could finish the original manuscript in time to meet a small boat in Africa and sail across the Atlantic Ocean to Brazil.

And to all the wonderful people at IDG who held my hand, advised and encouraged me, and worked hard and long on this book, especially: Holly McGuire, Acquisitions Editor; Jennifer Ehrlich, Senior Project Editor, Tracy Barr, "Dummification expert," Elizabeth Kuball, Copy Editor, and Heather Prince, Research Coordinator and Internet wizard. You are absolutely the best editorial team I've ever encountered. May the Fonts be with you!

Publisher's Acknowledgments

We're proud of this book; please register your comments through our IDG Books Worldwide Online Registration Form located at http://my2cents.dummies.com.

Some of the people who helped bring this book to market include the following:

Acquisitions, Editorial, and Media Development

Senior Project Editor: Jennifer Ehrlich

Acquisitions Editor: Holly McGuire

Copy Editor: Elizabeth Netedu Kuball

Technical Editor: Paul Dean

Editorial Manager: Mary C. Corder

Editorial Coordinator: Maureen Kelly

Production

Associate Project Coordinator: Tom Missler

Layout and Graphics: Lou Boudreau, Linda M. Boyer, J. Tyler Connor, Maridee V. Ennis, Kelly Hardesty, Angela F. Hunckler, Todd Klemme, Heather N. Pearson, Anna Rohrer, Brent Savage, Janet Seib, Rashell Smith

Proofreaders: Christine Berman, Kelli Botta, Michelle Croninger, Betty Kish, Jennifer Mahern, Nancy Price, Rebecca Senninger, Ethel M. Winslow, Janet M. Withers

Indexer: Ty Koontz

Special Help

Tracy L. Barr; Christine Meloy Beck; Nate Holdread; Paula Lowell; Heather Prince; Linda S. Stark

---

General and Administrative

IDG Books Worldwide, Inc.: John Kilcullen, CEO; Steven Berkowitz, President and Publisher

IDG Books Technology Publishing Group: Richard Swadley, Senior Vice President and Publisher; Walter Bruce III, Vice President and Associate Publisher; Joseph Wikert, Associate Publisher; Mary Bednarek, Branded Product Development Director; Mary Corder, Editorial Director; Barry Pruett, Publishing Manager; Michelle Baxter, Publishing Manager

IDG Books Consumer Publishing Group: Roland Elgey, Senior Vice President and Publisher; Kathleen A. Welton, Vice President and Publisher; Kevin Thornton, Acquisitions Manager; Kristin A. Cocks, Editorial Director

IDG Books Internet Publishing Group: Brenda McLaughlin, Senior Vice President and Publisher; Diane Graves Steele, Vice President and Associate Publisher; Sofia Marchant, Online Marketing Manager

IDG Books Production for Dummies Press: Debbie Stailey, Associate Director of Production; Cindy L. Phipps, Manager of Project Coordination, Production Proofreading, and Indexing; Tony Augsburger, Manager of Prepress, Reprints, and Systems; Laura Carpenter, Production Control Manager; Shelley Lea, Supervisor of Graphics and Design; Debbie J. Gates, Production Systems Specialist; Robert Springer, Supervisor of Proofreading; Kathie Schutte, Production Supervisor

Dummies Packaging and Book Design: Patty Page, Manager, Promotions Marketing

◆

The publisher would like to give special thanks to Patrick J. McGovern, without whom this book would not have been possible.

◆

Contents at a Glance

Cartoons at a Glance

By Rich Tennant

page 7

"Are you sure it's never been in an accident?"

page 23

page 89

"Frankly sir, issuing you reasonably priced auto insurance isn't going to be easy given the number of crashes you've been involved in."

page 217

page 171

page 279

page 377

Fax: 978-546-7747 • E-mail: the5wave@tiac.net

Table of Contents

Part III: Untried and True: Buying a New Car 89

Chapter 7: Deciding What You Want 91

Introduction

. . . .

*B*uying a Car For Dummies contains everything a car owner needs to know about cars and money. It's for anyone who wants to find out how to buy, sell, insure, drive, protect, or rent a vehicle.

This may be the most important book I'll ever write, and one of the most useful books you'll ever read. My original motivation was simple: Many of you feel like "Dummies" when you're buying, financing, insuring, renting, and repairing your vehicles because the Powers That Be have obscured the process with so much jargon, legalese, and just plain garbage that it's nearly impossible for even the most sophisticated consumers to understand exactly what they're buying and the terms they've agreed to. So I decided to translate all the useful data in these areas into simple terms, supply the questions you need to ask, and provide checklists and worksheets to help you keep track of the steps you have to take during those perilous excursions into enemy territory when everyone you encounter seems to be doing their best to confuse, mislead, and get the best of you. Surely writing such a book would be a great path of service and a fitting companion to *Auto Repair For Dummies,* which demystifies the exotic secrets of the internal combustion engine.

With a high heart I set to work without a clue that the process would involve more than five years of research and three tortuous years converting what I'd found into simple language and instructions that you can read without falling asleep from boredom. Next time I'll choose something really easy, like translating the complete works of Shakespeare into Early Ugaritic!

Enough *kvetching*. Here's what to expect in the following pages, and the easiest way to use them.

You're Driving a What?

Oddly enough, there are few generic words for what many of you consider your most-cherished companions after family, friends, and pets. (Where I live, most people spend more time with their vehicles than they do with anyone or anything else.) To avoid numbing repetition, I have used the terms "car," "auto," and "set of wheels" interchangeably to mean *any* type of vehicle. When something applies only to specific vehicles such as luxury cars, motorcycles, trucks, or SUVs, I say so.

How I Picture You

To make this book as relevant, readable, and enjoyable as possible, I envisioned it as a friendly conversation with the kind of person who would want to read it. Here's the mental portrait of my readers that I kept in mind:

- ✓ **You own — or intend to own — a vehicle.** If you already have one, maybe you're thinking of selling it or trading it in for a newer model. If you don't own one, you're in the market for a set of wheels.

- ✓ **You're smart enough to be determined to learn what you don't know.** You believe that you can improve your chances of getting a better deal if you learn the tricks that experts know and, too often, don't reveal.

- ✓ **You want to protect yourself and your best interests.** When you're dealing with buying, selling, insuring, renting, or just driving a vehicle, you feel the need to protect yourself from people and situations that can range from the dangerously ignorant to the downright dangerous.

- ✓ **You spend the major part of your time thinking about things other than cars and car deals.** In other words, you have a life and you want to enjoy it — preferably with a good, reliable vehicle at your disposal.

How This Book Is Organized

I've organized this book to mirror the events that most people experience in the course of acquiring and owning a vehicle: From the initial decision about whether or not to buy one, to finding it, to getting it insured, protected, and repaired properly. This book is the only one I know of that even explores the problems you encounter when you have to rent a vehicle because yours isn't available or suitable for the occasion.

IDG has cleverly divided the book into seven parts, each of which contains chapters that deal with a particular topic so you can speed right to the heart of whatever it is you need to know without getting lost or distracted. The following sections describe the type of information you can find in each part.

Part I: New or Used: Deciding Which Option Is Best

If you can't decide whether to give up your old vehicle in favor of a newer one, or you're having a hard time deciding between a brand-new car and a previously owned one, the information you need is here. In this part you learn the pros and cons about both new and used cars, and you get an eye-opener about how much your current vehicle *really* costs you and whether it's a good idea to keep it.

Part II: Auto Recycling without Tears: How to Buy a Good Used Car and Get Rid of Your Own

Too many people think that buying used means buying trouble. Well, it ain't necessarily so — not if you know what to look for and how much you should pay for something you like. In fact, buying a good used car often makes more financial sense than buying new. The first three chapters in this part tell you everything you need to know to get a good deal on a previously owned car: You discover where to find the best potential buys, what to look for, and how to negotiate the most advantageous deal.

If you want to get rid of your current vehicle, you can find that information here as well. From selling it, to trading it in, to donating it to a charity, this part explains what you need to do to say goodbye to Old Faithful (or Faithless) in the best possible way.

Part III: Untried and True: Buying a New Car

The allure of new cars is very hard to resist: the smell, the shine, the dandy new gadgets, the unsmudged carpets. But if you never look beyond the thrill of it, you're bound to make some very expensive — and easily avoidable — mistakes. Part III can help you think logically about this decision. With the checklists and advice you find here, this part can help you determine exactly which features and options you need, figure out what the current prices are, shop without sabotaging your budget, and negotiate a deal you can be proud of.

Part IV: Money, Money, Money, Money

For nearly everyone except the fabulously wealthy, buying a car ranks right up there with other major expenses: mortgages, college tuition, and weddings. Because getting a car often means spending large amounts of money, you may decide to finance the purchase. The chapters in this part take the mystery and risk out of leases, loans, and paying cash to help you determine which option is best for you.

Part V: Insuring Your Car: How to Cover Your Automotive Assets

If all you know about auto insurance is that you need it and it costs an arm and a leg, this is the part for you. By understanding the things that affect your rates, the types of insurance available, what you can negotiate, and how you can save money on premiums, you may discover that, although still not cheap, the right insurance doesn't have to break the bank. This part gives you all the information you need to find a policy and company that you trust. It also explains how you can review your present policy, how you can protect yourself when things go wrong, and what you can do if your claims are ever disputed.

Part VI: Protecting Your Investment

Buying insurance isn't the only protection you need; with chapters covering everything from warranties to car thieves to repair shops, Part VI proves it. This part explains what you can expect from warranties and why extended warranties and service contracts may not be worth the money they cost. You can also find the most common car scams and what you can do to protect your vehicle — and yourself — from thieves and carjackers, and take a close look at some of the latest antitheft devices. If you ever need to take your vehicle to the shop (and, believe me, you will), you can discover how to find a good repair facility, attain "favored customer" status, and get satisfaction on legitimate complaints about *any* purchase.

Finally, if you need to rent a vehicle because yours is in the shop or you're away from home, you can find information on the process and pitfalls of renting a car, including the extra charges to avoid that can save you almost half the standard rental rates. If, like most people, you drive rental cars under the dangerous illusion that you're covered for *any* contingency by personal, credit-card, or the rental company's insurance, you're in for some big surprises. Head for this part to find out what questions you need to ask and what kinds of insurance you should have before you hit the road in a vehicle that isn't yours.

Part VII: The Part of Tens

This part contains several informative chapters that offer information in short, snappy bursts. It covers things *not* to do during negotiations, Web sites where you can check out new and used vehicles and find a variety of other automotive information, and how to tell if a car is a lemon. Believe me, this part is one you don't want to miss.

Icons Used in This Book

Follow these little road signs to make reading this book a joy ride:

This icon points to suggestions or hints that can save you money, help you avoid hassles, and otherwise make your life a little bit easier.

This icon indicates information that was either covered earlier or may prove beneficial to keep in mind.

This icon appears beside information that you want to watch out for because it points out events or circumstances that either are dangerous, can end up costing you a lot of money, or can otherwise destroy your life as you know it.

This icon appears beside rules that you absolutely must follow if you want to achieve success in a particular situation. There aren't many of them, so pay attention!

This icon appears beside real-life stories that provide a relaxing respite from serious subjects and demonstrate what you should — or should not — do to avoid major trouble or to triumph in difficult situations.

This icon appears beside technical information that, although potentially interesting (if you aspire to be an automotive expert), you can skip without risking anything important.

Where to Go from Here

Use this book in any way you like to get the information you want. You can read it from cover to cover or jump from section to section as the fancy strikes you. If you're looking for a general topic, scan the Contents at a Glance page; it can give you a good idea of what topics are covered and where to find them. If you're looking for more specific information, head to the Index. Wherever you go, you're bound to find lots of interesting things about cars and money that you probably didn't know before.

One final word: We're definitely dealing here with life in the fast lane. The automotive world is in a state of constant change: New options, features, and gizmos that can save your life or drive you to the poorhouse at greater speeds are developed every day. New government regulations and laws are being enacted as we go to press, and established organizations not only change their addresses and phone numbers, but e-mail and Internet addresses, too. The good news is that most of the published and computerized sources mentioned in this book are updated constantly, so you should get current information whenever you consult them. Of course, this book will be updated, too, from time to time. So please write to me in care of IDG Books Worldwide, Inc., with your comments, personal stories, any new sources of information that impress you, and topics you'd like to see covered in future volumes.

May you and your car have a long and happy life together! As for me? Right now I'm going sailing!

Part I
New or Used: Deciding Which Option Is Best

In this part . . .

Some call it a fever — that rush of interest, anticipation, and anxiety that accompanies thoughts of shopping for an automobile. Whether your pulse picks up at the notion of a factory-fresh model or the idea of a new-to-you set of wheels, this part can help you decide which way to turn with your car-buying considerations. (Be aware that reading Chapter 2, "Figuring Out How Much Your Current Car Costs," may send your mind — and heels — racing toward public transportation!)

Chapter 1

Making the Right Decision

*U*sed cars are like mature people. They've been through the minor problems of youth and have either evolved into strong, time-tested, reliable partners, or they have succumbed to the wear and tear of life in the fast lane, lack of proper care, and unforeseen catastrophes and can no longer be relied upon to operate efficiently.

New cars, on the other hand, are like newborns. Sure, your chances of getting a new car that you're satisfied with are greater than your chances of getting a dud (especially if you heed the advice I give you in this book). But without a track record, you're the lucky soul who gets to discover and deal with everything — good and bad — first.

And the car you have? Well, it's like your teenager: You either hate to part with it or you can't wait to see it go.

This chapter can help you to decide whether to overhaul or replace your present vehicle — and, for those of you who decide that replacement is the best option, it outlines the advantages and disadvantages of both new and used vehicles.

Keep Old Faithful or Replace Her? Making the Decision

How satisfied are you with your present vehicle? Unless additional safety features, increased fuel economy, or other compelling reasons really justify the cost of a newer model — or you're sick of driving the same old workhorse year after year — repairing a good older vehicle and continuing to drive it is often a wiser move. The following sections can help you get a clear view of your car's condition. If your car is in relatively good shape, why not spend your money to restore Old Faithful to the peak of health rather than put it out to pasture in favor of an untried steed with potential problems of its own?

Evaluating owning and operating costs

What does your present vehicle cost to operate each year? Will you want to pay much more than that for a new one? Vehicle-related expenses include more than just the cost to purchase the vehicle; they also include ownership and operating expenses, which can vary greatly from one model to another:

- **Ownership expenses:** These expenses include things like the price of the vehicle, how much it costs to insure and finance; the cost of such government red tape as titling, licensing, and registration; and the value the vehicle loses over time from depreciation.

- **Operating expenses:** These expenses include things like what you spend on fuel, oil, maintenance, repairs, and new tires. They may be relatively low for the first few years while everything's new and warranties cover many repairs and some basic maintenance, as well. After that, as the vehicle ages and warranties expire, parts begin to wear and maintenance is definitely your responsibility, so operating costs will rise, especially if you're lazy about preventive maintenance.

Annual ownership and operating expenses vary greatly from one model to another. Chapter 2 provides methods and worksheets that can help you figure out what driving your present car really costs each year. (You can also use the information in Chapter 2 to get an estimate on the total annual cost of driving a particular new or used replacement.)

How much have you paid in interest on your car loan? How much did last March's brake job cost? How much money a month do you spend in gas when you stop here and there to put five or ten dollars' worth in? Unless you're the type who keeps diligent track of where all your money is going, you're probably going to have to wrack your brain to remember, and then end up guessing at, your car expenses. To get a really accurate picture of the amount of money going into your car, you need to keep track over a long period of time — preferably a year. The worksheets I use (see Chapter 2) give you an *annual* overview. In other words, don't wait until Saturday of the weekend you're heading out to car shop before you figure out how much green stuff your car guzzles.

Checking out your present vehicle

You may not like to think of it this way, but your present car became a used car the very day you bought it. Viewing your current vehicle as though you were considering whether to buy it again can provide you with the necessary objectivity to evaluate it accurately and decide whether it's worth any further investment of time, effort, and money. The section on how to check out a used car (in Chapter 4), and the checklist you'll find there will pinpoint the areas to concentrate on as you decide whether to restore your vehicle to top condition or sell it and buy a new or used replacement.

Unless you're madly in love with Old Faithful and cannot bear to part with it, it's usually foolish to spend more money fixing up an old vehicle than it will be worth on the present market when you've finished sprucing it up. Use one of the sources in Chapter 5 to determine the "blue book value" of your aging steed and compare it with your mechanic's estimate of what it will cost to return it to health. You remember the old adage about beating a dead horse, don't you?

Replacement Options: New or Used?

After you make the decision to replace your old car, you face another decision: whether to buy a new vehicle or a used one. Each option offers advantages and disadvantages, so keep an open mind until you have all the facts.

The advantages of buying new

The allure of new cars is certainly compelling: shiny paint in myriad rainbow colors; gadgets and doodads that blink and glow; and who can resist that new car smell? But there are more — and better — reasons than these to consider a new car.

Safety features

The best reason for buying a new vehicle is to replace one that lacks such vital safety features as air bags, integrated child seats, structural reinforcements and the like.

Other technological improvements

In recent years, innovations in steering and suspension, fuel injection, and basic equipment have resulted in vehicles that get better gas mileage, run cleaner, and can go for long periods of time between tune-ups and other periodic maintenance.

New car or toaster oven? Let me think. . . .

In a 1984 survey of consumer spending priorities, buying a new car rated second (taking a short vacation was first). A decade later, the same survey found buying a new vehicle in tenth place, after used cars and trucks, home computers, and home appliances. Recent surveys also show that high new-car prices would prompt 62 percent of consumers to consider buying a used car and 64 percent feel that there is little or no greater prestige in buying a new car than in buying a good used one.

In fact, many first-time buyers are choosing to purchase larger used cars instead of smaller new ones. Late-model or used sport-utility vehicles, minivans, midsized sedans loaded with options, and luxury cars have all become more attractive to many buyers, while sales of smaller new cars, which are often more expensive, have slowed. According to the U.S. Department of Commerce, while new-car sales have been relatively stagnant in recent years (averaging less than $100 billion annually), used-car sales have jumped 67 percent to $55 billion a year.

About 25 percent of new cars are leased, which has led to the return of between 1.4 and 2 million low-mileage, two- or three-year-old vehicles to dealerships every year. These "nearly new" cars are one reason that dealers currently sell three times as many used cars as new ones and make more money from them. Dealerships now tout leasing and financing programs for certified fully restored, guaranteed, and warranted "previously owned" cars almost as enthusiastically as they promote their new models. In Canada, the term for these vehicles is "newsed cars," and they are proving so popular that some experts fear that the supply of conventional used vehicles may be radically diminished. If you are interested in one of these deals, it pays to ascertain that the dealer's overhaul and resale program has been endorsed and controlled by the auto manufacturer.

You don't have to worry about past problems/neglect/repairs

It's nice to have a car that's all your own, free of the mistakes, mishaps, and poor choices of a previous owner. It should be pristine, rarin' to go, and free of the battle scars and aging components that can plague an older vehicle. Of course, some new cars have problems of their own due to faulty manufacturing or newfangled systems that may succumb to unforeseen circumstances. The choice of risks is yours. However, there's no denying that a new car is often considered more attractive and prestigious than an older model from the same manufacturer. You pays your money and you takes your chances.

The advantages of buying used

Although owning a brand-new car is nice, there are many reasons to buy a good used vehicle rather than a new one.

Used vehicles are often better buys

In 1998 the average price of a new car is almost $19,000. And a survey by University of Michigan researcher David Cole predicts that by the year 2005, that price will rise to $22,000 (excluding inflation), an increase of 40 percent over prices in 1994. At an average of only $8,000, a used car is definitely more affordable than a new one, which may cost more than half a year's salary.

Used vehicles cost less to own and maintain

Consumer Federation of America spokesperson and author Jack Gillis advises that "buying a used car will reduce your ownership and operating expenses by about 50 percent." Perhaps the best proof of this is that, currently, the average age of vehicles in the United States is nine years — the highest in half a century. And if that's not enough to sway you, consider the following tidbits of financial fodder:

- Registration, licensing fees, and insurance premiums for new cars are much higher than for used cars.

- When you buy a used car, you don't have destination, "dealer prep," and shipping costs to pay.

- You can keep a well-made vehicle running beautifully for a lot less than you'd spend on new-car payments, fees, and premiums, even if you rebuild the engine or restore the body.

- In addition to the fact that new cars can depreciate 30 percent to 40 percent in only two years, buying or leasing a new vehicle can continue to cost you several hundred dollars a month for an average of three years. As the Consumer Reports' *1996 Buying Guide* says, "A new car depreciates 20 to 30 percent the minute you drive it off the dealer's lot." Why not buy a two- or three-year-old used vehicle and let some other hotshot take the loss?

- A well-built automobile that has been properly maintained can stay on the road for over 150,000 miles, even though most of us think our cars are played out at half that mileage.

Used cars can be classics

While new cars devaluate, many older cars are gaining in value and prestige. Some of us view cars as works of art and dream about owning a really classic piece of automotive engineering. If you're in the market for a status symbol, it may be wiser (and more impressive) to forget about the new luxury models and look for an older classic car instead.

The same holds true if you consider your car an investment and not just a machine to move you and your brood from here to there and back again. Consider the following:

✔ I bought "Tweety-Bird," a '67 Mustang, for a little over $500 in 1973 and spent about $200 to fix her up, most of which went for a spiffy red paint job. Today, this model is considered a classic worth ten times what I paid for her.

✔ In 1975 I bought and restored "Honeybun," a 1959 Mercedes 190SL roadster, for under $5,000. After giving me twenty years and thousands of miles of sheer delight, she recently sold for more than four times what she cost when she was new.

Such oldies have increased in value because they're beautifully made — in many cases, by hand. And, although their owners usually love and pamper classic vehicles, in the long run, rust and accidents cause the supply to diminish and the value of the surviving ones to increase.

Chapter 2

Figuring Out How Much Your Current Car Costs

. . . .

In This Chapter

▶ Understanding the difference between owning and operating expenses

▶ Finding out where to go to get the information you need

▶ Figuring how much money you spend on your car annually

▶ Discovering ways to cut down on your owning and operating expenses

. . . .

*W*hen someone asks, "How much did your car cost?" after your initial reaction (the unspoken retort that dies on your lips), the sticker price — or price you negotiated — is probably the amount that pops into your head and out of your mouth. But that amount doesn't take into account financing, taxes, depreciation, and other things that you pay for when you buy or lease a car.

To understand what your car is truly costing you, you have to understand that vehicle costs fall into two categories: ownership expenses and operating expenses. These expenses do not necessarily go hand in hand. Ultimately, it all comes out of the same pocket: *yours*.

To help you make sense and take control of the myriad costs associated with owning and operating a car, this chapter explains both of these major areas of expense, gives you tips and guidelines on figuring out and recording what you spend in each area, and provides worksheets that you can use to calculate annual ownership and operating expenses for any vehicle that you own or would like to own. I also include suggestions for ways that you can control the cost of owning a car (selecting a vehicle that costs less to buy, license, and insure, for example) and save on operating expenses (like eliminating unnecessary trips to save on fuel, service, and tires).

Whether you are estimating your operating expenses so that you can deduct the business use of your present vehicle from your taxes, want to find out what it costs to drive a specific vehicle you'd like to own, or just want to get an accurate picture of what you're spending each year on your present car, you can use the guidelines and worksheets I offer in this chapter.

The Complete Car Cost Guide (Intellichoice) is packed with information about all categories of ownership costs, warranties, and dealer costs. If you feel like you want some in-depth information about the subject, check out that publication.

Ownership Expenses

Except for the effect on your insurance rates, the cost of *owning* a vehicle is not related to how many miles you drive; the meter keeps ticking even if you hardly ever use your car. Ownership expenses include the price of the vehicle; what it takes to insure and finance it; the cost of such government red tape as titling, licensing, and registration; and the value the vehicle loses over time from depreciation.

Financing

If you've financed a vehicle with a lease or loan, finance charges are part of your annual ownership expenses. One way to figure out how much you're spending on finance charges is to do the math yourself — presumably you know the interest rate of your loan and how much you borrowed — but there are easier ways: Your original paperwork, monthly statements, or payment book can provide you with the figures you need.

If you're leasing, whether or not you'll want to buy the vehicle at the end of the lease is a major factor here because it affects how much you'll pay over the time you possess the vehicle. Chapter 10 can help you evaluate the pros and cons of leasing and other financing options.

Licensing and registration, taxes, and insurance

To get a clear picture of how much a vehicle is (or will be) costing you, you must add these once-a-year items into your ownership expenses:

- ✔ **Licensing and registration fees:** What you pay in licensing and registration fees varies, depending on the model, the age of the car, and the state you live in. To get current information for a vehicle you own, take a look at your latest registration form (you probably keep this in your glove compartment) and remember that the amount due will change annually as the vehicle depreciates. For a car you're thinking about owning, you can call the Bureau of Motor Vehicles and ask someone, providing you know what the purchase price will be.

✔ **Taxes:** Remember to include any property or use taxes. (The sales and excise taxes were part of the purchase price.) Also, if you own or plan to buy a luxury car (one whose purchase price exceeds $34,000), figure in the luxury tax as well. For more information about luxury tax, see Chapter 7.

✔ **Insurance:** When you consider the cost of a vehicle, be sure to factor in insurance. If you can't remember how much your insurance premium is, look at your policy or your insurance bill. And if you pay in installments, add the installments together to get the annual premium amount. (See Part V for the lowdown on insurance, insurance premiums, and how to shop around for the best policy.)

Depreciation

Depreciation, or the value the car loses simply due to the passage of time, is the most expensive cost of ownership. As soon as you drive a new car off the lot, it begins to depreciate (and you'll be amazed at how much that drive over the last speed bump and out onto Main Street can cost). Most new cars depreciate from 30 to 50 percent over the first three to five years, depending on the popularity of the model and its availability. Happily, since the rate of depreciation drops sharply after the first couple of years, the longer you keep a vehicle, the less per year it will depreciate.

The reason depreciation is considered a cost is because it affects the resale value of the vehicle. The greater the depreciation, the less value your car has, and the less value your car has, the less you can get for it when you trade it in or sell it.

The *NADA Official Used Car Guide,* available at your local library or lending institution, is a good source of information on the projected trade-in value of a vehicle or how much it will depreciate over time. You can also find more information about depreciation in Chapters 7 and 10.

Operating Expenses

The cost of operating a vehicle includes what you spend on fuel, oil, maintenance, repairs, and new tires. These costs relate directly to your annual mileage — how far you travel and how often you're actually on the road.

Maintenance and tires

Regular maintenance items include changing the oil, oil filters, and coolant, and getting tune-ups, repairs, and new tires. If you do your own maintenance, don't forget the cost of oil, coolant, tools, and other automotive supplies — and the sales tax you pay on these items.

You can save a great deal of money by doing these simple tasks yourself and most of them are easier to accomplish than making breakfast. If you don't believe this, check out my step-by-step instructions in *Auto Repair For Dummies* (IDG Books Worldwide, Inc.).

Keep all your bills for regular maintenance in a folder for future reference. If you use financial software such as *Quicken,* create categories to keep track of these expenses.

Fuel

The easiest way to figure what you actually pay for fuel and how many miles per gallon (mpg) you get is to keep track of the following every time you buy a tank of gasoline: the mileage you got on that tank of gas, the number of gallons you bought, and how much you paid. Because your sales slip already shows the date, number of gallons, and price, all you need to add is the current mileage on the vehicle's odometer. Keep this information in a mileage log — most have special pages for recording operating expenses.

If you don't want to buy a mileage log at your local stationers, you can make a copy of the nearby Fuel Consumption and Cost Per Gallon Log for each of your vehicles. You can also use a regular notepad as a mileage log, as long as it contains the same information and is handy, accessible, and sturdy enough to withstand lots of use.

If you use your vehicle for business, keep a mileage log as proof for tax deduction; most have special pages for recording operating expenses.

When you're aware of how many miles per gallon your vehicle generally gets, you can better monitor your vehicle's condition and performance. If the number of miles per gallon suddenly drops and your driving habits or conditions haven't changed, watch your mileage closely for the next few tanks of gasoline. Take the car in for a checkup if the mpg doesn't go back to normal. The car may simply need an adjustment or a tune-up, but a change in mpg may also be an early-warning sign that, if heeded, can prevent the need for major repairs.

FUEL CONSUMPTION AND COST PER GALLON LOG

A DATE	B PRESENT MILEAGE	C LAST MILEAGE	D MILES DRIVEN	E NO. OF GALLONS	F MILES PER GALLON	G PRICE PER GALLON	H COST PER MILE
						$	$
						$	$
						$	$
						$	$
						$	$
						$	$
						$	$
						$	$
						$	$
						$	$
						$	$
						$	$
						$	$
						$	$
						$	$
						$	$
						$	$
						$	$
						$	$
						$	$
						$	$
						$	$
						$	$
TOTALS:			TOTAL MILES	TOTAL GALLONS	AVERAGE MPG.	AVERAGE COST	AVERAGE PER MILE
						$	$

INSTRUCTIONS

To find out your current usage:

1. Subtract LAST MILEAGE (C) from PRESENT MILEAGE (B) to get MILES DRIVEN (D).
2. Divide MILES DRIVEN (D) by NUMBER OF GALLONS (E) to get MILES PER GALLON (F).
3. Divide PRICE PER GALLON (G) by MILES DRIVEN (D) to get COST PER MILE (H).
4. To get your average miles per gallon and cost per mile for any given period of time, add columns (D), (E), (F), (G), and (H).

Keeping Track of Your Annual Driving Costs

To know how much you're spending on owning and operating costs — financing, fuel, taxes, maintenance, and so on — use a photocopy of the Annual Driving Costs Worksheet in this chapter to keep track of the annual owning and operating expenses for each vehicle you own. You can also use this worksheet to estimate the annual expenses for various vehicles that you're considering purchasing.

Lowering Your Annual Driving Costs

After you've tallied your annual driving costs (as explained in the preceding sections) and are no longer hyperventilating, take heart: If you think you spend too much each year on your car or if you just want to be more economical, you can try the following suggestions:

✔ **Buy a fuel-efficient vehicle.** According to *Common Sense Car Care,* an automotive consumer newsletter, for every 10 percent increase in weight, you lose 4 percent in fuel economy. If you drive 15,000 miles a year, that extra weight can cost you as much as $400 worth of gasoline (they don't call bigger cars *gas hogs* for nothing). Also, consider a car with a manual transmission. Vehicles with manual transmissions often consume less fuel than those with automatic transmissions. Check the window stickers on vehicles for sale at dealerships for fuel consumption ratings.

✔ **Hang on to the car for a while.** Because the rate of depreciation drops sharply after the first couple of years, the longer you keep a vehicle, the less per year it depreciates. Of course, as time goes by, repairs may increase, and if the car starts to require extensive repairs, it's not going to be a bargain for you, or for anyone else,

✔ **Use the fuel recommended for your vehicle.** Using high-octane premium fuel in a car that's designed to run on regular unleaded will *not* improve performance. As a matter of fact, it can impede performance and cause the engine to "ping" because the timing wasn't set for it. Using low-octane fuel on a high-performance vehicle may actually damage the vehicle. Consult your owner's manual for the proper fuel to use.

✔ **Practice preventive maintenance and follow the maintenance schedule outlined in your owner's manual.** To cut down on wear and tear and avoid unnecessary repairs, change your oil, coolant, other fluids, and filters regularly. Keep your tires filled with the proper amount of air and rotate them every 6,000 miles. You should find a schedule for servicing your transmission and other major maintenance tasks in your owner's manual, or you can get the information from the dealership or manufacturer.

ANNUAL DRIVING COSTS WORKSHEET

ANNUAL OWNERSHIP EXPENSES:	
1. Purchase price, including Cost to Finance[1]	$
2. Trade-in value after number of years you expect to own the car	$
3. Number of years you expect to own the car	
4. **Estimated Annual Depreciation** *(line 1 minus line 2 divided by line 3)*	$
5. Annual finance payments *(multiply monthly payment by 12)*	$
6. Annual auto insurance premium	$
7. Annual registration and licensing fees	$
8. Sales, titling, and property taxes	$
9. **TOTAL ANNUAL OWNERSHIP EXPENSE** *(add lines 4-8)*	$
ANNUAL OPERATING EXPENSES:	
10. Miles per gallon (MPG)	
11. Average cost of fuel per gallon	$
12. Average cost of fuel per mile *(multiply line 10 by line 11)*	$
13. Number of miles driven per year	
14. **Fuel cost per year** *(multiply line 12 by line 13)*	$
15. Maintenance (oil & coolant chages, tune-ups, etc.)	$
16. Washing, repairs, and accessories	$
17. Tires	$
18. Parking (total monthly fees plus parking meters and lots)	$
19. Tolls	$
20. **TOTAL ANNUAL OPERATING EXPENSE** *(add lines 14-19)*	$
21. **TOTAL COST PER MILE** *(divide line 20 by line 13)*	$
22. **TOTAL ANNUAL DRIVING COST** *(line 9 plus line 20)*	$

[1]See the Loan and Lease Comparison Worksheets in Chapters 11 and 12.

- ✔ **Do it yourself.** You can save lots of money by doing simple mainte-nance jobs yourself. *Auto Repair For Dummies* (IDG Books Worldwide, Inc.) contains instructions for most of the preventive maintenance procedures mentioned here, as well as a maintenance schedule to keep track of them.

- ✔ **Only run the air conditioner when you need it.** Air conditioning costs miles per gallon. On warm days, just run the fan or lower the windows.

  To prevent damage to the compressor, be sure to run your air condi-tioner for a short time at least once a week, all year long.

- ✔ **Drive "eco-logically."** No, this doesn't mean toss apple seeds from your sunroof as you pass by: It means that it makes logical sense to remem-ber that the way you drive not only has a major effect on your vehicle's fuel consumption, but affects the ecology of the entire planet, as well. To drive eco-logically, you should do things that save gas (like being a feather foot, that is, being light on the gas pedal) and avoid things that waste gas (like gunning the engine as soon as the light turns green). For more information on eco-logical driving techniques that can increase your car's mpg, see *Auto Repair For Dummies* or *Driving For Dummies: The Glove Compartment Guide* (both published by IDG Books Worldwide, Inc.).

Part II

Auto Recycling without Tears: How to Buy a Good Used Car and Get Rid of Your Own

The 5th Wave   By Rich Tennant

"Are you sure it's never been in an accident?"

In this part . . .

Did you know that the best time to buy a used vehicle is in autumn when people trade their cars for the newer models? Or that you may be able to talk a dealer into replacing tires and other worn parts, at no cost to you? Or that you can use different, but equally reliable, price quotes to make a car worth more or less, to serve your purposes? This part contains everything you need to know to get a good deal on a used car — from finding a prime candidate, to inspecting the vehicle, to negotiating an acceptable selling price. And, you discover how to bargain the best offer for your own vehicle as well!

Chapter 3

Good Places to Find Used Vehicles

*Y*ou've decided on a used car. Whether the primary motivator was finances ("I can't afford a new car"), sentiment ("I've always wanted to own a '68 Camaro"), or simply your good business sense ("All things being equal, a used car gives me more for my money"), you want to make sure that the car you get meets your expectations. And unless you're planning to rebuild a classic from the chassis up, you certainly want to find one that will perform reliably and well.

This chapter explains the different places where you can buy used vehicles (buying from dealerships and private parties are only two of many sources) and gives you pointers on how to make sure that you're not wasting your time with a disreputable or unreliable seller. Keep in mind that no matter *where* you finally end up buying your vehicle, you always have the opportunity to out-deal the dealers. Be sure to read Chapter 5 for tips on negotiating and closing your deal and check out its section "Independent pricing sources" to help build your pricing know-how.

Making Sense of the Ads

The best place to find a vehicle for sale by a private party— or a dealer, for that matter — is your local newspaper. However, just because the paper is the best place doesn't mean it's totally reliable. Used-car ads almost never deal with the most important aspects of the vehicle you're buying. In fact, these ads tend to reflect the uninformed concerns of the majority of potential auto buyers: They allude to air-conditioning (a/c), sound systems (am/fm/cass or CD), sunroofs (snrf), whitewalls (w/w), and "loaded," but they rarely, if ever, mention what's going on under the hood. What kind of engine does the vehicle have? Are service records available? — *that's* the type of information you want. After all, whether the exterior is cherry or candy-apple red is pretty irrelevant if the car can't make it down your driveway. For this reason, if you want to respond to a used-car ad, always call first and ask the questions in the section called "Getting the information you need."

Terms found in used-car ads can be misleading when sellers stretch the truth to make their vehicles sound better than they are. Here's my version of the real meanings hidden behind some popular terms:

Term	*Translation*
"Asking price"	The owners know they don't have a prayer in getting what they're asking for, but they'd love it if you made their dreams come true.
"Best offer"	The owners are praying for an oil sheik with a penchant for used cars.
"Firm"	The owners want you to think they won't bargain over the price, but they will.
"Negotiable"	What most "asking prices" and "firm prices" are.
"Clean"	This may mean that the vehicle doesn't have any major dings or rust and the engine isn't leaking anything in quantities large enough to deface your driveway. Or it can mean that the car may not be terrific, but at least it isn't dirty.
"Custom"	Refers to options that have been added after the car was purchased, such as sound systems with ear-splitting woofers, flashy hubcaps, leaky sunroofs installed by amateurs, and loud paint jobs that cost the world to insure. Unless you'd love a pair of steer horns on your front grille, custom stuff usually isn't a terrific deal. See also *Loaded*.
"Loaded"	The owner has sprung for — or gotten stuck with — every toy and gizmo the dealership could add to the base price of the vehicle. Be sure the goodies the vehicle is loaded with will not cost you more to insure, maintain, or replace after the car thieves have stolen them.
"Vintage"	Very old. If the car were a classic or an antique, the owner would probably say so.
"Cherry condition"	*Cherry* is supposed to indicate automotive perfection. It usually means that the car looks great in low light or as it flashes by on the freeway.
"Cream puff"	Canadian equivalent of *Cherry*.
"Mint condition"	Same as *Cherry* (although I prefer cars that are not described by flavors).

Term	Translation
"Excellent condition"	No major problems or damage. Probably more realistic than *Cherry* or *Mint,* unless the owner just isn't given to hyperbole.
"Good condition"	Not *Cherry, Mint,* or *Excellent* — but not bad, either.
"OK" (as in "looks OK" or "runs OK")	The equivalent of a large yawn. If the owner can't be more enthusiastic, you probably won't be either.
"Runs" (or "Driveable")	Worse than OK.
"Needs work"	A mess. Unless you're a passionate, shade-tree mechanic, need a high-school science project, or want a TV prop to drive off a bridge, forget it.
"Lemon"	A term you'll never find in a car ad. If you've just arrived from Madagascar, Chapter 4 helps you determine whether your car is a lemon.

Private Parties

Buying from a private party means that you're purchasing the car directly from its owner. When you buy from a private party, you can expect to pay at least 15 percent less than you would pay for the same model at a used-car lot. The reason for the difference is that, when you buy from a private party, you don't have the dealer's *overhead* (lot rent, salaries, and so on) built into the price. Buying from private parties does have drawbacks, however; keep the following in mind if you want to buy a vehicle directly from its owner:

✔ **Most private parties (wisely) refuse to accept a check from a stranger.**
So expect to pay cash. Because carrying a lot of money with you isn't smart, hide one or two hundred-dollar bills in your car for a deposit and arrange to give the owner the balance in cash after your mechanic has done the final inspection.

Be sure to get a receipt that says your deposit will be returned if, for *any* reason, you don't buy the vehicle.

✔ **Private parties may not be willing to let you take the car to your mechanic.** They may feel anxious about letting a stranger make off with a vehicle because they lack the resources to recover it if it's stolen. Or if they've had a good response to an ad, they may want to keep the vehicle close to home in case another, less demanding, buyer comes along. Offer a $100 deposit to prevent them from selling the car until after the inspection and try to arrange to meet the owner and the vehicle at your mechanic's shop at a mutually convenient time in the next day or two. That way, the seller can still show the car to other people and contact them if the deal with you falls through.

Always insist on an agreement in writing that allows you to return the car for a full refund in a day or two if the car fails to pass your mechanic's inspection. If a vehicle is as good as the owners say it is, they should be willing to agree to this refund. If they refuse, forget the vehicle.

✔ **If you buy a car from a private party and get ripped off, getting your money back can be difficult.** Unlike a car dealer, a private party has no reputation to protect, and most private deals carry no warranties, guarantees, or money-back promises. For this reason, there have been cases where unscrupulous dealers took used cars home to sell as a private party transaction. I know of no way to evade such a scam, your best defense is to check a vehicle's value and condition really carefully before committing to buy.

If you buy a used car in "as is" condition, you will lose your money and take your lumps if you choose poorly. A federal ruling states that if you buy something in "as is" condition, you own it without recourse. "As is" means that "what you see is what you get" and you can't complain if hidden defects reveal themselves after the deal is consummated. Of course, if the owner *lies* about the condition of the car you may get some satisfaction in small claims court.

✔ **You are at greater risk of buying a stolen car from a private party than from a dealer.** Never buy a car from someone who wants to meet on the street or in an empty lot. It's best to find out where the seller lives or works and check to be sure the information is accurate. That way you'll know where to go for recourse if the deal turns "sour." Be sure to read how to identify possibly stolen vehicles in Chapter 4.

✔ **Don't buy a used car from a friend, relative, or business acquaintance unless you need the car more than you need the former owner.** You may have better luck returning a lemon to someone you know personally, but the relationship may go sour in the process.

Guidelines for saving money and time

Of course, you shouldn't think that you *can't* get a good deal on a used car that you see advertised in your local paper. A lot of people get great deals on great cars when they buy from private parties. The trick is knowing what to pay attention to and what strategies to use to save time and money, as described in the following list:

✔ **Good deals tend to go quickly; make sure you're one of the first people inquiring about a car.** Find out when each publication hits the streets and check each new issue as soon as possible.

✔ **Never buy a car from a picture.** Always check the vehicle out personally and have an independent mechanic inspect it before you buy.

Although most "Auto Trader" publications and even such prestigious journals as *Hemming's Motor News* feature classified ads with photographs, unless an out-of-town dealer is willing to pay the cost of shipping it to you "on spec" and shipping it home if you reject it, it's worth the time and expense to check the vehicle out personally and have an independent mechanic inspect it.

✔ **Make an appointment to view the vehicle at the most advantagous time of day.** Be sure that you have at least an hour of full daylight for inspecting and test-driving the vehicle, more if the car's located in an unfamiliar area. If you decide not to keep the appointment, remember to have the decency to call and cancel.

Getting the information you need

When you call a private party to inquire about a car, you want to know whether the car is worth the time and effort to go see it. So instead of asking things like "What color is it?" and "Does it have stereo surround sound?" you need to ask questions, like the following, that can help you screen out the losers:

✔ **"How many miles are on the vehicle?"**

Divide the mileage by the age of the car to see whether it's been driven over or under the national average of 12 to 15 thousand miles a year.

✔ **"Are you the original owner?"**

This is usually the best possible situation. Original owners know the car's history and may have full service records. Second owners aren't too bad if the original owner or the dealership has provided full documentation of the car's past service and repairs. If the sellers are not the original or second owners, ask how long they've owned the car.

If a vehicle has passed through many hands, you'll have no idea what it's been through. This can lead to very unpleasant surprises on down the road.

✔ **"Does the vehicle have a salvage title?"**

A "yes" answer is reason enough to forget the car. See Chapter 4 for reasons to avoid salvaged vehicles.

✔ **"Does the vehicle have an out-of-state registration?"**

If the answer is "Yes," be careful. The car may have been stolen or may have emission violations that can make registration impossible or very expensive in your area. If you like the rest of what you hear enough to view the vehicle, be sure to check its Vehicle Identification Number (VIN) with the Department of Motor Vehicles (DMV) before you part with any money. (You can find the VIN on the title, the registration, and at the lower-left corner of the dashboard where it's visible through the windshield from outside the car.)

✔ **"What would you fix if you were keeping the car?"**

This question can give you an idea of where the current owners think the car needs work and — depending on the answer — can give you some negotiating leverage. For example, you may consider the asking price a little too steep for a car that needs a new set of tires.

✔ **"Does the vehicle need any other work that you know of?"**

Most people are honest and, if asked a direct question, will answer truthfully — albeit optimistically ("There's just a little ding in the door; most of the time, you can't even see it").

✔ **"Have there been any major modifications to the engine?"**

Unless you're in the market for a racing machine, a "Yes" to this question is not a good sign, especially if you live in a state with smog requirements that may have been violated by souping up the engine or disconnecting anti-pollution devices. If this is the case, you probably won't be able to register the vehicle unless you restore it to legal street condition.

✔ **"Has the vehicle ever been in an accident?"**

If the answer is yes, probe a bit: What kind of accident? What were the damages? What type of repair was done? If you're still interested in the car, be sure to tell the mechanic who inspects it everything you've learned.

✔ **"What sort of driving conditions has the vehicle seen?"**

What you're looking for here is an idea of how the car has been driven. Has it been exposed to mostly city or highway driving? (Stop-and-go city driving is much harder on vehicles than long commutes on the highway.) If the owner takes it off-road or carries heavy loads, the vehicle may have suspension wear and body dings. If it is often used to carry young children or pets, check the upholstery.

✔ **"Why are you selling it?"**

You may not get an honest answer, but it's worth a try. If you go to see the vehicle, ask this question again and see whether the answer is the same.

✔ **"Is the price negotiable?"**

Ask this question even if the ad says "firm." If you get a "No," don't bother to view the car unless you're willing to pay the price.

✔ **"Is the vehicle still under warranty?"**

Original manufacturer's warranties still in effect on two- to four-year-old vehicles may not be transferable between individuals. Call the automaker to find out what the rules are for transferring warranties from one private party to another. For more on warranties, see Chapter 16.

✔ **"Who's been doing the maintenance and repair?"**

If the answer is the owner and the vehicle is only a couple of years old, be sure that no warranties have been violated.

✔ **"What's your maintenance schedule?"**

Has the transmission been serviced regularly? Have the tires been rotated regularly? The answers to these questions give you important clues to the vehicle's real condition. If, for example, the oil and coolant haven't been changed at least every three thousand miles and the cooling system flushed at least once a year, the engine is probably a victim of premature old age.

✔ **"Are the service records available?"**

Even if the owner doesn't have the service records, the vehicle may still be worth viewing. If you find that you like the car, ask whether you can contact the shop that did most of the work for a look at its service records.

New-Car Dealers

New-car dealers usually have facilities for selling the best vehicles they take in as trade-ins and at the end of leases. Although new-car dealers tend to be higher in price, they are generally considered to be the safest sources for used cars, and here's why:

✔ **Quality used cars.** New-car dealers usually display on their used-car lots only the best vehicles they receive as trade-ins. They sell the others to independent used-car dealers or send them to the auction or to wreckers. Because they've spent years building a reputation in the community, they often go out of their way to see that you are satisfied if problems occur.

✔ **Previously leased vehicles.** Because it has become extremely popular to lease vehicles rather than buy them outright, dealers and car manufacturers are now faced with an increasing glut of vehicles that have been returned after 1- to 3-year leases have ended. As a result, they've begun to completely overhaul many of these "almost new" vehicles and offer them with the same 3-year/36,000-mile warranties as new ones. These are often the best buys available, for the following reasons:

- In order to avoid the expensive penalties for returning a vehicle that has suffered more than "ordinary wear and tear," or has been driven more than the allowed number of miles, most people who lease vehicles take very good care of them and keep an eye on mileage. And even if there were problems, the overhaul has probably corrected them.

- Because most new vehicles depreciate from 30 to 50 percent over the first three to five years, you'll be buying (or leasing) a nearly new car, in top condition and fully warrantied, for much less than its original price, because the person who originally leased the vehicle had to pay for its loss of value over the term of the lease.

✔ **Repair service.** On-site service facilities usually make repairs with original equipment from the vehicle's manufacturer (OEM) rather than with cheap after-market parts.

✔ **Financing and guarantees.** Varied financing options offered by many dealers on certified "previously owned" vehicles include the same or similar warranties, guarantees, and "creative financing" as they provide for new models. (For more information on leases, loans, and other financing options, see Part IV.)

Buying from a new-car dealer does have its drawbacks, however:

✔ **New-car dealers generally ask top prices for used cars — higher than independents and much higher than private parties.** But, usually you can talk them down a bit, and having safe recourse if trouble develops may be worth a slightly higher price up front.

✔ **If new-car sales are really down, a new-car dealer may become as hard-nosed as an unscrupulous used-car dealer about moving used merchandise.**

Following are some strategies you may want to use if you decide to buy a used car from a new-car dealership.

✔ If you want a fairly recent model of a particular vehicle, call several dealers in your area and ask whether a lease they hold on such a vehicle is due to expire shortly. Dealers love to turn these cars over quickly. They may even encourage the current lessee to get out of the lease a bit early to resell the vehicle to you.

✔ Go to new-car dealers in upper-class neighborhoods when shopping for a used car. There is usually little demand for used cars and a large turnover in new ones in high-income areas, so the dealers are eager to move the trade-ins off their lots.

Also, well-heeled people can afford to have maintenance work done regularly, with the best mechanics and the finest parts, so the used vehicles they trade in are often in pretty fine condition. Instead of running just one car into the ground, wealthy families often have several vehicles to choose from, and their vehicles may not have much mileage on them. This may be the only time you will find the best bargain in the high-rent part of town!

Used-Car Dealers

Used-car dealers buy cars for resale from the public as well as from new-car dealers and auctions. Used-car dealers range from purveyors of top-quality sports and luxury models to bottom-of-the-barrel lots that hawk little better models than wrecking yards.

Used-car dealers can be good sources for bargains if you find one that's been around long enough to have established a stake in being a reliable part of the community. To weed out the reputable from the less-reputable used-car dealers, follow these suggestions:

✔ Avoid the hit-and-run independent who springs up like a weed in an unused lot, unloads a group of lemons on the local public, and vanishes before the cars fall apart. These unscrupulous people have come to epitomize dishonest business practices to such an extent that, to point out how untrustworthy a person is, we often ask the rhetorical question, "Would you buy a used car from this person?"

✔ If you are unsure about the reliability of a particular dealer, call your local consumer protection office or Better Business Bureau to find out if any complaints have been filed against that dealership.

Dealer X

There is a hierarchy among used car dealerships, and I got a most accurate view of it years ago when I was trying to unload an 11-year-old "macho-mobile." The new-car dealer who sold such cars looked at mine and said, "I don't handle anything more than a year or two old. If I get a car that's a little older as a trade-in, I generally sell it to Dealer X on the next block. If he won't buy yours, try Dealer Y about a mile further down the street. Your car is over ten years old, and we sell those to him. If he turns you down, check out Dealer Z on the edge of town. He's the one who gets the cheapest and the oldest cars." Dealer Y bought my car. I hope it didn't end up with Dealer Z.

Superstores

The most recent phenomenon in car sales are huge auto sales centers created by major mass merchandisers. Although, at first, superstores concentrated on the large numbers of "nearly new" vehicles that are returned to dealers at the end of one- to three-year leases, some superstores also offer new vehicles from several major automakers. At these high-tech outlets, customers can use touch-screen computers to select — by make, model, price, and other criteria — from as many as a thousand vehicles (ten times the inventory of ordinary car lots). Superstores usually sell cars at fixed prices without haggling and can arrange financing and insurance on the spot.

Although being able to compare a wide range of vehicles side-by-side and conclude the deal without fighting a battle of wits with a battery of salespeople is very nice, superstore prices are generally higher than those you'd end up paying at a traditional dealership. (If this picture changes, traditional dealerships may become obsolete as superstores absorb them into their gigantic operations.) Your best bet is to determine the vehicles that interest you the most and check prices at superstores against pricing services and smaller dealerships before making a commitment.

Here are a few superstore chains to check out:

- ✔ **CarMax.** Circuit City's venture into the field, CarMax offers a 30-day warranty on used vehicles that are fewer than five years old with fewer than 7,000 miles. Its first store, in Richmond, Virginia, sold 4,000 vehicles its first year compared to 660 sold by the average dealer. CarMax should have stores in every major city before long.

- ✔ **AutoNation USA and CarChoice.** AutoNation USA and CarChoice, whose major backers include the creators of Blockbuster Entertainment and the nation's largest Toyota distributor, opened with plans for 100 superstores in the top 25 U.S. metropolitan areas.

- ✔ **Driver's Mart Worldwide.** Nine of the largest auto dealers in the United States have collaborated to build a chain with more than 100 used-car superstores in 31 states.

- ✔ **United Auto Group.** United Auto Group began with more than 40 dealerships under its control.

Car-Rental Company Resale Lots

Many car-rental companies acquire their vehicles through leaseback programs with auto manufacturers. Called *program cars,* these cars are usually returned to the manufacturer after six months to a couple of years and either end up at auctions or program-car sales at dealerships. Other rental companies offer their franchisers the option of buying program cars through their national organization or purchasing special cars directly from manufacturers and selling them "at risk" on their own. Some, such as Hertz and Enterprise, have used-car outlets that sell non-program vehicles to the public. Enterprise Car Sales does a 20-point safety and maintenance check to select the best cars and offers them with a 12-month/12,000-mile free warranty at non-negotiable window sticker prices with a buy-back plan that allows you to return the car within a week if you change your mind. They accept trade-ins and can arrange 100 percent financing with major lenders.

On the down side, many rental cars are basic, sparsely-equipped, low-powered vehicles with little in the way of frills. If you're looking for "car-isma" a former rental car won't have the glamour to attract you.

One thing to keep in mind if you're thinking about buying a former rental car is the many people who have driven it during its relatively short life: vacationers, business travelers, people who've had their own cars in the repair shop, and so on. Chances are that these cars, despite the fact that they're usually well cared for and maintained, have had pretty tough — and varied — use.

Independent Mechanics

Some independent mechanics sell used cars as a sideline. If you know the shop personally and have found it reliable, you may come up with a good buy. Perhaps the best benefit from buying a vehicle from a repair facility is that it may have the car's maintenance and repair record in its files.

As with any car purchase, either be sure to ask for a written warranty that covers both parts and labor to repair any defects that show up within six months to a year, or be prepared for the possible consequences of an "as-is" vehicle.

Auctions

Although cars may sell very cheaply at auction, you have little or no chance to inspect a vehicle, determine its past history, or get your money back if you find you've bought a wreck with a spiffy paint job. Dealers go to auctions prepared to take risks. But you can't, so forget them.

I have heard of agents who specialize in going to auctions to find good cars that fit their clients' specifications. Even these agents must buy vehicles under the conditions I've just described. So, at the risk of offending the legitimate members of this profession, I advise you not to take this route unless the rep has such an "inside track" with the auctioneers that he or she has been able to identify and procure excellent used vehicles for more than one of your acquaintances. Even so, I'd only play this risky game if I were committed to restoring a particular model from the ground up.

Buying across the Border

Canadians have often headed for the southern United States to look for classic and good used cars that are corrosion-free (no salt is needed on roads in the southern U.S. because it rarely or never snows). Depending on the current value of the dollar, these buyers may also find better prices or a larger selection in the United States. The North American Free Trade Agreement (NAFTA) phased out the age embargoes and duties that had previously prevented the importation of autos across the Canadian/U.S. border, but the following restrictions still apply:

- ✔ To prevent "gray markets," which slip European vehicles into Canada through U.S. ports, the vehicle must have been owned and operated in the United States.

- ✔ If you'd like to import a Canadian vehicle into the United States, remember that the speedometer and odometer will read in kilometers rather than miles. At .7 kilometers to the mile, you may run the risk of being pulled over for going too *slow!*

If you'd like to import a vehicle into Canada from the United States, be sure it meets import requirements before you buy. Since 1985, Canada's safety standards for seat-belt attachments, bumpers, daytime running lights, and child-safety seats are higher than those in the United States. As a result, some U.S. vehicles may not qualify for importation into Canada. Transport Canada, the agency whose mission it is to develop and administer policies, regulations, and services for the best possible Canadian transportation system, allows modifications to bring most of these parts up to Canadian standards, but they do not allow modifications to upgrade seat-belt anchorages. Check out the Registrar of Imported Vehicles Web site at www.riv.com for more information.

Chapter 4

What to Look for When Buying a Used Car

. . . .

In This Chapter

▶ Inspecting the car inside and out (and on the road)

▶ Finding out which problems aren't worth fixing and which are worth overlooking

▶ Understanding the cardinal rule of buying a used car

▶ Evaluating the news — both good and bad — and making a decision

. . . .

Y ou're at a dealership, in a seller's driveway, or walking around a used car at a superstore. The object of your attention has been spiffed up and the person trying to unload it is following you around, smiling expectantly. What you're probably thinking at this point is, "Well . . . it looks okay to me," followed quickly by, "I wish I knew what I'm supposed to be looking for!"

The fact of the matter is that, unless you know what to look for, you can easily be distracted by superficial things: the paint, the chrome, the cleanliness of the interior, the enthusiasm of the person who's trying to make a sale. To help you look beyond the glitter and make a wise decision, this chapter gives you a rundown and explanation of the things you need to examine before you commit to buying any particular used vehicle. (In fact, the step-by-step inspection you get in this chapter is similar to the way experts scrutinize classic cars.) The checks in this chapter can help you screen out all but the very best used vehicles — and, if you're trying to decide whether or not to keep your present vehicle, it can help you make that decision, too. The information in this chapter will also enable you to convince the seller that you are savvy about cars, and this can definitely work to your advantage, especially if you're female. Despite all the evidence to the contrary, car dealers still often assume that the only thing "a little lady" is interested in is the color of the car.

Vehicles to Avoid — No Matter What the Cost

The used-car scene changes from year to year, but following are a few general guidelines about what *not* to buy. If, for some reason, you have your heart or pocketbook set on one of these vehicles, make doubly sure that your mechanic does a thorough investigation before you buy it.

- **Police cars, fleet cars, or taxis:** Even if they're going for very reasonable prices and have been pretty well maintained, they've been driven for long hours over thousands of miles by people who neither owned them nor cared for them. As a result, they are often worn out and ready for pasture.

- **Used station wagons:** These are sometimes owned by traveling sales-people who put 50,000 miles a year on them. Unless you know the vehicle personally, a used station wagon should be checked out very thoroughly before you consider buying it.

- **Used trucks or commercial vans:** Be sure that the transmission and suspension haven't deteriorated from hauling too many heavy loads for too many miles. You may want to ask the owners, "If it's such a great truck, how come you want to sell it?"

- **Models that have gone completely out of production:** The only time you should consider getting one of these cars is if the one you want was so widely sold that there are still lots of parts available. Mercedes-Benz, for instance, usually stocks parts for 20 years.

- **Cars with engines that have been modified:** If a major change has been made by the owner, find out what went wrong with the original equipment and ask a professional mechanic what damage the defective part may have done to other parts of the car and what effect the modification may have on the rest of the vehicle.

- **Sports cars with racing modifications:** Most of these souped-up darlings are miserable in stop-and-go traffic and at low speeds. Many have been worn out by leading fast lives. Sometimes the addition of turbochargers or exceptionally powerful carburetion can place a strain on a transmission or differential that wasn't designed for such rapid acceleration.

- **Very new used cars:** Unless you're buying a previously leased vehicle that has been returned after only one year, these may be lemons or may have been wrecked. Of course, the owner may simply have lost a high-paying job rather suddenly. (It's not considered "prying" to ask why the owner has put a vehicle up for sale. Listen to the answer with your "inner ear.")

- **Old vehicles with very low mileage:** Unless you've met the "little old lady" personally and know her church-going habits, chances are the odometer has been set back.

✔ **Lemons:** Some states require that DMV titles show whether the vehicle has been returned to the manufacturer as a *lemon*. California, for instance, defines a lemon as any vehicle that has been held by a dealership for more than 30 days for repairs in the first year of ownership or that has a problem the dealer has been unable to repair after four tries. Despite this, automakers have consistently found ways of putting these losers back on the market disguised as ordinary used cars. The American Automobile Manufacturers Association (AAMA) has been lobbying for dealers to only have to identify cars as lemons if they are among the tiny fraction found to be lemons in court proceedings.

All 50 states in the U.S. have lemon laws. If you have access to the Internet and you'd like a summary of the lemon laws in your state, try Autopedia, the automotive encyclopedia at www.autopedia.com/html/HotLinks_Lemon.html. Autopedia.com. This site also has a direct link to the person in your state who would handle a complaint (usually the state attorney general) and lists lawyers who specialize in this area. Another good site is www.pond.net/~delvis/lemonaid.html (Lemon Aid).

Canadians outside of Quebec who believe they have been stuck with a lemon should contact the Canadian Motor Vehicle Arbitration Plan (CAMVAP) at 800-207-0685.

✔ **Any car that has been in a wreck:** Although the car may have been repaired, it's possible that the frame is bent and less stable, that spot welds or body filler will not hold, or that the steering is damaged. Remember, even though you may be convinced that the restored vehicle is as good as new, you can have trouble finding a buyer who feels the same way when the time comes for you to sell it.

✔ **Possibly stolen vehicles:** If you unknowingly buy a stolen vehicle, it's your loss if the police repossess it. For this reason, don't part with more than a small deposit until you've had your local DMV search the car's title by its current owner's name or, better still, by the Vehicle Identification Number (VIN) that can be found on the title, on the registration, and at the lower-left corner of the dashboard where it is visible through the windshield from outside the car. For clues to possibly stolen vehicles, see the nearby sidebar "Red-hot signs that a car may have been stolen."

✔ **Previously salvaged vehicles:** A *salvaged* vehicle is one that's been damaged to such an extent that an owner, leasing company, financial institution or insurer considers it uneconomical to repair it. Insurance companies automatically deduct 40 percent from the value of a salvaged car, even if it's in good condition. If a DMV or NICB (National Insurance Crime Bureau) search shows that a vehicle has been salvaged, either have the price lowered by that amount or don't buy it.

Red-hot signs that a car may have been stolen

Always be alert to these signs that a vehicle may have been stolen:

- ✔ The vehicle is from a region of the United States or Canada that is far away from the place where it is being sold.

- ✔ The VIN on the title doesn't agree with the VIN on the body or other parts.

- ✔ The VIN plate is missing, loose, repainted, or painted over.

- ✔ The license plate number doesn't match the one on a recent registration.

- ✔ The license plate is brand new or has been mounted with very new-looking bolts.

- ✔ The name on the title is that of the dealer rather than the previous owner.

- ✔ The ID numbers on the engine have been removed.

- ✔ The original keys to the vehicle are missing, and only duplicates are available.

- ✔ The ignition switch is loose or shows signs of tampering.

- ✔ The vehicle is priced far below what it's worth.

If something looks suspicious, call the National Insurance Crime Bureau (NICB) at 800-TEL-NICB. They can provide a vehicle's ownership history and salvage record from its VIN.

- ✔ **Cars that have been recalled for defective parts:** The National Highway Traffic Safety Administration's Auto Safety Hotline (800-424-9393) can tell you whether a car model has been recalled and will send you information about it. You can find a description of the many essential services NHTSA provides in the nearby sidebar entitled "The National Highway Traffic Safety Administration (NHTSA) and the Center for Auto Safety." If the car you want has been recalled, it may be difficult to tell whether the necessary replacements or repairs were made.

- ✔ **Pre-1992 vehicles with defective air conditioners:** Although many older vehicles built before 1992 are well worth purchasing, keep in mind that R-12, the refrigerant for their air conditioners, has been declared environmentally unsafe by the EPA. Though reserves of the refrigerant will exist for a while, R-12 will become increasingly expensive and hard to find. If you buy a pre-1992 vehicle from a dealer, ask to have the air conditioner serviced and refilled with R-12 as part of the deal. Conversions to R-134a, the new refrigerant, will be necessary when the supply of R-12 runs out, and that may cost you a pretty penny.

- ✔ **"Gray" cars:** These are foreign vehicles that do not meet emission and safety standards. If you unknowingly buy a vehicle that has been illegally imported, it can be impounded, and you can run into insurance problems. Since 1990, the EPA has been authorized to collect a "gas guzzler" tax on post-1980 vehicles with low mileage ratings. They must be imported through a DOT-registered importer and modified to meet U.S. regulations before they can be driven. Although these vehicles may come with valid titles, they only prove ownership and do not indicate that the vehicle is legally driveable. Be sure any foreign-built car under 25 years old has been certified to meet DOT and EPA specifications.

TIP

The National Highway Traffic Safety Administration (NHTSA) and the Center for Auto Safety

The National Highway Traffic Safety Administration (NHTSA), within the U.S. Department of Transportation, works to prevent deaths and injuries resulting from motor vehicle crashes by investigating alleged safety defects and ordering recalls when necessary. The NHTSA crash-tests about 40 new vehicles and 60 older models each year and publishes reports on its findings.

Call the NHTSA Auto Safety Hotline at 800-424-9393, Monday through Friday, from 8 a.m. to 10 p.m. (EST), or visit the Web site at www.nhtsa.dot.gov/hotline for any of the following reasons:

✔ To report problems with your present vehicle

✔ To get information regarding factory recalls, defects, and technical information

✔ For safety ratings drawn from the results of new-car crash tests

✔ For additional information on how to make your present vehicle safer

Your call will be welcomed. More than 75 percent of NHTSA's investigations are started by consumer complaints — sometimes from a single report! People who call about specific problems receive a questionnaire to help

NHTSA further evaluate the complaint and determine whether it merits investigation. The Hotline is available in English and Spanish. For Fax on Demand service, press 1. For TTY for the hearing impaired, dial 800-424-9153. You can also write to National Highway Traffic Safety Administration, Technical Reference Library, Room 5108, 400 Seventh Street SW, Washington, DC 20590.

The Center for Auto Safety is an independent, nonprofit organization funded by membership dues (60 percent of members are individual consumers) and the sale of such publications as *The Car Book* and *The Lemon Times* — a quarterly newsletter filled with information on current legislation and legal action relating to automotive defects, unfair and fraudulent marketing practices, and other consumer issues. To order publications, call 202-328-7700 or write to the address below. To receive a list of common defects, information and technical service bulletins, recalls, and "secret warranties," send a letter with your vehicle's make, model, year, and problems, plus a #10 self-addressed, stamped envelope with 55 cents postage to 2001 S Street NW, Suite 410, Washington, DC 20009 or try their Web site at www.autosafety.org.

Intimidating "Honest John"

The recent trend toward used-car sales and leasing by new-car dealerships has left some used-car dealers with only the less reliable models. Consequently, being able to judge a vehicle wisely is even more important. Sad to say, this goes double if you're female. Luckily, if you're a woman, you can turn this outdated thinking to your advantage.

When I first went used-car shopping and asked the salesman to open the hood, he said, "If I do, will you know what you're looking at?" His eyes popped when I proceeded to open the master brake cylinder and poke around. "What's she doing?" he asked the man who accompanied me. "Oh, she's a mechanic," my friend replied, "I'm just along for the ride." The salesman wiped his brow. "Now I've seen everything," he murmured. After I finished telling him what was wrong with the car and what it would probably cost to fix it, we left.

Be sure to follow the inspection I outline in this chapter. Doing so will not only provide a thorough view of a vehicle's strong and weak points, it will also show "Honest John" that he has a tough customer on his hands. He will assume that if you are that savvy about vehicles, you're probably going to be just as

smart when it comes to negotiations. Who knows, it just may keep him from using his entire bag of dirty tricks. Other tips to keep in mind:

- Wear casual clothing you don't mind getting creased or soiled when you go to look at prospective used cars. When you do the inspection, you will have to look under the car, and that's a bit hard to do in high heels and a skirt or light-colored slacks. Plus, if you're dressed in a way that says, "I plan to inspect this car thoroughly and I mean business," the dealer is less likely to underestimate you.

- Leave your Rolex watch or Versace blouse at home. If you look too well-off the sales staff will assume that money is no object and you'll have to try twice as hard to get the vehicle for a decent price.

- Take along several copies of the Used-Car Inspection and Test Drive checklists, which you can find in this chapter, so that you'll have one for each vehicle that seems worth inspecting. Also carry a pad to make further notes.

Inspecting the Outside of the Vehicle

When you check the outside of the vehicle, you look at the body of the car, the tires, and pay attention to any fluids that leak out of it.

Bring several photocopies of the Used-Car Inspection Checklist in this chapter, so you'll have one for each vehicle that seems worth a closer look, and carry a pad to make further notes. This will also impress the dealers and possibly prevent them from even attempting to sell you a car that isn't in good shape. It can also prompt a private party to either reduce the price because of needed repairs, or to make the repairs before selling you the car.

Check out the exterior

You check the outside of the vehicle for several reasons: The amount of dings, dents, and scratches will give you an idea of how hard the car has been driven. Ripples in the body can indicate that the car has been in an accident. And anything but minor rust is a great reason to walk away from a vehicle and not look back. To check out the exterior of a vehicle, follow these steps:

1. **Walk around the car to form a general opinion of it.**

   Does it have "good vibes" or do you get an impression of seediness? If the car looks crummy to you, that's how it will look to everybody else. If the vehicle doesn't impress you, forget it.

2. **Sight along the sides of the car to catch ripples in the light reflected by the surface.**

   A distorted reflection can reveal bodywork, spot welds, and paint cover-up after an accident. If you have reason to believe that the body has been repaired, a small magnet will distinguish between cheap plastic body filler and durable sheet-metal bodywork.

3. **Look at the chrome trim: bumpers, hub caps, grille, and so on.**

   If you find any problems, keep in mind that you can have a bumper re-chromed for about half the cost of a new one or, if the car is a popular model, you can find a good used bumper at a salvage yard. Trim is relatively cheap to replace, ditto some hub caps; but a grille is hard to find and very expensive.

   If a car you like is missing some chrome, find a local yard under "Automobile Wrecking" in the Yellow Pages *before you buy the car.* Give them the year, make, and model, and ask them to put a call out on their hotline to see whether the parts you need are available and what they cost. If you can get the parts, call a local re-chromer and ask what it costs to re-chrome them. Then decide if you still want to buy the vehicle.

4. **Look for dents and marred paint.**

   If the car has severe dents or chipped or blistered paint, add the price of body work and a paint job to the cost of the car and check thoroughly for signs of rust in the affected areas.

5. **Check for rust around the headlights and trim, on the underside of the car, in the wheel wells, and under the mats in the trunk.**

   Rust is "car cancer." It requires immediate removal and a paint touch-up because it tends to spread if it isn't checked immediately. If you just paint over rust, it continues to form under the shiny new surface. Reject any vehicle that has started to rust out because it may also be happening in places you cannot see.

6. **If you live in an area that gets snow in the winter, check the underside for corrosion due to salt on the streets.**

You may have trouble finding a car in such an area that has not rusted because of these conditions. If a vehicle is old and has recently had an undercoating, be careful: The owner may have undercoated the car to hide the fact that the bottom has rusted out.

7. **Look under the car for signs of a bent frame and/or spot welding.**

These are clues to accidents. If you see them, don't buy.

8. **Look at the windshield and the rear window.**

If the glass is cracked or has been severely scratched by wiper blades, you'll have to replace it. New windshields and rear windows are expensive, and even little cracks tend to enlarge with time. Side windows and side vents are generally much cheaper to replace.

9. **Look for sagging doors, loose door handles, and trunk and hood lids that don't fit properly.**

These could mean that the car has been thrown out of line in an accident. If the car's been driven a lot since the accident, vital parts can be dangerously worn.

10. **Check under the hood, in the trunk, and around the doorjambs for signs of repainting.**

A new vehicle that has recently been repainted has probably been wrecked and restored. If it's old and otherwise in good condition, consider the new paint a plus as long as a close check doesn't reveal an attempt to cover rust. Also note whether all the locks and latches work.

11. **Check for sagging springs by looking at the profile of the vehicle as it sits on the lot.**

The front and rear ends should be on the same level — also the left and right sides. Lean on each of the front and rear fenders and let go. Do you hear squeaks? Sometimes these just mean that lubrication is needed; sometimes they indicate that the suspension has had it.

12. **Check the shock absorbers and struts by stepping on the front and rear bumpers and placing your weight on them. Then take your weight off the car abruptly.**

The car should return to its former level and stay there without continuing to bounce up and down. Shock absorbers and struts are relatively inexpensive if you buy them on sale. If you want to save the cost of installation, consider doing it yourself at an auto class.

13. **Look for signs of water damage.**

Water can corrode vital parts of a vehicle. If your area has experienced flooding in recent years, check for moisture or water stains inside the trunk, on and under the seats, on the interior door and *headliner* (the fabric inside the roof), and under the carpeting. A musty or "over-deodorized" smell can also indicate water damage. If it looks as though the car's been inundated, don't buy it.

14. **Run your finger around the inside edge of the tailpipe (after you make sure it's not hot).**

   There's bound to be some brownish-gray soot but if black carbon comes off on your finger, the fuel/air mixture is probably too rich. A mechanic can easily adjust this. If you have an older model with a carburetor (instead of fuel injection), you can find instructions for doing this in *Auto Repair For Dummies*.

Check for leaks

Before you buy a car, you'll want to know whether the car leaks fluids, and if it does, what type of fluid is leaking. The type of fluid you find gives you a good idea of where the problem is — and how much effort and money it will take to fix it. Here's an easy way to check for leaks:

1. **Back the vehicle up and take a look at where it was parked.**

   Are there fresh spots or puddles on the paving? Ask how long the car has been standing in that spot; the leaks may have come from another car. If you take the vehicle for a test drive, park it and let it stand for about fifteen minutes. When you return, back up and check the pavement again for leaks. Try parking your own vehicle overnight on a clean patch of pavement and check it the next morning.

2. **Dip your finger into each substance you find, and then, depending on what kind of fluid it is, take the appropriate course of action, as explained in the following list.**

Substance	*Do This*
Water	Check the radiator and hoses for leaks.
Black oil	Figure out which part of the vehicle was over the puddle and look for leaks around the oil-drain plug, the crankcase, and the engine.
Light-colored fluid	Depending on which part of the car has been parked over the puddle or spot, check for brake fluid leaks around the master cylinder, around the brake lines, and in back of the wheels. Even if the leaks have dried, the stains should be visible.
Pink oil	It may be automatic transmission fluid. Run your hands around the transmission and feel for wetness.

3. **If you smell gasoline near the hood area, check around the fuel pump and the carburetor, if there is one. If the odor is coming from the center of the car, check the fuel lines. Check the fuel tank if the odor is strongest at the rear of the vehicle.**

Obviously, you don't want to smoke while you're doing this!

4. **Check under the car around the crankcase, around the oil pan, and under the transmission.**

If the car has front-wheel drive, all of these will be under the transaxle. Is anything leaking?

Pay special attention to the tires

New tires are expensive and can add a few hundred dollars to the cost of a car. More importantly, tires provide valuable clues as to how the vehicle was maintained and driven. For these reasons, always check the tires carefully before you agree to buy a car.

If you find a vehicle you like at a dealership, and the tires are very worn, request that they be replaced at no charge.

If any of the terms or conditions mentioned in this section are unfamiliar to you, check out *Auto Repair For Dummies,* which provides pictures and descriptions of each type of tire wear along with guidelines on buying new tires.

Follow these steps to inspect the tires:

1. **Look at the tires and make sure they're all the same size and type (such as radials).**

Ask the seller to provide a matching set or lower the price by the amount it will take to do so. If she refuses, decide whether you're willing to undertake the task yourself. Unmatched tires, especially radials, can take their toll in mileage, performance, and premature wear.

2. **Note the wear patterns on the tire treads.**

Outsides worn: If the outside treads of one or more tires are worn, the car is probably out of alignment. This can simply be the result of hitting a curb or pothole, or it can be a sign of more serious damage. If only the front tires are affected, you can probably have the car realigned for relatively little money. (If you just ignore the situation, you will have to replace the tires before long.) If the rear tires show outside tread wear, realignment may be more expensive, and the rear axle may be bent — a great reason to forget the car.

Centers or sides worn: If the tires show signs of over-inflation (center tread wear) or under-inflation (side tread wear), correction is no problem unless they are worn to the point of replacement. Simply release or add air to the correct level embossed on the side of the tire.

Unevenly worn: If the tires are unevenly worn, the wheels may be poorly balanced. Wheel balancing is not expensive, but you'll have to get new tires if the present ones are in bad shape.

Cupped tires: If the tires are worn very unevenly or "cupped," the steering, suspension, shock absorbers, or brakes may be defective. If the vehicle seems otherwise okay, draw this to the attention of the mechanic who performs the final inspection and be prepared to buy new tires.

3. **Note whether the tires have been replaced.**

If the tires have already been replaced or are very worn, no matter what the odometer says, the car has at least 25,000 miles on it — possibly over 40,000 miles if the tires are steel-belted radials. If the seller swears this isn't so, the vehicle has been driven *very* hard.

4. **Look at the spare tire.**

Is it in good shape? Is there a jack and a lug wrench? If you're shopping at a dealership, ask them to provide a good spare tire, jack, and wrench. If you're buying from a private party, you'll have to provide your own.

5. **Jack the car up high enough to take its weight off the wheels. Then grab the top edge of each of the front tires and try to pull it toward you and push it away from you.**

If you hear a clunking sound, or if there is a lot of movement, the suspension or wheel bearings may be worn.

6. **Now jack a rear wheel off the ground and jiggle it up and down.**

Any up-and-down-movement of the wheel while the axle housing remains stationary indicates that the rear axle bearing may be worn. The axle and the wheel should move as a unit. Personally, I'd have to absolutely love a vehicle to accept this condition, because it could also indicate greater problems with the axle. Be sure your mechanic checks this out.

Inspecting the Inside of the Car

When you inspect the inside of the car, you look at more than the upholstery and carpeting. You also pay attention to other features, like the seat belts, odometer, windshield wipers, headlights, and so on. To help you keep track of your impressions and findings, I've included the nearby Used-Car Inspection Checklist for you to use.

The following steps show you how to thoroughly check out the inside of the car:

1. **Open the door, get in, and look around.**

   Is the carpeting in good shape? Is the upholstery torn? Unless you are willing to settle for cheap mats and seat covers from an auto supply store, recarpeting or reupholstering seats costs a lot. Worn floor mats and pedal covers are cheap to replace, but they may indicate that the car has been driven for many miles, no matter what the odometer says.

2. **Try the seat belts.**

   Do all the seat belts lock and adjust properly? Don't forget to check the ones in the rear.

3. **Try all the seats.**

   Are the seat springs sagging or bumpy and uncomfortable? If they are, forget the car. New seats are expensive and may not be available for an older model unless you want to search the salvage yards and then reupholster whatever seats you find.

4. **Try all the manual and power mechanisms that adjust, and move the driver's and passengers' seats.**

   Do they work? It may cost a bit to repair or replace them.

5. **Look for tears or stains in the *headliner* (the fabric inside the roof) and the upholstery inside the doors.**

   Installing replacements is expensive, and stains can be a sign that leaks are coming in through ill-fitting windows, worn window or sunroof gaskets, or the roof itself.

6. **If the car has a sunroof, open and close it.**

   Does the sunroof work properly? Repairs or replacement can be very costly.

7. **Try all the door locks and window controls.**

   Repairing or replacing manual or power controls can be expensive, because they're located inside the doors.

8. **Check the glove box.**

   Does the lid close properly? Does it lock?

9. **Take a look at the odometer.**

   Does the number of miles on it seem suspiciously low? Yes, people do illegally tamper with them, and this is a great reason for wanting to see a vehicle's previous service records, which indicate the mileage at the time of each repair. If records are not available, you can locate the prior owners through the DMV.

10. **Try to move the steering wheel without starting the car.**

    If there are more than two inches of play in the steering wheel before the wheels begin to move, the steering is unsafe.

11. **Sound the horn.**

    Is it easy to find? To operate?

12. **Put the emergency brake on and turn the key in the ignition. Then, with the gearshift in Park or Neutral, look at the gauges on the dashboard to make sure they're working.**

    A broken gauge may be replaced relatively cheaply — if it's still available. If the gauges indicate low oil pressure, a discharging alternator, brake trouble, or other problems, be wary about buying the car.

13. **Try the dashboard controls.**

    Turn on the windshield washer and wipers, the sound system, the heater, the defroster, the air conditioner, and the interior lights. Are they all working properly? Is the clock working?

14. **Turn on the headlights and check the directional signal flashers on the dashboard and the interior lights.**

    Have a friend check to see if all the lights actually work. Do the front and rear turn signals blink? Do the headlights go to high beam when you turn on the brights? If the car has fog lights, check them, too.

15. **Have your friend look at the brake lights.**

    Do they go on when you step on the brakes? Do the backup lights go on when you back the car up? (Back up slowly — you're going to need your friend for a few more tests.)

Checking under the Hood

After you've inspected the exterior and the interior, it's time to get down to the nitty-gritty. And in a car, the nitty-gritty is the stuff under the hood. I know it looks horrendously complicated, but the parts you need to check should be easy to identify. Your objective is to find clues to potential or existing problems so that you can make a good decision about buying — or not buying — a particular vehicle.

To help you keep track of the things you find, use the "Used-Car Inspection Checklist."

Take a look inside

With the engine off, and the gearshift in Park, ask the seller to lift the hood. (The location and operation of the hoodlatch differs from one vehicle to the next so this is an easy way to keep your cool.)

Be wary if everything looks shiny and clean. Most used-car dealers have the engine area cleaned so that it looks as though the engine is in mint condition. Unfortunately, this cleaning can hide signs of repair work. To do a thorough under-the-hood check, follow these steps:

1. **Look for signs of leaks.**

   They don't have to be wet; sometimes dried stains can clue you in.

2. **Look at the radiator and run your hands across its grille.**

   Check your hands for rust from the grille. If you find some, pinch and rub the grille fins. If they're rusty or crumbly, it's new radiator time!

3. **Check the radiator hoses.**

   Are the clamps secure, or is there leakage around them? Are the hoses cracked or brittle? Sticky and gooey? Leaky radiator hoses can be replaced for a couple of dollars; a dealer should be willing to replace them free of charge.

4. **Open the radiator cap or the coolant bottle and check the fluid level and color.**

   The liquid should cover the radiator fins or reach the Full line on the bottle and should be yellow-green or blue. If it looks like water, it may be just that. Vehicles that have been running with little or no coolant have not been properly maintained.

5. **Check for rust floating around inside.**

   The radiator may simply need flushing (which is easy to do), but it may need replacing if it's rusted through. To learn how long that rust has been building up, ask when the coolant was last changed. If it hasn't been changed in a year, ask the dealer to flush and refill the system and have your mechanic check it with a pressure tester before you buy the vehicle. Leaky radiators can cost a lot of money to repair or replace.

6. **Check for oil floating on the surface of the liquid.**

   If so, this indicates that a cylinder wall is cracked, a good reason to forget the car.

7. **Look around the water pump (usually just behind the fan).**

   Rusty areas may indicate leaks, and leaky water pumps must be replaced, not repaired.

8. **Check the fan belts that run between the water pump and the alternator and air conditioner.**

   These belts should have about a half-inch of play in them. If you can, turn them over to see whether the inner surfaces are frayed or cracked. If they are, ask the dealer to replace the belts.

9. **Check the wiring.**

   Are any wires or electrical cables loose, cracked, brittle, or frayed?

10. **Wiggle the distributor to see if it's loose.**

    If there is a lot of play, the timing will be off. Check the distributor cap for frayed wires and cracks.

11. **Check the spark plug cables and boots.**

    Are they cracked or brittle? Do the boots fit securely over the plugs? These aren't very expensive to replace, but they may cause the engine to misfire if they aren't in good shape.

12. **Look at the battery.**

    If the terminals are very corroded you will need a new one. If someone has cleaned up the acid deposits on the terminals, check the battery cables to see whether they are frayed, cracked, or show signs of deterioration where they adjoin the terminals. If you think the battery needs to be replaced, ask the dealer to throw a new battery in as part of the deal or a private seller to deduct the price of a battery from the cost of the vehicle.

13. **Open the lid of the master brake cylinder and look inside.**

    Is the brake fluid clean? Is it up to the fill line? If it's low, there may be a leak in the brake lines or in a wheel cylinder or the brakes may be badly worn. Does the rubber diaphragm on the lid seem to be in good shape? Replace the lid and run your hands around the sides and base of the master cylinder. Are there any signs of leaks around the cylinder or on the fire walls behind and next to the cylinder?

Look for smoke signals

While the car is running, you can continue your inspection by noting and identifying any smoke that comes from the tailpipe (you'll need your friend back there to tell you what's happening). With the gearshift in Park or Neutral and the emergency brake on, race the engine. Have your friend check for smoke coming out of the tailpipe and note the smoke's color. The following table explains what the smoke may mean:

- ✔ **White vapor.** If it's a cold morning, you may see some white water vapor. Disregard this if it stops when the car warms up. If it continues after the car is warm, a cracked engine block or a leaky head gasket may be letting water leak into the engine. If you're unsure as to the cause and you really like the car, be sure to have your mechanic check this out. You could be in for some really expensive repairs.

- ✔ **Black smoke.** If you see black smoke, the fuel/air mixture may be too rich and need adjusting. Carbon in the tailpipe (refer to the section "Check out the exterior") means the same thing.

- ✔ **Light or dark blue smoke.** If the smoke is light or dark blue, the vehicle is burning oil, which can indicate that oil is leaking into the combustion chambers and the car either needs its piston rings or valve guides replaced or the engine rebuilt or replaced. Remedying this situation usually costs at least $1,000, which is probably why the previous owner dumped the car. Forget the vehicle.

- ✔ **Light gray smoke.** If the smoke is light gray, the car may be burning transmission fluid. Keep the engine running while you check the transmission dipstick. Is the fluid dark and burned-looking? Does it smell burned? If so, have the transmission checked carefully by your mechanic if you are still interested in the car; with luck, it may simply need the fluid changed.

A faulty vacuum modulator can suck transmission fluid into the engine where it is burned in the cylinders and causes the same type of smoke to come out of the tailpipe. If your mechanic tells you this is the case, you can usually replace the vacuum modulator quite cheaply.

If the transmission turns out to be marginal, reject the vehicle. Transmission work is just too costly to justify, unless you're buying a classic car that you intend to rebuild completely.

Look at the engine

The engine is the heart of the car, and as such, it deserves a thorough going over. Your mechanic will be able to electronically check the inner workings of a vehicle you'd like to buy — including the engine management computer, if there is one — but there are many things you can spot yourself that will help you eliminate losers from your shopping list.

1. **Run your finger around the edge of the cylinder head where it meets the rocker-arm cover.**

   If oil is leaking out, you may simply need a new gasket. That's not too expensive, if you replace it yourself. Be sure to ask your mechanic to check for signs of further damage.

2. **Check the engine block and manifolds for cracks or rust, which may indicate leaks.**

   If you find cracks, do not buy the car.

3. **Run your finger around the line where the head of the engine joins the cylinder block.**

   A sooty deposit there may mean that there's a blown head gasket, which is an expensive proposition. When you get to Step 6, be doubly sure there's no sign of water in the oil on the dipstick.

4. **Look at the core plugs on the sides of the engine.**

   Are there signs that these have been leaking? If only one plug looks rusty, the others probably have as much hidden rust and will soon begin to leak, too. Replacing them all can add up to a lot of money.

5. **Feel the hoses that run into and out of the engine.**

   Are they cracked or leaky? Sticky? Soft and mushy? Stiff or brittle? If they have any of these symptoms, they have to be replaced or they could blow at any time. Again, this isn't a big expense if you do it yourself. A dealer should replace these before you buy the vehicle.

6. **Check the oil dipstick. Note the oil level and whether the oil is clean.**

   To tell whether the oil is clean, dip your forefinger in the oil and rub the oil against your thumb. Oil turns black almost immediately, but does this oil have particles in it? Does it leave a black streak on your finger? If it does, this can indicate poor maintenance and a badly worn engine.

   A low oil level may also indicate a leak or poor maintenance, but if everything else looks spiffy you can probably take a chance on the car.

   Does the dipstick have drops of water on it or does the oil on it look spongy and gray? Either could be a sign of a blown head gasket or a cracked block that has allowed water to leak into the oil. Don't buy the vehicle.

7. **Ask when the oil, oil filter, air filter, and fuel filter were last replaced.**

   Most dealers replace these as a matter of routine when getting a car ready for resale. If they haven't, they should do it as part of the deal. If you're buying from a private party, you have to do it yourself.

8. **Remove the lid from the air cleaner. Remove the air filter and hold it up to the sun or a bright light.**

   Can you see light through it? If the air filter is really filthy, the car may not have been properly maintained.

9. **Remove the entire air cleaner and look at the carburetor, if the car has one (fuel-injected cars don't).**

   Are there signs of fuel leaking from the bottom or from the gasket where the top of the carburetor meets the float bowl? If you haven't run the engine yet, is the choke closed? It should be.

10. **Look at the underside of the hood, above the carburetor.**

     If you see a black "blow-by" stain on the underside of the hood, have the PCV valve and the compression checked.

11. **With the gearshift in Neutral or Park and the emergency brake on, start the car.**

     Then go back under the hood and take a look down the carburetor barrel. Did the choke open after a while?

     Be careful about looking down a carburetor barrel while the engine is running; it could possibly backfire in your face.

12. **Move the throttle linkage with your finger.**

     Does the throttle linkage move easily? Does the car rev up promptly? It should. If it doesn't, that may mean that the carburetor may simply need adjusting to make it run well — or it could mean that the carburetor needs to be taken apart and cleaned (that's called *rebuilding*). If you think the carburetor needs to be rebuilt or replaced, think twice about buying the vehicle.

13. **Replace the air cleaner.**

14. **Unscrew the oil filler cap and listen to the engine.**

     Are the valves ticking? Do you hear rattling or clunking noises coming from inside the engine? If so, the car may need a valve job. Valve jobs are expensive, and even worse things could be happening in there.

15. **Notice whether the engine seems securely mounted or is shaking.**

     If the engine shakes around a lot, one or more cylinders could be misfiring because of a loose connection, bad wiring, or carburetor or fuel injector problems. If the shaking occurs only when you are stepping on the gas and accelerating, the cause could be the engine mounts. Ask your mechanic to check this one out before you buy the car. Repairs can vary from next-to-nothing to very expensive, depending on the problem.

16. **If the car has an automatic transmission, with the engine still running, check the transmission dipstick.**

     Does the fluid reach the Full level on the dipstick? Is it pink or does it look or smell burned? If it does, the transmission could need service, repair, or replacement.

17. **Turn on the air conditioner and stick your head under the hood to listen to it.**

     Clanks and thumps can be very expensive noises.

USED-CAR INSPECTION CHECKLIST

Make, Model & Year: _____ Odometer Mileage: _____

Owner: _____ Asking Price: _____

Address: _____ Phone: _____

Source: _____ Date: _____

Service Records Available? _____ Owners Manual? _____ Service Manual? _____

Safety Features: ABS Brakes? _____ Dual Air Bags? _____ Side Air Bags? _____ 3-Pt. Seat Belts? _____

AREA INSPECTED	LOCATION	REPAIR COST
Exterior		
Ripples in body?		$
Chrome peeling? Pitted? Dented? Rusty?		$
Paint: Chipped? Blistered? Signs of repainting?		$
Dents?		$
Poor body restoration?		$
Rust?		$
Underside corroded? Dented?		$
Frame OK?		$
Windshield & rear window OK?		$
Side window & vents OK?		$
Doors sagging? Poorly aligned?		$
Door handles loose? Missing?		$
Trunk & hood lids aligned? Locks OK?		$
Springs squeaky? Vehicle's profile even?		$
Shock absorbers & struts OK?		$
Water damage?		$
Tailpipe(s): Black carbon deposit inside?		$
Leaks		
On pavement under car? From where? What kind?		$
Tires		
Same size & type?		$
Abnormal wear? What kind?		$
Mileage on tires *(if not the original tires)*		$
Spare tire OK? Jack and lug wrench?		$
Signs of worn wheel bearings?		$

USED-CAR INSPECTION CHECKLIST *(continued)*

Make, Model & Year:

Owner:

AREA INSPECTED	LOCATION	REPAIR COST
Interior		
Carpets OK?		$
Pedal covers worn or missing?		$
Floor mats OK?		$
Upholstery OK?		$
Seat springs OK? Seat controls OK?		$
Headliner & door upholstery OK?		$
Does sunroof work? Does it leak?		$
Door locks OK? Glove box OK?		$
Window cranks or power controls OK?		$
Steering wheel "play" before wheels turn?		$
Horn OK?		$
Start Engine: *(Car in Park or Neutral w/emergency brake on)*		
Gauges missing? Broken? Any problems indicated on gauges?		$
Dashboard Controls:		
Windshield washer & wiper OK?		$
Clock? Sound system?		$
Heater? Air conditioner? Defroster?		$
Lights:		
Dashboard, map & interior lights OK?		$
Turn signals on dashboard & exterior OK?		$
Headlights and brights OK?		$
Brake, backup & fog lights OK?		$
Smoke Signals: *(race engine & check tail pipe emissions)* What color are they?		
Turn Engine Off & Open Hood:		
Radiator leaking? Rusty?		$
Hoses secure? Leaky? Cracked?		$
Coolant sufficient? Rusty? Clear? When was it last changed?	Date:	$ $
Water pump leaky?		$
Belts: 1/2" play? Cracked or frayed?		$

USED-CAR INSPECTION CHECKLIST *(continued)*

Make, Model & Year:

Owner:

AREA INSPECTED	LOCATION	REPAIR COST
Wiring cracked? Brittle? Unattached?		$
Distributor loose? Cap & cable OK?		$
Spark plug cables & boots OK?		$
Battery corrosion? Cables OK?		$
Master brake cyclinder level OK? Fluid clean? Lid diaphragm OK? Leaks?		$
Cylinder head: Gasket leaking?		$
Core plugs leaking? Rusty?		$
Engine block, manifolds: Any leaks?		$
Hoses leaky? Cracked? Sticky? Soft? Brittle? Clamps in place?		$
Oil dipstick: Oil level OK? Oil clean? Spongy? Watery?		$
Filters: Can you see through air filter? When were air filter, oil and oil filter, and fuel filter last replaced?	Air Filter: Oil & Filter: Fuel Filter:	$
Power steering dipstick: Level OK? Does fluid look or smell burnt?		$
Carburetor: *(If car is not fuel-injected)*		$
Leaks? (Check around gaskets)		$
Blow-by on underside of hood over carb.?		$
Start the Engine: *(Car in Park or Neutral w/emergency brake on. Watch hair, clothing & jewelry)*		
Choke: (Should be closed until engine starts, then should open in a short time.)		$
Does throttle linkage move easily? Does engine rev promptly?		$
Valves ticking? (With oil-filter cap off)		$
Engine shaking?		$
Transmission dipstick: Level OK? Pink? Or brown & burnt-smelling?		$
Leaks: *(Upon return)* Anything leaking around engine? Where?		$

See How It Runs: Test-Driving the Vehicle

If you're still interested in a vehicle after you've inspected it inside, outside, and under the hood, now's the time to take the show on the road. I've provided a Test Drive Checklist to help you follow these steps while you test drive the car:

1. **Adjust the seats.**

   Are you comfortable? Do you feel at home?

2. **Look around, out the windows, and in the mirrors.**

   Can you see the road well? Can you see through the right rear window when you look in the rear mirror? Are the side mirrors okay?

3. **Drive slowly down a quiet street with your seat belts on, make sure there's no one behind you, and then hit the brakes.**

   If the car pulls to one side, that may indicate a hydraulic leak, air in the system, or worn linings.

   If the brakes squeal, they may need to be replaced or serviced or they may just be noisy. Your mechanic will check them and decide.

   Notice how long it takes to stop the car comfortably. Can you stop quickly enough to avoid an accident without putting yourself through the windshield?

   If the car has ABS (an Antilock Braking System), this is the time to see whether it's working properly. If you've had no experience with ABS, be sure to read about them in Chapter 7, so you know what to look for, and how to use them properly.

4. **Step on the brake pedal again.**

   The pedal should stay put after you have pressed it. If it continues to sink slowly toward the floor, the master cylinder is probably defective. Check the brake lines around the master cylinder and behind each wheel for leaks.

5. **If the car has a manual transmission, add the following to your test-drive routine:**

   - While the car is at rest with the engine still running, engage the hand brake, shift into second gear and try pulling away.

     If the engine stalls, the clutch is probably okay (this is one of the few circumstances when stalling out is good news); if the engine races, the clutch is shot.

   - Run through the gears to check the clutch for slippage.

     Notice whether the gearshift works smoothly. If the car hesitates or makes grinding noises when you shift, this could signal clutch or transmission problems.

- Is there "free pedal play?" (Can you press the clutch an inch or two before the gears engage?)

- Does the clutch chatter?

- Release the hand brake and drive the car down the block. Vary your speed. Stop, shift from forward to reverse, and back up a little. The engine shouldn't race, and there should be no slams, jerks, or howls from the transmission during any of these shifts.

6. **Drive slowly down the block with your hands off the wheel.**

   If the car pulls to one side, the steering linkage may be damaged, or the front end may just need alignment. The former is a no-no; the latter isn't too costly.

7. **Have your friend get out and watch to see whether any wheels wobble while you drive the car slowly.**

   If the wheels wobble, the cause may be a bent wheel. If you really want the car, change to the spare tire and try again. If the wobble is gone, chances are it was the tire that was bad — not a big problem if you don't have to replace more than one. If the wobble remains, it probably means that the wheel is off-kilter. Wheels are relatively expensive to replace.

8. **Drive down an alley or driveway with the windows open.**

   Clanking or grinding noises coming from the rear wheels can indicate worn rear-axle bearings. You can check them by following the easy instructions in *Auto Repair For Dummies,* or have your mechanic take a look.

9. **Head for the nearest highway and get up to speed.**

   Does the car handle well? If the front wheels shimmy or the car pulls to one side, it may need alignment, or the front end may be badly worn. Front-end alignments usually cost under $100, but front ends are expensive to replace.

   Also note the car's "pickup" when you accelerate, pass, or start. Does it feel lively and powerful?

   Does the vehicle have overdrive, fifth, or passing gears?

10. **If the car has an automatic transmission, note whether it moves smoothly from low to higher gears.**

    If you hear clunking or feel hesitations a mechanic should check the transmission to see whether it just needs service or has to be replaced. I wouldn't pay for a high-ticket item like a transmission unless I intended to rebuild a classic car.

11. **Drive up the steepest hill or driveway you can find.**

    Does the car sail up smoothly with power to spare?

TEST-DRIVE CHECKLIST

Make: _____   Model: _____   Year: _____

Source: _____   Phone: _____

TEST:	YES	NO	1-10 RATING
Road Test on Quiet Street or Alley:			
Feel comfortable? Seats adjust OK?			
Visibility OK? Right rear window? Mirrors?			
Brakes: *(Drive slowly and stop suddenly)* Does car pull to side? Squeal? Stop OK?			
Brake pedal sinkage?			
ABS working properly?			
Steering: *(Drive slowly)* Does the car pull to one side?			
All transmissions: *(Vary speed & shift from forward to reverse)* Engine racing? Slams, jerks, howls?			
Manual transmissions: *(Run through gears)* Gearshift smooth? Hesitations? Grinding?			
Clutch: Is there 1/2" pedal play before it disengages? Chatters? Hand brake test OK?			
Wheels: *(Drive slowly)* Do wheels wobble?			
Axle bearings: *(Drive up alley or driveway w/ window open)* Clanking or grinding?			
Highway Road Test:			
Handling OK? Front wheel shimmy?			
Does car pull to one side?			
Pickup on acceleration OK? Powerful?			
Smooth shifting? Overdrive/5th gears OK?			
Hills: Power OK?			
Curves: Oversteering? Understeering?			

12. **Let the car coast down the hill for a few seconds without stepping on the gas. Then accelerate and look in the rearview mirror.**

    If there's a puff of blue smoke from the exhaust, oil may be getting past the valve guides or seals. This is *not* a good sign. Have a mechanic check carefully to see whether they need to be replaced.

13. **Find a safe opportunity to take some tight curves at the speed limit.**

    Does the car *oversteer* (turn more sharply than you expected it to when you moved the steering wheel)? Does it *understeer* (require more effort with the steering wheel than is usually necessary to make such a turn)? Do you feel in control of it?

14. **When you return from your test drive, look at the engine again for signs of leaks that may have opened up under the pressure of driving.**

    If the car seemed to lack power or felt "funny," you may want to run a compression check on the engine, which can tell you how well the cylinders, pistons, rings, and valves have worn. Look for easy instructions in *Auto Repair For Dummies* or have your mechanic do this.

Arranging for the Final Inspection

When you've found the vehicle you'd like to buy, even though you've checked it out yourself, be sure to follow the absolutely primal rule of used-car buying:

> *No matter how well any used vehicle seems to perform, always have an independent mechanic do a final inspection before you buy.*

A good mechanic has the ability to hear things you'd miss, a sixth sense to diagnose them, and the hoists and electronic equipment to check a vehicle more thoroughly than you can. For obvious reasons, you don't want the seller's or dealer's mechanic to do this inspection. (If you don't already have a mechanic you can trust, check out Chapter 18 for tips on how to find a mechanic who's honest and competent.) Call several shops and ask them if they'd be willing to check out a used car and provide a written report of their findings.

Be sure the inspection includes a cylinder compression test as well as a look at the frame, suspension, alignment, brakes, emissions, and a test-drive to check performance. The inspection should take about an hour, so be prepared to pay $35 to $50. It definitely shouldn't cost more than $100.

Many private parties and dealers may be reluctant to allow you to take a vehicle you haven't paid for to your mechanic. Suggest that they allow you to schedule an appointment with your mechanic at a mutually convenient time and meet you at the shop. If they are willing to let you take the car if you leave a deposit, a couple of hundred dollars should suffice. Be sure you get a receipt that stipulates that the deposit is refundable if, *for any reason,* you decide not to buy the car. Most private parties will insist on cash, but do your best to give dealers a check. That way, if they try any funny business or insist that the deposit be applied to another of their vehicles, you can simply stop payment on the check.

Photocopy the checklists on the previous pages and use them for every vehicle that interests you (and save the lists you filled out for other vehicles you liked in case the deal for your favorite falls through). Give the lists to the mechanic who does the final inspection. Because he or she won't profit from the sale of the vehicle, you can rely on the impartiality of the survey. Arrange for the mechanic to report to you privately when the owner or dealer isn't there. The insight from the mechanic can provide you with a valuable tool for final negotiations.

Evaluating What You've Found

The Repair Evaluation Chart that follows gives you an idea of what it would cost to repair some of the defects you've discovered. If you've been checking out your own car, it tells you whether repairing it pays, and if you decide to sell your car, you can use this chart to identify minor repairs you can make to increase the selling price, as well as those problems that cost more than they're worth. If you're shopping for a used vehicle, the chart enables you to screen out those with expensive defects and estimate the cost of repairs needed to bring the car into good condition. If the seller won't repair the vehicle, ask to have the cost of the repair deducted from the selling price.

Unless the vehicle is advertised as "needing work," a reputable dealer should be willing to take care of all these items as part of the deal. A used car bought from a dealer is supposed to be in good condition. Some states require a recent state inspection sticker before a car can be sold or re-registered. If the dealerships in your state are required to furnish this, they will have to fix anything found to be below standard even if you have the car reinspected after you buy it. If you are buying from a private party or must do the work yourself, a good rule is this:

> ***If any defects are listed on the chart as a major problem, forget the car.***

The problems in the first column are either unsolvable and will lead to the quick demise of the vehicle, or they are much too costly to handle. Only classic vehicles that will go up in value by thousands of dollars after they are restored are worth the time and trouble. In such cases, add up the probable cost of the required work plus the cost of the vehicle and see if it compares favorably with the current price for such restored vehicles in recent ads.

Repairs in the center column of the chart can cost a couple of hundred dollars, maybe more. Investing may be worthwhile if only one of these repairs is needed; more than one of them will mean a considerably larger outlay of money, even if you do the work yourself. If you really love the car, ask your mechanic to estimate the cost of the repairs in question before making a decision. But be prepared to find another vehicle that doesn't require such expensive repair.

The last column lists the repairs and replacements that many used cars require. If you're buying from a dealership they should be willing to remedy all of these. If not, some of these jobs can be done with little or no expertise; if a lot of work is required, the vehicle is probably more trouble than it's worth.

Repair Evaluation Chart

Major Problems	*Think Twice About These*	*Relatively Cheap*
I. Wreck Indicators	Needs new shock absorbers	Minor dents
Extensive dents, rust, and chips	Needs new springs	Needs front-end alignment
Misalignment of hood, trunk lid, or doors	Needs new carburetor	Needs new throttle linkage
Welded or bent under car	Needs new master cylinder	Needs carburetor frame adjustment
New paint job on a new car	Needs complete brake job	Needs new gauges, knobs, switches, wiper blades, lighter, and so on
II. High Expense Items	Self-adjusting brakes out of adjustment (possibly expensive)	Radio needs to be repaired
Transmission leaks or poor performance	Needs new alternator, radiator, starter, muffler, flywheel, or distributor	Clock doesn't work
Blue smoke coming from tailpipe (unless due to faulty vacuum modulator)	Needs seats recovered	Needs horn, lights, or signals repaired
Cracked block, head, or manifold	Needs new side windows or vents	Needs hoses replaced
Valves need to be reground or replaced	Needs new carpets	Needs a tune-up
Grille missing or damaged	Needs new chrome or bumper	Needs manual brakes adjusted

(continued)

Repair Evaluation Chart *(continued)*

Major Problems	Think Twice About These	Relatively Cheap
Needs four new tires	Needs pollution device required by law	Needs a spare tire, or just two tires
Needs new windshield or rear window	Cracked plastic bumpers need replacing	Needs new fan belts
Clutch worn or defective		(The dealer should definitely supply all of the above. In some states the law requires that the brake system, muffler, pollution devices, steering, suspension, horn, and lights be in safe condition before the car is sold.)
Rear axle worn or damaged		
Steering linkage and front-end suspension worn or damaged		
Needs extensive bodywork or complete paint job		
Needs new seats because seat springs are shot		
Needs new convertible top or interior		
Needs new crankshaft, driveshaft, and so on		

Smog Certification

If you live in an area that requires smog certification each time a vehicle is registered to a new owner, be sure that the vehicle you choose will pass the emissions test. Even if you don't have to recertify the vehicle immediately, sooner or later, you're going to have to have it tested. The seller may show you recent proof of certification, but there are tricks that enable defective vehicles to fool the diagnostic equipment just long enough to pass the test. For this reason, be sure that any agreement you sign with a private party or a dealer specifies that you can return the vehicle if it doesn't pass the emissions test.

Be sure to ask the mechanic who does your final inspection to test the car's emissions against smog certification requirements. If it doesn't pass, find out whether a simple tune-up will remedy the situation. If it will, the current owner or dealer may be willing to have the car tuned to make the sale. If more expensive repairs are necessary, you may want to look for another vehicle.

Chapter 5

Shopping for Value and Negotiating the Deal

. . . .

In This Chapter

▶ Figuring out the real value of a used car

▶ Knowing which features increase or decrease a car's value

▶ Knowing which vehicles to steer clear of

▶ Dealing with sales staff and getting the best price

▶ Getting the most for your trade-in

▶ Wrapping up the deal

. . . .

*B*efore you buy or sell a vehicle, you need to have a realistic idea of what the car is worth. If you don't know the value of the model you want, you may overpay or lose a great vehicle by bidding too low. If you set too high a price on your own car, you may never get rid of it. This chapter helps you determine the going rate for a particular year and type of vehicle; Chapter 4 guides you through a complete inspection of a used car. Both factors together — the value of the make and model and the inspection of the particular vehicle — can help you determine whether the price you're being quoted is reasonable or ridiculous.

Of course, after you determine the real value of a used car, the challenge becomes convincing the dealer or owner that your price is the right one. To make sure that you get the best deal possible, this chapter also offers tips and pointers for handling the negotiations.

Determining the True Value of a Used Vehicle

The following sections explain the types of things that affect resale value, offer resources you can use to compare the price of the car you're looking at with others like it, and tell where you can get additional information about price and hidden costs. Armed with this information, you'll be able to recognize a good — or bad — deal when you see it.

Factors that affect resale value

Some things increase the value of a used car; some decrease it. Before you begin to negotiate a price for the vehicle you want (or want to sell), take a look at the following items to see where your car stands:

- ✔ **Mileage:** Most used-car prices are based on an average of 15,000 miles per year of wear and tear. If a car you like shows greater mileage, ask for a discount of 15 to 20 cents per mile over the average. Of course, you should also be willing to pay more for a vehicle that's seen less than average use.

- ✔ **Special features:** Automatic transmission, air conditioning, power steering, security and safety systems, extremely powerful engines, air bags, antilock brakes, traction control, and four doors increase the value of a vehicle.

- ✔ **Expensive accessories:** Custom sound systems, designer wheels, and car phones only attract extra bucks from buyers who share these priorities.

- ✔ **Wild colors:** Exotic colors or decorations are not attractive to most buyers and may raise insurance premiums; therefore, unless you are lucky enough to find someone with the same taste as you, these things can actually decrease the value of the car.

- ✔ **Rarely used features:** Heated or electronic-memory seats and digital or "computer screen" dashboards are not worth paying for and are expensive to repair. I wouldn't reject a vehicle just because it has them, but don't let anyone try to convince you that they justify a higher price for a used vehicle.

Independent pricing sources

When you're buying a used car, don't take the used-car dealer's or current owner's word for what the car is worth on the current market. And if you just rely on your own opinion of the car's worth you may discover too late that you either paid too much, or bid too low and lost a great car. Instead, use independent pricing sources to obtain an informed, objective opinion. It doesn't cost much in time or money, and the knowledge you gain can save you a bundle — in cash or heartache. Reliable pricing sources include the following:

✔ **Classified and dealership ads.** These ads appear in local and major newspapers, trade publications, recycling publications, and "Auto Trader" publications. They can give you an idea of what the makes and models that interest you are going for.

Keep in mind that most asking prices you see in these publications are a bit inflated to give the owner or dealer a chance to negotiate.

✔ **The Internet and other online services.** The Internet offers several sites that will locate used vehicles in your area that satisfy your priorities concerning age, make, features and price. Some offer other useful data as well. Here are some sites to get you started:

- **Auto Trader Online** (www.traderonline.com/auto) lists car dealers, parts sources, and more. If you'd like to place an ad of your own, they offer tips on how to advertise.

- **Autoweb.com** (www.autoweb.com) enables you to search thousands of used cars and place an ad to sell your own. You can research prices at *Kelley Bluebook* and *Car & Driver's Buying Guide* via links to those sites, find information on automotive financing, insurance, specifications, and reviews — and compare opinions in their Auto Talk chat area.

- **Online Auto** (www.onlineauto.com) can be used to search for cars, and more. You can place an ads or buy a new or used car using their photo classifieds, or locate a dealer in your area.

- **Used Car Net** (www.usedcars.com) provides classifieds for finding or selling cars, plus information on dealers, financing, parts, auctions, clubs, activities, and services. They also have a link to the Kelley Bluebook site (www.kbb.com).

✔ **Blue books.** These books, such as the *Kelley Blue Book Used Car Guide* (Kelley Blue Book Co.), the *N.A.D.A. Official Used Car Guide* (National Automobile Dealers Used Car Guide Co.), the *Automobile Red Book* (National Market Reports, Inc.), and *Edmund's Used Car Prices* (Edmund Publications Corp.), are the most popular sources for wholesale ("low") and retail ("high") prices — sometimes referred to informally as "blue-book prices" — for foreign and domestic used cars. *Sanford Evans Gold Book of Used Car Prices* (Sanford Evans Communications) does the same for antique and classic cars. Blue books break down the price by year, make, model, accessories, body condition, engine size, 2- or 4-doors, transmission type, 2- or 4-wheel drive, mileage, and so on, so you can zero in on the price range for a vehicle by age, quality, and general condition.

- The *Consumer Guide Automobile Book* (Publications International, Ltd.) lists the retail price, dealer invoice, and a fair price to pay for most vehicles.

These books help you estimate how much you can expect to get for your car and how much you can expect to pay for a vehicle you want. *Wholesale* refers to what a dealer may offer for the vehicle as a trade-in or what it may bring at auction; *retail* is what a dealer may charge you for it. Private-party deals fall somewhere between the two.

Estimates vary from one publication to another so check more than one for greater accuracy. Kelley's prices are usually higher than Edmund's, so you may prefer to quote Kelley if you're selling a vehicle and Edmund if you're buying one.

You can find blue books at banks, insurance and loan companies, and public libraries. Be sure you are reading the most recent copy. Car values can change drastically, depending on competition, economic conditions, and current fads, so these books may not be as accurate as the classified ads in your local paper. Kelley's information is also available on the Internet at www.kbb.com.

- The *Consumer Reports* Used Car Price Service. This service provides current prices for your geographical region. The price estimates are based on age, mileage, options, condition, reliability, and frequency of repair. Have the following data handy when you call: your zip code; the year, make, and model of the vehicle you're considering, as well as its mileage, number of cylinders, major options, and overall condition. This service is open seven days a week from 7 a.m. to 2 a.m. EST and costs $1.75 per minute. Call 900-446-1120 to see if the service is available in your area.

- The *Consumer Reports* Facts by Fax. To receive a specially edited report by fax or first class mail, use a Touch-Tone phone to enter any topic code from the cumulative index at the back of an issue of *Consumer Reports* or its annual Buying Guide. The fax line (800-896-7788) is open 24 hours a day.

- The *Consumer's Digest* Used Car Price Fax Service. This service offers current market prices for 1976 to current-year used cars, trucks, vans, and optional equipment. Prices are adjusted for condition, mileage, and repair, and include trade-in and private-party listings. The service's toll line is 900-884-CARS, and they say an average call lasts four minutes. To save time and money, be ready to supply the year, model, body style, mileage, and condition of each vehicle you'd like to buy or sell.

- The CAA Consumer Advisory Department. This department provides current blue-book value for used cars to members of the Canadian Automobile Association.

Places to get more info about used cars and hidden costs

Although not strictly related to the cost of the car, hidden costs, like insurance, frequency of repairs, and reliability, can affect how much owning a car costs. And when you're negotiating, you want as much information as you can get regarding the car you're looking to buy or sell. So use the following sources for information on current prices and hidden costs.

- ✔ *Consumer Reports* **Annual Buying Guides.** These guides feature lists of the best and worst used vehicles, as well as frequency-of-repair records.

- ✔ *The Used Car Book,* **by Jack Gillis (HarperCollins Publishers, Inc.).** This book lists insurance rates for major models of domestic and foreign cars as "Discount," "Regular," or "Surcharge" and provides auto-theft, complaint, repair, and occupant-injury data. The book is updated annually.

- ✔ *Injury, Collision, and Theft Losses by Make and Model.* This booklet published annually by the Highway Loss Data Institute in Arlington, Virginia, rates recent vehicles from "Substantially Better Than Average" to "Substantially Worse Than Average." It's available free by calling the National Insurance Consumer Helpline (NICH) at 800-942-4242.

- ✔ **Carfax.** This service will do a computerized title search on any used vehicle (except motorcycles) manufactured from 1981 to the present and let you now whether it has been salvaged, has had the odometer rolled back to indicate fewer miles than it's actually traveled, or is a new car that was returned to the manufacturer as a lemon and has found its way back on the market. If you call them at 800-274-2277 they'll fax you the information within 20 minutes for $20 per vehicle. Their Web site (www.carfaxreport.com) is an even better deal at $12.50. After offering a preview report on a similar vehicle (so you can decide whether the data is what you're looking for) they'll put your report on screen and/or send you a faxed hard copy.

Other resources

In addition to the books, the ads, the pricing services, and any other source you may glean information from, there's one you may not have considered: people who own vehicles like the one you're considering.

After you've determined how much the model you want should cost, take the time to find out what it's like to own one. Car-watch on the street and ask the owners of the models you like for a firsthand view of the pleasures and problems they've experienced with that particular vehicle. Look those models up in the sources listed in the section "Places to get more info about used cars and hidden costs" to make sure they are reliable and carry no hidden costs.

Don't limit your choice to just one model unless you have plenty of time to search for it. However, if you have a favorite manufacturer, their new-car dealerships tend to have more used cars of that make, which have been traded in for new models.

Out-Dealing the Dealers

After you decide on a vehicle, you're ready to start negotiating to buy it. Negotiating means dealing with salespeople. Unless you're comfortable negotiating (and many of us aren't) or can negotiate well (and many of us can't), you may find yourself — and your bank account — at the mercy of the dealership's sales staff. Just remember: The key to successful car shopping is to keep in mind that you want to buy, not be *sold,* a car. This should give you a cocky attitude that can unnerve the dealers. Armed with this attitude and the following tips, you'll be able to negotiate a better deal than you could have otherwise; at the very least, you'll be able to protect yourself from being fleeced:

- ✔ **Never negotiate under pressure.** Car dealers love customers who are in a hurry because these eager beavers overlook defects, accept higher prices than they need to, and sign contracts without reading the fine print. Never negotiate *any* deal when you're in a rush or very tired. If your present vehicle breaks down and you don't have time to negotiate properly for a replacement, rent one until you've got at least a weekend free to do the job right.

- ✔ **Take your time.** Car salespeople often deliberately waste time by disappearing for lengthy "conferences" with their superiors to wear down their customers. They believe that if you've spent a lot of time at the dealership, you'll buy a car just to end the ordeal. But the reverse is also true: The more effort a dealership invests in helping you find a vehicle, the more they will want to close the deal. This puts you in a position to drive a harder bargain. I usually bring along a good book and come prepared to sit around and wait or engage in idle chatter. This relaxed attitude really unnerves the dealers who thought they were going to control the situation with these tactics.

- ✔ **Set boundaries and limits on what you will or will not put up with.** If the sales personnel are really stretching out the time by repeated and lengthy "conferences" and you'd rather not play the waiting game, simply say, "I'll give you five minutes to talk to your boss and then I'm out of here." Then stroll into the showroom or get a cup of coffee, look at your watch, and when five minutes have passed, head for the door. Don't worry, they'll catch you before you leave the lot.

- ✓ **Wait to talk trade-in.** Park your old car about half a block away and walk to the dealer's lot, especially if you intend to trade it in. Be vague about whether or not a trade-in is part of your plans. Most dealers will mentally appraise your old vehicle to decide how much they'd have to give you in trade for it and how much profit they can expect on its resale, whether or not you say you want to trade it in. This can seriously affect the prices they quote for the vehicles you are considering. It's better to negotiate the lowest price and then talk trade-ins to lower the cost even further. So keep your old vehicle an unknown quantity until you are almost ready to close the deal.

- ✓ **Ask for extras (new tires, battery, filters, hoses, fan belts, and the replacement of any existing equipment that looks worn out).** Remember that, if a dealership is selling the car, the sales staff may be willing to replace some of the defective or worn items as part of the deal. Most private parties prefer to sell "as is," but you can use the defects you find to negotiate a lower price.

Be sure to ask the dealer to service and refill the air conditioner before you buy a car made before 1992. The section "Vehicles to Avoid — No Matter What the Cost" in Chapter 4 explains why.

- ✓ **Agree on what the vehicle is worth *before* you have your own mechanic inspect it.** That way, if defects exist, you can negotiate a price reduction if the dealer refuses to make repairs.

- ✓ **Get everything in writing.** Oral promises by dealers are difficult — if not impossible — to enforce.

- ✓ **Bargain for the most comprehensive warranty you can get.** In the past, although most dealers provided some sort of guarantee on used cars, very few used vehicles carried full warranties. Today, because leasing has become such a major factor in car ownership, many two- and three-year-old vehicles are turned in when their leases expire. As a result, many dealerships now offer full warranties on the "nearly new" vehicles they've brought up to mint condition and limited warranties on older ones. They also offer service contracts, most of which should not be necessary if you have the vehicle checked thoroughly by your mechanic before you buy it. Chapter 16 provides full details on warranties and service contracts.

- ✓ **Take a friend.** Thoroughly checking a vehicle requires two people, so take a friend along who knows something about cars, especially if you don't know where to find some of the parts.

✔ **Wear casual clothing.** Be sure it's something you won't mind getting creased or slightly soiled when you go to look at a prospective used car. Although you won't have to crawl under it, you will have to get a glimpse of its nether regions, and that's hard to do in high heels, a fitted skirt, or light-colored trousers.

✔ **Shop during daylight hours.** Floodlights tend to make cars look more exotic, and they can hide a lot of damage, especially to the underbody of the vehicle. After you've had a look at the vehicle in full sunlight, it's okay to return after sunset to negotiate for it.

✔ **Be indefinite about exactly what you want.** If you indicate that you are passionately interested in a particular make and model, the asking prices for those vehicles will rise. Browse around before casually zeroing in on the ones that really attract you.

✔ **Make it clear that you are looking for a car in fine condition and that you value condition over price.** This will prevent dealers from trying to foist lemons on you. They'll know that you'll be very upset if they sell you a vehicle that isn't in good shape.

✔ **Meticulously check out each vehicle that you really like.** This inspection includes giving it a road test according to the instructions in Chapter 4. Doing so not only pinpoints the ones that you want to consider seriously, it impresses the dealer, especially if you are female.

✔ **Shop several places and make sure the dealer knows that you are shopping around.** Car dealers probably coined that old phrase about a bird in the hand. Because the dealers know that customers who leave the showroom seldom return, they will be eager to offer you a good deal to keep you out of the hands of the competition.

Negotiating the Best Trade-In

When the vehicle you want has passed your mechanic's inspection, return to the dealer, trot out your trade-in (if you have one), and negotiate the final deal. Following are tips for how to get the most for your trade-in:

✔ Be aware of the oldest trade-in gambit in the book, what *Los Angeles Times* Automotive Editor Paul Dean calls "the ancient method of swings and roundabouts": If you're offered an extremely high trade-in value for your car, the dealer probably plans to cover the loss by keeping the price of the new car high, as well. If you're offered a really low value on your trade-in, the dealer may plan to sell the new vehicle at the lower end of its price range.

✔ It's your turn to be the car dealer here, so really talk up your old vehicle. Sell its virtues creatively. Don't lie about its defects; just don't mention them if you don't have to. Keep in mind that repairs will cost a dealership less than *you'd* have to pay for them.

Financing a used car

These days you can lease or finance the cost of a used vehicle as though it were a new one. Car financing is very complex, and leasing offers a great opportunity for you to be ripped off, but either alternative may provide the means to own a vehicle you couldn't otherwise afford. If you lack the ready cash to buy the vehicle you've chosen, be sure to read Chapters 10, 11, and 12 very carefully.

✔ If you feel your car is being undervalued — and it probably will be undervalued at first — say that you've had better offers, even if you haven't. Two can play at the same game.

✔ Let the dealer know if the offer is below blue book wholesale value, or whatever value other dealers are paying for that model. Eventually, you will reach a price that is less than you'd like to get but more than the original offer.

✔ You can probably sell your car privately for more than its trade-in value because there'll be no dealer involved who has to make a profit. But your time is worth money, so if the dealer's new price seems fair, take it.

Closing the Deal

Whether you buy a vehicle from a private party or a dealership, when the time comes to "sign on the dotted line," be sure to take the following precautions:

✔ **Allow plenty of time for signing documents.** If you decide to buy a vehicle, and you're late for another appointment, give the dealer or owner a deposit to hold the car and put off signing anything until you have enough time to do it properly.

Remember the rule for signing any agreement:

> *The smaller the type in any contract, the more attention you should pay to it.*

✔ **Read the purchase agreement slowly and carefully before you sign it.** Then do the same with every other piece of paper they shove at you. Don't let anyone rush you or distract you. If you find anything that is not exactly what you agreed to, discuss it until you're satisfied. If anything isn't clear, make them clarify it. Don't be afraid of sounding stupid or naïve — the most foolish thing you can do is sign an agreement you haven't checked out thoroughly.

✔ **Draw a line through any blank spaces in the agreement.** That will prevent anyone adding anything to the contract without your knowledge.

✔ **Recheck the vehicle**. If time has lapsed since you first inspected it, give it another test-drive before you sign the final papers. Go out for 15 to 30 minutes, drive at the speed limit on the highway, do a bit of stop-and-going on surface streets, parallel park, try a 3-point turn, and test the ABS on an alley, deserted street or parking lot to be sure it performs correctly during emergency stops. If you notice any adjustments or corrections that still need to be made, have them recorded in writing, together with how, when, and by whom the repairs will be made. If possible, delay signing the sales agreement and taking possession of the vehicle until it's in completely satisfactory condition.

✔ **Remember, a purchase contract isn't binding until both parties sign it.** Be sure that any paperwork is signed by both you and the seller, and don't leave without a copy of everything you sign.

Chapter 6

Saying Good-Bye to Old Faithful

- -

In This Chapter

▶ Understanding what it takes to sell a car yourself

▶ Attracting prospective buyers

▶ Writing truthful ads that make your car sound good anyway

▶ Handling prospective buyers and protecting yourself at the same time

▶ Going the easy route: Using your car as a trade-in

▶ Doing the altruistic thing and getting a tax credit, too: Donating your car to charity

▶ Freshening up your vehicle before it faces the buying public

- -

You've decided to get rid of your current vehicle. Maybe your third child pushed you out of your mid-sized sedan and into a van; maybe your midlife crisis is over and you've decided that you'd rather have a rugged sports utility vehicle instead of that little red sporty thing (okay, so your midlife crisis isn't quite over yet); or maybe you've just decided that you're tired of your old car and want a new one.

Whatever the reason, if you're looking to rid yourself of your old vehicle, you have several options: You can sell it to a private party or a dealer, trade it in on a new or used vehicle, or give it away and take a charitable tax deduction. All of these options are explained in the following sections.

Selling to Private Parties

When you sell to private parties, you take on the burden of advertising to attract potential buyers, answering call after call from the serious and the not-so-serious, being stuck at home to meet with people who say they want to come by and see the vehicle (and sometimes never show up), and then negotiating the deal and arranging for payment. All of these things add up to a lot of work. But the work may be worth it. If you sell your car to a private party, you can usually get more for it than if you sell or trade it to a dealer, who would have to make a profit on its resale. The following sections explain the things you should do if you decide to sell the car yourself.

If you buy a vehicle from a private party, that doesn't mean that you have to sell it to a private party; you can still sell it to a dealership, which would involve less work (and less profit) than selling it to an individual. Ask yourself, "Which matters more to me, time or money?"

Incidentally, convertibles are notoriously hard to sell during cold weather or the rainy season. So if you want to sell a sports car or a convertible, try to wait until spring.

Getting yourself ready

Before you place the first ad or attract the attention of that first potential buyer, you need to do a few things:

- ✔ **Determine the price.** Figure out how much you're going to ask for the vehicle, and remember that what you ask for and what you're willing to accept aren't necessarily the same: Add 15 percent to your asking price to give yourself room to negotiate. To set a fair price, see Chapter 5, where you can find out how to determine the true value of a used vehicle. If you just want to move it quickly at the going rate in your area, you can check the local classifieds and, if there are several vehicles with the same make, model, and year as yours for sale, add all their asking prices together and divide by the number of vehicles advertised to get an average asking price quickly.

  Be willing to make counteroffers. Don't reject offers for less than your asking price. Suggest a compromise and keep bargaining until you reach an agreement.

- ✔ **Get the maintenance records together.** Have the receipts from past maintenance handy to prove mileage and show the car's history of maintenance and repair. Also, try to have an up-to-date service sticker on the car to show that the oil has recently been changed.

  Tuning your car and getting it into good working order before you put it up for sale is a good idea so that test-drives are a positive experience for prospective buyers. Avoid major repairs, however; they very rarely raise the price enough to compensate for what they cost. The same goes for new tires.

- ✔ **Get the paperwork together.** This includes the title or pink slip, the registration, and the owner's manual, if you have it. Find out ahead of time how to transfer the title, registration, and license plates so things will go smoothly after the sale is made. You'll find step-by-step instructions later in this chapter in the "Taking care of business" section.

- ✔ **Practice your sales pitch.** Although you should present your car honestly, be sure to stress its good points and respond to criticisms by emphasizing positives such as, "Sure it's old, but the body and interior are in great shape, and it gets 28 miles to the gallon."

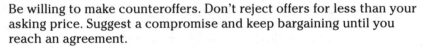

You may present your best case to potential buyers, but still lose the sale if your car isn't well-prepared for show. Before you make the move to the marketplace, check out the "Taking a Shine to Your Trusty Vehicle" section later in this chapter. After all, years of Old Faithful service deserve nothing less than a proud fresh start!

Protecting yourself

Everyone's heard the horror stories: A guy goes for a test drive with a prospective buyer and ends up mugged (or worse). Or a guy doesn't go on a test drive with a prospective buyer, and he never sees his car again. Or how about the one where the guy test-driving the car got into a wreck and sued the owner for damages? Even though you're more likely to encounter prospective buyers whose only ulterior motive is to talk you down to the lowest price, you should always play it safe and smart. The following pointers can help you:

✔ **Make certain that your insurance covers prospective buyers who test-drive your car.** As the owner, you share the liability for any accidents, so be sure the buyer can safely operate your car.

✔ **Check out claims by the prospective buyer's mechanic.** If a prospective buyer has a mechanic inspect your car, verify that any defects noticed by the mechanic really exist. It may be worth it to have your own mechanic inspect your vehicle before you put it up for sale so that nobody can con you into lowering the price or paying for phony repairs.

✔ **Make sure the car passes mandatory safety or smog tests before you put it on sale.** Otherwise, you limit yourself to buyers who are willing to purchase it in "as is" condition for low prices.

✔ **Beware of car thieves.** The only sure way to prevent some culprit from making off with your vehicle during a test-drive or an inspection trip to an independent mechanic is to demand to go along. If you're concerned for your safety, take a friend along as well. It's a choice between paranoia and convenience.

✔ **If you must let the car out of your sight, ask prospective buyers for security against its return.** Just remember that the name and address on the driver's license they show you could be false. You can hold their car keys, credit cards, or Rolex watch hostage until they return, but these could be phony, too. A cash deposit is nice, but it won't compensate you completely for the loss of your vehicle.

✔ **Follow your instincts and refuse to deal with anyone who really seems suspicious.** After all, you don't want to end up on the next *Jerry Springer* or *Geraldo*, explaining to a hostile audience why you thought hopping in a car with a psycho who had "Born to Raise Hell" tattooed across his forehead was a good idea.

Placing an ad for your vehicle

It pays to advertise in order to attract the widest range of buyers for your car. And when it comes to advertising, you have a lot of choices — many you may not be aware of. The following sections tell you everything you need to know about putting the word out that your vehicle is for sale.

Free advertising

How can you sell something if nobody knows it's for sale? The cheapest forms of advertising are free:

- **Place a For Sale sign** with your phone number, in large numbers that can be read from across the street, in the driver's-side rear window where it won't obstruct your vision. Then drive the car around town or park it in a large shopping mall lot or on a well-traveled street where it will get lots of exposure. To avoid a lot of silly inquiries, put a price on the sign — if you'd rather wait for the best deal, just your phone number will do.

  Do not put your address on the sign: You don't want prospective burglars disguised as prospective buyers to check out your home as well as your car. Also keep in mind that it's illegal to place a For Sale sign on a parked car in some localities. If you're not sure about the statutes in your area, check with your local police or city attorney's office.

- **Trade and recycling publications** accept free ads from people who want to get rid of secondhand stuff. Many specialize in vehicles for sale. Some will print ads free but demand a percentage of the selling price if you make a sale. Check out the possibilities and go for the publication with the largest circulation.

- **Bulletin boards** at schools, churches, shopping centers, community centers, or workplaces can reach hundreds of prospects. Write your sales pitch on 4-x-6-inch index cards and fringe the bottom into tabs with your phone number so that prospective buyers can tear them off. Use colored cards, borders, or lettering to make your card stand out from the crowd. Stick them up all over town and check them regularly to be sure nobody has tacked signs over them or removed them.

Cheap advertising

Although not free, advertising is relatively inexpensive in the following places:

- **Bargain boxes in local newspapers:** Bargain boxes, or columns for the sale of secondhand merchandise by private parties, can be found in most local newspapers. Most of these cost about $1 per line, and most are one-liners. Just the make, year, price (if you like), and your phone number are necessary. It's worth a couple of bucks.

✔ **The classifieds in your local paper:** Newspaper classified sections are a prime source for car advertising. Choose a paper that is read by people who live fairly near you — or by very large numbers of people all over town. Take ads in weekend issues and also on weekdays in the summer, when people tend to get out of town on Fridays. Rates vary, and you can get a cheaper rate if you agree to run the ad for several issues. To estimate how many prospective buyers you will hit per dollar of advertising cost, divide the circulation of the paper by the cost of the ad.

✔ **Local specialty papers:** Some cities have special, smaller newspapers that are dedicated solely to buying, selling, and trading property. This type of paper can be very useful because it focuses solely on the buying, selling, or trading audience. Another plus is that some of these publications don't charge you for advertising unless you sell what you're advertising.

Writing your ad

What can you say about Old Faithful? It's been carrying you around for years, and you have a personal love for it, but to the eye of a stranger, Old Faithful may be just another heap. Compose your ad before you call to place it. Don't mince words when describing your vehicle; an extra line or two can more than pay for itself by attracting a larger number of responses.

The best ads convey the fact that the owner cares about the vehicle, so establish this with copy such as that shown in Figure 6-1.

Figure 6-1:
With an ad like this, who can refuse?

Faithful Mustang convertible needs good home. High-spirited 6-yr-old w/fuel-saving V-6 eng., auto trans., FM/AM/cass. & a/c. Lovingly maintained and housebroken. Currently stabled at 310-555-1234. Best offer.

Describe the car — honestly, but positively

Be positive, but honest (use the list of terms that are found in used-car ads in Chapter 3 for inspiration). Convey whatever enthusiasm you can muster, but don't misrepresent what you are selling; dishonest advertising is against the law. If the vehicle is only in fair shape, don't say "mint condition." "Needs minor body work" and other bad-news items are better left unsaid, but tell the truth when asked. Some buyers are quite willing to undertake some work themselves if they know the vehicle will be worth the effort in the long run. List the vehicle's condition only if it's good, the mileage only if it's low, the price if it's average or low; otherwise, specify "best offer." It's better to describe the selling points of an expensive luxury or classic car in person before talking about money.

If you specify "best offer," be sure you have the time to wheel and deal. You'll have to put up with a lot of silly phone calls and tire kickers because many people are going to try for a bargain at a price that's much lower than one you'd accept. Still, a golden goose may fly in and make it all worthwhile.

Your ads must contain the vehicle's year, make, model, and special equipment such as air conditioning, automatic transmission, and power stuff. Be sure to include your phone number and the license plate number if it's mandatory in your locality.

Tailor your ad to the publication

Write a master ad that includes everything you'd like to say about the vehicle and then modify it to suit the style and format of each publication. If the classifieds are listed alphabetically by carmaker, begin with "Ford" rather than "Faithful Mustang." If you abbreviate, make sure people can understand it; the classified representatives who take your ads can be helpful here. After you specify the wording for each ad, ask the specialists to abbreviate everything they can.

Don't divulge personal info

If your home is empty while you're at work, don't identify phone numbers as "Day" and "Evening" or "Home" and "Work" because you may attract burglars. Taking messages on your answering machine while you're away is better. Say something like "If you're calling about the ad, please leave your name, number, and a good time to reach you" on your outgoing message so callers will know they've reached the right party.

While the ad is running

Plan to stay at home on the weekends your ads are running. Otherwise, the perfect buyers may end up finding another vehicle before you get back to them. Because most people work during the week, you'll be better off if you are available to show the car during weekend daylight hours.

Closing the deal

After you and the prospective buyer have agreed on the price, completed the inspections to everyone's satisfaction, and shaken hands all around, you're ready to close the deal. And closing the deal means more than handing over the keys and waxing nostalgic as Old Faithful zooms — or putts — into the sunset. Be sure you do the following:

✔ **Demand payment in cash.** If the buyer insists on using a check, only accept a certified or cashier's check and call the bank to verify it before giving up the vehicle.

Never accept personal checks! Ask buyers who insist on using a personal check to make it out to themselves, cash the check themselves, and then bring you the money.

✔ **Get payment in full.** To allow a private party to pay you in installments is courting disaster. If you are foolish enough to get into such a deal, do not simply hold the pink slip (certificate of ownership) until the full amount is paid, unless you also retain possession of the vehicle.

If you transfer the vehicle without endorsing and delivering the pink slip, you may be liable for accidents and traffic tickets that the car is involved in.

✔ **Get it in writing.** Make out the bill of sale in duplicate. You don't need a fancy invoice; any kind of paper with the sales terms laid out in longhand will do as long as you both sign and date all copies of the agreement. The bill of sale should include the following:

- Names, addresses, and phone numbers of both you and the buyer.
- Vehicle's make, model, year, and VIN (vehicle identification number).
- Full sales price and how it was paid.
- Exact mileage on the car, if you know it. If not, specify "exact mileage is unknown." (This may occur, for example, if you originally bought the car from someone else.)
- The fact that you are selling the car in "as is" condition without any guarantee or warranty — if that is the case.
- Time limits, if you are willing to guarantee that the buyer can return the car for a refund if it doesn't pass a mechanical and/or smog inspection. A day or two should suffice.

Taking care of business

Take care of the following as soon as you close the deal on your car:

✔ **Contact the bank and clear the title, if you have an existing car loan.** You must contact the lender to clear the title when you sell the vehicle because they "own" a piece of it, too. You can either arrange to pay the lender back with the proceeds from the sale or continue paying the loan after the car is sold by putting something else (your next vehicle?) up for collateral.

✔ **Transfer the title.** Supervise the transfer of the title in person or by mail at your local DMV. If you live in a state where the license plate goes with the vehicle, the car remains your responsibility until the pink slip, registration, fees, smog certificates, and any other documents required in your locality are received by the DMV and transferred to the buyer. Here's how to do it:

TIP

1. **Contact your local DMV**. Have them send you all the forms necessary to transfer ownership and registration.

2. **If possible, have the buyer meet you at the DMV.** Before your name can be removed from the DMV's records, the new buyer must complete the transfer with the DMV, using your ownership documents. Meeting the buyer at a DMV office with all the necessary documents and fees and transferring the vehicle there is the best strategy. If this is impossible, either bring your paperwork to the DMV in person or send it as soon as you can by certified mail, return receipt requested. If you belong to the American Automobile Association (AAA), Auto Club offices at some localities can handle the transfer for you.

3. **Completely sign and date DMV documents before turning the pink slip and the vehicle over to the buyer.** Be sure to include the name and address of the buyer, the date of the transaction, the vehicle license number and VIN number, the selling price, the last odometer reading, and your name, address, and signature. Make copies for your records.

4. **Cancel your insurance on the car.** Notify your insurance company to cancel coverage on the vehicle as soon as the transfer of title takes place. The new owner may be driving under your insurance policy until you notify your company that the title has been transferred! Besides, the sooner you cancel, the larger the refund you will receive.

Enjoy your profit! Hopefully, you've made enough on the sale of your car to justify the time and work it took to sell it.

Dealing with Dealers

If you don't have the time and patience to sit through dozens of phone calls, answer silly questions, and stay home so prospective buyers can kick your tires, selling your car yourself to a private buyer probably isn't for you. Remember that time is money, and selling or trading the car to a dealership may be a more profitable alternative.

Trading it in

If your vehicle needs major work — unless it's a classic model that would attract a do-it-yourselfer or car restorer — you can probably do best if you trade your car in on a used or new vehicle. The dealership won't give you much, but it should be worth its while to give you *something* in order to make a sale. The dealer will then either repair your trade-in and make a profit on reselling it, send it to auction, or sell it to a lower-caliber used-car dealer or a wrecking yard.

If you're going to use your old vehicle as a trade-in, follow the instructions in Chapter 5 to get the best trade-in offer. Also make sure that you compare the trade-in offer from the dealership with your vehicle's blue-book value (also explained in Chapter 5) to decide whether looking for a private buyer is worth the time and trouble.

Selling to a dealership

If you aren't in the market for another vehicle, you won't be able to trade Old Faithful in. But you can still unload your old car at a dealership if the idea of selling it privately doesn't appeal to you. As I've said before, don't expect to get as much as you would have from an individual because the dealer will have to absorb the cost of fixing the car up for resale and then make a profit on it. Also, the glut of previously leased vehicles on the market has considerably reduced the demand for older used cars at lots that are probably overstocked anyway. However, it still may be worth a try, so here are a few tips to help you get the best possible price:

- ✔ **Spruce up Old Faithful.** Use some of the suggestions in the "Taking a Shine to Your Trusty Vehicle" section of this chapter to spiff up your car, but stick to stuff that will cost you little more than elbow grease. A dealership can replace parts and do body work for much less than you can, so why invest money you'll never get back? In other words, don't paint it, wax it, or have anything repaired or replaced. Just get it looking clean and well-cared for, inside and out.

- ✔ **Choose a dealership that will appreciate your car.** Drive past the used-car lots in your area, including those at new-car dealerships, to see what kind of vehicles are on sale. Choose a place that is selling vehicles of the same quality—or not quite as good—as yours.

If you're selling a fairly expensive vehicle that's only a few years old, a new-car dealership for the same manufacturer may be interested in offering it to customers who can't afford a brand-new model. And, if they're not already maxed out with used cars of their own, new-car dealers are usually willing to put used vehicles by other manufacturers on their lots, if they feel they can make a profit on them.

- ✔ **Do your homework.** It's especially important to have a very accurate idea of the blue-book low-end or wholesale price for your vehicle's make, model, year, accessories, and condition *before* you hit the dealerships. In fact, take the trouble to photocopy the pages that list those prices and bring them with you to prove you know the worth of the car.

> ✔ **Be prepared to settle for less than blue-book value.** Unless you're greeted with open arms by a dealer who just loves your car, don't expect to get even low-end value for it. The dealership will want to hedge their bets because if they can't move your car off their lot they'll have to resell it to a lower-quality used-car lot at a rock-bottom price. But don't despair: If you can't get much for your monster, the next section provides another alternative that can give you a more satisfying return than mere money can provide.

Putting Old Faithful Out to Pasture

If your vehicle is terminally ill, or virtually worthless, don't try to unload it on an unsuspecting stranger. I'm firmly convinced that deeds like that eventually come home to roost. You can turn bad "car-ma" into a blessing by donating your vehicle to a charitable organization and taking the tax deduction for a non-cash charitable contribution in the amount of the vehicle's current retail (fair-market) value. Such a deal!

Here are a few organizations that would like to have your vehicle:

> ✔ **The American Red Cross** has accepted donations of five to six thousand vehicles per year in Southern California alone. Now the Red Cross is rolling out its program to all major U.S. cities. It will pick up your vehicle, whether or not it's in running order, and will provide blue-book figures to help you determine the current value of your donation. Call your local chapter to see whether this program exists in your area.
>
> ✔ **The Polly Klaas Foundation** accepts cars and boats, running or not, and handles all the DMV and IRS paperwork. The foundation will pick up vehicles anywhere in the United States and Canada. The proceeds are used to support searches for missing children, child-education seminars, and lobbying for child-safety legislation. The foundation's number is 800-380-5257.
>
> ✔ **The National Kidney Foundation** doesn't care whether or not your vehicle is in running order — they'll be happy to pick it up and sell it for parts. Call 800-488-2277 or reach them on the Internet at `www.kidney.org`.
>
> ✔ **Goodwill Industries** offers vehicle donation programs at many of their sites throughout the United States and Canada. You can find a local Goodwill office in the Yellow Pages or at `www.goodwill.org`.
>
> ✔ **The Salvation Army** now has vehicle donation programs nationwide as well as in Canada. Most territories will accept vehicles that aren't running. Call your local office for details or try the national Web site at `salvationarmyusa.org`.

- **Your Local United Way** may accept RVs, boats and real estate, as well as cars. They often advertise such services through local radio and newspapers. Contact them through your local telephone directory.

- **Missing Kids International,** a nonprofit organization that televises daily Missing Kids Alerts nationwide, currently has vehicle donation programs from Washington D.C. north to New York, in the metropolitan Chicago area, and in Los Angeles and San Diego. The operation is constantly expanding, so try them 24 hours a day at 800-353-6477, or e-mail them at mki@access.digex.net.

Local charitable organizations in your area may offer similar programs. For instance, most missions and other agencies for the poor and homeless are grateful for vehicles, computers, jewelry, furniture, and anything else of value you'd care to donate. Churches and thrift shops are worth contacting, and your local Chamber of Commerce may have suggestions, as well. Remember, recycling your vehicle by either selling it or giving it away is better than adding it to the overwhelming amount of trash that's polluting our planet!

Some cases of bogus foundations selling donated cars and then pocketing the money have been discovered, so check to be sure that any unfamiliar organization has a legitimate program.

Taking a Shine to Your Trusty Vehicle

Whether you're selling your car or using it as a trade-in, you increase the chances of getting a good deal if you bring out the best in your vehicle. Well-kept cars command higher resale prices. When prospective buyers come around or you go looking for the best trade-in deal, you want to show your vehicle to its fullest advantage. What's more, knowing how to make an older car look really spiffy can alert you to similar tactics used by those who want to sell you *their* cars. The following sections tell you what you can to do help Old Faithful make the best possible impression on prospective buyers.

Clean the interior

Although cleanliness may or may not be next to godliness, a clean car has a better chance of attracting buyers than one that looks likes it's never seen the end of a hose. So, for starters, clean the interior thoroughly. Spot-clean the upholstery, dust the dashboard and other surfaces, and vacuum the rug. Remember to clean the ashtrays, the glove box, and the trunk. Make it look loved!

Don't forget the windows: Wash them — *all* of them — inside and out. Most people drive around with a layer of dirt on their windows, the only relatively clean spots being the wiper areas of the front windshield and the rear window — *if* they remember to keep the window washer tanks filled. If the owner smokes, a grayish film forms on the inside of the windows, and that rarely gets cleaned. When a prospective buyer gets into a car with clean windows, the effect is scintillating: the vehicle seems spacious and roomy, the world looks brighter. No kidding, this really works!

Repair torn upholstery and worn pedal covers, and cover worn carpets with floor mats. But don't wait until the last minute to make these replacements. Do it a couple of weeks in advance so the replacements will be a bit scuffed. Just as a badly worn pedal cover or floor mat is a sure sign of high mileage, a sparkling new pedal or mat may prompt a buyer to assume that the old one must have worn through even if it didn't.

If you're selling the car to a dealer or trading it in, it doesn't pay to invest money in repairs or new parts. Just clean everything thoroughly so that your faithful steed can look its best when it comes time to haggle for the highest possible price.

Take care of the exterior

Wash the outside of the car, polish up the chrome, and clean the sidewalls of the tires. If the paint is in decent condition, have the car waxed. A shiny finish can add a couple of hundred dollars to the price.

But *don't* have the car painted. Most prospective buyers will assume that you did it to cover up bodywork due to an accident.

Pay attention to the engine

If your engine looks *really* cruddy, clean it with an aerosol can of engine degreaser. Do this at a do-it-yourself car wash so that the nasty stuff doesn't end up in the municipal storm drains and be sure to cover the distributor with a plastic bag before you wash the stuff off. However, before you turn the *entire* under-the-hood area into a Mr. Clean fantasy, be aware that many buyers consider a totally clean engine an indication that a mechanic opened the engine, found a terminal illness inside, closed it up, and eliminated the signs of exploratory surgery by cleaning everything in sight. Despite this possibility, do clean the worst parts, because a well-kept engine is generally a good selling aid.

Give your car a well-maintained look

Here are a few other things you should do to make your vehicle look like it's been well cared for:

- Sponge off battery deposits with a tablespoon of baking soda in a cup of water.

- Take a look at the underside of the hood. A sure giveaway of a poorly functioning PCV valve or bad rings is a huge greasy spot on the undersurface of the hood right over the air cleaner. This is called "blow-by." Use a nonflammable grease-cutting household cleanser to tidy up the area. Even though you'll want to be honest about major flaws, it still can't hurt to get the car looking as good as possible.

- If your vehicle needs minor repairs or replacements, be prepared to knock a few dollars off the price to cover the stuff you should have done in the first place.

- Check the oil and coolant as well as the transmission, power steering, and brake fluid levels. If they're low, top them off. If the oil or coolant hasn't been changed in a while, change it. A recent oil change and lube job gives a vehicle an air of having been well-maintained.

Now Old Faithful will be able to put its best wheel forward when it's time to meet potential new owners!

Part III
Untried and True: Buying a New Car

In this part . . .

*I*f you're planning to buy a new vehicle, brace yourself for one of the more expensive investments of your life — and a highly enlightening experience. The purchase process plants you squarely on the playing field of an exciting game, one in which you're pitted against well-trained and intelligent professionals. The prize: the best possible vehicle at the lowest possible price. You can walk away a winner if you pay close attention to all the advice in this part. Remember, all's fair in love, war, and buying a car!

Chapter 7

Deciding What You Want

The process for buying a new car is quite simple: Be very clear about exactly what you want; investigate thoroughly to see what your options and alternatives are and which vehicles offer them; find out who has the lowest prices; and then deal wisely from a position of enlightened power to get the best quality at the lowest possible cost. Sounds easy enough. But the sheer volume of choices you have can make this seemingly simple process more difficult than it has to be.

And although it's not hard, if you're serious about your decision, buying a new car does take more than cruising through a dealer's lot and choosing between blue metal flake and candy-apple red paint. You need to know what features you want, how you plan to use the vehicle, and how much you can afford to spend. That's where this chapter comes in handy. When you know that nothing can make you happy except a brand new set of wheels, this chapter can help you to pick the right vehicle for your needs.

Getting Clear on What You Want

Before you even set foot on a dealer's lot — or talk to any salesperson about buying a car — you need to decide what kind of vehicle you want and what options and features that vehicle should possess. If you make the mistake of going unprepared into a new car showroom, be prepared to come out with a car that has more or less than you wanted and that costs more than you wanted to spend. The following sections explain what types of questions you should ask yourself.

How will you use the vehicle?

Does your driving usually involve a lot of extended trips or just short home-school-shopping excursions? Do you commute to work? Do you drive mostly at highway speeds or in city stop-and-go traffic? Manufacturers design their models to meet specific markets. To be sure the vehicle you choose can accommodate your needs and driving habits, consider the following:

- ✔ **If you travel a lot,** you need sufficient enclosed trunk space so that your luggage isn't exposed to public view. You'll probably also want larger interior space and a more cushy ride for those long hours on the road. Fuel-efficiency can be a factor here: You may want a fairly large gas tank so you won't have to fill 'er up so often.

- ✔ **If you use the car mostly for short local errands,** a shorter wheelbase and power steering can help you squeeze into tight parking spots and negotiate crowded shopping centers.

- ✔ **If you often drive off-road or on unpaved roads,** a car or sport utility vehicle (SUV) with all-wheel or four-wheel drive may be a good idea.

If you only want an SUV because they're trendy, think twice before you pay a premium price for a vehicle that consumes more fuel, costs more to register and insure, offers less comfort and protection from the elements, and may not be as safe as an equally attractive and high-status car. SUVs not only have scary roll-over statistics, but they can also wreak havoc on the drivers and passengers of cars that are involved with them in accidents.

How much can you afford?

How much money are you willing to pay to buy, own, and operate a vehicle? Annual ownership and operating expenses vary greatly from one model to another. Don't mistakenly think that the only expenses you incur when you buy a car are the price of the vehicle and other obvious expenses like maintenance and fuel. You also have interest payments on financing, insurance premiums, registering and titling costs, and, in some states, excise taxes. Another cost that most people don't even think about is how much value the vehicle loses over time — in other words, how much the car *depreciates.* To help you estimate the total annual cost of owning and driving a vehicle, refer to Chapter 2, and use the methods and worksheets in that chapter to compare your favorite candidates. You may be surprised by what you find out.

In general, new cars have more safety features than older models and can go longer between tune-ups. But, they also cost much more, depreciate more swiftly, are more expensive to register and insure, and some new features may have hidden "bugs." Buying a used car can reduce your ownership and operating expenses by half, so if you haven't done so already, be sure to read Chapter 1 *before* you rush off to the dealership. You may discover that buying a good used vehicle or restoring the one you already own is a better option.

After you get a good overall picture of how much each car is going to cost in owning and operating expenses, take a look at the following sections for a few additional financial factors to consider.

How much power do you really need?

Many vehicles come in both four- and six-cylinder models. Is the larger engine really worth the price? If you often have to travel on the highways, trying to charge up the on-ramp in a four-cylinder car and get up to speed for joining a 65 mph stream of traffic can be hazardous to your health. In such cases, although a V-6 engine won't save you money, it just might save your life.

On the downside, big engines burn more fuel — often the expensive premium variety — both for high performance and because they weigh a lot. If an automobile is EPA-rated as getting fewer than 22.5 miles per gallon (mpg), the manufacturer incurs an excise tax called "the gas-guzzler tax," which ranges from $1,000 on vehicles that only get from 21.5 to 22.5 miles per gallon, to $7,700 for those that get less than 12.5 mpg. Obviously, this tax seriously affects the purchase price. (***Note:*** Right now, this tax does *not* apply to trucks or vans or some sport utility vehicles, but this exclusion may change. Be sure to check out the most recent excise-tax rulings if you're interested in one of these vehicles. Your dealership should have the figures for you.)

If you think you can get past the tax by buying your car outside the United States, forget it. The U.S. customs department collects the gas-guzzler tax when you bring the car into the country.

Here's another thing to think about before buying a high-powered gas-guzzler: Some optional big engines fit so closely under the hood that you cannot reach spark plugs and other parts without hoisting the engine right out of the car! You'll not only have to rely on a mechanic for basic maintenance, but also pay the professional more for the additional time and labor involved. And, the stability of the engine certainly isn't going to be improved by repeatedly removing and reinstalling it.

So before you buy that fuel hog, ask yourself, "Do I often carry heavy loads? Climb steep hills? Have access to roads where I can hit high speeds?" If the answer is yes, a big engine may be right for you. If the answer is no — you're usually tied to 65 miles per hour or less no matter what you drive — save yourself some money and go for a smaller engine.

How much is the prestige of a luxury car worth to you?

At present, dealers who sell expensive cars must pay the federal government an excise tax called a "luxury tax." This tax currently amounts to 9 percent of the selling price that is in excess of a basic amount, which is adjusted annually for inflation. The basic amount is currently $34,000, so luxury tax on a $36,000 car costs $180 (9 percent of $2,000, the difference between the total cost of the car and the basic price). On a $44,000 car, 9 percent tax would be $9,000. This tax will decrease by one percentage point a year until the year 2002, when it will be eliminated.

Although dealers are responsible for paying the tax, they definitely figure it into the price of the car. You can't get around the tax by leasing or renting because the lessor or rental agency passes the cost of the tax on to you. Luxury tax also applies to any modifications you make within the first six months of ownership. So if you buy a cheaper model and add expensive accessories that bring its value above the base amount, the luxury tax still applies.

One bright spot is that modifications to accommodate disabled people, like wheelchair accessibility or hand controls, are exempt from the luxury tax. Like gas-guzzler taxes, luxury taxes currently apply only to automobiles, not to trucks, vans, and *some* sport utility vehicles. But this may change, so check with your dealership before you buy one of these vehicles.

What will insuring this vehicle cost?

Insurance is always a factor when considering the cost of a vehicle. Every state requires that any car you own and drive be insured, and if you finance a car, the bank holding your loan can stipulate the type of insurance you get. If you buy a sport or luxury model, you can spend well over $1,000 more per year to insure these cars than you would to insure less flashy vehicles. If you want to research the minimum insurance requirement in your state, call the National Insurance Consumer Helpline (NICH) at 800-942-4242, Monday to Friday, 8 a.m. to 8 p.m. (EST) or visit 4insurance.com at `www.4insurance.com/resource/minimum.html`.

If saving on insurance is important, keep in mind that turbocharged cars, luxury cars, vehicles on the "Most Stolen" list, and snazzy sports cars command the highest premiums. Some insurers won't insure particularly risky models at any price.

To find out which things impact how much you'll pay to insure your car, and for tips on getting the best deal on insurance, regardless of the model you drive, read Chapter 13.

Can you wait until the most favorable time of year to save money?

In the old days, most new cars were released around September, but increased competition has resulted in the release of new models all year long. Nevertheless, timing is still a factor when it comes to buying a car. Try to wait for sales, for the end of the month, quarter or year, when salespeople are trying to fill their quotas, or until the arrival of new models motivates a dealership to discount their predecessors.

If you stay abreast of ads and articles about your favorite automotive candidates, you may find a bargain on a vehicle that's about to be replaced by a newer model. True, the vehicle may be considered older in terms of depreciation, but if you intend to keep it for quite a while, this difference may be insignificant compared to what you can save up front.

Is resale value important?

All things being equal, you want a car that has a good resale value or that depreciates the least over time. A good resale value makes the car worth more later, whether you plan to sell it or trade it in for another vehicle. When you're choosing options and features, keep in mind that some actually increase the car's resale value, and some decrease it.

The following features have a positive effect on resale price:

✔ Air-conditioning.

✔ Antilock brakes and other safety options, like air bags. We really get into these options in the upcoming section, "Safety Features."

✔ Automatic transmissions.

✔ Sunroofs and moonroofs.

✔ Power steering and adjustable steering wheels.

✔ Power windows and door locks.

✔ Remote-entry and antitheft systems.

✔ Traction control.

✔ Leather upholstery.

✔ Adjustable steering wheels.

Custom wheels, high-tech sound systems, programmable seats, and built-in phones are only attractive to fellow enthusiasts, and wild colors (except for red) are generally a turnoff.

To check the rate of depreciation for models that interest you, read the *Consumer Reports* Annual Auto Issue, which is released every April, or contact the magazine's New Car Price Service at 800-933-5555. For a complete list of sources to contact regarding new cars, see Chapter 8.

Who else is going to drive?

If you'll be sharing your vehicle with someone who is very different in size or too frail to move the seats easily, you may find it worthwhile to pay extra for a vehicle that can "memorize" more than one seat position or one with power adjustments for seat height and tilt as well as distance from the dashboard.

If you're going to be the only person driving, paying for something you'll probably use once and never need again is foolish.

What sort of passengers and gear do you usually carry?

Do you have kids who need child-safety seats? Do you chauffeur amateur athletes and their gear? Elderly people? A large dog? Who rides along is an important factor to consider. For example, you may be leaning toward a less expensive compact car, but if you transport your kids or your folks, you may want to reconsider: Loading small children or aging adults into the tiny rear seat of a two-door model is difficult. And if you or your children go in for surfboarding, skiing, camping, bike riding, or any other activity that requires bulky equipment, you need a vehicle that can handle all the stuff.

What are your priorities?

What's your main reason for wanting a new vehicle rather than a used one? Fuel economy? Status? (Be honest; this is just between you and me!) The tax benefits of business depreciation? Have you been struck by the beauty and power of a newcomer to the automotive field?

Because weighing the merits of different models is often like comparing apples and oranges, you have a better chance of finding out what really matters to you if you make a list of such things as low cost, high power, fuel economy, safety, versatility, prestige, trunk space, and so forth, and then prioritize the list, weighting each item from one to ten. Doing so can help you remember what's really important to you, even when a multicolored dashboard display hypnotizes you with its beauty.

What features and options are important?

The assortment of standard and optional equipment available on vehicles today staggers the mind. Some of the new safety features are critically important for everyone because they can prevent injury or death. Other options are vital only for those who drive under specific conditions, and still others are basically just status symbols.

The Features and Options Checklist at the end of this chapter can help you thread your way through this maze of opportunities to spend money. Photocopy it and jot down your preferences as you read the following sections. The checklist has space to check availability and cost on several vehicles that interest you. If the equipment is part of a package, be sure to see how many of the package's features you really want and how much stuff you can happily do without. You may find that ordering just the individual features you want and forgoing the package is cheaper. Later, when you're ready to make your final choice, this checklist, in addition to the Test Drive Checklist and the Price Comparison Worksheet (both in Chapter 8), can provide you with the data you need to choose wisely and negotiate your final deal.

Safety Features

In recent years, "crashworthiness" seems to have overtaken fuel economy as the most vital automotive concern. In a recent U.S. survey, almost 80 percent cited air bags, and 71 percent cited traction control as other safety features that could influence their choice of new vehicle.

Because safety devices have proved to reduce serious injury and death by 50 percent, federal laws in both the United States and Canada now mandate that all new cars must be equipped with crash protection that works *automatically* to prevent the driver and front-seat occupants from injuring themselves by striking the interior of their vehicles during an accident. Currently, automakers can satisfy these requirements with automatic seat belts or air bags. Safety features, such as dual air bags and passive seat restraints, that used to be optional are now standard on most vehicles, and at least minimal side-impact protection is required on all models from 1997 on.

Other safety features are becoming increasingly available. In 1996, a National Research Council report, prepared at the request of the U.S. Congress, proposed that new cars be required to have safety labels that include "a safety score of crashworthiness compared to other vehicles, plus a list of crash-avoidance features." As of now, this excellent recommendation is still being researched by NHTSA (the National Highway Traffic Safety Administration). I hope that by the time you read this, the proposal will have become a law. You can keep track of its progress via the NHTSA Auto Safety Hotline (800-424-9393) or Web site (www.nhtsa.dot.gov). Figure 7-1 shows you the NHTSA's Motor Vehicle Safety Standards.

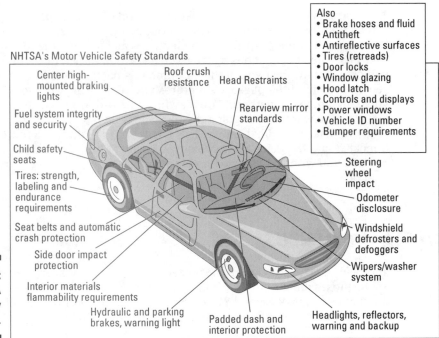

NHTSA's Motor Vehicle Safety Standards

Also
• Brake hoses and fluid
• Antitheft
• Antireflective surfaces
• Tires (retreads)
• Door locks
• Window glazing
• Hood latch
• Controls and displays
• Power windows
• Vehicle ID number
• Bumper requirements

Center high-mounted braking lights
Roof crush resistance
Head Restraints
Rearview mirror standards
Fuel system integrity and security
Child safety seats
Tires: strength, labeling and endurance requirements
Seat belts and automatic crash protection
Side door impact protection
Interior materials flammability requirements
Steering wheel impact
Odometer disclosure
Windshield defrosters and defoggers
Wipers/washer system
Headlights, reflectors, warning and backup
Hydraulic and parking brakes, warning light
Padded dash and interior protection

Figure 7-1:
The NHTSA list of safety standards.

Because innovative safety features are among the few reasons for buying a new vehicle rather than a good used one, be sure that the vehicle you choose has a high safety rating. The following sections provide a look at the most popular automotive safety features.

As I explain in Part V, "Insuring Your Car: How to Cover Your Automotive Assets," some of these features qualify you for special discounts on your premiums. So be sure to notify your insurance company about the safety features on the vehicle you select.

Sources for safety information

The best things in life are free, and so are many excellent sources of vehicle safety information:

✔ **The Insurance Institute for Highway Safety (IIHS)** rates recent models according to occupant deaths per registered vehicle. Get a free copy of *Shopping For A Safer Car* by sending a self-addressed, stamped envelope to IIHS, Dept. P, P.O. Box 1420, Arlington, VA 22210-1420, calling 703-247-1500, or visiting them online at www.highwaysafety.org.

✔ **The Highway Loss Data Institute (HLDI)** collaborates with the IIHS to publish comparisons of insurance claims for particular vehicles and the comparative amount of damage and injuries. The Institute's findings are available from the sources provided previously.

✔ **The National Highway Traffic Safety Administration (NHTSA)** provides crash test results for about 40 new vehicles and 60 used ones each year and collaborates with the AAA and the Federal Trade Commission (FTC) on *Buying a Safer Car,* a pamphlet that rates new vehicles for safety features, crash tests, and theft. You can reach the Auto Safety Hotline at 1-800-424-9393 or at www.nhtsa.dot.gov.

✔ **Annual vehicle comparison publications,** such as *Consumer Reports, AAA AutoGraph,* and *The Car Book,* also feature annually updated, detailed, safety ratings.

You can find more information about these and other sources in Chapter 8.

Importing cars in the United States and Canada

All vehicles imported into the United States or Canada from anywhere in the world must meet the country's current safety standards. Be sure the vehicle you choose complies *before* you buy.

Since 1986, the Canadians have outstripped the United States in setting safety standards for seat belt anchorage, bumpers, daytime running lights, and child-safety seats. As a result, although the North American Free Trade Agreement (NAFTA) has eliminated former embargoes and duties, vehicles imported from the United States into Canada must be upgraded to meet Canadian safety standards.

However, Transport Canada *does not allow* upgrade modifications on seat belt anchorage, which must meet Canadian standards in its original form. NAFTA provisions also do not allow vehicles from other countries to be imported into Canada via the United States.

The bigger the better (but is it worth it?)

As a general rule, people suffer fewer injuries in larger vehicles than in smaller ones. According to the IIHS, which rates recent models according to occupant deaths per registered vehicle, small vehicles account for more than twice as many occupant deaths as large vehicles (see Figure 7-2). Small utility vehicles have the highest death rates of all, in part because of their greater involvement in fatal rollover crashes. And they're not the only ones who suffer. Recent IIHS findings show that the occupants of cars hit by SUVs are four times more likely to be killed than the occupants of SUVs or trucks. This is because the higher and heavier front-ends of the SUVs strike the cars above the underbody with greater force. Nearly half of all new vehicles sold these days are SUVs. By 1998, light trucks (which include SUVs) accounted for one-third of the vehicles owned in America. Of 5,249 people killed in 1997 in crashes involving light trucks and cars, 81 percent were car occupants. As a result, NHTSA is currently urging automakers to make their SUVs and other light trucks more "crash-compatible" with cars. If the automakers don't comply voluntarily, you'll probably see legislation to that effect before long.

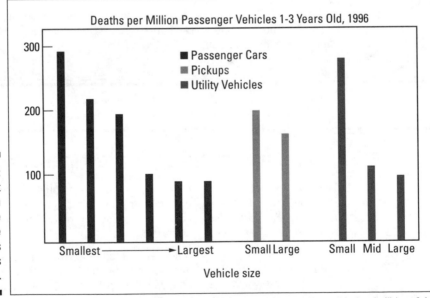

Figure 7-2: This chart shows you the relative safety rate of vehicles of various sizes.

Reprinted with permission from the Insurance Institute for Highway Safety

Structural design features

Safety cages, crumple zones, and crush zones are now being incorporated into the bodies of new vehicles (see Figure 7-3). Unlike the old rigid frames, "unibody construction" now features a rigid occupant compartment (the safety cage) and structural members in the front and rear crush zones that crumple on impact to absorb the force of the crash and direct it away from occupants. Roll bars are built right into some vehicles and are especially important on convertibles, which otherwise offer very little or no protection in rollover accidents, and, of course, on sport utility vehicles. Mercedes offers an automatic roll bar that pops up in a third of a second if sensors detect an impending rollover. The bar can be manually deployed as well.

Figure 7-3:
This unibody construction offers more protection in an accident.

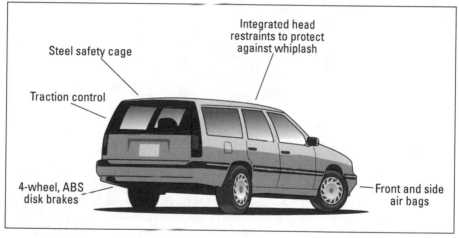

Integrated head restraints to protect against whiplash

Steel safety cage

Traction control

4-wheel, ABS disk brakes

Front and side air bags

Air bags

Air bags are *passive restraints* designed to prevent injuries to the driver and front seat passenger in impacts with vehicles that are moving at speeds over ten miles per hour. They are called "passive" restraints because they operate automatically, and require no effort on the part of the individual. ("Active" restraints would be like seat belts you have to buckle up yourself.) Most air bags deploy from compartments in the steering wheel and the passenger side of the dashboard. An increasing number of vehicles now feature side-impact air bags as well (see Figure 7-4), with many more carmakers promising them within the next few years. (Air bags are filled with harmless gas, not air. But *gas bags* just didn't seem an attractive name for them.)

ROAD RULE

Air bags are not substitutes for seat belts. They can cause injuries if seat belts are not worn.

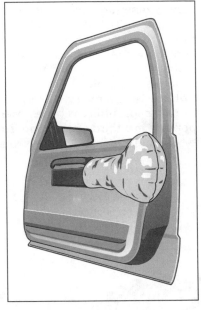

Figure 7-4:
More and
more auto
companies
are using
side-impact
air bags.

According to the Insurance Institute for Highway Safety (IIHS), the rate of driver deaths in frontal crashes is about 20 percent lower in cars with air bags than in similar vehicles that have only seat belts. By January 1999, the bags had already saved nearly 3,500 lives nationwide. However, although they definitely improve your chances of walking away from an accident unscathed, recent findings show that air bags can also cause injuries, especially to children. Because of this, newer "second generation" air bags are designed to deploy at slower speeds and an increasing number of vehicles feature air bags that can be disarmed to prevent injuries (see the sidebar "Safety concerns about air bags" for more on this). Great emphasis is now being placed on developing "smart" air bag systems that can automatically sense the presence, weight, and position of passengers, and whether the passengers are wearing seat belts. These systems can decide, on a situation-by-situation basis, whether or not to deploy and the deployment speed and direction. For instance, Mercedes-Benz now uses a "dual threshold" system that deploys at speeds that vary depending on whether seat belts are being used or not. If they are, the air bag is released in a crash impact of 18 mph; if occupants are unbelted, that is reduced to 12 mph. Because children have been killed in vehicles that were only going 5 mph, consumer groups are also calling for "dual level" systems that would deploy more gently in lower-speed crashes and more forcefully at speeds over 18 mph. Until smart air bags are more readily available, the upcoming bulleted list gives you several tips to help you prevent injuries from air bags.

Again, air bags are not substitutes for seat belts; they should always be used in conjunction with them. Belts protect you from being thrown around — or out of — the vehicle and keep you from being injured by the air bag when it deploys. The National Transportation Safety Board says that if seat belt use rose from 68 percent to 85 percent, there'd be 4,200 fewer deaths each year — that's more than all the deaths from all other forms of transportation combined! Most of the people who were killed or injured were not properly restrained by car seats or safety belts, and/or were sitting too close to the dashboard when the air bag deployed.

The Auto Club of Southern California has rated 80 models of cars, light trucks, and vans for vehicle safety features, including air bag cut-off switches, rear center-seat lap-shoulder belts, and built–in car seats. The information is available in a new American Automobile Association brochure called "Buying a Safer Car for Child Passengers" — a companion piece to "Buying a Safer Car."

Safety concerns about air bags

Many older air bags deploy at speeds as high as 200 mph and can strike children and small adults in the head, according to the *Los Angeles Times*. In the 1990s, air bags were considered to have caused the deaths of 68 children and 54 adults. As a result, the National Highway Traffic Safety Administration (NHTSA) prescribes a lower force by which newer air bags deploy, requires air-bag warning labels for new cars, and allows vehicle owners who obtain government approval to have on-off switches that enable bags to be disarmed installed by independent mechanics and dealerships. The switches must have a warning light that indicates that the air bag has been turned off and must turn back on, automatically, when the occupant leaves the seat, so it will be armed for the next occupant.

To obtain permission to install a switch, you must be able to meet at least one of these four criteria:

- Unable to sit at least 10 inches from an air bag

- At risk from an air bag because of a medical condition

- Transporting children in a vehicle without a rear seat

- Transporting more children than can fit in a rear seat

- You can obtain permission by writing to NHTSA at 400 7th Street SW, Washington, DC 20590-1000; faxing to 202-366-3443; or downloading from NHTSA's Web site at www.nhtsa.dot.gov. Include your name and address, your reason, and any supporting documentation.

✔ **When driving, sit with your face and chest as far back from the steering wheel as possible while still being able to reach the pedals.** The center of your breastbone should be at least 10 inches from the wheel (12 is better). If you have trouble reaching the pedals, look for a vehicle with an adjustable steering wheel that can be telescoped away from you, which will aim the bag at your chest rather than at your face and neck.

✔ **To move further from the air bag, try tilting your seat back slightly.** If the position makes it difficult to see through the windshield, either raise the seat — if it can be adjusted vertically — or sit on a firm, non-slippery cushion.

✔ **Passengers should also sit as far back from the air bag as possible (at least 10 inches away) — even if you end up talking to the back of the driver's head.**

> *Never put a child safety seat in a front passenger seat that has an air bag.*

✔ **Always place children under 12 in the back seat (unless the vehicle doesn't have one). Many states now make this mandatory because so many kids have been severely or fatally injured in front seats.** Infants and small children who are seated in the front passenger seat are particularly vulnerable to injury caused by air bag deployment.

For more information about the do's and don'ts of child placement, seating, and restraints, write to the Insurance Institute for Highway Safety, Box 1420, Arlington, VA 22210. Include a self-addressed, stamped business-sized envelope.

Whether or not you have children of your own, be sure to read the following section, "Child-safety seats," for detailed advice on how to insure the safety of young passengers, including those who are too old for special seats.

✔ **Don't drive with your hand between the steering wheel and the dashboard or your arm draped over it or through it.** Your arm could be broken if the air bag deploys and traps it.

✔ **Don't smoke.** An air bag can cause accidental cigarette burns, and dropping ashes or having them fly into the rear seat can start a fire, even under ordinary circumstances.

✔ **Have the air bag checked after ten years.** If you keep your vehicle longer than ten years, you must have the bags checked by a qualified dealership technician.

✔ **If the air bag light doesn't come on when you turn the key in the ignition, stays on for more than eight seconds, or suddenly lights while you're driving, have the dealer check the system.**

✔ **After they are deployed, air bags must be replaced so they can be on the ready to deploy again.**

If you feel that it's necessary to disarm your air bag, you can get up-to-the-minute information by calling the NHTSA Hotline (800-424-9393) or, better still, by visiting the Administration's Web site at `www.nhtsa.dot.gov/` and check out the terrific information in their air bag brochure at `www.nhtsa.dot.gov/airbags/brochure`.

Because they are so expensive, air bags have become prime targets for thieves and unscrupulous mechanics, who have been known to buy air bags cheaply on the black market and then charge their customers full price. The danger exceeds simply being ripped off: Mechanics that are crooked enough to use stolen air bags often install a bag that wasn't made for your vehicle. In an accident, such a bag usually fails to deploy and protect you. If you need to replace an air bag, have the work done at the dealership, or, if you go to an independent shop, ask to see the original sales receipt for the replacement bag. To be sure that your mechanic has obtained an air bag that is specifically designed for your vehicle's make, model, and year, check the part number on the receipt with the parts department at your dealership.

Child-safety seats

It is against the law in the United States to allow children who are either 4 years old or under 40 pounds to ride in cars unless they are placed in child-safety seats.

After the first weeks of a child's life, vehicle crashes are the single leading cause of death and serious injury for children. In the United States, 1,400 children die and 280,000 are injured in automobiles every year. Nearly 80 percent of those deaths could have been prevented by proper seats and belts, yet only about 60 percent of the 35 million children under 8 years of age ride with such restraints. Of the kids who are restrained, 80 percent are not properly buckled up.

Integral child-safety seats are now included in some cars and vans. These optional built-in seats fold out when you need them and convert back to adult seating when you don't. These seats are great, but some aren't suitable for infants.

You should be able to fit only one finger between your child and the harness straps, and the harness clip should be fastened at the child's armpit level. Some auto makers provide an anchor point on the rear parcel shelf to which some child seats can be tethered. If you buy such a vehicle, be sure to get a seat with the appropriate tether strap.

How to ensure that *all* children are seated safely

The following reminders, tips, and advice suggest how you can ensure the safety of your youngest — and most precious — passengers:

✔ **All young children, even those who are too old or big for child-safety seats, are safest in the center of the *rear* seat.** If you often carry small children, buy a four-door vehicle. You'll be able to stash the kids easily in the middle of the rear seat where they'll be visible in the rearview mirror. If they act up, don't turn around; instead, drive off the road, park, and attend to them.

✔ **Children who weigh fewer than 20 pounds or are less than a year old must be placed in the *rear* seat of the car, in infant-safety seats that face *backward*.** Too many infants have been killed when their seats were placed facing backward in the *front* seat of a vehicle and an air bag deployed.

✔ **If you *must* place an infant in the front seat of a vehicle, move the seat back as far as possible and have the child properly buckled up. Never place a rear-facing child-safety seat in a front passenger seat in a vehicle with air bags.** Placing the seat with the child facing *forward* (rather than to the rear) can also result in severe or fatal injuries unless the air bag has been disabled.

✔ **Choose the correct seat for your child's age and size.** Some child-safety seats are designed solely for infants, while others convert from infant seats to toddler seats. Booster seats allow larger children to ride safely when they are still too little for seat belts. Although some infant car-safety seats can be used outside the vehicle, do not attempt to use indoor infant seats as car-safety seats; they aren't built to withstand the stresses of an auto accident.

Four out of five child-safety seats are not installed or used correctly. If they were, they could reduce the risk of death by 69 percent in children younger than 1, and by 47 percent in kids ages 1-4, who account for nearly 40 percent of all the children killed while riding in motor vehicles. General Motors, in partnership with the National Safe Kids Campaign, are sponsoring car-seat safety checks at GM dealerships nationwide. For the nearest site or additional instructions on how to restrain children properly, write to National Safe Kids Campaign, 1301 Pennsylvania Ave., N.W., Suite 1000, Dept. P, Washington, D.C. 20004 or go to www.safekids.org and ask about the "Safe Kids Buckle Up" program.

About 75 percent of crashes occur within 25 miles from home — 60 percent on roads with posted speed limits of 40 mph or less!

Shopping for kid-friendly cars

The AAA offers the following checklist to take along when shopping for a child-safe vehicle:

✔ Are there enough safety belts for everyone?

✔ Do lap safety belts fit children who have outgrown safety seats and booster seats?

✔ Can a child safety seat be installed correctly in the back seat?

✔ Do safety belts have locking features for safety seats?

✔ Is head restraint protection available?

✔ Does the vehicle have safety door locks?

✔ Can individual window controls be overridden by a master safety lock?

When buying a safety seat, keep these things in mind:

✔ **Buy a safety seat that is easy and uncomplicated to secure safely.** You're going to have to take your kid in and out of that seat several times during an average shopping trip, and you don't want to get frustrated or lazy. Generally speaking, seats with T- or tray-shields are the easiest to use, but they're not appropriate for infants. Also, be sure your child can't unbuckle the seat without your assistance.

✔ **Look for a seat-certification label that says the seat meets or exceeds Federal Motor Vehicle Safety Standard 213 (FMVSS 213).** (Every car seat should have this certification.)

✔ **When your child is too big for a safety seat, be sure the standard seat belt is buckled snugly across the hips.** Don't put kids on pillows or cushions to raise them; the children can slip right out from under the lap belt and be injured.

✔ **Never ride with a child in your arms or strap the belt around both of you or around two children.** Doing this substantially increases the risk of injury.

✔ **Call the NHTSA Auto Safety Hotline (800-424-9393) to verify that your present child-safety seat, or one you are considering buying, is really safe.** When you buy a new seat, fill out and mail in the manufacturer's registration card so they can notify you in the event of a recall.

Seat belts

NHTSA estimates that seat belts save 9,500 lives every year and notes that fears about belts trapping a victim in a burning or submerged car are largely unfounded. Yet, despite government pressure, in recent years seat-belt use has leveled off and even lessened in several states. Compared with usage rates above 90 percent in such industrialized countries as Canada, Australia, and Germany, NHTSA finds seat-belt usage in the United States "pathetic." The Transportation Department estimates that, if the U.S. achieved a goal of 85 percent, we could save an additional 42,000 lives a year, prevent 102,000 injuries, and reduce medical insurance and other costs by $6.7 billion.

Seat belts come in various configurations, but because so many people are negligent about using them, the only ones that are considered *bona fide* safety devices are the type that work *automatically* (passively.) Within that category, some belts are designed to be more comfortable than others, and I strongly suggest that you test out the automatic belts on every vehicle you consider. Also, remember the following:

- ✔ **Look for belts that are *not* door-mounted.** "Three-point" belts that anchor at three locations and restrain across the hips and shoulder offer easy access and egress to the car. Door-mounted belts not only make it extremely awkward to get in and out of the car with packages, but they also have been known to let you fly out of the car if the door should open in an accident.

- ✔ **Make sure the fit is comfortable.** Belts should fit you comfortably and buckle as low as possible across your hips and pelvis rather than your abdomen. Because people come in a variety of sizes and shapes, *adjustable* shoulder belts ensure both comfort and safety.

- ✔ **Look for a model with automatic crash-tensioners.** Automatic crash-tensioners and inertia reels that keep seat belts from becoming slack reduce the distance you move forward in an accident and prevent you from injuring yourself. You can tell if a vehicle is equipped with these if it automatically tightens up when you lean forward or if you brake suddenly. (If your vehicle lacks automatic crash-tensioners, sit as far from the steering wheel or dashboard as possible and be sure seat belts are snug at all times.)

- ✔ **Pregnant women should always wear seat belts, but they must wear them correctly.** If you're pregnant, place the lap belt around your hips rather than across your stomach and keep it as low as possible; put the shoulder belt so that it rests on your breastbone but not on your stomach. Remember, too, that when you go the hospital to have your baby, bring an infant-safety seat along for the journey home. By the way, NHTSA does *not* consider pregnancy to be a good reason to disable an air bag. The risk of injury is much greater without one. Just be sure to belt yourself in securely and sit as far back from the bag as possible.

In Canada as well as the United States, the terms "active" and "passive" are used instead of "manual" and "automatic," respectively. Canadian safety regulations stipulate either passive belts or air bags. Canadian standards for seat belt anchorage are higher than those in the United States.

Ruby and me

"Ruby," my present car, has what I've come to call "anxious mother seat belts." When I turn on the ignition, the shoulder belt slams across my chest and pins me into my seat the way my mother used to block me with her right arm every time she had to brake abruptly. Despite their overzealous behavior, the belts really aren't very safe because I still have to remember to buckle the lap belt myself. To make matters worse, they are attached to the door, which is in many respects an inconvenient and unsafe design. I wish I'd done this research before I bought her. The good news is that those mechanical, mouse-on-a-rail seat belts have been sent to the oblivion they so richly deserve. They survive only as relics on older models.

Antilock braking systems (ABS)

A *factory-installed* antilock braking system (ABS) helps avoid accidents by preventing wheels from locking and by controlling the speed of the wheels on wet, slippery surfaces. An ABS's biggest asset is allowance for *steering* while emergency braking, even on gravel and icy surfaces. The system may also shorten the distance it takes to stop under wet conditions, because ABS uses electronic sensors to judge the speed of each wheel and pumps the brakes many times per second, much faster than any human can. ABS works about as well as conventional brakes on dry pavement. It may not stop your car in as short a distance as traditional brakes on gravel or loose, wet snow, but it should enable you to maintain enough control to steer the vehicle out of danger. The downside is that many drivers aren't prepared to continue steering while in this mode, and some of them simply drive right off the road. If you're in the market for ABS-equipped vehicle, be sure to read the tips I provide on how to use the system properly. ABS is standard on some models and optional equipment on others. Most ABS-equipped cars have it connected to all four wheels. Some trucks and vans only provide it for the rear wheels.

> *Never pump ABS brakes, and don't be gentle with them. It takes hard continuous pressure on the brake pedal to activate them.*

If you purchase a vehicle with ABS, you must be aware of the proper way to use it: In other words, when you're careening into something, you have to consciously forget what just about every driver's ed teacher ever taught you and follow these tips for using ABS brakes:

- ✔ **ABS brakes do the pumping for you.** Just step firmly on the brake pedal, hold it down, and keep steering precisely, even during a panic stop.

✔ **Practice this new way of braking.** Take the vehicle to a location that's free of traffic and brake it hard. You may feel the brake pedal pulsating when ABS takes over. This is totally normal; ABS is simply releasing and reapplying pressure. In some cases, you may not feel the pulsating, and that's okay, too. Practice steering while the ABS system is functioning.

✔ **Never take risks you wouldn't otherwise attempt just because your vehicle has ABS.** These are not "super brakes," and they *won't* enable you to stop on a dime under all circumstances.

✔ **In a skid, if your vehicle is equipped with 4-wheel ABS, steer in the direction in which you want to go.** Vehicles with rear-end ABS or no ABS at all should be steered in the direction of the skid. In other words, if the tail of the car is going to the right, steer to the right (into the skid). If the tail is going to the left, your steering input should be to the left. Try, however, not to understeer or oversteer.

✔ **If your ABS system fails, pump your brakes as you would with a traditional braking system and steer in the direction of the skid.**

✔ **Replace tires on ABS-equipped vehicles with the same size tires as the original equipment.** Automakers make a great effort to determine the optimum size and design when selecting tires for ABS-equipped vehicles, so don't get creative when shopping for new tires and be sure to follow the manufacturer's instructions.

✔ **Don't buy after-market ABS brakes.** Be aware that after-market products billed as antilock brakes have not proved reliable; in fact, some are downright dangerous and the courts have ruled that they cannot be called ABS. If your present vehicle lacks ABS, either continue to get along without it or buy a vehicle that is *factory* equipped with ABS.

For more information about ABS brakes, check out the Web site at www.ABS-education.org. It provides detailed information about how ABS work. While you're there, click the link to "America Brakes for Safety," a curriculum developed by the Alliance that teaches you how to use them properly.

Traction and other control issues

The IIHS is unclear to what extent traction control and multi-wheel drive features actually help *prevent* crashes because drivers may react to the better handling or braking capability by taking chances or driving in bad weather that they otherwise may not have attempted. However, if you often drive in wet, slippery, or off-road conditions, these features can be very valuable indeed. Several different systems are available:

- **Limited-slip differential** is designed to improve traction in slick conditions, but it can cause side-slipping. It usually costs less than other control options, but it's not as efficient as traction control or multi-wheel drive.

- **Traction control** senses when one wheel is spinning faster than the others and may automatically apply the brakes, cut off power to that wheel, and/or reduce acceleration to improve traction and maintain stability. It is available in various configurations as standard equipment on some vehicles or as an option on others.

- **Four-wheel drive** allows a driver to manually adjust the vehicle to operate in difficult terrain. How that is accomplished differs from one model to another. Formerly, the driver had to get out and lock each wheel. Today, on many vehicles, the shift from two- to four-wheel drive can be accomplished almost as easily as changing gears. In its purest form, four-wheel drive involves a second, separate gear box that takes the vehicle into very low gear ranges for extreme conditions. These are heavy, expensive vehicles designed for traveling through really goopy stuff or chasing rhinos across Tanzania. In any form, four-wheel drive should only be used when needed, because it doesn't work efficiently under normal road conditions.

- **All-wheel drive** is the easiest to use of these options. Traditional vehicles offer either *front-wheel* or *rear-wheel drive,* which means that those wheels are powered directly by the engine while the remaining set just travels along. All-wheel drive powers all the wheels simultaneously. *Full-time* all-wheel drive operates constantly and improves handling even on dry pavement. *Selectable* all-wheel drive requires very little effort to engage. All-wheel drive is standard on some models, but is an option on others.

Head restraints

Head restraints (also known as headrests) help to prevent whiplash in rear-end collisions. They are mandatory on the front seats of new passenger vehicles, and many models now feature rear-seat head restraints as well. Some head restraints are adjustable; others are fixed in place. Although both usually provide adequate protection, adjustable ones are sometimes too small for tall people, and some are set too far back. The IIHS suggests that you look for high, fixed head restraints or adjustable ones that are high enough to protect you in their lowest position and placed as close as possible to the back of your head to prevent it from snapping back in a rear-end crash (see Figure 7-5).

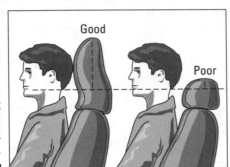

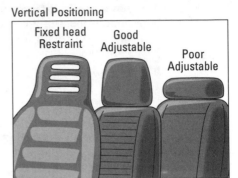

Figure 7-5: Head restraints, properly built and used, help prevent head and neck injuries.

Side-impact protection

Side-impact crashes account for close to 30 percent of all passenger vehicle occupant deaths, and many serious injuries occur when the force of a side impact drives a door into an occupant. As a result, side-impact protection became mandatory on American cars made after 1997. It will become mandatory on utility vehicles, passenger vans, and pickups by 1999.

Side guard beams have proved somewhat effective in protecting people in single-vehicle collisions with objects, but they have not made much difference in accidents where one vehicle hits the side of another. Federal standards now include side-impact crash tests and automakers must meet "dynamic side impact" requirements equivalent to being broadsided while traveling at 15 mph by a vehicle moving at 30 mph. To do this, some carmakers are adding more energy-absorbing padding inside doors, and others are installing side-impact air bags that deploy from doors, side pillars, or seats.

Damage-resistant bumpers

Damage-resistant bumpers protect a vehicle from damage during accidents. Because federal bumper standards were reduced in 1983 from "no damage at five miles per hour" to "no damage at two and a half miles per hour," new cars often feature sleek-looking colored plastic bumpers that provide very little protection at all. At today's prices for labor and parts, even a minor collision can cost anywhere from a few hundred to several thousand dollars. By mid-1998, campaigns were underway to reinstate the 5 mph requirement. Hopefully, by the time you read this, it will have become law.

Ask your dealership how the bumpers on their models are constructed, and pay special attention to the following:

- **What material absorbs the impact.** Bumper systems usually feature a reinforcing bar and some energy-absorbing material such as polypropylene foam, but better bumpers incorporate hydraulic shock absorbers in addition to, or instead of, foam.

- **How far the bumper is from the vehicle's body.** The distance from the bumper to the body of the vehicle is another important safety factor. The farther away, the greater the bumper's ability to absorb the shock of an accident and reduce damage.

By the way, *no* bumper standards apply to passenger vans, and pickup trucks can be sold with no rear bumpers at all — I found *this* out the hard way.

Oh, say, can you see?

The ability of a driver to see everything that is going on around the vehicle is a major safety factor. So is the ability of other drivers to see your vehicle in low light and inclement weather. Here are a few things to look for:

- **Head restraints, roof structure, and the size and location of windows** can seriously impair your ability to see what is going on to the rear and each side of you. Get behind the wheel and check the visibility. Then check it again during road tests.

- **Right-side mirrors** are still considered optional equipment by some automakers. In view of the fact that, on many vehicles, it is impossible to see through the right rear window when you look into the rearview mirror, a right-side mirror is necessary to be sure nobody is approaching on your right before you change lanes or make a right turn. Demand mirrors on *both* sides of any vehicle you buy.

- **Halogen driving lights and fog lamps** improve visibility under extreme conditions. If you do a lot of night driving on dark or difficult roads or in foggy or misty areas, these are worth paying for.

- **Daytime running lights** that are automatically activated by the ignition switch are an increasingly popular way to enhance vehicle visibility and can prevent accidents by 7 to 40 percent. They are currently required on new cars in Canada and are "allowed" in the United States.

- **HID (High Intensity Discharge)** are the latest improvement in headlights — usually available only in upscale, expensive cars.

- **Color** is an important visibility factor. It is not surprising that gray cars get fewer tickets than red or white ones; the cops may not see them easily, but neither do other drivers. For this reason, gray cars get into more accidents than red or white ones do. What are *your* priorities?

Safety features in the works

Safety features are continually being added to new car models. The following list includes items not available at the time this book was written, but be sure to ask the dealership whether the vehicles you consider can be equipped with any of these innovations:

✔ **Warning devices** that alert drivers to an impending collision by flashing or sounding an alarm or applying the brakes automatically. (Some vans can warn you if you're about to hit something while backing up, but that's not quite the same thing.)

✔ **Crash recorders** that record the way air bags and other safety mechanisms function during a car crash in the same way that they provide information about what happened during airplane accidents.

✔ **Driver monitors** that keep track of the car's behavior and even shut down the vehicle if the driver is driving drunk or irresponsibly. At least one major automaker has developed a warning system that monitors the steering and pulse of the driver. If it senses that you are drowsy or asleep, the monitor uses lights and sound and even shakes your seat to alert you. If you still don't wake up, it automatically stops the car!

✔ **911 emergency calls**, triggered whenever an air bag deploys, transmit the vehicle's location automatically using an onboard navigational system and a cellular phone.

✔ **Vision enhancements**, developed by the military, that use radar, video, or infrared sensors to help drivers see obstacles that may be obscured by snow, fog, rain, and darkness; or to detect potentially dangerous individuals lurking in dark parking lots.

✔ **"Super brakes"** that sense and automatically compensate for over- and understeering or use radar to detect objects in front of your vehicle and sound a warning to tell you to brake. They may even apply the brakes automatically if you fall asleep while driving.

A word about newfangled gadgets and systems: I like to wait until a new model or system establishes a track record before I buy. If a vehicle has unusual or innovative features, ask how long they've been in use. It can take a year or two to work the bugs out of a new mechanism and to provide the service department with enough experience and training to deal with it efficiently. Find out if a new electronic system consists of components that can be replaced or repaired, or whether the entire unit has to be replaced if anything goes wrong.

Theft prevention systems and cellular telephones

The increasing prevalence of car thieves and carjackers has produced many types of antitheft devices. More automakers are including alarm systems as standard equipment; others offer them as options, and a large after-market business has developed to install or upgrade antitheft equipment on vehicles that lack it.

Cellular phones have powerful advantages and disadvantages as safety devices. They may be linked directly to 911, emergency road service, or stolen-vehicle tracking agencies. On the other hand, studies show that using a car phone can lower your attentiveness by 20 percent, and an intense conversation can cut your concentration by a third. Be sure all phones are safely anchored when you carry them in your vehicle — in an accident, they can be formidable projectiles. The good news is that cellular telephones are being linked to automated service and security systems such as GM's OnStar system, which is described in detail in Chapter 17. This chapter also tells you more about alarms, cellular phones, and other antitheft devices.

If the vehicle you choose doesn't offer what you want as *standard* equipment, a quick survey of current ads can help you decide whether to pay the car dealer to install the equipment or have it installed by an independent specialist. Just be sure installation doesn't affect any manufacturer's warranties.

Other Features to Consider

Safety features are among the more important considerations when you're defining what you want and need in a new car. But plan to give some thought to a few other key points and options that may sway your decision. Although these features may not save your life or let you stop on a dime, they can certainly affect the satisfaction — and expense — involved in owning a new car.

Can alternatively powered vehicles save the world?

Consider an alternatively fueled vehicle if the environment really means a lot to you. These vehicles not only substantially reduce emissions or eliminate them entirely but are quieter as well, so you can prevent two kinds of pollution at the same time.

- **Electric cars** developed by major domestic and foreign automakers are emission-free and provide steadily increasing range and performance. The major drawbacks — high cost and lack of convenient recharging facilities — may be eliminated soon. There's talk of federal and state income tax credits of up to $4,000 for purchasers of electric vehicles, and some local governments are offering rebates of as much as $5,000. As demand goes up, prices will go down. Advances in battery technology are making electric vehicles more efficient. The new Honda EV can accelerate to over 80 mph with EPA estimates of as much as 100 miles between charges, longer-running vehicles are being developed, and an increasing number of recharging stations are being built. Ford and Honda are funding the development of public recharging stations at malls, airports, hospitals, and parking structures, and Edison EV has similar plans. Electric vehicles are silent, which makes me hope

(continued)

(continued)

that electric-powered motorscooters and motorcycles will return many relatively undeveloped areas to their former serenity. Today, electric cars have a range of 50 to 100 miles, so if you do most of your motoring within an hour from home, an electric car may be a wonderful way to do your bit to protect Mother Earth.

✔ **Fuel cells** were invented in 1839 and already provide electricity on spacecraft. They are now considered by many experts to be the "most likely to succeed" of all alternatives to conventional engines. Fuel-cell systems electrochemically convert gasoline to hydrogen and combine it with oxygen to generate electricity, which is then used to power a vehicle. The only by-products are heat and water vapor. Estimated to be twice as efficient as internal combustion engines, fuel cells can provide the equivalent of 80 miles per gallon while reducing exhaust emissions by 90 percent. Unlike electric vehicles, they can be refueled at any gas station. The need to use gasoline turns off many environmentalists, but fuel-cell systems that use methanol and ethanol are being developed. Once established, fuel cells may be used to power trains, submarines and portable PCs and even provide electricity for homes and offices in remote locations. Many domestic and foreign automakers are developing these systems: By the end of March 1998, they'd committed more than $1 billion to fuel-cell research. Ford and Mercedes (Daimler) have announced plans to put over 100,000 fuel-cell powered cars on the road by 2004. Let's keep our fingers crossed!

✔ **Natural-gas-fueled cars, trucks, and vans (NGVs)** that reduce emissions by as much as 60 percent are used mainly by fleets, taxis, and police departments. Passenger cars that can run on either natural gas or gasoline are available from major auto makers and may qualify for substantial rebates

and incentives. Although over 1,000 NGV fueling stations are located across the United States, and natural gas costs only a fraction of what gasoline costs, the lack of easy access to natural gas has limited the popularity of these vehicles with private owners.

✔ **Cars that run on liquid hydrogen, ethanol, and methanol** have also been developed, as well as "hybrid cars" that combine gasoline or diesel engines with electric motors. In January 1998, Chrysler unveiled a plastic-bodied, electric-diesel hybrid that is capable of getting 70 miles per gallon while reducing emissions by 50 percent. Unfortunately, diesel fumes have recently been identified as a cause of cancer, so the future of even efficient diesel-powered vehicles is uncertain.

✔ **Ultra low-emission gasoline engines** are also undergoing a surge of new development. Honda is now marketing the world's first gasoline-powered car that is so clean that it qualifies as an Ultra Low-Emission Vehicle (ULEV). These Civics and Accords produce less emissions than any gasoline-powered car ever built and meet a California standard, which reduces hydrocarbons by an incredible 85 percent. To top that, Honda recently announced an engine that will emit essentially no smog precursors at all.

As federal and state governments become more insistent on the necessity for clean-burning vehicles, many of these alternative systems will become increasingly efficient and cost-effective. Right now, fuel-cell systems seem to be the most promising. I urge you to support *all* state and federal legislation for alternatively fueled vehicles that reduce consumption of our dwindling supplies of petroleum and fulfill the mandates of the federal Clean Air Act. Even if you don't feel that one of the existing alternatives currently fills *your* needs, you'll benefit — along with the rest of the environment — from having more of them available to replace the millions of gas-gulpers currently on the road.

Fuel economy

If you do a great deal of driving, make fuel efficiency a high priority. Even if you can afford to pay for the extra gasoline, you certainly don't want to be a major contributor to air pollution. Federal law demands that a window sticker with EPA mileage estimates appear on every new vehicle (see Figure 7-6). To compare the fuel consumption of models from various manufacturers, ask for a free copy of *Passenger Car Fuel Economy: EPA and Road* at a dealership, or ask the Government Printing Office for a copy of publication #460380010. (Publications Service Section, Washington, D.C. 20402 [202-512-1803] 7:30 a.m. to 4 p.m. EST. While you're at it, get on the mailing list for a catalog of other free and low-cost consumer publications.)

Factors that affect fuel economy include the load, road conditions, power options, type of transmission, size of the car or the engine, air conditioning, design, tire pressure, and driving habits. If you really care about saving fuel, you can find detailed chapters on driving ecologically in *Driving For Dummies: The Glove Compartment Guide* (written by me and published by IDG Books Worldwide, Inc.).

Don't expect the vehicle you buy to achieve the EPA estimates on the label. These estimates are really averages for comparison purposes only, and they are arrived at under test conditions that are probably more favorable than the ones you're likely to encounter. Tests are limited to short seven- to ten-mile trips, on warm days, over level or gently rolling routes, at speeds of from 20 to 55.5 miles per hour, with no fast acceleration, air conditioning, cargo, or passengers.

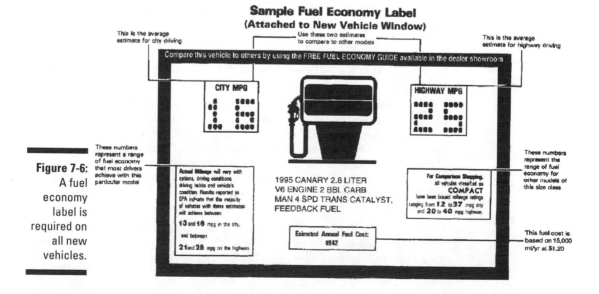

Figure 7-6: A fuel economy label is required on all new vehicles.

Fuel economy is more than just miles per gallon. It has to do with the *financial* economy of driving a vehicle that runs on low-cost, low-octane gasoline instead of a gourmet diet of high-priced, high-octane, premium fuel. And don't forget the "gas-guzzler tax" that the federal government imposes on voracious fuel hogs!

Manual versus automatic transmissions

The type of transmission you choose is pretty much a matter of taste. Automatic transmissions are standard on many models. As options they can add from $100 to $1,000 to the price. Each type has pros and cons, as explained in the following sections.

Manual transmissions

These transmissions are great if you love to fine-tune your driving to every situation, and you don't spend a lot of time in stop-and-go traffic. I really loved the manual transmissions on my truck and my classic car. I felt such rapport with my vehicles as I glided the stick shift through the gears, downshifting on curves and hills like a race driver. Of course, in those days, I spent a lot of time on the highway and lived in a rural area with little traffic. When I moved to the Big City and had to manually shift from gear to gear at every stoplight, having a manual transmission wasn't nearly as much fun. Now, I really love the convenience of an automatic transmission for city and freeway rush-hour traffic, and the overdrive feature works like a manual fifth gear to reduce strain on the engine and save fuel on long stretches of highway.

A manual transmission is a mixed blessing. Here are some of its advantages and disadvantages.

- Manual transmissions are generally cheaper on a new-car purchase, especially if they are standard on a particular vehicle (rather than an option).

- They are also often cheaper to run because most of them are more fuel-efficient than automatic transmissions of similar size, especially the 4-speed and 5-speed models, which provide extra higher gears to use when you're barreling merrily down the highway and the vehicle's momentum is almost all you need to maintain your speed. By being able to shift manually into a higher gear as soon as possible, you can get the engine turning fewer times for each turn of the wheels, which means you need less fuel to keep that engine going.

- Generally speaking, manual transmissions have more power on tap when you need to jump into heavy traffic at a freeway entrance, climb a steep hill, or carry a heavy load. That's because you have the option of shifting into a lower, more powerful gear and really pouring it on.

- Again, generally speaking (because there are many models out there) a manual transmission can be less expensive to repair than an automatic transmission of similar quality.

- Although manual transmissions may require less fuel, they demand a lot more energy from you. You must stay alert in order to change gears at the appropriate times. You also have to do the physical work involved in stepping on the clutch and moving the gear shift every time a change of speed requires it, and this can be exhausting in stop-and-go traffic. If you can see it as dancing with your car, terrific. If not, read on, an automatic transmission is probably just what you're looking for.

Automatic transmissions

I find it interesting that automatic transmissions have become standard on an increasing number of vehicles to the point that you sometimes have to order a manual transmission as an option, instead of the other way around, as it was in the past. Models designed as family cars are usually the ones equipped with automatic transmissions; the high-performance, sporty models still assume you're going to want to drive the car every inch of the way in order to put it through its paces in the finest style. If your tastes put you somewhere in the middle, consider the pros and cons of owning a vehicle with an automatic transmission:

- Automatic transmissions make driving easier: You just step on the gas to go, step on the brake to stop, and steer the car in any direction that appeals to you.

- But automatics usually cost more — especially if they're optional — and they usually get fewer miles to the gallon. There are, however, automatic transmissions that work in conjunction with computers that are so sensitive to speed and "load" that they can fine-tune performance more efficiently than a human mind. As time goes on and these are more generally available, they may prove cheaper than manuals in the long run.

- Automatic transmissions are generally less responsive than manual transmissions for the same size engine, because they have to "think" about what the vehicle needs in terms of power and speed through a variety of changing road conditions, instead of being "popped" into the proper gear as fast as you can make your choice. They are also generally less powerful than their manual counterparts and won't perform as well during initial acceleration, especially on small four-cylinder vehicles.

- Some automatic transmissions may be cheaper to repair than manual transmissions; sometimes it's the other way around. You pays your money and you takes your choice. . . .

Air-conditioning

If you want air-conditioning, buy a vehicle that comes equipped with it. Factory-installed A/C units take up less space and are designed to cool a specific vehicle more efficiently than after-market units can. If you live in a cool or moderate climate, air-conditioning may be a *disadvantage* because the unit weighs enough to cost you a couple of miles per gallon — even when you aren't using it. If fuel economy means a lot to you, forgo air conditioning and simply open the vents, windows, or sunroof. In a hot climate, air-conditioning is a necessity, not just for comfort but for safety. Some models feature a separate switch that lets you defrost your windshield without running the A/C compressor.

If you suffer from allergies or drive in regions with highly polluted air, an *air filtration system* can keep microscopic dust, pollen, and diesel particles from entering the passenger compartment. The system also eliminates odors caused by mold and bacteria growing inside heating and air-conditioning units.

Power options

Today a variety of power gizmos are included as standard equipment within "luxury packages" or are sold separately. Take the time to consider each of the following features and decide which you need and whether or not you are prepared to pay in dollars and fuel for "conveniences" you can do without:

- ✔ **Power brakes and power steering are standard on most vehicles and not really options at all.** Because both features substantially increase safety and handling, you may even want to reject vehicles that lack them. After years of driving a pickup that lacked both, I consider them indispensable, especially on large or heavy vehicles.

- ✔ **Variable-assist power steering systems are becoming increasingly popular.** These systems regulate the efforts required to turn the wheels in relation to the speed of the vehicle. You get more assistance when you're parking and less help at high speeds, so you don't oversteer.

- ✔ **Power seats may add significantly to the up-front cost of the vehicle,** and the mechanisms that power them can weigh enough to lower the car's fuel economy by a couple of miles per gallon. Unless you share your car with someone who is very different in size, or a driver or frequent passenger is too weak to adjust a seat manually, you're better off refusing to pay for the dubious privilege of hauling power seats around.

✔ **Power windows and door locks used to leave me cold, but I've come to adore them.** I can shut the windows every time I park, without cranking my life away, and drop them with the flick of a finger at toll booths. Driver's-side universal locks keep kids from opening car doors and windows. Remote control door locks are not only convenient when my hands are full, they allow me to open and lock the passenger-side doors, without having to lean across the car, and to enter swiftly and safely without having to fumble with a key after dark. If your present vehicle has power locks, you can buy a remote control device for under $100.

All of these controls vary from one vehicle to another. Be sure that power locks on your vehicle can be overridden manually so you can exit if your vehicle's power systems fail in an accident.

✔ **Power-operated side mirrors can save your life if the right-side mirror is out of adjustment when you're driving alone.** If power mirrors aren't available, at the very least, make sure the models you look at have little levers that allow you to adjust both side mirrors without having to lower the windows.

Sunroofs, moonroofs, T-roofs, and "no-roofs" (convertibles)

I really enjoy the way my car's sunroof lets in fresh air without the need for drafty open windows. Having a sunroof is almost as good as having a convertible, at a fraction of the cost, and without the prematurely aging blasts of sun and wind on my face. If you share my preference for sunroofs, keep the following in mind:

✔ **Choose a vehicle with a factory-installed sunroof.** After-market roofs may leak and can detract from resale value.

✔ **Buy a vehicle with an opaque shield (often called a *moonroof*) that slides into place automatically to block the sun from heating up the interior of the car or baking your brains on hot, sunny days.** Another alternative is a sunroof that comes with a shield you can easily insert manually, when you want to block the sun from the interior of the car. In both cases, the shield should not prevent you from opening the roof for air.

✔ **T-roofs were designed to offer the open feeling of a convertible and the protection of a closed roof.** Before you settle for T-roofs, be sure you want to go through the hassle of removing and stowing them often enough to justify the expense.

✔ **When your car's warranty expires, power versions of these roofs can be very expensive to repair.**

Windshield equipment

Intermittent windshield wipers have become standard on most cars. Some have one setting; others offer several or variable settings. On some luxury models, they automatically increase with the speed of the vehicle. Cadillac's Rainsense Wiper System senses the presence of moisture on the windshield by changes in light reflection. Will wonders never cease?

Wet wiper blades on some vehicles integrate the windshield-washer nozzle into the wiper blade arm. This keeps the washing fluid right in the area you need to clean rather than spraying it over the window. Rear window wipers, washers, and defoggers are safety devices as well as conveniences. They really increase visibility, especially on hatchbacks, vans, and RVs.

Cruise control

Cruise control is useless in stop-and-go traffic and on city streets. Its extra cost can be justified only if you often drive a big gas burner for many miles at sustained highway speeds. Even then, cruising along, mile after mile, without having to operate the gas pedal may make you careless or drowsy, whereas having to watch your speed may help to keep you awake. Pay extra for this option only if you tend to be terribly lead-footed on the accelerator pedal and prone to speeding tickets. If the dealer has to install it, be sure that it won't void the factory warranties on your vehicle.

Sound equipment

Many of us consider a sound system an indispensable driving companion. I love to drive to music; it's like dancing. Books on tape transform long trips into opportunities for entertainment and education. Although most vehicles come with a no-frills system, in most cases, more sophisticated equipment is available — at a price. Ask yourself: Do I need a more powerful FM receiver to bring in my favorite stations? Would I get my money's worth of enjoyment from a multi-disc CD player? How many powerful speakers do I need to satisfy my soul?

Some car manufacturers will give you a credit if you buy a vehicle without a sound system, and the wiring for the speakers and the system will still be in the vehicle for use with after-market equipment. Also worthy of note: If your kids' musical tastes drive you crazy, systems with rear-seat headphones can keep them "rap-happy" on long trips.

After-market sound systems can provide more features — often of higher quality — at a lower price than factory-installed systems. If your taste runs to high-tech sound, take the time to investigate the after-market before you opt for an expensive factory-installed system. Check consumer publications to see which systems are the most efficient and compare sale prices in Sunday or special advertising supplements against the cost of factory-installed equipment. Be sure the after-market price includes installation and that the system will fit into the space provided in your car.

If security is an issue, consider that factory-installed sound systems are usually harder for thieves to remove. So, if a vehicle comes with a system that suits your taste and budget, you may want to go for it. Systems that hang under the dashboard are not only targets for theft, they can also be hazardous in an accident. Avoid spectacular LED readouts and many-buttoned electronic gizmos, not just because thieves adore them, but because the following rule applies to *anything* you buy:

> **The simpler the equipment, the less chance it will need repair.**

Or, as we sailors say, KISS! (Keep It Simple, Stupid!)

Those exterior antennas that vandals love to break are being eliminated by an increasing number of carmakers who are concealing them in the body of the car and rigging them to raise and lower automatically when you start and stop the engine, or incorporating the antenna in the upper windshield. If you live or work in high-vandalism areas, one of these options should be a priority.

If you are planning to finance a vehicle, remember that the price of expensive factory-installed high-tech sound options is included in your loan and will cost you substantial interest over time. In this case, you'll probably be better off with after-market equipment, *if* you can pay it off completely, at better rates, in a shorter time.

Radial tires

All new cars come equipped with radials these days, and they are definitely an advantage because they actually save fuel. If the vehicle you choose lacks them, bargain to have them included at no additional cost. Request *steel-belted* radials rated for *at least* 40,000 miles. Worthwhile options are the 50,000- or 80,000-mile radials, even if you drive as little as 10,000 miles a year. If you live in an area where the winters are severe, ask for all-weather radials so that you won't have to bother with snow tires.

Don't get conned into buying too much tire for your vehicle. Just because a tire is more expensive doesn't necessarily mean it offers better quality and longevity under all conditions; it may have been intended solely for high-speed performance. And what's the use of driving around on tires designed to run continuously at 150 mph when you're constrained by 55 to 65 mph speed limits?

Most basic new-car warranties do *not* include tires, which are warranted separately by the tire manufacturer. See Chapter 17 for more information about warranties.

Seating and upholstery

How many people do you have to carry in the *front* seat of your car? Seating configurations vary from one model to another. Large sedans and trucks often have bench seats up front, while coupes and sports models feature bucket seats. Rear seating also varies widely, from roomy couch-like seats in large sedans to tiny vestigial shelves that offer little more than package room in smaller cars and nothing at all in most standard pickup trucks.

- ✔ Bench seats can accommodate three fairly slim adults, provided no gearshift is in the way and the vehicle has three sets of seat belts. Bench seats are fine for four-door vehicles, but a pain to lower for rear access on two-door models and trucks.

- ✔ Bucket seats accommodate only two people, but can be individually adjusted for comfort, leg room, and ease of access.

- ✔ Some models offer a "split bench" option that combines the best features of each: room for three up front, plus the ability to adjust each side separately.

If you often chauffeur infants or small children, look for a vehicle with built-in child-safety seats that fold back into conventional seating when not in use.

Do you like to sit in the lap of luxury? Most carmakers offer luxury packages that include high-tech ergonomically designed seats and leather upholstery.

Do you often carry large loads or long objects such as skis and surfboards? The seats in many station wagons and passenger vans fold and slide away to make room for large loads. My hatchback features rear seats that can be folded down, with access from the rear, which gives it the same capacity for stowing long objects that I loved in my truck.

Upholstery options may include gorgeous leather, washable vinyl, and a variety of fabrics. What you choose depends on your budget, your taste, the people and animals who are regular passengers in the vehicle, and where you live. Leather and vinyl can get hot and sticky in scorching weather or icy cold in sub-zero climates. Little kids and animals are lethal to leather or velour upholstery. If you tend to carry messy passengers or drive in wet or unpaved areas, vinyl is probably your best bet. (Getting removable mats to protect both front and rear carpeting is also wise.)

Dealers may try to foist a fabric-protection package on you. Forget it! If the upholstery can't hold up to normal wear and tear, you probably don't want it at all. Go for vinyl instead.

Adjustable steering wheels

An increasing number of vehicles provide steering wheels that can tilt up and down and/or telescope forward and backward. This option is worth paying for if

- ✔ You can't see over a normal steering wheel.
- ✔ You risk air bag injury because your face would be too close to a standard wheel.
- ✔ You are too large to slip easily behind a standard wheel.

Electrically adjustable steering wheels have a memory that automatically adjusts the car's wheel to the individual needs of drivers who vary greatly in size, but can be expensive to repair. If this consideration fits your family's profile, this kind of steering wheel may be worth the cost.

Electronic dashboard displays

We seem to have entered Wonderland when it comes to fancy electronic dashboard gadgets. Animated monitors that graphically display everything from speed, mileage, and fuel consumption to the load on the engine in scintillating colors may be fun, but they're also very distracting. They can literally leave you in the dark if they go out of whack, and they are expensive to repair. In some vehicles, a lush feminine voice coos, "Your oil is getting low," and "Please buckle your seat belts." If I have to put up with some stranger telling me how to run my car, they can at least offer me a sexy *male* invisible companion!

To return to the real world: Be sure to give high priority to vehicles with *calibrated* oil, water, and temperature gauges — which indicate a range of levels and show your vehicle's current status — rather than "idiot lights" or voices that alert you when it's already too late to avoid possible damage to the engine. If you're looking at vehicles with manual transmissions, make sure the cars include tachometers (gauges that indicate at how many revolutions per minute your engine is operating) for efficient shifting. *All* controls must be easy to use, without distracting you from the road. Be vocal about your preferences. If we gripe enough about the growing number of new cars that offer only idiot lights, perhaps the manufacturers will find it worth their while to return to the calibrated gauges that were standard equipment for most of automotive history.

Navigation systems

As a sailor, I owe my life to navigational devices. When our sailboat was dismasted in the mid-Pacific, we traversed the empty ocean for six weeks and landed safely on a small island because one member of the crew was proficient with a sextant, which is an instrument used to manually determine the latitude and longitude of your current location. Today, electronic navigational devices are considered to be essential equipment on most boats, and these systems have begun to appear on vehicles as well. Just as GPS (global positioning systems) use data beamed from satellites to provide boats with current latitude and longitude, estimate the distance and time needed to reach a particular "way point," and alert you when you get there, automotive navigational computers also use GPS data to tell you where you are.

But navigational systems in automobiles can provide much more information, including how to get to specific addresses, restaurants, theaters, hotels, hospitals, airports, police stations, and places of interest. Other options include traffic warnings and the ability to send for the police, a tow truck, or an ambulance. Navigation systems are standard or optional equipment on an increasing number of new vehicles and are also available as after-market equipment.

These systems vary greatly in quality and cost, so do your homework carefully before choosing from those currently available to you. Because they are a relatively new technology, navigational systems are expensive, often error-prone, and not easily updated. Some are programmed to be of use only in large metropolitan areas, and will not function in some states and many cities. Some are free-standing electronic devices that work off your cigarette lighter. (I wonder when lighters will become as optional as ash trays, and their power sources transformed into "electronic access ports.") Before long, some form of navigational system will be as standard on all vehicles as a sound system; it will be interesting to see what form it takes.

Undercoating and rustproofing

Good quality vehicles are protected against corrosion and rust before they leave the factory, and carry long-term rust-through warranties. If a dealer tries to convince you to pay extra for additional undercoating or rustproofing, tell the dealer that if the vehicle can't stand up to *normal* wear and tear, perhaps you'd better find one that does.

If salty ocean breezes or salted snowy roads regularly eat away at vehicles in your area, a professional who specializes in this kind of protection can do the work at a lower price than a dealership can, and with better materials than do-it-yourself products. Do-it-yourself after-market polymer generally lasts about half as long as the substances used by reliable professionals, and you run the risk of clogging drain holes and damaging exhaust and brake systems if the coating isn't applied correctly.

If you decide to have anyone — including a dealership — rustproof your vehicle, be sure that doing so does not void the automaker's warranty.

If you *do* allow someone to rustproof your car, be sure the work is guaranteed, not only for the cost of the rustproofing, but also for the repair or replacement of any rusted body panels. Some rustproofing guarantees demand that the vehicle be checked annually, on a specified date, to maintain the guarantee. Ask for at least a month's leeway and find out if you'll have to pay "refresher" fees on those occasions.

Never have older cars undercoated. Existing rust will continue to eat away unseen beneath the coating and hasten the demise of the car. Use only genuine factory replacement body parts. After-market parts often do not have rust-resistant protection.

Fancy trim packages

These packages are strictly for rich kids who couldn't care less about money. Pinstriping, wild paint jobs, spoilers, and other racing equipment on vehicles that will never see a track not only add to the initial cost of the vehicle, but their effect on your insurance rates will go on forever. Expensive custom wheels may attract more thieves than compliments.

Remote engine starters

Remote engine starters are becoming quite popular in Canada and the northern United States because they allow drivers to start and warm up their vehicles without having to leave their cozy homes or offices until the car is comfy to sit in and ready to go. If you'd like one of these dandy gizmos, compare the cost of having it installed by an independent professional with the dealership's price.

Trailer-towing packages

If you plan to tow a trailer, pick a vehicle with a large transmission and have it delivered with a trailer-towing package already installed. This option usually includes a heavy-duty suspension system with springs and shock absorbers that can cope with the extra weight and shifting loads, a cooler to prevent the transmission from overheating, a rear bumper that can be hitched to a trailer, and a high output alternator. You may want to buy one of these packages, even if you have no immediate plans but may want to tow a trailer in the future. Trailer-towing packages are usually priced very reasonably — certainly less than what it would cost to buy all that stuff separately — and your vehicle will be tougher and easier to handle. At the very least, find out what the towing capacity of your vehicle is (there are varying degrees), if there's any chance at all that you may need one.

Use the Features and Options Checklist on the next two pages to identify the stuff you want and compare prices for several vehicles with that equipment.

FEATURES & OPTIONS CHECKLIST

Model #1	Model #4
Model #2	Model #5
Model #3	Model #6

In the first box, write **Y**(es), **N**(o), or **M**(aybe) to indicate whether or not you want the feature. In the box for each model, insert code letters to indicate whether the feature is **S**(tandard), **O**(ptional), or part of a **P**(ackage), and whether the transmission is **A**(utomatic) or **M**(anual), and so on.

STANDARD/OPTIONAL EQUIPMENT	Y, N or M	Model #1	Model #2	Model #3	Model #4	Model #5	Model #6
Safety Features:							
Does vehicle project your "image?"							
Dual air bags							
Integral child-safety seat							
Automatic seat belts							
Anti-lock brakes (ABS)							
Traction control							
Four-wheel drive							
All-wheel drive							
Head restraints (**F**ixed/**A**djustable)							
Side-impact protection							
Damage-resistant bumpers							
Visibility:							
Through windshield							
Through rear mirror							
Right-side mirror							
Halogen and/or **F**og lamps							
Daytime running lights							
Theft-prevention Systems Type:							
Cellular telephone							
Warning devices*							
Windshield displays*							
Crash recorder*							
Driver-monitor*							
Auto 911*							
Vision enhancement*							
Tire monitors*/**R**un-flat tires*							
Super brakes*							
Fuel (EPA estimate/Low-lead or Premium?)							
Auto or Manual Transmission							
Air Conditioning							
Air-filtration System							
*May not be available yet							

FEATURES & OPTIONS CHECKLIST (continued)

Model #1	Model #4
Model #2	Model #5
Model #3	Model #6

In the first box, write **Y**(es), **N**(o), or **M**(aybe) to indicate whether or not you want the feature. In the box for each model, insert code letters to indicate whether the feature is **S**(tandard), **O**(ptional), or part of a **P**(ackage), and whether the transmission is **A**(utomatic) or **M**(anual), and so on.

STANDARD/OPTIONAL EQUIPMENT	Y, N or M	Model #1	Model #2	Model #3	Model #4	Model #5	Model #6
Power Options:							
Power brakes							
Power steering/**V**ariable-assist							
Power seats							
Power windows							
Power/**R**emote door locks							
Sunroof/Moonroof/T-roof Power or Manual?							
Windshield Equipment:							
Intermittent wipers							
Wet wiper blades							
Rear window wiper							
Rear window washer							
Rear window defogger							
Cruise Control							
Sound Equipment:							
Size & # of speakers							
# of watts per channel							
# of AM/FM station presets							
Tape deck (Auto-reverse?)							
CD (**S**ingle? **M**ultiple? in **T**runk?)							
Radial Tires (rated for #-miles)							
All-weather radials							
Seating (# of **F**ront/**R**ear passengers)							
Upholstery (Leather? **V**inyl? **F**abric?)							
Adjustable Steering Wheel							
Electronic Displays							
Voice Messages							
Navigation System							
Undercoating/Rustproofing							
Fancy Trim Package:							
Custom paint							
Spoilers							
Custom wheels/**W**heel covers							
Remote Engine Starter							
Trailer-towing Package							
Other Options & Packages:							

Chapter 8

Finding and Testing a New Car

· ·

In This Chapter

▶ Narrowing your list to the models that offer what you want

▶ Referencing sources that give you information about new cars

▶ Investigating other sources for new cars

▶ Staying in control while you shop for a car

▶ Test driving cars as part of the shopping process

· ·

*W*hen you know what features you want (options and features are explained in Chapter 7), you need to find out which models offer them. Unless you know where to look, evaluating the new models can be overwhelming. But, fear not, this chapter gives you a list of publications and resources that can help you narrow your car search to the vehicle that's just right for you.

After you've chosen the vehicle you want, it's time to investigate and compare a variety of sources for the best deal you can get. In recent years, the new-car market has changed considerably. Dealerships are no longer the only source for new vehicles; you can get cars through brokers or buying services, at superstores, through clubs and organizations, even via the Internet. These purchasing options offer unprecedented opportunities to leverage a better deal than most of us could command if we were limited to the whims and salesmanship of our local new-car dealers. In this chapter, I get into the pros and cons of each purchasing option.

This chapter also provides tips and pointers for what to do and *not* do when you're finally ready to begin shopping for the car so that you can stay in control of your senses, your pocketbook, and your decision in spite of aggressive sales tactics and the seductive sparkle of showroom lights on gleaming paint jobs.

Evaluating the New Models

The best way to evaluate which model is best for you is to keep abreast of new models and features by reading articles and ads in newspapers and automotive publications and visiting auto shows in nearby cities. You can also talk to people about the cars they drive. Ask about their experiences at various dealerships and whether they're satisfied with their vehicle's performance. Word of mouth only goes so far, however. It cannot substitute for accurate and unbiased information about a vehicle's safety, reliability, depreciation, and true cost. To get the latest and most comprehensive data, check out the following sources:

Automotive consumer publications

Almost too much information is published in the United States on each year's new models. *Car & Driver, Motor Trend,* and other magazines for auto enthusiasts review new vehicles each month and pick their favorite "Car of the Year." Automotive publishers such as Chilton and Edmund put out a wide variety of new- and used-car guides. *Hemming's Motor News* deals with classic cars, and many specialty publications cover new features and developments in vans, RVs, and motorcycles. You can find these and more at your library or newsstand:

- *Consumer Reports Annual Auto Issue* comes out every April. It provides color photos, test results, base price, cost factors, and depreciation data. It also charts the performance, safety, and reliability ratings for the year's new models.

- *AAA AutoGraph,* the national American Automobile Association's annual publication, covers more than a hundred new vehicles. It provides large, black-and-white interior and exterior photos; full-page reviews; safety features; performance, passenger-environment, and workmanship ratings; as well as full specifications, options, and pricing data for each vehicle.

- *CAA Autopinion,* published annually by the Canadian Automobile Association, profiles and reviews cars, light trucks, and vans. It provides exterior color photos, reviews, pricing, and specifications, in addition to comparison charts for durability, cost, customer satisfaction, frequency of repair, and fuel consumption. One of this publication's most useful features is a list of manufacturer's recalls by model year.

- *The Car Book,* by Jack Gillis, et al., provides similar data to that provided by *Consumer Reports* Annual Auto Issue and *AAA AutoGraph,* including insurance, warranty, maintenance, safety, and fuel-economy comparisons.

✔ *Consumer Guide* publishes many magazines and books that rate new and used cars.

✔ *Consumer's Digest* features new vehicles throughout the year. Its Annual Buying Guide issue compares the next year's new cars, trucks, vans, and 4x4s by NHTSA crash-test results, ownership costs, and warranties.

✔ *CarDeals* is a newsletter that lists current rebate and incentive programs on new cars and light trucks. It's published biweekly by the Center for the Study of Services, a nonprofit consumer organization. Call the organization at 202-347-7283 for a copy of the newsletter.

✔ **"Injury, Collision, and Theft Losses by Make and Model,"** a free pamphlet published by the Highway Data Loss Institute (HDLI) rates most cars, trucks, vans, and utility vehicles in those vital areas. You can get a free copy from the National Insurance Consumer Helpline (800-942-4242).

✔ *Kelley Blue Book* lists vehicles by make, model, and year, with basic factory invoice prices plus the cost of options such as air conditioning. *Kelley Blue Book* is available at your local library, bank, loan office, or credit union. It does *not* cover current rebates or dealer incentives.

New-car data services

In addition to the sources listed in the preceding section, the following may also be available to you (note that some of them charge a fee for their services):

✔ **AAA (American Automobile Association) clubs** sometimes offer their members a vehicle services program that may include assistance with auto pricing, buying, leases, and loans. You can find full details about AAA AutoEase and AAA Car Network in the "Buying services" section of this chapter.

✔ **ADM (Automotive Dealers Marketing) CarFax Reports** (800-916-2887) provide AAA and AARP members with manufacturer's suggested retail prices (MSRP) and invoice prices, tax and freight costs, current rebates and dealer's incentives, standard and optional equipment, plus package prices, safety equipment, extended warranty and complaint ratings, a pricing worksheet, insurance, theft and crash-test data, fuel-economy estimates, expected maintenance costs, and projected five-year resale values. Reports run from 10 to 15 pages in length. You can find more ADM services in the "Buying services" section.

✔ **The CAA (Canadian Automobile Association)** does not have a national pricing service, but check with your regional CAA affiliate to see if they can provide pricing information. Canadians currently have no free access to manufacturer's invoice prices, so pricing services must rely on MSRP and current auction prices for quotes.

✔ *Consumer Reports'* **New Car Price Service** (800-933-5555) provides comparisons of sticker versus factory-invoice prices, factory rebate information, depreciation ratings, and options recommended by the *Consumer Reports* Auto Test Division. You can call seven days a week from 8 a.m. to midnight EST with the year, make, model, and style of the vehicles that interest you. They will fax or mail the data to you.

✔ **IntelliChoice** (800-369-4436) will send you "Just the Facts," a customized report on the complete model line of your choice. It includes dealer's invoice price, factory-installed options, dealer's incentives and customer rebates, suggested retail prices, safety information, warranties, and the invoice and retail prices for up to six competitor's models.

✔ **NHTSA (The National Highway Traffic Safety Administration)** crash-tests about 40 new vehicles each year and makes their findings available free of charge. They also have information on factory recalls and safety defects. Call their hotline at 800-424-9393 Monday through Friday from 8 a.m. to 10 p.m. EST to see whether they have current data on a new vehicle you're considering. (To use TTY for the hearing impaired call 800-424-9153.)

✔ **Transport Canada's Defect Investigation Office** (in Canada, call 800-333-0510) investigates suspected safety defects and requests the manufacturer issue a "notice of defect" (the Canadian term for "recall"). Automakers that do not comply face federal charges. If you find a safety-related defect in a vehicle or have a problem with a recall, they encourage you to call them and report it. Please supply the vehicle's make, model, year, and VIN (vehicle identification number).

When you have a pretty good idea of what you're looking for, you're ready to visit the dealerships and interview the pretty new models.

Going to Alternative Sources for New Vehicles

Unless your family owns a dealership, I'd strongly recommend that you check out some alternative sources explained in the following sections *before* you buy a vehicle. Even if you end up getting a better deal at your local dealership, the effort you put into research can pay off in two ways: Your dealership will have to compete with some pretty low price quotes, and you'll know you've found the best bargain around.

The sources mentioned in this chapter are *not* endorsements, and they're not the only games in town. Additional national sources are constantly becoming available, and local services may be available in your area as well.

Nonnegotiable deals

Some dealerships and carmakers offer "hassle-free," take-it-or-leave-it, nonnegotiable prices. If you hate to bargain, this is definitely the simplest way to go, but consider carefully what a deal like this is worth to you. In a NADA survey of potential new-car buyers, 60.5 percent said they like to negotiate the purchase price of a new vehicle and about 88 percent said they would visit a dealership that advertises a single, nonnegotiable price only to obtain the quote and try to get other dealerships to beat it. These people probably had the right idea. Studies have found that buyers who negotiate the price usually pay less than if they purchased through a nonnegotiating source.

Auto brokers

An auto broker buys vehicles at volume rates from dealers and may offer you a better deal than you could negotiate alone. However, because some brokers' fees are built into the sales price, and many brokers tend to rely on sources with whom they've built up volume, be sure you can't do better elsewhere before you commit to a sale. To find a broker, consult your local Yellow Pages under "Automobile Brokers."

Nationwide Auto Brokers (800-521-7257) straddle the line between brokers and pricing services. They furnish current automotive pricing data to *Consumer Guide, Edmund,* and *Pace* publications and will mail you a printout with the factory invoice price, MSRP, and a guaranteed selling price that is roughly $50 to $125 over factory invoice, more for rare or high-demand vehicles. If you want your data fast, either call 900-884-6800 for telephone quotes or fax them at 248-559-4782 for data within the hour. Fees vary for each type of service. If you want them to broker the vehicle for you, they'll do so at no additional charge and drop-ship anywhere in the United States to a dealership near you. They say you can save from $150 to $4,000 because their dealer-to-dealer process eliminates the salesperson's commission.

Buying services

Most car-buying services rely on competitive bids from dealers and put you in touch with those who are willing to sell the vehicle you want at discounted prices. Some then leave the formalities up to you and the dealer, while others negotiate for you and arrange delivery or issue a certificate that you can exchange at the dealership for the vehicle. Some of these services are free to members of a particular organization; others either charge a flat fee or a percentage of what you save over the sticker price.

Although many of these deals are supposed to be non-negotiable, if you enter the game armed with a clear picture of current factory invoice prices and the cost of various optional equipment, you may be able to insist on a price that's even lower than the original bid.

- **AAA AutoEase.** At least one-quarter of the AAA clubs offer their members this integrated "one-stop shopping" program. It provides pricing and buying services, competitive leases and financing rates, and extended service and warranty contracts. Check with your local AAA club for more details. If your club does not participate in the AutoEase program, try the AAA Car Network.

- **AAA Car Network and Mature Advantage (800-916-2887).** These refer AAA and AARP members to participating dealers for special discounts off pre-negotiated prices. Their other services include the ADM CarFax pricing reports (explained in the section "New-car data services"), extended warranties through Travelers Group that are valid at any licensed repair facility, and loans through participating banks at special discount rates.

- **AutoAdvisor (800-326-1976).** AutoAdvisor, the oldest car-buyer's service in the U.S., originated as an automotive information source. Their services range from providing information and advice on new vehicles to locating the lowest-priced source for a vehicle and/or negotiating the deal for you. Fees vary with the service and your time requirements. They can provide service in one day or one, two, or four weeks. Specially-ordered vehicles may take from 8 to 16 weeks. AutoAdvisor guarantees that if you find an *identical* car at a lower price within seven days, your fee will be refunded.

- **Auto Insider (800-446-7433).** This is a national service that charges nothing to put you in touch with dealers near you that offer discount prices. It's then up to you and the dealer to conclude the deal.

- **AutoVantage (800-876-7787).** For an annual fee, this division of CUC International provides car pricing and buying services from a nationwide network of over 2,000 dealers, as well as discounts on car repair, parts, and rentals, plus emergency towing and travel services.

✔ **CarBargains (800-475-7283).** CarBargains is a service of the Center for the Study of Services/Consumers' CHECKBOOK, a nonprofit organization. Give them the make, model, and style, and they'll ask at least five dealers in your area to bid against each other. They provide the factory invoice price for the base vehicle and each available option, plus each dealer's quote and the sales manager responsible for it. They also evaluate any vehicle you'd like to trade in. Visit as many dealers as you like, and if the vehicle you want isn't on the lot, a dealer can order it from the factory or from another dealer and sell it to you at an agreed-upon price. Because CarBargains makes nothing more than their fee, they feel clients get better prices from them than from buying services and brokers who may steer customers to dealers who pay them high commissions.

Canadian vehicle purchasing sources are just beginning to appear in some regions. CAA clubs carry ads for dealerships that promise low prices; and huge auto sales centers, such as Auto Mall in British Columbia, offer buyers "one-stop shopping" at a large number of dealerships in the same location. Can auto superstores be far behind?

Fleet sales

Fleet sales used to be restricted to companies that bought huge numbers of vehicles for their employees. Now, large purchasing organizations such as Fedco, Price Club, Costco, credit unions, and some regional AAAs offer their members fleet-sale prices from dealers who do high-volume business with them. Visiting the Fleet Sales Manager at the dealership when it's time to negotiate price is wise. He or she can sometimes provide lower prices than you'll get through regular channels, especially if you want to lease a car.

Buying cars abroad

In the past, people who traveled to Europe and bought foreign luxury cars right from the plant not only paid less than they would have at home, but had a nifty new vehicle to travel and sightsee in. Whether or not this still works today depends on several factors:

✔ **The current exchange rate.** If the dollar is seriously devalued, Europe and Japan can be very costly places to go car shopping.

✔ **Taxes and other expenses.** The tariffs, duties, and shipping costs involved in bringing the car home can be prohibitive.

✔ **Safety and environmental standards.** U.S. or Canadian safety and environmental requirements may bar entry to a vehicle that doesn't meet them.

Online sources

America Online, CompuServe, and other online sources provide links to new-car sales sources, or you can access them through the Internet. Although these sources promise the lowest possible prices, I'd do my homework elsewhere to ascertain the current list price and dealer cost before buying a vehicle from them. Here are a few sites that are currently available:

- ✔ **Auto-By-Tel** (`www.autobytel.com`): Auto-By-Tel is a group of more than 1,000 U.S. dealers that offer to supply new vehicles at wholesale prices. Simply type in the make, model, and features you want, and they'll provide non-negotiable, guaranteed lowest-price quotes from several dealers in your area. After that, you deal with the dealer directly. Financing packages are also available.

- ✔ **AutoVantage** (`www.autovantage.com`): AutoVantage is another network of dealers providing low prices. (Check out the "Buying services" section for more information.)

- ✔ **Consumers Car Club** (`www.carclub.com`): Consumers Car Club offers unique options to Internet car shoppers. You can be referred to one of its affiliated dealers offering no-hassle, preset prices, pay to have the company do the shopping and paperwork for you, obtain several firm price quotes on the model you want, or order a vehicle custom-built from several major manufacturers. Carclub.com also has a wide array of options if you are shopping for a used vehicle. This site is linked to a large used car classifieds site with thousands of vehicles to choose from. You can also list your own vehicle for sale. Carclub.com has been rated the best Internet site for car shoppers by two respected consumer technology publications.

- ✔ **Edmund's** (`www.edmunds.com`): Known as the granddaddy of auto Web sites, Edmund's provides data from its many publications that deal with new and used cars.

- ✔ **PersonaLogic** (`www.personalogic.com`): PersonaLogic is a "personalized decision guide." When you go to this site, you answer a series of questions about the cost, size, and special features you're looking for in a new vehicle. The site helps you to weigh your priorities and then narrows the field down to those vehicles that best meet your needs. When you click on a particular vehicle, it magically transports you to Edmund's Web site, where you'll find all of the specifications, options, MSRP and dealer's invoice prices, and a host of information that help you make your choice.

- ✔ **Price Auto Outlet** (`www.priceautooutlet.com`): Price Auto Outlet is a service that enables you to buy cars from leasing companies, which is often a good deal.

Virtually all the automakers have Web sites that are easy to find (just type the manufacturer's name into your Web browser and you're ready to go). If you want more information on great automotive Web sites, check out Chapter 21.

Shopping for Cars: A Study in Creative Paranoia

Your first visits to dealerships are just rehearsals. No matter what you see or what they offer you, keep in mind that *you are not there to buy, just to do research.* Visit dealers to test-drive models that interest you and try out the techniques in this chapter so that you'll be really sharp when it's time to negotiate at a later date.

> *Never buy until you've checked out the competition and located the source for the lowest possible price.*

That source may not turn out to be a dealership at all. As explained in the preceding section, "Going to Alternative Sources for New Vehicles," an auto broker, buyer's service, or dealer referral service may come through with a better deal. Even if you do end up buying from a dealership, it pays to make them worry about whether they can make the sale.

Don't let them check your credit until you're ready to buy!

If you're out shopping for a vehicle and find one you'd like to test-drive, be sure to warn the salesperson that he cannot legally check your credit until you give him written permission to do so. And if you're asked to give such permission before you specifically apply for credit, refuse.

In early 1998, the Federal Trade Commission (FTC) issued a warning to car dealers that, if a customer hasn't actually applied for credit, the dealer is prohibited by law from checking credit without the customer's written permission. The FTC set the penalty for each unauthorized credit check at $2,500, under the Fair Credit Reporting Act.

The FTC's reasons for this ruling — reasons you should be aware of — include the following:

✔ Dealers are not permitted to request a credit report simply for the purposes of negotiating, because knowing whether you can afford to pay a higher price for the vehicle gives the dealer an unfair advantage.

✔ Multiple credit checks by car dealers can have a negative effect on the credit rating of a customer who is simply out "window shopping," because the implication is that the individual is applying for credit and being turned down repeatedly. If you end up with a bad credit rating, it not only may hinder your ability to get financing when the time comes to lease or purchase a vehicle, but it can also reduce your chances of qualifying for a mortgage or another type of loan.

If you live in a fairly small city, you may want to visit dealers in a larger city. Big-city prices are usually lower, and you can have warranty service done at local dealerships and even at qualified independent shops. Besides, if you negotiate with your local dealer, you can always say, "I can buy the same car for such-and-such in the city" and challenge them to meet the price. Be sharp. This is a game of wits.

Here are a few preliminary tips that can help you get a better deal.

Plan your strategy

By following these tips, you'll give the impression that you're informed and not easily intimidated. These techniques also improve your chances of getting the best deal:

- **Play it cool:** If you're crazy about a particular model or feature, don't let it show. Wander around and look at several vehicles including those that cost more — and less — than the one you want. Then saunter back and indicate a willingness to discuss any that "just might interest you."

- **Do not wear expensive clothing or jewelry:** Obviously, you want to look as though you are capable of paying for a vehicle, but salespeople are trained to size up a customer. There's no point in being quoted a higher price just because you look extremely well-to-do. Your usual office or casual clothes will be fine.

- **Don't go alone:** Bring along someone else for two reasons: First, if you're going to share the driving with someone else, that person's input is important. Second, if you're afraid that your passion for a particular model may carry you away, your friend can help you keep in touch with reality.

Assemble your ammunition

After you've contacted as many purchasing sources (such as dealerships, pricing services, brokers, and so on) as you feel necessary, you will end up with a large bag of apples and oranges to compare. The easiest way to unscramble all the data and come up with the best price is to use the handy-dandy Price Comparison Worksheet I provide in this chapter. Include the name of the sales representative you dealt with and the phone number.

The difference between the base price and the invoice price of each vehicle or option should reflect any sales incentives and discounts that the source can command. The quote from each source represents the best price they can offer you. (See Chapter 9 to find out the difference between the base price, the invoice price, and the sticker price.) The totals at the bottom should be everything you'll ultimately pay, so be sure that the lowest quote includes *all* the options you want and every dime they'll charge you.

PRICE COMPARISON WORKSHEET

Make:	Model:	Style:	Year:

Source #1 _____ Rep: _____ Phone: _____
Source #2 _____ Rep: _____ Phone: _____
Source #3 _____ Rep: _____ Phone: _____

ITEM	MSRP	BASE PRICE	INVOICE PRICE	SOURCE #1 PRICE	SOURCE #2 PRICE	SOURCE #3 PRICE
Basic Vehicle:						
Option Package 1:						
Option Package 2:						
Other Options: (Mfr. Code)						
Destination Fees:						
Other Fees:						
Rebate:						
Trade-in:						
License & Registration:						
Taxes:						
TOTALS:						

Carry — and use — your checklists

Carry copies of the Features and Options Checklist (included in Chapter 7), the Test-Drive Checklist (in this chapter), and the Price Comparison Worksheet (in this chapter) on a clipboard. These checklists are more than just props. Use them to list your impressions of each model that interests you and whether or not it has all the features you want. You can copy the base price and the cost of all the optional extras, warranty coverage, EPA mileage estimates, and other data right off the window stickers. Be sure to note any charges for preparation, transportation, fees, and taxes they plan to add to the sticker price. If you like what you see, ask for a brochure for that model. The brochure serves to jog your memory and provides all the vehicle specifications you'll need when you're narrowing down the field to your final choice. Brochures from another dealership will also strongly motivate salespeople to capture your business.

Tell the salespeople that you're serious about buying a car and that you intend to visit several dealerships before you make up your mind. This tactic spurs the dealers to quote their most competitive starting prices because a basic tenet of the trade is "After a customer gets out the door, chances are he'll never return."

No matter how good their first offer is, you can bargain for an even better deal later on. This first visit is just to look at vehicles at several dealerships and pick the one(s) worth negotiating for. You are *not* going to negotiate for or buy a car until you've seen all the candidates. Trust me, this strategy will pay off . . . big time!

Check out these things

In addition to all the checklist stuff you're paying attention to, be sure to check out each of the following items, as well. They all can affect both how much you end up spending and how happy you'll be with the vehicle. By checking them out, you also let the dealer know that you're not someone who is easily hoodwinked.

Availability of options

Compare the standard equipment on various vehicles to see whether the features you want are included. If not, ask to see a list of optional equipment for the models you like. Is the dealership willing to supply them? At what cost? Some options packages can raise the price of a vehicle by as much as 50 percent!

Ask to see the factory invoice which lists the manufacturer's price for these options. This invoice can tell you whether the dealer has marked these options up excessively. The markup on options is usually 10 to 11 percent. It can go as high as 16 percent on luxury cars or SUVs. Unscrupulous dealers have been known to mark some options up by several hundred percent! If the dealer refuses to show you the invoice, you can assume the prices quoted are too high. Head for another dealership. Of course, if you've used a pricing or data service (explained in the section "New-car data services"), you'll know the factory invoice prices of the options before you arrive at the lot. If the dealer (rather than the manufacturer) is providing the options you want, be sure that the basic warranty covers them or that they are covered by separate warranties.

Check out all available options packages to see whether the savings on the options you desire is greater than what you'd pay for them individually. A high-performance, sports, or luxury package may provide those options at a lower price, but you may be forced to accept features that you neither need nor desire. However, you may decide to put up with the unnecessary stuff if accepting the package saves you money.

If a vehicle with the features you want is not on the lot, or if they have a vehicle that features options you don't want to pay for, find out whether they can special-order a vehicle that suits your requirements and how long you'll have to wait for it to arrive. You may find some dealers reluctant to special-order a vehicle because they're afraid of being stuck with it if you back out of the deal. If this is the case, an auto broker or car-buying service may be your best bet for obtaining exactly what you want. (See the section called "Going to Alternative Sources for New Vehicles" and for information on how to handle a special order, see Chapter 9.)

When dealers try to sell you a model equipped with unnecessary optional equipment, either demand that they special-order a vehicle without it or ask that the cost of the unnecessary equipment be deducted from the price. If the dealer refuses to accommodate you, call the automaker or other dealers to see whether they have "no-frills" models in stock, or ask an auto broker or buying service to find exactly what you want. You can also check out different models of the same basic vehicle and nearly identical vehicles marketed by different manufacturers.

Different models of the same vehicle

A basic car usually comes in several models, each of which features standard and optional equipment designed to please a specific market segment. For instance, my Ford Probe came in SE and GT configurations. The SE was a basic vehicle with a smaller engine and fewer features. (I doubt that SE stood for "Smaller Engine." It probably indicates "Standard Equipment.") The "souped-up" GT (Grand Touring) model had a more powerful engine and was designed to provide superior handling and performance. If the standard equipment on a more expensive GT model includes a lot of the options you want, it may prove cheaper than paying to have those options installed on a less expensive SE model. Brochures, window stickers, and buying services can help you sort this stuff out. Other automakers' acronyms include DX (Deluxe), EX (Executive), GS (Grand Sport), GP (Grand Prix), LS (Luxury Sedan), LX (Luxury), SL (Super Light), and STS (Super Touring Sedan).

If a particular model is extremely popular, you may have to pay a premium price for it. Ask whether a less sought-after model with the features you want is available at a more reasonable price. You can find information on the sales performance and availability of new vehicles at your local library in current issues of *Automotive News.*

Siblings, twins, or clones

These are all terms for nearly identical vehicles that are marketed under different names by different carmakers. (For example, the Honda Passport is the same as the Isuzu Rodeo and the Lincoln Navigator is a plusher version of the Ford Expedition. GMC's Jimmy, the Chevy Blazer, and the Oldsmobile Bravada are all clones. Ditto for Chevy's Camaro and the Pontiac Firebird. And the VW Passat borrows most of its hardware, chassis, and power train from the Audi AD.) Because prices and options vary, you may pay less for a higher-priced vehicle with ABS and dual air bags as basic equipment than you'd end up paying for a low-end clone that only offers these as expensive options. You can find lists of "Automotive Twins" in the AAA's annual *AutoGraph, The Car Book,* and other publications.

Warranties

Warranties differ from one model to another, so ask about warranties on standard and optional equipment. You can find a detailed analysis of all types of basic, limited, implied, and extended warranties in Chapter 16. Be sure to read that information before you go shopping so you can ask the right questions.

The service department

You can usually have required maintenance done at any of the manufacturer's dealerships, by a qualified independent, or in some cases, even do the work yourself without voiding the warranty. However, your local dealership will most likely do the maintenance, at least for the warranty period. While you're car shopping, check out the dealership's service facilities. Chapter 18 can help you evaluate what you see.

✔ **Have a chat with the service writer.** The service writer is the person with the clipboard who meets you when you first drive in for repairs, asks you what is wrong with your car, and hands you an estimate that is usually lower than what you end up paying. (Consider the service writer a diagnostician, who will then pass you on to the proper specialist for surgery.) Ask whether the service department is certified by the automakers it represents and if the mechanics have been trained to handle any radically new features on the vehicle you'd like to buy. Ask for a tour of the repair shop.

✔ **Visit the parts department and ask about the availability of parts.** The independent mechanics who are waiting for service at the counter are an excellent source of unbiased information.

TEST-DRIVE CHECKLIST

Make: _____ Model: _____ Year: _____

Source: _____ Phone: _____

THINGS TO CHECK	YES or NO	NOTES	Rate 1-10
WALK AROUND THE VEHICLE:			
Does vehicle project your "image?"			
Paint OK? Color choice available?			
Chrome finish and trim OK?			
GET THE "FEEL" OF THE VEHICLE:			
Easy to get into?			
Upholstery choice available?			
Seats comfortable?			
Head room? Leg room?			
Seats adjust OK? Head restraint OK?			
Seats belts comfortable? Easy to use?			
180° front & side visibility?			
Rear mirror visibility OK?			
Right rear window visible in rear mirror?			
Side mirrors easy to adjust?			
Pedals and gearshift easily accessible?			
Dashboard gadgets easy to reach & read?			
Sound system OK? How much to upgrade?			
Interior lights, cupholders, glove box OK?			
Easy to get into rear seating?			
Rear seats comfortable? Seat belts OK?			
Easy exit from front and rear?			
CHECK THE TRUNK:			
Cargo room ample? Is cargo concealed?			
Back seats fold to increase trunk space?			
Full-size spare tire?			
Decent jack and lug wrench? Tools?			

TEST-DRIVE CHECKLIST (continued)

Make: _____ Model: _____ Year: _____

Source: _____ Phone: _____

THINGS TO CHECK	YES or NO	NOTES	Rate 1-10
DRIVE DOWN A QUIET STREET OR ALLEY:			
Steering wheel comfortable? Adjustable?			
Steering & handling at low speeds OK?			
(Run Transmission through gears) Gearshift smooth? Hesitation? Grinding?			
Clutch easy to operate?			
(Stop suddenly, when it's safe to do so) Brakes OK?			
(If ABS-equipped, test system) ABS OK?			
(Try a couple of U-turns and 3-point turns) Is it easy to maneuver?			
(Parallel park the car in a small space) Is it easy to park? Visibility OK?			
DRIVE ON HIGHWAY OR FREEWAY:			
Powerful acceleration from full stop?			
Powerful acceleration to pass?			
Steering OK? Does it pull to one side?			
Smooth shifting at higher speed?			
Powerful overdrive or 5th gear?			
Brakes OK? Do brakes pull to one side?			
(On hills) Power in lower gears OK?			
(On curves) Oversteers? Understeers?			
Engine, wind & road noise levels OK with windows/roof open? Closed?			
Sunroof/convertible top easy to operate?			
Heater & A/C work OK?			
Windshield washers and wipers OK? Rear windshield washer, wiper, defogger?			
DRIVE ON UNPAVED ROADS, SPEED BUMPS AND/OR RAILROAD TRACKS:			
Suspension too soft? Too hard?			
PARK ON STEEP HILL:			
Emergency brake OK facing downhill? Uphill?			
DRIVE AT NIGHT:			
Visibility good with headlights? Brights? Fog lights? Back-up lights?			
TOTALS:			

Preventive maintenance

The amount and cost of regular maintenance can differ greatly from one vehicle to another and significantly affect the amount of money you'll lay out for a vehicle over time. Although the owner's manual for each vehicle contains a preventive maintenance schedule, some dealers have schedules of their own that may call for more frequent or extensive service. If the maintenance schedule specified in the owner's manual differs from what the dealership requires, find out what you *really* need to have done under the terms of the warranty. If it's a toss-up between one vehicle and another, the maintenance requirements may help you decide between them. You can also consult the maintenance cost comparisons in *The Car Book* and the reliability tables in *Consumer Reports* for more clues on how much a vehicle may cost you *after* you buy it. Chapter 5 will help you keep track of these costs.

If you plan to do the basic maintenance yourself, be sure you'll have easy access to the oil filter and drain plug, *every* spark plug, and most hoses and belts. Even if you don't intend to do the work yourself, ease of access will mean lower costs for a mechanic's time and labor.

Test-Driving Strategies

Whenever you find a vehicle that attracts you, ask to take it for a test drive. To make sure you don't miss anything, use the detailed Test Drive Checklist I provide in this chapter. Make several copies of this checklist and use one for each vehicle you test-drive. After a busy day of car shopping, these completed checklists can help you to remember the positive and negative points of each candidate.

- ✓ **If a salesperson must accompany you, insist on doing the driving.** If someone else will be sharing the car frequently, take him or her along, too. Not only will you get someone else's input, having a friend along is a great reason for sticking the salesperson in the backseat where she can't influence you as readily.

- ✓ **Test each vehicle thoroughly.** Find a deserted street or alley, make sure everyone is seat-belted, and put the car through some short stops and hard turns to see how well it responds. Try to duplicate the traffic and road conditions that you will encounter most often as closely as possible. Make sure you test the vehicle's performance on steep hills, at higher speeds, in stop-and-go traffic, and so on. Don't forget parallel and curbside parking.

- ✓ **Don't waste time negotiating.** When you return from a test drive, the salesperson will try hard to make a sale. Refuse to negotiate. Say it's a waste of time because you haven't finished comparing vehicles, prices, *and* dealerships. You are just there to test-drive and gather data.

✔ **Resist being lured into one of the sales cubicles.** If you end up in one, you're only going to have to talk yourself out of there to get away. Just thank the salesperson who assisted you and take a business card.

✔ **After you leave, jot down your impressions of the salesperson on the card and clip it to the checklist you filled out on the car.** If the sales staff is wise, they'll make some notes about you, too: "Smart buyer. Very price- and performance-conscious. Definitely *not* a pushover!"

Over the river and through the woods. . . .

Before I test-drove my truck, I told the salesman that because I intended to use it for camping, I had to see how well it could handle steep hills and rough roads. He agreed and soon found himself out of town, climbing a mountain pass that leads straight into the wilderness. "Where are we going?" he asked nervously, positive that I was abducting him. "My boss is going to be upset if we're gone too long." "Well, I told you I have to check it out on country roads," I said as I gained the top of the mountain and headed down a winding dirt road that led back toward town. When we returned to the dealership half an hour later, I was convinced that this was the truck for me. The salesman was relieved to be back in civilization and mighty glad that I had decided to buy the truck, which was too dusty to show again without a bath!

Chapter 9

Getting the Best Deal on a New Vehicle

. . . .

. . . .

*T*oo many people go into a new car showroom thinking that they're ready to buy if they can find the vehicle they like with a sticker price that doesn't make them hyperventilate — and if a salesperson is willing to assure them, in the most sincere voice, that he's offering them a deal to beat all deals. Others go in, knowing that they want to negotiate but having as their only weapon the conviction that they don't want to pay as much as the dealer is asking.

If you take nothing else away from this book, I want you to remember this: *You* are in charge when it comes to buying a car. Armed with the necessary information (what you want, what is a reasonable price to pay for a particular vehicle, what other dealers and new car sources are charging for the same vehicle, what the extra charges are that dealers slap onto the sticker price, and so on), you can walk into any showroom and negotiate from a position of authority. Blanket terms like "additional dealer mark-up" and "market value adjustment" — which dealers use to keep the price of a car up — don't sound so intimidating when you know what they mean and what services they include.

This chapter tells you what you need to know to negotiate the best deal you can get, and it gives you strategies to follow for making sure that the price you're quoted is actually the price you can expect to pay. I also include what I like to think of as an inspirational story or, if you prefer, a sort of "how I turned the tables on an unscrupulous dealer and drove away a winner" tale, which shows that if you arm yourself with information, sometimes you can get the last laugh — and the car.

How Much Is That Auto in the Window?

Such a simple question. Unfortunately, the answer is obscured by the huge number of pricing terms you encounter. Before you can find out the "real" price, you'd better know what these terms mean.

Manufacturer's suggested retail price (MSRP)

The manufacturer's suggested retail price is just what it says it is: a number the manufacturer came up with to give the dealers a uniform place from which to start bargaining. What it *isn't* is even more important: It is not the price the dealer expects you to pay (unless you are unusually soft in the head or the model is the hottest thing on the market). The MSRP simply tells you where negotiations will probably start. It's obviously not the price the dealership paid for the vehicle. What they did pay is harder to ascertain. If you think it's the factory invoice price, read on.

The factory invoice price

The factory invoice price (also known as the *dealer's invoice price* or *dealer's cost*) never appears on window stickers, but most pricing services provide it. Some dealers promise to sell you a vehicle for "less than dealer's invoice" and tell you what a great bargain you're going to get. Such a deal! The truth is, the factory invoice price doesn't usually represent the true dealer's cost. Why? Because of the following:

- ✔ Most manufacturers give dealers a 2 percent to 3 percent "holdback" on the price of the vehicle. (Sounds a bit like "kickback," doesn't it?) You can find out how to use holdbacks to negotiate a better price in the section called "Nailing Down the Best Possible Deal."

- ✔ Carmakers also provide discounts, allowances, and incentive payments to dealers that range from a few hundred to several thousand dollars for selling specific models. So the dealer can still make a tidy profit by selling "below invoice."

Be aware that the factory invoice price often includes *freight* (also referred to as "delivery" or "destination" charges), so if a dealer offers a vehicle to you at factory invoice price, be sure they don't add freight costs to the final price of the vehicle if they're already included in the factory invoice price.

You may have no way to find out what the true dealer's cost is unless a relative or really close friend owns the dealership and wants to do you a very big favor. The only source I know of for what a dealer really lays out for a vehicle is its "green sheet." A friend of mine, who used to work for a dealership, asked to see the green sheet when she was looking for a car at another dealership. The sales manager swiftly ushered her to the door!

One way to negotiate is to request a copy of the factory invoice and make an initial offer of between $200 and $500 more, then haggle until you or the dealer runs out of gas.

The base price

The base price is what the car would cost with no options, frills, fees, or taxes — with just standard equipment and the factory warranty.

The sticker price

The sticker price is the total amount that appears on the vehicle's window stickers, which are called the Monroney sticker and the Dealer's sticker. Read both stickers carefully to ensure that you don't get "stuck" with — or without — features you may or may not want, and also for valuable clues for negotiation.

The Monroney sticker (see Figure 9-1) is required by federal law. No one can remove this sticker except the person who buys the vehicle. It shows the base price, the factory-installed options and their MSRP, the manufacturer's transportation charge, and the fuel economy mileage.

The dealer's sticker (see Figure 9-2) represents the dealer's asking price — usually 5 percent to 23 percent above factory invoice — plus the dealer's suggested price for any dealer-installed options, plus any or all of the following:

- Additional dealer mark-up (ADM)
- Additional dealer profit (ADP)
- Dealer preparation ("dealer prep")
- Undercoating and other extras
- Market value adjustment (MVA)

Be sure to read all about this alphabet soup in the section entitled "Beware of hidden charges."

STANDARD FEATURES

Items featured below are included at NO EXTRA CHARGE in the Standard Vehicle Price shown at right.

SAFETY FIRST

*ALL-WHEEL DRIVE (AWD)
*DRIVER & FRONT PASSENGER AIRBAGS
*4-CHANNEL ANTI-LOCK BRAKING SYSTEM (ABS)
*POWER-ASSISTED FOUR-WHEEL DISC BRAKES
*REAR WINDOW WIPER/WASHER & DEFOGGER
*SIDE-IMPACT DOOR BEAMS
*CHILD SAFETY LOCKS, REAR DOORS
*REAR-SEAT HEADRESTS
**********PERFORMANCE GROUP**********
*2.5L HORIZONTALLY OPPOSED 4-CYLINDER
16-VALVE, MPFI, DOHC ENGINE
*HOOD SCOOP
**************WARRANTIES**************
*3YR/36,000 MILE BUMPER TO BUMPER
*5YR/60,000 MILE POWERTRAIN
*5YR/UNLIMITED MILAGE RUST PERFORATION
*SEE WARRANTY BOOK FOR DETAILS

***************KEY FEATURES***************
*TWO-TONE EXTERIOR BODY PAINT
*RAISED "STEP" ROOF DESIGN
*HEAVY DUTY INDEPENDENT SUSPENSION
*REAR BUMPER COVER/SPORT TAILPIPE
*HALOGEN FOG LAMPS W/STONE SHIELDS
*ROOF RACK / OUTBACK CARPETED FLOORMATS
*205/70 R15 ALL-SEASON RADIAL TIRES
*ALLOY WHEELS & SPLASH GUARDS
*CARGO AREA 12 VOLT POWER OUTLET
*CARGO AREA HOOKS/COVER/STORAGE TRAY
**********COMFORT & CONVENIENCE**********
*AIR CONDITIONING (NON-CFC REFRIGERANT)
*POWER WINDOWS, DOOR LOCKS, & SIDE MIRRORS
*80-WATT AM/FM STEREO CASSETTE W/4SPKRS
*CRUISE CONTROL / OVERHEAD MAPLIGHT
*HEADLIGHTS OFF VIA IGNITION SWITCH
*60/40 SPLIT FOLD-DOWN REAR SEAT
*FACTORY UNDERCOATING AND RUSTPROOFING
*PROTECTIVE CLEARCOAT FINISH

Compare this vehicle to others in the FREE GAS MILAGE GUIDE available at the dealer.

CITY MPG	HIGHWAY MPG
21	**27**

Actual Milage will vary with options, driving conditions, driving habits, and vehicle's condition. Results reported to EPA indicate that the majority of vehicles with these estimates will achieve between 17 and 25 mpg in the city, and between 22 and 32 mpg on the highway.

2.5 LITRE ENGINE, 4 CYLINDERS,
4-SPD AUTO TRANS,
MULTI-POINT FUEL INJECTION,
(FEEDBACK FUEL SYSTEM)
CALIF. EMISSION CONTROL SYST
ESTIMATED ANNUAL FUEL COST:
$783.00

For comparison shopping.
ALL MID-SIZE WAGON VEHICLES
have been issued
milage ratings
ranging from
18 to 38 mpg city
and
25 to 47 mpg highway.

STANDARD VEHICLE PRICE

Manufacturer's Suggested Retail Price
$22,495.00

OPTIONAL EQUIPMENT AND OTHER ITEMS

ELECTRICALLY CONTROLLED	$800.00
4-SPEED AUTOMATIC TRANSMISSION	
KEY STANDARD FEATURES	
*ALL-WHEEL DRIVE (AWD)	INCLD
*DUAL AIRBAGS	INCLD
*4-CHANNEL ANTI-LOCK BRAKING SYSTEM (ABS)	INCLD
*2.5 LITRE DOHC BOXER ENGINE	INCLD
*HEAVY DUTY INDEPENDENT SUSPENSION	INCLD
*HALOGEN FOG LAMPS / ROOF RACK	INCLD
TWEETER KIT	$100.00
REAR CUP HOLDER	$40.00
DUAL POWER OUTLET SOCKET	$88.00
REMOTE KEYLESS ENTRY SYSTEM	$225.00
DIFFERENTIAL PROTECTOR	$159.00
GLACIER WHITE/SLATE PAINT	$495.00
DESTINATION AND DELIVERY	

TOTAL SUGGESTED RETAIL PRICE   **$24,402.00**

THIS LABEL HAS BEEN APPLIED PURSUANT TO FEDERAL LAW. DO NOT REMOVE OR ALTER PRIOR TO THE DELIVERY TO THE ULTIMATE PURCHASER.

Figure 9-1: The Monroney sticker.

SOLD TO: 140/100
FRED'S AUTO EXTRAVAGANZA
4030 S. ASTRID EXPRESSWAY
AUTOVILLE, WA 98411

FINANCING ORGANIZATION
FIRST INTERSTATE BANK OF BIG BUCKS
P.O. BOX 73210
MONEYVILLE, WA 98124

		MANUFACTURED SUGGESTED RETAIL	DEALER COST
VBV	1997 WAGON AWD 4EAT	$23,295.00	$20,901.00
WXM	GLACIER WHITE/SLATE PAINT		
	DUAL AIRBAGS		
	AIR CONDITIONING		
	PS/PW/PDL/ABS CC		
	AUDIO SYSTEM		
DSB	TWEETER KIT	100.00	65.00
MVC	REAR CUP HOLDER	40.00	26.00
MVD	DUAL POWER OUTLET SOCKET	88.00	57.00
RVA	REMOTE KEYLESS ENTRY SYSTEM	225.00	146.00
TVB	DIFFERENTTIAL PROTECTOR	159.00	104.00
	FREIGHT AND HANDING	495.00	495.00
HB 0466 FPA 0220	TOTAL VEHICLE PRICE	$24,402.00	$21,794.00

VEHICLE IDENTIFICATION	ENGINE NUMBER	KEY CODE	PORT
5S2BG6849	233445	6479X	LAFAYETTE, IN

ORIGINAL

Figure 9-2: The dealer's sticker shows you how much the dealer would like to stick you with.

The "real" price

The only "real" price is the one you end up paying. It's the lowest possible price you can negotiate including discounts, rebates, options furnished free or at reduced prices, trade-ins, and the best available financing.

Nailing Down the Best Possible Deal

Whether you've found the vehicle you want through your own research or have been steered to a dealership by a buying service, you're still going to have to do some negotiating before you drive away in your new car. Even "one-price" dealerships and those who "commit" to "lowest possible prices" through buying services leave some room for making more profit, and it's up to you to recognize and resist the pitfalls that await you. If you do, you may save thousands of dollars and really pay the lowest possible price.

I'm very proud of the technique I used when I bought "Ruby" a couple of years ago. The results were so impressive that they were one of my major motivations for writing this book. After plowing through so many pages of instructions and caveats, you deserve a rest, so here's a chance to relax and listen to a story. You'll find "Outsmarting 'Honest John'" at the very end of this chapter because I didn't want to interrupt those who were in such hot pursuit of information that they couldn't take the time to digress.

Keep the following tactics and games in mind every time you find yourself in the process of buying anything expensive. Car dealers aren't the only sharpies out there, you know.

Take advantage of rebates

Many auto manufacturers offer rebate programs on new vehicles. Call the car manufacturer for up-to-date information on available rebates and keep an eye on the car ads on television and in local newspapers to spot special, limited-time offers. You can also get rebate information from some of the pricing services and Web sites mentioned in Chapter 8. Rebates are often attached to financing packages or come with other strings attached, so check the fine print closely before committing yourself to purchasing a vehicle under one of these deals. Don't discuss rebates with dealers until you've negotiated the lowest possible price without one.

Always deduct the rebate from the price you actually pay rather than letting them send you a check after the sale. If the rebate is deducted from the purchase price, you don't have to pay sales tax on it. If you're financing the vehicle, avoid paying interest on the rebate by making sure they deduct it from the amount you have to finance.

Choose the best time to buy

In the good ol' days, the best time to buy a vehicle was in early autumn when dealers were eager to get the current year's cars off the lot to make way for new models. These days, new models are released all year long, and "next year's models" may arrive as early as the spring or summer of the current year. However, any time new models are announced the dealers are anxious to clear the showroom of older models, so they may be very willing to sell at a discount.

In addition to new model time, you have other windows of opportunity to get a vehicle at a lower price. Car salespeople have quotas to meet and are judged by their performance at regular intervals. Arrange to negotiate when the pressure on them is at its greatest:

✔ **The end of the sales week, usually on Saturday.** If your salesperson or sales manager has had a slow week, you could have cause to celebrate on Saturday night.

✔ **After the 25th of the month.** At this point, the sales staff at many dealerships gets antsy about making their monthly quotas. As a result, they may be quite willing to shave a bit off their normal commissions to make a sale.

✔ **The end of the year.** This is the last chance for good annual figures. If you can wait until the end of December, you may really give yourself a great holiday present.

Keep your cool

> *Never negotiate a deal when you're pressed for time.*

Arrange to visit the dealership when you have plenty of leisure. Tell the salesperson you dealt with before that you are now ready to *negotiate* and will buy the car that day only if you get a satisfactory deal. Then pull out your Features and Options Checklist (located in Chapter 7) and state exactly what you want. The Price Comparison Worksheet, located in Chapter 8, will also come in handy.

If a vehicle you saw previously had everything you desire and nothing you'd want to pay extra for, ask whether it's still on the lot. If not, find out if they have a similar model and go over it closely to be sure it fills the bill. If the car is equipped with options you can do without, tell the dealer right up front that you won't pay a penny extra for anything you don't need. If necessary, find out whether a suitable vehicle is available or whether they can special-order one for you. If they can, ask how long you'd have to wait to *see* (not *buy*) it. You can find the reasons for this distinction in the section called "How to Special-Order a Vehicle" later in this chapter.

Keep your old vehicle out of sight

Whether or not you want to trade in your old car, park it down the street and walk to the dealership. The salesperson will probably ask you early in the game whether you have a vehicle to trade in. Whatever the case, tell them no and refuse to discuss it further until you are in the final phases of negotiation. Arriving at the lowest possible price without a trade-in, before you allow the possibility of negotiating one, is very important.

To get the most for your old vehicle, you must have an accurate idea of its value. See Chapter 2 and Part II for detailed instructions on checking out your present car, establishing its wholesale and retail value, and advertising and selling it. In Chapter 5, you can find tips on negotiating the best trade-in deal and a whole section in Chapter 6 tells you what you need to do to command the highest possible price for your vehicle.

Let them know they're not the only game in town

If you want to get the lowest price from a dealership, flaunt the fact that you're comparing their quotes with those you've obtained from alternative sources and dealerships. Refer to your notebook, checklists, and work-sheets to see whether their quotes for options agree with what you've heard from other sources, but don't let them see the actual data. It'll drive them crazy.

Also, keep asking, "Can't you do better than that?" Constantly tell them, "I can do better at so-and-so's," or "According to the such-and-such pricing (or data) service, the dealer's cost (or factory invoice) on this model is such-and-such." Doing that should eliminate some of the finagling right away.

Don't let them pressure you

Don't be swayed by sales pressure tactics. Dealers love to make you feel that ten other people are just waiting to get their hands on the only model you like. Sometimes they'll arrange to receive phone calls from a colleague down the hall: "The red Voomer? Yes, we have it. As a matter of fact, I have a possible buyer with me right now. . . ."

They may tell you that if you don't act today, the "special deal" they've proposed will no longer be offered. Don't believe it. To any good salesperson, closing a deal is the most important thing. If they can't do it now, they will be just as eager to make the sale on the same terms another day. If a vehicle with the options you want is no longer on the lot by then, they will turn heaven and earth to find a similar one for you rather than lose the sale to someone else. So relax and refuse to be high-pressured into a commitment until you're certain it's the best deal you can get.

Don't let them ignore you

Salespeople often subject customers to long delays to wear down their resistance. They've been known to excuse themselves for long "conferences with management" and spend the time drinking coffee and talking sports with their cohorts while your energy and resistance wears down. You can deal with this in several ways; the one you choose depends on how much time you have and how much other action is going on at the dealership:

- ✔ **Arrive an hour or two before closing time.** Get there while you still have plenty of time to negotiate, but close enough to closing time to pressure the sales staff into cutting their stalling tactics short. They'll probably be anxious to offer the deal, make the sale, and go home. Behave as though you have all the time in the world and refuse anything but the absolutely lowest price you can get. Even if you seem willing to finish the process another day, the dealers won't want to run the risk of letting you leave the showroom without a signed contract.

- ✔ **Play the waiting game.** No matter when you arrive, if you show that you're in no hurry to close a deal, you rob the salesperson of one of their primary weapons. Act quite unruffled by the delays. Bring along a good book, or better still, spend the time looking at ads and brochures from other carmakers. You may have time to burn, but they know that their wasted time could be spent dealing with other customers.

- ✔ **Play the "catch me if you can" game.** The opposite tactic is to say, after the first delay, "Look, I'm not going to sit here very long. If we can get this deal consummated quickly, fine. If not, I'm out of here." The next time the salesperson is "called away," wait a few minutes and then stop any member of the staff and ask them to tell your salesperson that you got tired of waiting and left. Then head for the door. Believe me, they'll never let you leave the lot, and things will go much faster afterward.

Don't provide the enemy with ammunition

Salespeople try hard to find out how much you're willing to pay. They appraise your clothing and jewelry. They ask you what your price range is. Be vague. Refuse to discuss financing; say you don't want to even consider it until you know how much the vehicle you want will cost.

Never deal in terms of the sticker price

The sticker price can represent a profit of as much as 7 to 20 percent for the dealer. That may not seem like much until you realize that 7 percent of $20,000 is $1,400. If that seems like a hefty profit on just one sale, a 20 percent profit on a $35,000 vehicle is $7,000! There's plenty of room to negotiate. Both the AAA and *Consumer Reports* advise that you should always follow this rule:

> *Always negotiate* **up** *from the factory invoice price, not* **down** *from the sticker price.*

This rule illustrates why coming armed with a good idea of factory invoice prices from the sources listed in Chapter 8 is so important. Many car-buying experts suggest that an offer of $200 over factory invoice is often quite acceptable. If you really have chutzpah, try making an offer *below* factory invoice. If you're told that they won't make a profit on such a low offer, just say, "Well, you'll have to dip into the holdback for your profit. How much is it on this vehicle, anyway?" They may not love you for this, but they'll respect you and probably try harder to meet your offer.

A *holdback* is money that the car manufacturer provides to be used *at the dealer's discretion* to advertise and promote the vehicle. In reality, the dealers can use that money any way they please — including putting it into their own pockets. So, although they may not make a profit on the factory invoice price, the holdback can provide more than an ample profit anyway. To find out ahead of time whether there's a holdback on a vehicle and how much it amounts to, ask to see the factory invoice and look for an item that says something like "HB1050." This means that the automaker is giving the dealer a holdback of $1,050. (Now you can see why some dealers can advertise vehicles at "below factory invoice" prices.)

If you're having difficulty finding the proper figure to offer, look at the sticker price and deduct 2 percent, which is the average dealer's profit margin. You can usually use that as your negotiating room, but keep in mind that the margin is larger for luxury cars and trucks, and smaller for inexpensive imports.

If the demand for the model you want exceeds the available supply, a dealer may refuse to accept less than full sticker price. If you encounter this, be sure to check out buying services and brokers before you buy. If they fail to get you a better deal, at least you'll know you gave it your best shot.

Never discuss price in terms of monthly payments

Often, a salesperson will ask you, "How much do you think you can pay a month?" You never want to answer this question with a figure because they'll then work out a lease or loan deal that allows you to pay exactly that amount each month. If you accept it, you'll still be paying more for the vehicle than you want to in the form of a larger down payment and/or interest over a longer period of time.

Vehicles have become so prohibitively expensive that most buyers either cannot afford to pay for them in cash or prefer to keep their money in profitable investments. As a result, many people now prefer to lease vehicles or pay for them over time. But you should never discuss trade-ins or financing until you've arrived at the lowest price you can get — and even then, you have to watch your step and be sure the loan or lease isn't based on a higher price than the one you negotiated! Because the procedure is so fraught with opportunities to be seriously ripped off, I devote an entire part to it in this book. If you're considering a lease or loan, be sure to consult the chapters in Part IV before you go shopping.

When the big gun comes in for the final deal

When the salesperson feels you're ready to close a deal, the heavy honcho — usually a sales manager — takes over for the final negotiations. His or her job is not only to get as much money for the vehicle as possible, it is also to sell you additional services and goodies. If the big gun attempts to raise the price by offering you additional options or trying to steer you into a higher-priced model, be very firm about sticking to your original choice and refuse to be conned into unnecessary expenditures. (In Canada, the sales manager's office is sometimes referred to as the "glue factory" because that's where they really stick it to you.)

Reject all offers of service contracts, extended warranties, special paint, or upholstery protection. Most cars don't begin to need major repairs until after 50,000 miles — which is when an increasing number of basic and power-train warranties run out. Even if the vehicle is only warranted for 3 years or 36,000 miles, unless you drive much more than most people do, basic warranties and an occasional helping hand from Lady Luck should see you through; the cost of any repairs you may need should be less than a service contract or an extended warranty would cost.

If you really intend to brutalize the car, consider buying a used one and replacing it often, or go for a high-quality vehicle with a 5-year, 50,000-mile warranty that may even include regular maintenance. Chapter 16 covers extended warranties and service contracts on new and used vehicles in detail.

If their "absolutely rock-bottom price" is still too high, hang in there. Smile ruefully and say, "Gee, I sure would like to buy that car, but it's just more than I can spend." Then have another cup of coffee and talk about the weather or the local sports scene. Salespeople can be amazingly creative when it comes to closing a deal that is threatening to dematerialize at the last moment. They may be willing to throw in an option you'd considered but dropped as too costly, or they may come up with additional discounts to save the deal.

Beware of hidden charges

Be sure the price you're quoted is the full price you have to pay. Ask, "*If I wrote you a check for this amount, would I have to pay* anything *else in connection with buying and owning this car?*" Be sure the quote includes the optional extras you want, plus tax, licensing, and registration fees. Taxes and fees can add over 10 percent to the cost all by themselves! Dealers often try to impose other "fees" to pad your bill. Many of them are never mentioned until you find them on the final paperwork. Unless you know exactly what a quote includes, you may turn down a good deal in favor of a lower quote that suddenly inflates when all these gimmicks are added in at contract-signing time. Here are a few to look out for:

- ✔ **Dealer preparation fees** are included in the factory invoice price for most domestic cars. Nevertheless, some dealers stick it on *again* to the final price. Strongly resist this. Ask what the dealer did to deserve even the non-negotiable "dealer prep" charge on the factory invoice. Do we pay furniture or clothing stores for unpacking their wares and keeping them in good condition?

- ✔ **Conveyance fees** do not have anything to do with shipping the vehicle to the dealership. Sometimes called "documentation" fees, they are supposed to repay the dealership for their "computer costs" and the cost of doing the paperwork to get the title transferred or register the vehicle in your name. Challenge this. It's like paying a merchant to write a sales slip or to forward the sales tax to the government.

- ✔ **Freight** (also known as "destination" or "delivery") charges are already included in the factory invoice price. It's bad enough to have to pay the shipping costs to bring the merchandise from the manufacturer to the store. Challenge these fees, and don't let the dealer add them on again!

✔ **Advertising fees** of from 1 to 3 percent are often imposed by manufacturers, who usually include them in the factory invoice price. If a dealer adds such a fee to the final cost of a vehicle, be sure you aren't paying it twice. Also look on the factory invoice to see if there's a holdback. Resist paying a dealer's advertising fee on the grounds that it is part of their overhead. If you can't get the fee eliminated, tell the dealer you want to check other dealerships to see whether they are charging the same amount.

✔ **Other "alphabet soup" fees** may appear on the dealer's sticker. These fees are usually negotiable, so start by refusing to pay any of them. The dealership may try to tough it out, or they may magnanimously offer to "waive all fees." Thank them kindly (for nothing) and get back to the serious haggling. Here are a few fees you may encounter:

  • ADM (additional dealer mark-up)

  • ADP (additional dealer profit)

  • MVA (market value adjustment)

According to *Consumer Reports Car Buyer's and Leaser's Negotiating Bible,* these artificial charges, which can range from zero to $5,000, are sometimes added by dealers to provide a higher asking price from which to start negotiating. The charges are usually added to cars that are in relatively high demand and short supply, especially imports. The charges may be found on a window sticker that is next to or near the Monroney sticker and may even look similar to it. Tell the dealer to remove the charges or you will buy elsewhere. Because these unnecessary charges are not as prevalent as they used to be, you should have no trouble finding a dealer who doesn't try to impose them.

Nonnegotiable deals

Some dealerships and carmakers offer "hassle-free," take-it-or-leave-it, nonnegotiable prices. If you hate to bargain, this is definitely the simplest way to go, but consider carefully what such a deal is worth to you. In a NADA survey of potential new-car buyers, 60.5 percent said they like to negotiate the purchase price of a new vehicle, and about 88 percent said they would visit a dealership that advertises a single, nonnegotiable price *only to obtain the quote and try to get other dealerships to beat it.* These people probably had the right idea. Studies have found that buyers who negotiate the price usually pay less than if they purchased through a non-negotiating source.

Hard-to-get vehicles

Sometimes a particular make or model is so much in demand that dealers have more trouble obtaining them than selling them. If you want one of these vehicles badly, you have to accept the fact that none of the strategies in this chapter will work. Dealers will act as though they're doing you a favor, will take the hard line, and will refuse to give an inch. Some dealers add premiums to the sticker price if they have a waiting list for a hot car in limited supply. The first Mazda Miatas went for up to $10,000 over the sticker price! Brokers and purchasing services may get you what you want, but they, too, may have problems in obtaining the vehicle at a decent price. If you are determined to have that model, be prepared to wait as long as six months, and then pay whatever the market demands. I hope it turns out to be worth it.

How to Special-Order a Vehicle

If a dealer is going to special-order a vehicle for you, you need to be doubly careful. If the vehicle turns out to be unavailable or fails to meet your specifications, dealers have been known to refuse to refund deposits; to demand they be applied to another vehicle at that dealership; to deduct fees and penalties from the deposit for the time, trouble, bookkeeping, and so on that the special order involved; or to lose checks, delay repayment, and otherwise drive you crazy rather than to give up one penny. Here are some ways to protect yourself from these tactics:

- ✔ **Never give a deposit in cash.** Use a credit card so you can contest the charges, if necessary. Failing that, at least write a check. Ask for a signed statement that says that they will not bill your credit card or cash your check until the vehicle is delivered and the final papers are signed.

- ✔ **Don't lay down more than a *minimum* refundable deposit or sign a contract for a special-order vehicle unless there is an ironclad clause that says you won't have to pay more than the quoted price under any circumstances and that the vehicle must have all the options you've requested.** You don't want to arrive to pick it up only to find that the price has gone up due to "market fluctuations" or because the vehicle arrived equipped with options you didn't ask for.

- ✔ **Have the contract stipulate that you will get your full deposit back if the vehicle fails to meet the specifications you agreed upon at the quoted total cost.** If they try to convince you that they deserve to keep at least a portion of the deposit in the event the vehicle isn't satisfactory, remind them that they, too, have to take some risks. If they don't feel they can deliver what you've asked for, at the price you've agreed on, then perhaps you should take your business elsewhere. After all, purchasing services will special-order directly from the manufacturer at very good prices.

✔ **Try to have the contract specify a delivery date, with penalties for late delivery.** This can prevent a dealer from selling your special-ordered vehicle to another customer who is willing to pay a higher price — and then making you wait a long time for another one. It never hurts to ask. . . .

When to Discuss Trade-Ins

When the dealership has come down as far in price as you believe it can, then — and only then — it is time to mention the possibility of a trade-in. ("Well, it still seems a little high, but I guess I *could* trade in my old car. I was hoping to sell it to my kid brother, but if you can give me a good price for it, I guess he could find something cheaper.")

Although you can probably get more for your old vehicle by selling it personally than you can by trading it (see Chapter 6), the time and trouble involved may not be worth the effort if you can get almost as much from the dealership. Ask how much your old car would be worth to the dealer as a trade-in. If the trade-in price you're given is close to the blue-book wholesale price or within a couple of hundred dollars of the current retail price of your old car, have the salesperson subtract the trade-in price he's offering from the *lowest* price he's quoted for the new car you want to buy.

If you don't feel they've offered you enough, tell them you can't buy a new vehicle until you've sold your old one at a better price. They're not going to want you to walk out at that point, so they may increase their trade-in offer.

Closing the Deal

After you've settled on a final price, including options, financing, trade-ins, registration, and licensing fees, and your new vehicle is available to drive off the lot, you are ready to sign the sales agreement. You are also at that crucial point where you can really get ripped off, if you don't take the following precautions.

Oops! Did I mention I wanted a steering wheel?

I'm ashamed to admit that, several years ago, when I bought my truck after a day of negotiations, I drove it home and then discovered that it lacked a rear bumper and side mirrors! It never occurred to me that a rear bumper could be considered an optional extra, and I had simply forgotten that I wanted extra-large mirrors on both sides for better visibility. When I called the dealership, the sales manager said soothingly, "Don't worry. I'll give them to you at our cost because I want you to be a satisfied customer."

Luckily, before I returned to the dealership I took the precaution of calling their parts department for the retail price of those items because, when I arrived, the sales manager wanted about 20 percent more! "How can this be your cost when your own parts department is selling them retail for less?" I asked. The manager exhibited great shock and surprise. "The prices must have changed recently," he gasped and proceeded to call the parts department for "verification." I ended up paying about 50 percent less than I would have if I had blindly accepted his "cost" prices!

Check the vehicle carefully

Arrange to take possession during the day. Moonlight and floodlights can hide a multitude of imperfections.

Refer to your Features and Options Checklist (see Chapter 7) to be sure the vehicle has everything you want.

Test-drive again before you take possession to be sure the vehicle starts easily and runs well and that you know how to operate all its bells and whistles. Be sure the doors, trunk, and hood fit and work well; that the exterior and interior are whole and unblemished; and that there's a spare tire, a jack, a lug wrench, an owner's manual, and a maintenance schedule.

Check the VIN (vehicle identification number) on the left-hand corner where the dashboard meets the windshield. Make sure that it's the same as the VIN on the window sticker and on all the paperwork.

Check the contract carefully

In any business deal, there is no substitute for caution and for hard, written facts. The less chance there is for a misunderstanding when you buy the car, the better the chances of a good relationship with the dealership in the future.

Absolutely refuse to sign the contract and take possession of the vehicle until you're certain that all the items mentioned previously have been accounted for. Otherwise, after the deal is done, you'll have much more trouble getting problems resolved.

> *Get everything in writing.*

Never accept verbal estimates or agreements. Be sure you get all the relevant documents, including all warranties, registration and licensing forms, window stickers, and, of course, the sales contract, in writing.

Sales managers have been known to tell customers who are ready to sign a contract that "management" has just told them the price they've quoted is too low, does not apply because the only available vehicle has additional optional equipment on it, or that a special-ordered vehicle has arrived without options you asked for or with unrequested stuff that raises the price. If this sort of thing happens, just get up and head for the door. Then call the Better Business Bureau and the carmaker and report the dealership.

> *Read the fine print.*

Make sure the final contract lists every option you asked for and contains the warranty terms you've been promised. Compare the contract with your Feature and Options Checklist to be sure that it doesn't include the cost of any options you didn't request, *even if the car has been equipped with them.* If it does, refuse to pay for them.

Draw lines through any blank spaces and initial all changes in the contract. Have the dealer initial them, too.

Have discounts or rebates deducted from the sales price of the vehicle rather than letting them send you a check later on. Otherwise, you'll have to pay taxes and licensing fees based on the full sales price shown on the contract. If you're financing, you'll pay interest on the full sales price as well.

Be sure the contract includes the following items:

- ✔ **The exact price you agreed to pay** for the vehicle, including optional equipment.

- ✔ **The amount of any down payment,** which should include the value of your trade-in.

- ✔ **Any fees and surcharges you've agreed to pay** that were not already included in the factory invoice price.

- ✔ **The proper sales tax,** which you should check for your locality *before* you pay for your new vehicle. States and local governments vary not only on the amount of the sales tax, but also whether it is imposed on the full price of the vehicle or after any trade-in has been deducted.

✔ **The terms of any loan you've negotiated,** including the actual amount you're borrowing broken down into principal and interest, the interest rate (APR), your monthly payment, and how many months it will take you to pay off the loan. If you are leasing, be sure the agreement measures up to the criteria in Chapter 12.

✔ **The absolutely final** *total* **cost of the vehicle** that you've agreed to pay.

Register the vehicle in only one person's name. If the registered owner should die, transferring the title to the surviving spouse is easy; just show up at the DMV with a death certificate. But if a vehicle that is jointly registered is in an accident, the victim may be able to go after both spouses' assets and incomes in a lawsuit.

Extending the Life of Your New Vehicle

After all the time, effort, and expense that went into finding and purchasing your new vehicle, I'm sure you want it to perform well for a long time. Here are the two most important things you can do to ensure a long and happy life for any vehicle (for more tips on protecting your vehicle, read the chapters in Part VI).

Break it in properly

Although you may have heard that the newest cars don't have to be broken in, this is emphatically *not* the case. During the first 500 miles (and especially during the first 50 miles), you should treat your vehicle as gently as a newborn baby. I know seeing what your spiffy new set of wheels can do is tempting, but give the piston rings a chance to get properly seated first.

Avoid high speeds — you can play race-car driver when the car is a little older. Stay within the speed limits and vary the speed on the highway so the engine can get used to driving conditions. Don't over-rev the engine and don't "lug" the transmission by driving up hills in high gear or when carrying heavy loads. If possible, pick the car up at the dealership yourself to avoid having some speed demon burn up the roads to get it to you quickly.

New brakes should be broken in carefully. Treat the brakes gently on a new vehicle and whenever you get new brake pads. For the first 50 to 100 miles, try not to stop short or hit the brakes hard. This helps to "seat" the brakes (burnish the rough surfaces of the new brake pads so they'll have optimum contact with the brake discs) and prevent the glue, which may still be soft, from being squeezed through the pads and glazing their surfaces.

Maintain it faithfully

Pay attention to the care and feeding of your vehicle. Regular maintenance is a form of preventive medicine — it can keep the engine and body from wearing away prematurely. If you don't maintain your vehicle properly, you can void the warranty or be charged hundreds of dollars for repairs at the end of a lease.

Before you drive away from the dealership, here are some final tips that may pay off in the future:

- ✔ Maintenance schedules vary. Be very clear about what — and when — basic maintenance must be done to keep from voiding the warranty.

- ✔ Find out whether the dealership will contact you when the vehicle is due for warranty service or whether you must keep track of time and mileage requirements yourself.

- ✔ Be sure you have an owner's manual and buy a service manual as well so that you'll know what's involved in any repairs that become necessary and can deal with your mechanic from an informed point of view. If you lend the service manual to independent mechanics who don't have one for your vehicle's year, make, and model, you can save yourself time and labor charges and ensure that the work is done properly.

- ✔ Ask the service manager or the lubrication specialist whether the vehicle has grease points and where they are located. Find out whether there are any trouble areas that could benefit from having additional grease fittings installed to prevent squeaks and keep parts from wearing away. This step shouldn't be necessary on most new cars.

- ✔ If you're going to park your new vehicle outside on a regular basis, invest in a good 100-percent cotton car cover to protect it. Although some new synthetic fabrics on the market can "breathe," plastic, nylon, and vinyl covers retain moisture and encourage rust.

Outsmarting "Honest John"

Several years ago, I was in a serious auto accident. My doctor flatly told me that unless I drove only vehicles with power steering and automatic transmissions, I would continue to suffer from my injuries for a very long time and perhaps never recover completely. Because my automotive stable consisted of "Honeybun," my classic sports car, and "Baby Blues," my little truck — neither of which had either feature — I was forced to buy another vehicle. I was in too much pain to go through the time and effort of hunting down a good used car, so I resigned myself to buying a new one. After schlepping myself to the library to read up on the new models, I narrowed the choice down to a couple of sporty hatchbacks with powerful engines, and when I was well enough to get around, I test-drove the major candidates and identified the one I liked best.

The car came in a variety of colors, but to paraphrase Henry Ford, I'll drive any color car, as long as it's red. Unfortunately, none of my local dealerships had a red model in stock, and I really couldn't afford to wait for them to special-order for me. One day, on my way to visit my kids, I saw a red beauty at a dealership about ninety miles from my home, and I stopped off to check it out. The test drive went well, but the sales manager, whom I'll call "Honest John," put me through every subterfuge and scam that has given car dealers such bad reputations. What's more, although I'd told him I intended to pay cash, he offered me a "special first-time buyer's loan" with a rate that was so low I could make a profit by keeping my car money invested at a higher rate.

"But how can I qualify for a first-time buyer's loan when I've owned and driven cars for twenty years?" I asked. "Aren't they just for college kids?"

"Oh, no!" HJ assured me. "They're for people who have never bought a new vehicle from our manufacturer before." It sounded weird, but I thought, if they're willing to do it on those terms, why should I complain? If I'd known then that the first-time buyer's loans usually carry *higher* interest rates than standard financing, I would have suspected him immediately.

The vehicle lacked a sunroof, which was one of my priorities, but HJ said they'd have one installed by a local authorized specialist and add the cost of the sunroof to the sales price. I told HJ I'd think it over and went on my way.

When I asked a friend in the automotive field what she thought about the first-time buyer's loan, boy, did I get an earful! HJ had lied about the requirements for loan qualification. It was, indeed, limited to those who had never bought or financed a vehicle.

"But what would they have done if I'd signed the contract?" I asked. "Wouldn't they have been stuck with the terms of the deal anyway?" My friend gently set me straight. "Auto contracts usually have fine print stating that if the buyer proves to be unqualified for the financing stipulated in the contract, the buyer must either return the vehicle or buy it for the price quoted and seek financing elsewhere. If, after not qualifying, you decide to return the car, you would have been stuck with the cost of the sunroof to the tune of several hundred dollars. The dealership would have ended up with a new car equipped with a classy sunroof to sell at a profit, and you would have ended up holding the bag!" She suggested that I ask an auto broker to find me a red model.

The broker offered to find me what I wanted at the lowest possible price in return for a very reasonable fee. Before long, she called to say that she'd contacted every dealership within a hundred-mile radius, and nobody had a red model. However, if I wanted to settle for white or burgundy, she could get one for $3,000 less than the price I'd been quoted by Honest John.

When she'd called HJ's dealership, they'd told her they didn't have a red one in stock. "That's bull," I protested. "When I drove by on my way home yesterday it was right out front." "Maybe those creeps just didn't want to sell the car at a broker's discount, so they lied to me," she said. "You know, you can turn their own game against them. It'll be worth it to me in satisfaction if you can pull it off. Here's what you have to do. . . ."

When I called HJ's dealership and asked if they still had that gorgeous red Probe, they assured me that they did. A day later, when I arrived prepared for battle, it was nowhere in sight. I brushed off the boy in the fake Italian suit who waited in the parking lot to snag potential buyers.

"Take me to your leader. I'm here to buy, and I don't want to horse around with any preliminaries!" He ushered me into the showroom and turned me over to a salesman who looked more experienced — or at least a little older — than he did. I told him I knew what I wanted and suggested that we get right down to business. He seemed a bit surprised, but he ushered me into his cubicle and pulled out his pad.

I have found over the years that the best way to defeat a powerful and accomplished opponent is to be everything they *don't* expect you to be: friendly, open, charming, and utterly inflexible. Kind of puts 'em off their stride. I smiled sweetly and told him that I'd been there before, had test-driven the red model and just loved it. "You do still have it, don't you?" He assured me that they did. "Could I see it? I just want to be sure it's as beautiful as I remember."

He was only too happy to drive me around to the back of the lot where they'd hidden it behind a shed. Were they afraid the broker might come by to check up on it? We hopped in the car and I drove it around to the front of the lot. Now that they couldn't say it didn't exist, I was ready for Phase II of my strategy. We went back to the cubicle to negotiate.

"I must tell you something," I confided. "The last time I was here, your sales manager pulled some dirty tricks on me. He offered me a loan for which I was utterly unqualified, and I was just lucky I didn't buy the car that day because I would have wound up in deep financial trouble. Since then, I've had a broker searching for the car, and your people lied to her and said you didn't have one on the lot. I don't know if that's actionable, but the only reason I'm here now is that I would really like the car in red, and you have the only one around."

The salesman protested that there must have been some misunderstanding, he couldn't believe that HJ would do anything underhanded. I smiled warmly into his eyes. "I'm sure you wouldn't work here if you thought there was anything shady going on. So here's my deal: I'm going to write a number on a piece of paper. That number is the total out-the-door price the broker quoted me for this make and model. It's several thousand dollars cheaper than what I was quoted when I was here before, and if you can't meet it, I'll walk out of here and buy the car through the broker, in white. The number represents exactly what I'm willing to pay with no last-minute surprises. It must include taxes, registration, and licensing fees, the sunroof, and any other equipment that's already on it, plus any little extras that you usually try to tack onto the price. I intend to pay for the car in cash, and I have nothing to trade in. If you can meet my offer, I'll buy the car today and pick it up as soon as the sunroof is installed. After that, you'll never see me again because I really don't trust this dealership. One more thing, I don't want to have to go through the usual routines with several levels of management, and I don't want to even *see* HJ. I'm so angry with him that I may change my mind and split."

The salesman was literally gasping with astonishment, but he recovered quickly. Now, *he* smiled warmly into *my* eyes. "I can't believe that HJ would try to cheat you, but that's neither here nor there. You have my word that I'll do my best to get the car for you for the price you want and do it with the least amount of 'formalities.' However, I do have to go through a certain . . . er . . . protocol, so I'm going to make you comfortable and then go talk to Honest . . . er . . . my boss. I may have to stop in to ask you certain questions, even though I already know what your answers will be, but please bear with me. Okay?"

"Okay, but don't horse around too much. If we haven't gotten this settled in half an hour, I'm out of here." I passed him the paper with the price the broker had quoted. The salesman looked at it, winced, and left. I settled down with a cup of coffee and the local paper. A few minutes later, he popped back in again. "He wants to know if you'd be willing. . . ."

"No!"

"Right." He popped back out. Five minutes later, he reappeared. "Have you considered . . . ?"

"Forget it."

"No problem." He disappeared.

After one or two more equally useless trips, he returned with sales documents in hand. "Management" had agreed to sell me the car for the price I'd stipulated. I read the contract carefully, signed it, and left.

A couple of days later, when the salesman picked me up at the bus station and brought me to the dealership to take possession of the car, he said, "You know, I really shouldn't tell you this, but you deserve to hear it. In the five years I've been selling cars, I've never seen anyone do what you did. My boss told me that never in the history of the dealership have they ever sold a vehicle for as little profit as they made on this sale. And frankly, if he really did try to pull the tricks you say he did, he richly deserved it. I salute you!"

I drove "Ruby" home, and when I received the manufacturer's customer satisfaction survey in the mail, I praised the salesman by name, lambasted HJ as unethical, and hoped that copies of the survey would find their way to the executive offices of the dealership as well as the carmaker.

Part IV
Money, Money, Money, Money

The 5th Wave
By Rich Tennant

In this part . . .

If you're like most people, you probably don't have thousands of dollars sitting unused in a savings account or stuffed between the mattress and the box springs. For many of us, buying a car means relying on a finance or lease agreement to put ourselves in the driver's seat. If an other-than-cash arrangement applies to your purchasing power, check out the information in this part. These chapters can help you navigate through the financial morass and come out intact — and financially solvent — on the other side.

Chapter 10

Should You Borrow, Buy, or Lease?

In This Chapter

▶ Taking into account factors that affect leases and loans

▶ Pre-qualifying for a loan before you talk to the dealer to ensure that you get the best financing arrangement

▶ Taking advantage of manufacturer's rebates and financing offers

▶ Understanding why shorter financing periods are usually better

▶ Upcoming legislation that may affect your financing decision

*B*ecause vehicles now cost tens of thousands of dollars, most of us pay for them the same way we buy houses: We have a financing institution pay the bill and we repay the financer in installments that include the price plus interest.

Unfortunately, compared to the average person, finance and mortgage companies have relatively unlimited funds. In the case of housing, after mortgaging became established, the price of houses soared, at least in part because buying a house was no longer limited by how much money the average family had at its disposal. Automotive sales prices have also risen at an unprecedented rate and many of us have turned to loans and leases in order to afford the vehicles we want and need.

Higher prices for vehicles are partially due to the higher cost of labor and materials, as well as the research and development of fuel-efficient engines. Safety features such as air bags, antilock braking systems, and reinforced structural components also contribute to higher prices. But I believe that prices are also influenced by the fact that many financing institutions and dealerships have seized the opportunity to make inflated profits by literally charging us "as much as traffic can bear" for auto leases and loans.

However, the positive sides to financing are that, when you finance a car, your own funds are freed up to invest elsewhere — hopefully at higher returns than the financing costs. And although interest on auto loans is no longer tax-deductible, you can use the equity in your home as a source of tax-deductible funds with which to purchase vehicles (this method of financing is explained in Chapter 11).

There are three primary ways to pay for a vehicle: leases, loans, and cash. This chapter provides general information and advice relating to both loans and leasing agreements. For more detailed information about borrowing money to finance a car, see Chapter 11. For details on leasing, see Chapter 12.

To negotiate the best possible financing and avoid the numerous pitfalls that lie in wait, you must understand the jargon used in these contracts. The following section not only provides definitions for the financing language you'll encounter, it also contains vital advice on how to deal with the issues that involve these terms. Because it contains information that applies to all three financing options, you'll get the most out of these chapters if you read through the entire Jargon Jungle section right now, instead of only referring to it when you encounter an unfamiliar term. Yes, it's untraditional to place a glossary right in the beginning of a chapter, but understanding these terms is so vitally important that I'm willing to abandon all tradition just to get your attention.

How to Find Your Way through the Jargon Jungle

If you're afraid you'll forget what all the following terms mean, fear not. I've placed the terms in a different font, like this, throughout the chapters in this part, so when you encounter them, you can come back to this section to refresh your memory.

Administrative fees: These fees offer financers a very creative area for increasing profits. They can include set-up fees, documentation charges, security deposits, and a host of other add-ons. Read Chapter 9, which covers additional fees and charges, and strongly challenge any you feel are unfair or redundant.

APR (annual percentage rate): The rate of interest you pay each year to finance the vehicle with a loan, expressed as a percentage of the principal. A reduction of as little as 1 percent of the APR can save you thousands of dollars over the life of the loan contract. (Auto leases are no longer allowed to allude to the cost of funds as an APR. Leases now express the APR as a rent charge, or use a money factor to determine the equivalent of the amount of interest you'll have to pay.)

If you add up all the financing costs, you may find that these total as much as 20 percent of the vehicle's base value! *Determining the APR of a loan and demanding an itemized list of all additional fees and charges is extremely important.* I provide worksheets throughout the book to help you compare the costs of loans from several sources.

Balloon payment: These loans allocate little — or none — of your monthly payments toward the outstanding balance. Instead, one huge lump sum is due when the loan matures.

Base value: The price of a vehicle before taxes, fees, charges, and financing costs have been tacked on to it. Most finance contracts use the MSRP as the base value, but unless the vehicle is much in demand, you can usually negotiate a lower price.

"Buy here, pay here" financing: People with poor credit ratings often must pay off a used car by going into the dealership every week with a payment, in cash. If they haven't got the cash, they risk having the vehicle repossessed.

Buy-out price: Often called "cost to purchase," this is what you have to pay to buy the vehicle at the end of a lease. Be sure it includes *every* dollar you'll have to lay out in order to own the vehicle.

Capitalized cost (cap cost): This figure includes the sales price of the vehicle, taxes, administrative fees, mandatory insurance, service contracts, and any additional options or services you want to pay for over time. It may not include hidden charges, so always ask for a quote — in writing and signed by the dealership sales manager or an officer of the financing company — that itemizes *all* the charges (including insurance) that are capitalized in the lease. The cap cost is usually based on the sticker price or MSRP, so keep in mind that if you negotiate a lower sales price for the vehicle, the cap cost must be adjusted to reflect the new price plus any reduction in fees based on the lower price. Why is the cap cost so important? It not only provides an easy way to tell how much profit each lessor would make on your car (and therefore serves as a yardstick with which to measure other offers or determine whether you're better off leasing the vehicle or financing it in some other way), it also comes into play in the event of early termination. *Before* you start to negotiate a lease, check the current fair market value with the car pricing services (listed in Chapter 8) and use it to bargain for a lower capitalized cost.

Capitalized cost reduction: Sometimes called an equity lease, this allows you to lower your monthly payments by making a larger down payment. Unfortunately, it also negates the main advantage of leasing: For the term of the lease, you lose the use of the down payment and any dividends you may earn by investing the money. Some contracts refer to the down payment as a capitalized cost reduction — but it's still a down payment. The term is sometimes also used to cover the manufacturer's or dealer's discounts because they, too, lower the amount that is capitalized over time.

Closed-end lease: Sometimes called a *walk-away lease,* this is a contract that gives you the option to purchase the vehicle at the end of the leasing period or return it and walk away. For more details, see Chapter 12.

Collateral: A borrower's money or property that financers can appropriate to pay themselves back in the event of a default on a loan.

Cost of funds: Instead of disclosing the APR, some lessors specify a cost of funds figure, which is *not* expressed as a percentage. In order to be able to decide whether to lease a vehicle or purchase it with a loan, insist that this cost be expressed as a percentage so you don't have to compare apples and oranges. See Rent charge and Money factor.

Dealer discount: Car manufacturers and dealerships may offer discounts on specific models to promote sales or clear out last year's models before the newest ones arrive. Ask the dealer what discounts are available and whether they apply to leases as well as sales. To avoid problems, get the discount offer and its applicability to the lease in writing and make sure it's taken into consideration on the lease contract before you sign.

Dealer prep: An additional up-front charge to compensate the dealer for getting the vehicle ready for sale after it has arrived in the showroom from the manufacturer. For full details on this and other hidden charges, see Chapter 9.

Default: Failure to meet the payments or other conditions of a finance contract.

Depreciation: The loss of value that vehicles undergo as they grow older. The rate of depreciation is a major factor when you buy, lease, or finance a vehicle because it determines how much the vehicle will be worth when you sell it, pay off the loan, or buy it at the end of a lease. Some vehicles depreciate more quickly than others, and financers generally require higher monthly payments for vehicles with faster rates of depreciation. *Be sure to check price guides and pricing services for the vehicle's estimated rate of depreciation before you begin negotiations.*

Destination fee: Believe it or not, most contracts include a charge for getting the vehicle from the manufacturer to the dealership. In what other business do vendors charge their customers to get the merchandise into the store? Unless you've chosen a custom-made vehicle or need fast delivery that requires more expensive shipping than usual, object to this fee. In any case, be sure this charge has not already been included in the factory invoice price as a "freight" or "delivery" charge.

Disposition fee: If you don't purchase the vehicle at the end of the lease, lessors try to charge you $250 to $500 or more to prepare the vehicle for resale, ship it to a used car dealer, or sell it at auction. Sometimes called a *termination fee,* this charge is negotiable and can even be waived completely, so strongly object to paying it on the grounds that getting the merchandise into salable shape is part of every retailer's cost of business and is tax-deductible as an operating expense. You are already subject to penalties if the vehicle you return has suffered more than normal wear and tear, so why should you also pay to have the dealer slick it up in order to make a higher profit on its resale?

Documentation charges: Dealerships have been known to impose additional fees for doing the paperwork on the sale or financing of a vehicle. Definitely challenge this one — the dealer's tax deductions for the cost of doing business include what they pay their personnel to do this kind of thing.

Down payment: Sometimes referred to as a capitalized cost reduction, this is a lump sum you may be required to pay when you sign a financing contract. One of the advantages of leasing is supposed to be that you don't need to make a down payment, as you would with a loan.

However, today more and more lease ads seem to require a down payment. I'm willing to bet that, in most cases, the down payment is actually optional, so negotiate this issue. Dealers will tell you that a down payment will lower your monthly payments, and this is true, but it negates one of the main motivations for financing the car in the first place: to free large amounts of cash for personal investment or other purchases. Lessors love an opportunity to use your money for as long as possible, but you don't have to provide them with one. You can usually avoid having to come up with a down payment by opting for higher monthly payments or extending your payments over a longer period of time. Of course, if your income varies and you're afraid you may not be able to meet higher monthly payments consistently, a down payment can be a form of forced savings. Frankly, I'd rather invest the money at a good rate of return and draw my monthly payment from it during lean periods.

Early-termination penalties: Charges for canceling a lease or loan ahead of schedule. You may plan to keep the vehicle for the entire term but, if the vehicle is stolen or so badly damaged that repairs cost more than the repairs are worth, your finance contract probably will be terminated. To make matters worse, even if your auto insurance covers the entire value of the vehicle, your contract may still impose penalties for early termination. These penalties vary. In addition to the difference between the vehicle's current wholesale and retail value, you may be forced to pay one of the following: the difference between its depreciation to date and the amount of principal you've already paid; the equivalent of two to six monthly payments; or *all* your remaining payments. See Prepayment penalties and GAP insurance.

On the other hand, sometimes a dealer will contact you and offer to terminate your lease ahead of time. This usually means that the vehicle has become so popular that the dealership hopes to sell it at a substantial profit. If this happens, and the lease period ends within a year or two, I recommend refusing the dealer's offer. Because the vehicle will probably still be worth more than the residual value on your lease when the lease period ends, you may want to buy it, resell it, and pocket the money yourself.

Earnings-to-debts ratio: A comparison between how much you earn and how much you owe that is used to determine whether you earn enough to be able to pay back additional loans or purchases on credit.

Equity lease: See Capitalized lease reduction.

Excess mileage charges: Penalties you pay for exceeding the specified mileage allowance. These can run from 10 cents to as much as 30 cents per mile or kilometer and can really add up to big bucks.

Factors: See Financing costs and Money factor.

Fair market value: The current retail price for the vehicle at the *end* of the lease period. This is often predetermined by the lessor when you sign the contract. If you have a closed-end lease and you disagree with the lessor's estimated fair market value when the time comes to decide whether to buy the vehicle or return it, you can resort to blue books, pricing services, and advertisements to determine current fair market value and refuse to pay a penny more.

Fees: See Administrative fees, Destination fee, and Disposition fee.

Financer: A catchall term I've invented to cover whoever is responsible for financing a lease or loan. Some automakers have their own financing divisions, but banks, credit companies, leasing and loan organizations, or even your father-in-law may be the financer of your new vehicle. See Lessor and Lender.

Financing costs: The cost of borrowing funds for a lease. Rather than a loan, this is usually called a rent charge, the money factor, or the lease factor. A cooperative dealer or finance company can usually translate financing costs into an APR percentage. See Implicit lease rate.

First-time buyers: Although dealerships usually present special finance packages for first-time buyers as though the rates are cheaper than traditional financing, be warned that you will *not* get a better deal if you accept one. In fact, you're going to pay *more* than the average buyer would! The only advantage these packages have to offer is that the dealership is willing to finance you at all. Here's why: On the sliding scale that most financing companies use to determine what dealers should pay them for finance packages, the APR rises dramatically from low rates for vehicle buyers with excellent credit records, to higher, subprime rates for people with credit problems, and then to very high rates — or total rejection — for first-time buyers who have never proved their ability to pay off a vehicle.

If your credit is good, or if you have substantial collateral, you'll probably get a better deal from a bank, credit union, or finance company than from a dealership (see Lessor for the reason why). On the other hand, if you have no previous credit history and can't pre-qualify for a lease or loan from an outside source, a first-time buyer's package may be the only financing you'll be able to obtain. This doesn't mean you have to accept any terms the dealer offers you. There's always room to negotiate a lower price for the vehicle and optional equipment as well as for lower interest rates and down payments. And you can always challenge every fee and charge.

Fixed (guaranteed) residual: A predetermined price at which the lessor has promised to sell you the vehicle at the end of the lease. See Guaranteed buy-back.

GAP insurance: This covers the difference between the vehicle's stated value in a loan or lease and what an insurance company will pay if the vehicle is stolen or damaged beyond repair, after it has depreciated. You can find detailed information on other types of automobile insurance in Part V.

Grace period: The period of time between when a payment is due and when penalties for non-payment begin.

Guaranteed buy-back: The lessor's promise to sell you the vehicle at a predetermined price at the end of the lease period. This means that if the fair market value is higher than the fixed residual, you will be able to buy the vehicle for less than its current retail price. Unfortunately, the reverse is also true — and much more likely. See Fixed residual.

Home equity line of credit: Similar to a home equity loan, but instead of drawing the full amount you've qualified for and paying interest on all of it, you simply spend the money as you need it and only pay interest on the amount you've spent. You are usually given a checkbook so you can easily access these funds. See Home equity loan.

Home equity loan: A loan based on the difference between the present value of your home and its original price, less any unpaid balance on your mortgage. If your home is worth more now than it was when you bought it, that extra equity is considered to be collateral for this loan. You can receive the entire principal as a lump sum or opt for a home equity line of credit that allows you to pay only interest on money you've actually spent.

Look for a *no-fee* home equity loan at a competitive rate of interest that allows you the option of just paying interest each month and does not require any repayment of the principal for 10 or more years.

Although home equity loans are attractive because the interest you pay is tax-deductible, keep in mind that the lender can sell your home if you fail to repay the loan! There is also the risk that someday the U.S. Congress could decide to restrict or eliminate this tax deduction. Therefore, if possible, try to repay a home equity loan in two to three years, the same term as for most traditional financing. See Home equity line of credit.

Implicit lease rate: Because borrowing money for leases is technically different from borrowing money for loans, leases can no longer express interest as an APR, and lessors may legally refuse to quote one. Instead, because a lease is really a long-term rental contract, the dollar amount of interest is now often called a rent charge, or you may see a money factor, expressed as a decimal, which is a formula that can enable you to compare the cost of a lease with the APR or interest on a loan if you multiply it by 2400. (For example, multiplying a money factor of .00321 by 2400 would give you an interest rate of 7.7 percent.) See Financing cost.

Interest: Money paid to lessors or lenders for the use of the principal during a loan or lease. See APR and Pre-computed interest.

Lease period: The length of time a lease is in effect.

Lender: The person or organization that finances a loan. See Lessor.

Lessee: The person who is leasing a vehicle.

Lessor: The financing institution responsible for the lease. Even if you lease through a dealership, the lessor is the one to whom you send your monthly payments. Automobile dealers "buy" a financing package from a finance company, which may or may not belong to the manufacturer. They then mark up the terms of the contract and make a profit on the difference. In this way, a loan package that calls for an APR of 6 percent can be marked up as high as 12 percent (the highest APR currently allowed by law). The dealer could then pocket an extra $1,200 of your money on a $20,000 vehicle. On a $50,000 vehicle, you'd pay $3,000 more. This situation is also true for leases, so *always* ask to see what the dealer is paying for the financing. The dealer should be willing to show you the paperwork — if you aren't being cheated. A good dealer shouldn't make more than 2 or 3 percent on financing. If it comes down to whether or not you'll take the car, they may even be willing to break even on it just to make the sale. For this reason, pre-qualifying for outside financing before you begin negotiations at the dealership is always best. See Lender.

Lifetime rate cap: The highest rate you can be charged during the life of an adjustable-rate loan. Because most car loans have fixed rates, this usually applies to mortgages and home-equity loans and lines of credit.

Loan period: The length of time a loan is in effect.

Mileage allowance: The maximum amount of miles (or kilometers) you may drive the vehicle during the lease term without paying excess mileage charges. In the United States, yearly mileage allowances range from 10,000 to 15,000; in Canada, yearly allowances range from 20,000 to 24,000 kilometers. If you know you will drive more than the specified mileage allowance, negotiate to have it raised. If the lessor refuses to raise it, or wants to raise your monthly payments as compensation for the possibility that the vehicle's depreciation may increase because of the extra miles you may drive, try to have the excess mileage charges lowered instead. Failing that, buy extra miles up front. They will cost you less than the penalty you'd have to pay if you exceed the mileage allowance, and they are usually refundable if you don't use them all. Make sure any changes to the mileage allowance or excess mileage charges you've negotiated are written into the contract before you sign it.

Money factor: Sometimes called a lease rate, this is a mathematical formula sometimes used to get the equivalent of an interest rate on a lease. A money factor is expressed as a decimal, which you can multiply by 2400 to find out what the interest rate would be. Most leases now state the cost of financing as a dollar amount called a rent charge instead of a money factor. However, if you want to compare the amount of interest you'd pay on a lease, versus the interest on a loan, the money factor of the lease will give you a percentage that is comparable to the APR on the loan.

Monthly payments: Monthly lease payments are largely determined by the vehicle's base price, its rate of depreciation, and the profit the lessor wants to make on the deal, which is often determined by the vehicle's residual value. Monthly payments are figured in this way: If a $40,000 vehicle's residual value at the end of a 36-month lease is set at 40 percent of its original value ($40,000 × .40 = $16,000), the residual will be based on the remaining $24,000 worth of depreciation by the end of the lease ($40,000 − $16,000 = $24,000), and the depreciation portion of each monthly payment will be $667 ($24,000 ÷ 36 = $667). Monthly interest payments on a lease are determined by adding the purchase price to the residual value of the vehicle and dividing the total by a money factor. They also may include some taxes, and an assortment of fees that are payable over the life of the lease.

MSRP (manufacturer's suggested retail price): A figure that the carmaker provides to give dealers a uniform place from which to start bargaining. It is usually lower than the sticker price (which is basically the same but includes additional fees and charges) and higher than the price the dealer expects you to be willing to pay unless the vehicle is in great demand or you were born yesterday.

Open-end lease: A contract that *requires* you to buy the vehicle at the end of the lease period. Open-end leases are generally more attractive to fleets and large companies as opposed to individuals. For details, see Chapter 12.

Option to purchase: The right to buy the vehicle at the end of the lease for a predetermined price. Closed-end leases give you an option to purchase the vehicle; open-end leases *require* you to buy it. You can find out more about both types of leases in Chapter 12.

Originator: The company with whom you negotiate the lease and sign the contract. The originator is not necessarily the lessor; it is often the car dealership.

Points: An interest fee charged by the lender. One point is equal to one percent of the loan. The use of points allows the lender to raise its yield above the apparent interest rate.

Pre-computed interest: The equal allocation of finance charges to each monthly loan payment. These charges should be partially refunded if you pay off the principal ahead of time.

Prepayment penalties: A charge for paying the principal ahead of schedule. Because interest is determined by the amount of unpaid principal, paying off the principal as fast as you can is often a good idea. Any good financing deal should *not* include penalties for prepayment or early termination.

Pre-qualify: To have a financing institution verify that you are eligible for a lease or loan from them without committing yourself to accepting one. *Pre-approved* is another word for being pre-qualified.

Principal: The amount you've borrowed, excluding interest or any other additional charges. Monthly loan payments may include both principal and interest or just interest, with the principal to be paid by another date. Good financing allows you to pay all or part of the principal with no early termination or prepayment penalties.

Rebate: A refund offered by carmakers or dealers to customers who buy or lease a vehicle. Rebates can be deducted from the sales price of the vehicle or paid by mail after the contract is signed. Because the nature of the rebate can cost or save you thousands of dollars, be sure to read the section on rebates in Chapter 9.

Rent charges: Because a lease is really a long-term rental contract, these charges for the use of the money that the vehicle represents are listed as a dollar amount instead of an interest rate or money factor on some leases.

Residual value: The *estimated* value of a vehicle at the end of a lease. This is usually based on its estimated rate of depreciation when you sign the lease contract. Some leases require you to pay the residual value if you want to buy the vehicle when the lease ends — even if that estimate was higher than the vehicle's current fair market value. See Chapter 12 for advice on what to do in this situation.

Security deposit: An up-front payment imposed by some lessors. Make sure that this deposit is fully refundable at the end of the lease. I think the law should require that all security deposits — for apartments as well as vehicles — must be placed in a bank account, and the interest earned (less the tax the account holder had to pay on it) be paid to you when your deposit is refunded. Why should the lessor profit by the use of your money when you re losing the use of it in order to protect the lessor's assets?

Simple interest: Interest charges based on the *daily* unpaid balance of a loan. Because this is the most advantageous for borrowers, lenders rarely offer it.

Sticker price: The price for a vehicle stated on the Monroney sticker, which is required to be placed on the window of a new vehicle. Always try to negotiate a price that's lower than the sticker price.

Subprime loans: Customers who insist on buying vehicles that are more expensive than they can realistically afford are often rated in the "subprime" category when the dealer does a credit check. Subprime borrowers end up paying higher interest rates and larger down payments than they would have paid on an affordable vehicle. In addition, the higher price of this ego trip results in higher registration fees, insurance, and taxes.

Taxes: Some states may require the lessee to pay sales tax on the full price of the car, even though the lessee only plans to keep it a few years. (Ask the dealer what the regulations are in your state.) If you choose to lease another vehicle when the first lease ends, you'll have to pay sales tax *again*. If you buy the vehicle at the end of the lease, you may also have to pay tax on the purchase price. Other special taxes include monthly use taxes, gross receipt taxes, and so on, depending on where you live or lease the vehicle. Check your state laws carefully because taxes can amount to thousands of dollars. The federal government gets into the act as well: A luxury tax is imposed on certain specialty vehicles and luxury cars, and gas guzzlers are subject to an excise tax. For details on how these taxes are computed, see Chapter 2.

Term: This word is used in several ways. *Financing terms* refers to words and phrases used in financing contracts. The *terms of a lease or loan* are the conditions and requirements in the contract, and the *term of a lease* is the length of time until the lease period ends. To keep you on your toes, *term* is used in all three ways in this book.

Termination fee: See Disposition fee.

Total cost: Sometimes called *gross cost,* this is the *full* amount of money you'll have to pay, including all interest, charges, and fees, to buy a vehicle outright or finance it with a lease or loan. Contracts have often relegated extra fees and charges to "small print" that boggles both the eyes and the mind or have failed to mention some hidden charges at all. U.S. federal regulations require that the total amount you have to pay to buy or lease a vehicle be prominently and accurately displayed on the contract.

Up-front costs: The total amount you have to pay before you can drive a leased vehicle off the lot. This can include the first monthly lease payment, any down payment and/or security deposit you've agreed to, plus taxes, first-year license and registration fees, and GAP insurance. Check up-front costs carefully before you sign, because lessors can be very creative.

Walk-away lease: See Closed-end lease.

Wear and tear: Most contracts specify that you must pay to repair or replace any damage to the vehicle "in excess of normal wear and tear." Because the definition of "normal" can vary drastically from one contract to another, under new legislation, leasing companies must tell the customer what types of wear and tear they will consider to be "excessive." Nevertheless, you should always ask the dealer for a specific definition, even if you both have to take a walk around the used-car portion of the lot and look at different types of damage and what they cost to repair. Get these costs and a specific definition of what normal wear and tear involves *in writing,* signed by the sales manager. Don't forget to ask who's responsible for wear on brakes and tires.

Things to Think about Before Making Your Decision

Your three major alternatives when acquiring a vehicle are leasing it, financing it with a loan, or using your own cash to pay for it. Of course, when you pay for a car with your own cash, you're not beholden to any person or institution. But if you lease or borrow, keep the following information in mind.

Depreciation is a major factor

When deciding whether to finance a new vehicle with a lease or loan, keep in mind that the cost of a lease or loan is partially determined by the vehicle's rate of depreciation (or how much value the vehicle loses as it grows older) during the duration of the contract. For this reason, make sure that you check the pricing sources listed in Chapter 8 to determine how much the vehicle you want will depreciate over the first two or three years you own it.

A new vehicle usually depreciates from 30 to 50 percent in the first three years in the United States, and an average of 2 percent per month in Canada. For this reason, you may decide to let someone else absorb the depreciation by selecting a two- or three-year-old previously owned vehicle rather than a new one.

Also, the higher the purchase price, the more you'll continue to pay for licensing, registration, insurance, taxes, and interest. Be sure to read the next two chapters on leasing and loans for more information on how depreciation affects these arrangements and how you may end up paying for depreciation *twice*.

Credit or leasing companies require insurance

When you lease a car or purchase one with a loan, the lessor or the creditor can stipulate the kind of insurance you must get for your car. However, according to the AAA (American Automobile Association), although a credit or leasing company can require you to insure the vehicle for fire, theft, collision, and so on, it cannot force you to purchase a policy through a specific broker, agent, or company.

Look for the best coverage you can find before agreeing to purchase insurance through a dealer or financer, the person responsible for financing a lease or loan. If you decide to insure through one of these sources, *do not let them include the insurance premiums in the cost of the lease or loan.* If you do, you have to pay interest on your coverage.

You may need more than one type of insurance if you choose to finance a vehicle. You may consider getting some of the following types of insurance, for example:

- ✔ **Auto insurance coverage:** Financer-required insurance usually does *not* include any minimum liability insurance that your state or province requires, or anything else besides comprehensive and collision coverage to repair or replace the vehicle if it is damaged or stolen. Chapter 13 shows you how to find the best and least expensive auto insurance coverage. Verify that *all* insurance policies are in effect before you take possession of the vehicle.

- ✔ **GAP insurance:** This type of insurance covers the difference between a vehicle's stated value in a finance contract and what an insurance company will pay if the vehicle is damaged beyond repair or stolen before the end of the finance period or lease. Some financing contracts provide GAP insurance free of charge; others include it as part of the up-front cost (the total amount you have to pay before you can drive a vehicle off the lot), and still others require you to purchase the insurance yourself. Although GAP insurance shouldn't cost more than a couple of hundred dollars, some policies can be much more expensive — especially if they're obtained through the financer.

Because a vehicle begins to depreciate as soon as you take possession of it, its replacement value soon may be substantially less than when you bought it, and your insurance policy may not cover the full amount that you'll have to come up with to compensate the financer, if the need arises.

✔ **Credit life or credit disability insurance:** These policies make your payments if you die or become disabled while your financing is still in effect. This coverage is usually optional and extremely overpriced. If you feel that your estate could not cover the payments in the event of your death, you can buy this type of insurance at a better price from an outside source.

Some credit unions supply this insurance at no charge because the rules in many unions specify that loan obligations are canceled in the event of death. Because unscrupulous financers sometimes slip this coverage in whether you want it or not, be smart and recalculate the monthly payment shown on the final contract to be sure they do *not* include this coverage as a hidden charge.

Manufacturer's rebates and financing offers

Car manufacturers with their own financing departments may offer lower interest rates on loans and leases than rates that are available from outside credit sources. To insure goodwill, some pay the security deposit and first monthly payment when you lease the next car from them after a previous lease contract with them expires. Others offer perks such as free maintenance, auto club and towing services, emergency hotlines, stolen-vehicle tracking, and other goodies. Generally speaking, the more expensive the vehicle, the greater the perks offered by the manufacturer.

Auto manufacturers run frequent promotions that offer you the choice between a rebate or a low-interest deal. Ask your accountant or a friend who's good with numbers to work out which alternative would be the most profitable arrangement for you.

If you go for the rebate, ask the dealer to base the sales or lease contract on the price of the vehicle *after* the rebate has been deducted, instead of writing the contract for the original price and mailing you the rebate later on. Doing this enables you to avoid paying higher taxes, interest, registration fees, and perhaps insurance, on the *pre*-rebate price of the vehicle, which may be a couple of thousand dollars more than the vehicle actually costs you. If they try to wiggle out of this, read "Getting Satisfaction When You're Not Happy with the Job," in Chapter 18, and use those techniques to locate someone who has the power to get the contract written using the *post*-rebate price.

Research Financing Sources

Many carmakers and dealerships offer extremely low-interest deals to stimulate sales. These are rarely bargains, because a low interest loan is inevitably coupled with a higher than necessary purchase price for the car, but knowing what their terms are can be useful. If you intend to finance or lease a vehicle, first do some thorough research at banks, credit unions, lending and leasing institutions, auto clubs, and other organizations to find the lowest interest rates and financing fees available. Then compare these with the terms offered by dealerships and automakers.

Follow these steps to find the best financing deal:

1. **Determine the type of vehicle and optional equipment you want.**
   Refer to Chapter 7 to determine your priorities and for details on available features. Use the Features and Options checklist in Chapter 7 to keep track of everything.

2. **Inspect and test drive vehicles at dealerships (see Chapter 8 for details), but refuse to discuss buying or leasing.** Tell them you may return to negotiate at a later date. Most financing institutions only quote on a specific make and model.

3. **Get an idea of the estimated rate of depreciation for the vehicle you want to buy, plus its current retail price and its factory invoice price, if the vehicle is a new one.** If you're looking to buy a previously owned vehicle, refer to Chapter 3 for a list of pricing sources. If you want a new vehicle, refer to Chapter 8.

4. **Ascertain which financing sources are reliable and offer good rates.**
   Consult your local Better Business Bureau to find out who the bad guys are and ask friends for recommendations.

5. **Call the best of the sources you turn up in Step 4 and ask about the requirements and costs of their loan or lease.** To avoid comparing apples and oranges, be sure to always specify the same year, make, model, and options, as well as the same lease period, down payment (if any), price range, and estimated depreciation. Be sure to get the following information:

   - APR (Annual Percentage Rate)

   - Length of the lease or loan

   - Size of your monthly payments

   - Whether there are any administrative fees or other charges, and which ones have to be paid up front, at the end of the contract period, or are pre-computed monthly

   - *Total* amount the loan or lease will cost

   - Whether there are prepayment penalties (a charge for paying the principal off ahead of schedule) or early-termination penalties (a charge for canceling the lease or loan ahead of schedule)

   - Whether any GAP insurance or other coverage is required and what it will cost if you obtain it through the financer

   - Who can drive the vehicle besides yourself

   - Whether you can take the vehicle out of the province or country

6. **Ask to take home a sample copy of the contract with the terms you've negotiated filled in so you can look it over carefully.** If you are told that you can't have a copy because their contracts must be used in numerical sequence or because each contract is "written" by a computer for a specific agreement, suggest that they photocopy one they've generated in the past, cross out any information specific to that agreement (the number, name, address, pricing, and so on), and mark it "sample" to avoid any confusion.

   If *any* prospective lessor, lender, or dealer refuses to let you have a copy of their financing contract, you can assume that potential traps are hidden in the small print that they don't want you to look at too carefully. Cross these sources off your list of potential financers.

7. **Negotiate better rates by placing calls to financers whose terms you like.** Ask if they can give you a better rate than the lowest one you've found so far.

8. **Get yourself pre-qualified for financing from the source with the best terms so you'll know exactly what you can afford to pay for a vehicle.**

After you take these steps, you are ready to negotiate with dealerships to see if you can get a better financing deal than the one you've pre-qualified for — or a better price for the vehicle by using a loan to pay cash up front.

Select the Shortest Financing Period You Can Afford

Although a long-term lease or loan requires smaller monthly payments than one with a shorter life, you actually end up paying substantially more interest on it. Also, the chances of incurring costly repairs increase for every extra year you drive a vehicle. A clear picture of your financial situation can help you determine whether having more ready cash is worth paying more in the long run.

Keep Your Eyes Open for New Financing Legislation

In response to great public pressure for government reform of leasing practices, a new set of regulations that updates the Consumer Leasing Act took effect on January 1, 1998. The regulations stipulate that lessors must provide uniform cost and other disclosures in consumer lease transactions and in lease advertising. Before entering into a lease agreement, lessors must give consumers 15 to 20 disclosures, including the amount of initial charges to be paid, an identification of leased property, a payment schedule, the responsibilities for maintaining a leased property, and the liability for terminating a lease early.

The new regulations also require lessors to disclose the total dollar amount of all official and license fees, registration, title, or taxes required to be paid in connection with the lease; and the insurance specified in the lease, regardless of whether it is required or voluntary. With open-end leases, lessors now have to tell you the gross capitalized cost, the residual value of the vehicle, and the total lease obligation up-front, rather than at the consummation of the lease (as they did before the regulations took effect).

The bad news is that the original recommendations by the Federal Trade Commission called for a dollar figure that included the total cost of leasing the vehicle — including the final sales price and *every single penny you'll have to lay out* — to be prominently displayed on the contract. But this seems to have been lost in the horse-trading that produced the final regulations. If this annoys you as much as it does me, you may want to consider calling your congressional representatives and asking them to lobby for it.

Because additional reforms may be legislated to correct the fact that leases are still basically unreadable, I strongly suggest that, before you finance your next vehicle, you familiarize yourself with the current regulations by keeping an eye on the newspapers, consulting your local library's reference sources, accessing the information on the Internet, or asking the Federal Reserve Board for a copy of any changes to "Regulation M" that may have occurred after January 1, 1998.

Chapter 11

Buying a Car with Your Own — or Someone Else's — Money

*Y*ou have two main sources of cash: your own funds and money you've borrowed. Using your own funds to pay "cash on the barrelhead" has always been the simplest — and often the cheapest — way to buy, but whether it's the right option for you depends on several factors, which I cover in a minute in the section called, "Paying Cash." Although loans are more costly, they are probably the most popular way to finance a vehicle. Before deciding how to pay for any major purchase, take a close look at your investment income and tax status to decide which option is better for you. This chapter can help you make sense of these options. Here you can find the advantages and disadvantages of both paying cash or borrowing. If you opt to borrow money to purchase a vehicle, you can find advice on negotiating the best terms (yes, loans *are* negotiable) and information that can help you steer clear of particularly bad deals. (If any of the financial terms — which are set in a special font — in this chapter are unfamiliar to you, check out the first section in Chapter 10 for a fuller explanation.)

Paying Cash

A vehicle depreciates at the same rate whether you lease, finance, or pay cash for it. However, if you use your own money, you pay no interest or financing charges and you own the vehicle outright, with no strings attached. If you pay for the vehicle with cash you've acquired from a mortgage or home equity loan or line of credit (see the section "Using the equity in your home"), the interest you pay for the use of the funds is usually tax-deductible.

On the other hand, if you use your savings to pay for a vehicle, you don't enjoy the benefits of tax deductions that you would get if you used a home equity loan, and you lose the ability to profitably invest a great deal of money.

Paying cash up front for a vehicle is a good idea if any of the following apply to you:

✔ You intend to keep the vehicle for a long time.

✔ You have plenty of cash on hand.

✔ You'd prefer to avoid paying interest and financing charges on a loan or lease.

✔ You don't want to pay more taxes on capital gains from additional investments.

If none of these descriptions apply to you, consider the other alternatives: loans, covered in the following sections of this chapter, or leases, covered in Chapter 12.

Borrowing Money

Borrowing the money to pay for a vehicle may not be a bad idea if you intend to keep it for a long period of time and you can't or don't want to lay down cash for it. When compared to leasing a vehicle, borrowing money to purchase one has other potential advantages: First, the vehicle will belong to you at the end of the finance period with no residuals to pay. Second, although you risk paying a higher price for the car, if the car manufacturer sponsors a special low-rate loan through its own finance division, the terms may be better than you can obtain anywhere else. (On the other hand, the reverse may be true.)

Of course, borrowing money does have disadvantages:

✔ Although the total cost of using a loan to purchase a vehicle is generally lower than leasing it, your monthly payments will usually be higher, and you may fall into the depreciation trap, in which the car depreciates so quickly that you end up owing more on it than you can get out of it if, for some reason, you need to sell it.

✔ Unlike leases, loans are considered debts and may lower your earnings-to-debts ratio, which can disqualify you when you try to finance something else, such as a home.

✔ The option of financing a vehicle may encourage you to overspend or live beyond your means.

✔ Most lenders keep the legal title to the vehicle in their name until the loan is paid off. If you can't make payments, the lender may be able to repossess your car and sell it. Banks and credit unions may also be able to withdraw money from other accounts that you have at the same institutions to reimburse themselves if you default on the loan.

If, in spite of these caveats, you still feel that borrowing money for a car purchase is the best option for you, remember that the best type of loans charge simple interest and have a low *APR* with no prepayment penalties. Home equity loans, described in the section called "Using the equity in your home," may prove to be even less expensive, if you're *sure* you'll be able to repay them.

How much can you borrow?

The amount of the loan you can qualify for depends on your current credit status, the size of your down payment, and the vehicle you're buying. Other considerations, outlined in the following list, can also affect how much a creditor is willing to lend you:

✔ **Open credit lines.** Credit agencies consider the total amount you're able to charge on a credit card as an outstanding debt, even though you may have no current charges on the card at all! They do this because they have no way of knowing whether you'll suddenly decide to use the card to its full credit limit. Therefore, you may want to cancel any credit cards that you don't use before you apply for any type of financing or, at the very least, have the credit limits on the cards lowered.

✔ **Blue book value.** You can usually cover up to 90 percent of the current blue book value of a used vehicle that's less than five years old. You can cover even more if the vehicle is an expensive luxury model. New-car financing can cover up to 80 to 100 percent of a vehicle's cost. However, you'll usually have to pay a higher APR if you borrow the entire purchase price.

✔ **Age of the vehicle.** As a general rule, financing rates are usually lower for new cars than for used ones.

✔ **Cost of the car.** Loan periods usually run from two to five years, but you can often finance a higher-priced vehicle for a longer length of time. Just remember that the longer the loan period, the more interest you pay.

Negotiating the most advantageous terms on a loan

Many people are woefully unaware that loans are negotiable. Even if your negotiating strategy is simply to shop around for loans that meet your criteria, you can still impact how much you end up paying, both in the short- and long-term. Read the following sections for pointers that can help you get the most advantageous terms on a loan.

Pre-qualify with several different institutions

Get yourself pre-qualified for the best loan available from banks, credit unions, finance companies, and other sources *before* you negotiate with a dealership. Use the Loan Comparison Worksheet in this chapter to keep track of various terms and conditions that you get from different sources.

Pre-qualification does not mean that you have to accept the loan — unless you signed a contract. But it does enable you to narrow down the search for vehicles to those within your borrowing capacity and give you the security of knowing that you can negotiate a lower price for a vehicle based on your ability to use the loan to "pay cash on the line."

Use the Loan Comparison Worksheet to compare the loan you've pre-qualified for with the financing terms offered by dealerships and carmakers to see which offers you a better deal. Remember that APRs and monthly payments quoted in TV and newspaper promotions are only starting points for bargaining.

Don't tell dealers that you've been pre-approved for a loan from an outside source. Simply say that you haven't made any decision about whether or not to finance the vehicle, and refuse to discuss *any* kind of financing until after you negotiate the lowest possible purchase price for the vehicle. Doing so motivates the dealer to lower the sales price in the hope of compensating for it with profit from financing the transaction.

Talk financing only after you've agreed on a purchase price

After you agree on a purchase price for the vehicle, ask to hear the *best* financing terms the dealership has to offer. If their loan is not substantially cheaper than the one you've pre-qualified for, tell them that you'd rather pay cash or that you've been offered better terms by another source.

Refuse to reveal the other lender's identity or the terms of the loan you've been offered. Just tell them the length of the loan and ask them to come up with their lowest simple-interest loan for the same period of time.

If you've pre-qualified for a home equity loan (see the section called "Using the equity in your home"), remember that the tax deduction you get for the interest you pay on the loan may make it a better bargain than a lower APR from a dealer.

LOAN COMPARISON WORKSHEET

LOAN	SOURCE	AGENT	PHONE #
#1			
#2			
#3			
#4			

ITEM	LOAN #1	LOAN #2	LOAN #3	LOAN #4
Amount needed	$	$	$	$
Down Payment	($)	($)	($)	($)
Amount to be financed	$	$	$	$
APR (Annual Percentage Rate)	%	%	%	%
Fixed or Adjustable Rate?				
Annual/Lifetime Ceilings (If adjustable rate loan)	/	/	/	/
Length of Loan	months	months	months	months
Monthly Payment	$	$	$	$
Total Monthly Payments	$	$	$	$
Finance Charge	$	$	$	$
Other Fees & Charges	$	$	$	$
	$	$	$	$
	$	$	$	$
MANDATORY INSURANCE: Who provides? Part of monthly payment?				
GAP Insurance?	$	$	$	$
Comprehensive Insurance?	$	$	$	$
Death/Disability Insurance?	$	$	$	$
TOTAL COST OF LOAN	$_____	$_____	$_____	$_____

If a dealership insists on raising the price you've negotiated for a vehicle if you refuse to accept their financing, you may still have another card to play. If there are no prepayment penalties, you can buy the vehicle for their lowest price by accepting their loan, and then pay it off completely the very first month with money from the better loan for which you pre-qualified. *Major* savings would have to be involved before I would resort to this rather devious strategy, but if you feel that all's fair in love, war, and car sales, you may want to consider it if you have sufficient assets to qualify for both loans.

Challenge documentation charges

Finance charges are usually imposed on loans, but some lenders also demand documentation charges and other fees. Challenge these, especially if other lenders you've contacted don't require them.

Using the equity in your home

Your home can be a tax-deductible source of cash. As the real estate market rises and falls, homes increase and decrease in value. If your property is now worth more than you paid for it, the difference between its original price and its current value is called *equity*. You can use this equity as collateral on a no-fee home equity loan that enables you to purchase a vehicle for cash. Because the interest on mortgages and home equity loans is usually tax deductible, you'll not only be in a better position to negotiate a lower purchase price, but you'll also get a tax deduction for your interest payments that can be worth more to you than a lower APR for a traditional loan. What's more, with a no-fee loan you can avoid paying most financing charges, as well.

If you'd like to consider this option, here are a few words of caution:

- ✔ *If you default on a home equity loan, you can lose your house!* Don't borrow more than you need and be sure you can handle the monthly payments.

- ✔ Borrowing against your home isn't wise when the price of housing is falling. If the equity used as collateral disappears, you may be forced to repay the loan ahead of time.

- ✔ Even if the real estate market is rising, beware of adding too much to your mortgage debt. If the market suddenly falls, you may find yourself with a big debt hangover.

- ✔ Be sure that your tax deductions and any income from investing the cash you would otherwise have used to buy the vehicle is greater than the interest you pay on the loan.

- ✔ Beware of home equity loans that have higher fees than traditional loans. Look for *no-fee* home equity loans offered as special promotions by banks and credit companies.

Using my house to buy my car

I was brought up on the advice Polonius gave to his son in *Hamlet:* "Neither a borrower nor a lender be." And I've found that using my own funds to pay cash up front usually gives me a bargaining advantage and doesn't saddle me with the hassle of monthly payments. However, the last time I needed a car, my accountant suggested that I get a no-fee, low-interest, long-term home equity line of credit and defer paying off the principal for as long as possible. The monthly interest-only payments were quite a bit lower than what my own money was earning from investments, and because the payments were deducted electronically from my bank account and the principal was eventually figured into the sales price when I sold my house, I hardly noticed that I was paying for the car at all.

When you're getting a home equity loan or line of credit, be sure to ask the following questions:

- What is the highest rate I can be charged during the term of the loan? (This is called the *lifetime rate cap.*)
- What is the smallest amount I can borrow against my line of credit?
- If I don't use my credit line at all for a year, will I be charged an inactivity fee?
- Are there annual fees for maintaining the line of credit?
- Are there prepayment penalties if I decide to pay off the loan ahead of time?
- What will the total cost of the loan be, including points and closing costs?
- If I ever have trouble making payments on time, is there a grace period and/or a notification process before drastic action is taken?

Loan Traps to Avoid

As with leasing, loans also offer opportunities to be ripped off. The following sections list some obvious and not-so-obvious traps to watch out for.

The depreciation trap

Most lenders require a down payment that includes depreciation by as much as 20 percent of the vehicle's value, plus administrative fees and other up-front costs. On top of that, you have to make payments each month based on the full purchase price of the vehicle, plus taxes, destination fees, interest, and so on. I can understand that lenders want to protect themselves against the possibility of getting stuck with a depreciated vehicle if you fail to make your loan payments, but unless they refund the depreciation portion of your down payment at the end of the loan, you end up paying for it twice when you eventually sell the used vehicle at its depreciated resale value.

Adjustable-rate loans

Adjustable-rate loans rise and fall with various economic factors. If you get an adjustable rate loan, make sure it has a reasonable ceiling (or limit). Beware of those that have no ceilings on how much the interest rate can increase each year and over the lifetime of the loan. Extremely high ceilings can be as bad as no limits at all. Fixed-rate loans may have higher rates up front but may prove cheaper over time.

Hardship loans

If you have trouble qualifying for a loan, be wary of dealers who promise to find a way to finance the vehicle. Many of these "hardship" loans may force you to pay all the interest within a year, charge you interest on interest, or have a high APR and a lot of hidden extra fees. Be especially leery of the following deals that can really sock it to you:

- ✔ **Subprime loans:** If you insist on buying a vehicle that is more expensive than you can realistically afford, you may end up in the "subprime" category when the dealer does a credit check. As a subprime borrower, you end up paying higher interest rates and larger down payments than you would have paid on an affordable vehicle. In addition, the higher price of this ego trip results in higher registration fees, insurance, and taxes.

- ✔ **"Buy here, pay here" financing:** People with poor credit ratings often must pay off a used car by coming into the dealership every week with a cash payment. If they haven't got the cash, the dealership can repossess the vehicle.

Vendor-related loans

Some dealers may refer you to a specific finance company for the low-interest loans they've advertised. Others may offer *split loans,* for which the dealer finances a large down payment and a particular finance company lends you the balance. In both of these cases, because of the dealer's reciprocal relationship with the finance company, you may not be offered terms that are as good as other sources can provide.

Be cautious about dealership ads that feature low-interest loans. Scrutinize the small print at the bottom of the ad and then call the toll-free number in the ad for a detailed account of *all* the terms and conditions of the offer. Be sure to ask the following questions:

- Will I have to pay a higher price for the vehicle to qualify for this loan than I would if I paid cash or financed it elsewhere?

- Does this deal require a larger down payment than usual? (Some can go as high as 25 to 30 percent of the loan!)

- Are there limits on the length of this loan? How long can I take to pay it off? Are there prepayment penalties?

- Are there extra points tacked on to the loan that would cost me more than the published interest rate?

- Are there balloon payments involved? I don't want any surprises when the loan matures!

- How long will this offer be in effect? (Some specials only last a couple of days; others give you very little time to take possession of the vehicle.)

- Must I relinquish a manufacturer's rebate in order to qualify for the lower rates? (If you are required to choose between a rebate or lower interest rates, be sure the loan saves you more money than the rebate would provide. Bear in mind that you get the use of the rebate money immediately, which means you can use it to pay off a traditional loan more quickly, or you can apply the interest you earn by investing it toward paying off the loan.)

- Does this offer only apply to certain models? Can I special-order a vehicle, or must I buy one off the lot?

- Do I have to buy additional services or merchandise to qualify? (Some special offers involve the purchase of a service contract, extended warranty, rustproofing, or other dubious extras that cost more than you'd gain from the lower interest rate.)

If you decide to accept the loan, read both your contract and your sales invoice carefully to make sure that *all* the terms agree with the dealer's special offer.

Signing a Loan Contract

If you decide to finance the purchase of a vehicle with a loan, take the following precautions before you sign anything:

✔ **Ask the financer to supply you with a Credit Disclosure Statement that lists all the charges and fees.** Be sure you understand this statement before you sign anything. Check to be sure the APR is the one you agreed upon and that additional charges or fees haven't raised the cost above the rate you were quoted.

✔ **Read the contract slowly and carefully.** If the terms or language are unclear, insist on taking it home to read at your leisure or to show to your accountant. If the dealership or potential financer refuses (a common excuse is "the forms are computer generated in numerical order and can't be printed until you're ready to sign"), ask for a photocopy of a similar contract, as described in Chapter 10. If you're not allowed to take even a copy of the contract home with you for review, cancel the deal and leave.

✔ **Make sure the contract has no blank spaces left.** If you find any, draw a line through them and write N/A (not applicable) in each space.

✔ **Have the dealership or financer initial any blanks and changes — and initial each one yourself as well.**

✔ **Insist that there be no prepayment penalties.** You definitely want the option to save interest by paying off the loan as swiftly as possible without having to pay to do so.

✔ **Contest documentation fees.** Who pays you to do the paperwork associated with your job?

✔ **For that matter, contest *all* fees and additional charges.** What have you got to lose?

✔ **Check the numbers.** Be sure the contract shows the following:

   • Proper APR format (a nine-and-a-half percent loan should be stated as "9.5% APR")

   • Specific amount you are borrowing or financing

   • Full amount of each monthly payment

   • Term of the loan, expressed in months or in the maximum amount of time you have in which to pay it off in full

   • Total cost of the deal, including points, fees, down payments, balloon payments, and so on

✔ **Refuse to pay *anything* until the sales contract has been approved by the loan company.** Most sales contracts specify that if the financing involved is not approved, *the customer is responsible for finding other financing.* If you've put down enough of a down payment to take the vehicle home, you've been driving it, you've added accessories or — heaven forbid — you've damaged it, you are going to be in for a nasty time if you find out that financing it elsewhere is going to cost more than you'd planned to pay, and you can't return the vehicle!

Chapter 12

The Perils and Pleasures of Leasing

Many people have misconceptions about leasing cars. They think that leasing is not substantially different from financing a car purchase with a loan; and, because their monthly payments are often lower, they may be under the impression that leasing a car is less expensive. Both of these assumptions are wrong. Leasing a vehicle is very different from buying one: The vehicle you lease isn't yours at all; it's owned by someone else, and, among other things, that someone can stipulate the maximum number of miles you can drive the car without penalty, and the condition it must be in at the end of the lease.

Leasing a car is like renting it for a really long time.

Leasing is usually the most expensive way to obtain a vehicle, and it is fraught with perils. A 1996 survey by the National Association of Consumer Agency Administrations and the Consumer Federation of America found that around 30 percent of all new cars are leased, and a substantial number of rip-offs are taking place (the number of complaints related to auto leasing had doubled in the previous year at the 17 agencies they polled). The top complaint associated with auto leasing was that people did not understand the complicated contract. Many customers were unaware of substantial charges for early termination or excessive wear and tear. And, believe it or not, some consumers thought that they were purchasing, not leasing, the automobile!

The survey found that, if English is not the customer's native language, the chances of fraud increase dramatically. Questionable auto-leasing arrangements and deceptive practices aimed at Latinos have emerged as major new sources of consumer fraud complaints. The survey cited cases where

Spanish-speakers negotiated a car lease in Spanish, but then were asked to sign contracts in English that did not adhere to the verbal agreements they'd made.

Watch out for the following leasing traps, too:

- Some senior citizens who think they are buying cars have been conned into leases that were disguised as "special financing arrangements."

- The cost of some vehicles have been raised (sometimes by thousands of dollars) above the negotiated purchase price when customers were persuaded to lease them instead.

- The agreed-upon credit for a trade-in may be omitted from the final lease contract.

- A lease may include undisclosed charges or terms different from the ones you and the dealer agreed upon earlier.

- Leases have been foisted on customers who thought they were buying the vehicle when dealers referred to the lease as "the plan" or "the installment contract."

- In some cases, optional equipment included in the contract is omitted from the vehicle itself. Comparing the description of the vehicle on the lease with the itemized list of equipment on the window sticker is important for this reason.

Despite all of these instances of fraud, for certain people, leasing can be a sensible and financially sound way to get a vehicle. If you're interested in leasing, this chapter can help you understand leases, determine whether leasing is a good or bad alternative for you, and negotiate the most reasonable leasing terms possible. It also explains the options you have at the end of the lease and gives you pointers for making the most of them.

Although a lease may be right for you, because the opportunities for being ripped off are legendary, read this chapter very carefully if you're even considering leasing.

Note, too, that I've placed some financial terms in a special font. When you come across an unfamiliar word in that font, turn to the first section in Chapter 10 for a full explanation.

Leasing Defined

A lease is a contract by which the owner of a property (the lessor) allows another person (the lessee) to use it for a specified term. This is true for vehicles, apartments, and other items. In most cases, when you lease a vehicle, an outside credit source that the automaker or dealership is affiliated with actually buys the vehicle and then leases it to you. That's why your monthly payments generally go to the lessor rather than to the dealership. Most leases only cover the cost of the vehicle; you will usually have to pay for maintenance, repairs, and insurance yourself.

The first thing you need to know to make a good decision about leasing is that there are two types of vehicle leases, discussed in the following sections.

Closed-end leases

Closed-end leases (contracts that give you the option to purchase the vehicle at the end of the leasing period or return it and walk away) are the most popular with individuals. Some are quite straightforward — you simply return the vehicle at the end of the lease period. Other closed-end leases set a residual value at the beginning of the lease and offer you the option at the end of the lease of either returning the vehicle or purchasing it for the residual value. If you're interested in purchasing the car, keep the following in mind:

- ✔ Some lessors do not require you to pay them the current fair market value (the current retail price for the vehicle at the end of the lease period) — if you want to buy the car — if their estimate of the residual value was too low.

- ✔ Others set the buy-out price (the amount you'd have to pay to buy the car) at the vehicle's fair market value at the end of the lease, even though they estimate that amount *before* you sign the lease. (Talk about precognition!)

- ✔ Still others stipulate that, if you want to buy the car at the end of the lease, you must pay either their estimated fair market value or a fixed (guaranteed) residual value, whichever is higher.

You may get around the last two maneuvers when the lease period ends by refusing to exercise your right to purchase the vehicle for anything more than you'd pay to buy a similar model elsewhere. Anyone who insists you pay a higher price for a vehicle than its current value has little hope of getting another buyer to agree to do so, so they may agree to your terms.

Open-end leases

Open-end leases (contracts that *require* you to buy the vehicle at the end of the lease period) usually have lower monthly payments, but they obligate you to purchase the vehicle at the end of the lease, and you must pay the predetermined, fixed residual value. If the fair market value at lease-end is higher than the fixed residual, you've got a bargain. If it's lower, you'll be forced to buy the vehicle for more than its actual value.

If you accept this type of lease, not only do you risk having to pay a higher total price than you would have been able to negotiate if you'd bought the vehicle outright, but you'll also be buying a vehicle that has depreciated considerably for more than the highest price the dealer could have gotten for it when it was new. Open-end leases are mostly chosen by fleets and large corporations who can negotiate much better terms than individuals are able to because corporations usually buy in quantity. An individual person would usually have little reason to go for this option.

Strategies for getting the best deal

Unless you expect a vehicle to stay in high demand and not depreciate to any extent by the end of the lease, or if you think the price of most used vehicles will rise dramatically in the near future, I advise you to go for a **closed-end lease** on a previously leased two- to three-year-old vehicle that has already gone through its major depreciation, has been driven no more than 36,000 miles, and has been thoroughly refurbished and fully warranted by the dealer or manufacturer.

At the end of the lease, return the vehicle and lease another that's two or three years old. That way you'll always drive a vehicle that's younger than four or six years old, and you'll be able to invest the cash you would have paid to buy a vehicle at higher rates of interest than you're paying on the lease.

Advantages and disadvantages of leasing

Despite the potential pitfalls, leasing a car can offer the following advantages:

- ✔ Leasing allows you to drive a more expensive vehicle than you can otherwise afford and leaves the bulk of your cash available for other uses.

- ✔ Unlike loans, leases are not considered debts, and therefore, leasing a car doesn't lower your earnings-to-debts ratio, which can disqualify you when you try to finance something else. (Of course, the vehicle is not considered an asset, either, because you don't own it.)

- ✔ Leases usually require little to no down payment.

- ✔ Some experts believe that you should buy what appreciates and lease what depreciates. If you agree with this, then leasing a car makes good sense for you.

- ✔ Because you only pay for the depreciation of the vehicle over a limited time, monthly lease payments can be lower than loan payments.

- ✔ Taxes and interest are spread over the term of the lease as part of your monthly payments.

✔ The large number of two- and three-year-old previously leased vehicles has had a positive effect on the availability of "nearly new" cars, which are often fully warranted and can be leased on much the same terms as new ones.

Of course, leasing a car also has a negative side:

✔ You will have spent a lot of money and have nothing to show for it unless you decide to buy the vehicle at the end of a lease period.

✔ In most cases, you pay more to lease a vehicle than to buy it with cash or finance it with a loan (though other aspects of your financial picture may make this quite worthwhile; see the section "When Leasing May Work to Your Advantage").

✔ Even if no down payment is required, most leases ask for various administrative fees, for processing credit applications and other paperwork. (Whatever they call them, there's usually enough competition for your business to enable you to request that these fees be waived.)

✔ Many leases require a security deposit, which is payable when you sign the lease. Before you sign, make sure that the lease stipulates that the security deposit will be refunded to you when the lease ends.

✔ Although a new vehicle may have depreciated as much as 30 to 50 percent by the time the lease period is over, through your monthly payments you will have paid interest on its full original price.

✔ Lemon laws may not cover some leased vehicles, so check the laws in your state or province before deciding whether or not to lease. (For more on lemons, see the section in Chapter 4 that covers vehicles to avoid.)

When Leasing May Work to Your Advantage

To determine whether leasing would be of value to you or a waste of your money, take a close look at your financial picture and the uses you envision for the vehicle. Generally speaking, you may benefit from leasing if you fit into the following categories:

✔ Are self-employed and can deduct all or part of the cost of the lease from your income tax as a business expense.

Keep in mind that the miles you commute to and from work are not considered business use.

✔ Drive fewer than 15,000 miles a year.

✔ Get a high return on your investments.

✔ Simply cannot live without a new car every couple of years.

If you don't feel up to negotiating a lease . . .

A nonprofit consumer group called the Center for the Study of Services, based in Washington, D.C., has created a program, called LeaseWise, which provides consumers with reliable bids for leases. If you give them the make and model of the vehicle you want, for $230 they will negotiate with five dealerships for the best leasing terms and send you a report. You can either pick the dealerships yourself, or they will locate the five nearest you. If you find a better deal with lower terms, they will refund your fee. The dealers are committed to honoring the terms for any vehicle of that make and model on their lot that has the same optional equipment. If you're interested, call LeaseWise at 800-475-7283 or visit their Web site at consumer.checkbook.org/consumer/.

A Ford pamphlet, "Leasing and Tax Benefits: a Business Opportunity," provides a comparison of the tax deductions you can claim if you purchase a vehicle primarily for business or lease one. In one example, the two-year depreciation tax deduction on a $30,000 vehicle amounts to $5,222 if you buy the car — and $13,860 if you lease it. A more complex example, involving the cooperation of your employer, produces a deduction of $19,800. However, both the Ford pamphlet and I agree that you should consult your accountant to see whether leasing is the most profitable option for you.

Negotiating a Lease

Many dealers try hard to convince customers to lease a vehicle rather than buy it because the dealers usually make a better profit on a leased vehicle. Although dealers and lessors generally behave as though the terms of a lease are inviolable, the truth is that virtually every requirement can be negotiated (unless the vehicle is extremely popular and difficult to obtain). You can save several thousand dollars by carefully negotiating the provisions of a lease. If that got your attention, the following sections explain some things you need to know in order to get the best possible terms.

The Lease Comparison Worksheet, provided in this chapter helps you compare leases from various sources.

Negotiating the cost of the vehicle

Believe it or not, up until recently, only 9 percent of the people who planned to lease a vehicle bargained for a lower sales price, compared to 75 percent of those who intended to buy a car outright. This may change, but the fact remains that customers are still largely unaware that leases are negotiable.

LEASE COMPARISON WORKSHEET

Make, Model, and Year:		Estimated Depreciation[1] %	Open- or Closed-end?
Lease	**Source**	**Contact**	**Phone #**
#1			
#2			
#3			
#4			

ITEM	LEASE #1	LEASE #2	LEASE #3	LEASE #4
1. Length of Lease	months	months	months	months
2. Mileage Allowance	miles	miles	miles	miles
3. Excess Mileage Charges	¢/mile	¢/mile	¢/mile	¢/mile
4. Rent Charge	$	$	$	$
5. Money Factor				
6. Sticker Price	$	$	$	$
7. MSRP	$	$	$	$
8. Dealer Discount?[2]	($)	($)	($)	($)
9. Vehicle's Base Value[3]	$	$	$	$
10. Cost of Options[4]	$	$	$	$
11. Cost of Vehicle[5]	$	$	$	$
12. Monthly Payment	$	$	$	$
13. Total Monthly Payments[6]	$	$	$	$
14. Down Payment?	$	$	$	$
15. Destination Fee?	$	$	$	$
16. Disposition Fee?	$	$	$	$

[1] Obtain this from blue books or pricing services.

[2] Question marks indicate conditions that do not apply to every lease. Challenge any fees with question marks.

[3] Subtract line 8 from line 7.

[4] Be sure that all quotes are based on the same optional equipment. Don't pay for any options you don't want!

[5] Add lines 9 and 10.

[6] Multiply line 1 (Length of Lease) by line 12 (Monthly Payment).

LEASE COMPARISON WORKSHEET (continued)

Make, Model, and Year:		Estimated Depreciation[1] %		Open- or Closed-end?	
Lease	**Source**	**Contact**		**Phone #**	
#1					
#2					
#3					
#4					

ITEM	LEASE #1	LEASE #2	LEASE #3	LEASE #4
17. Other Fees & Charges[7]				
18. a. GAP Insurance	$	$	$	$
b. Comprehensive Ins.?	$	$	$	$
c. Life/Disability Ins.?	$	$	$	$
19. Total Insurance[8]	$	$	$	$
20. License & Registration	$	$	$	$
21. Taxes	$	$	$	$
22. Security Deposit[9]	$	$	$	$
23. Total Initial Payment[10]	$	$	$	$
24. Early Termination Fee?	$	$	$	$
25. Residual Value[11]	$	$	$	$
26. Acquisition Fee?	$	$	$	$
27. Purchase Option Fee?	$	$	$	$
28. Trade-in Allowance?[12]	$	$	$	$
29. Total Cost to Lease[13]	$	$	$	$
30. Capitalized Cost	$	$	$	$
31. Total Cost to Buy[14]	$	$	$	$

[7] Ask for itemized list of test charges and fees to compare with other quotes. Be sure list includes everything you'll have to pay to satisfy the terms of the lease.

[8] Add lines 18a., b., and c.

[9] Get written verification that Security Deposit will be refunded at end of lease.

[10] Add lines 14 (if down payment is required), 12 (the first monthly payment is usually included in the initial payment), and any lines from 15–17 and 19–22 that contain items that are to be paid at lease signing. Does this agree with the initial payment the lessor specified?

[11] Is this based on an estimated value, or the real Fair Market value at lease end?

[12] If you plan to trade in your old vehicle, how much will each source give you for it?

[13] Subtract line 12 from line 13, add result to line 23. Subtract line 28 (if it applies). The total will probably differ from the Capitalized Cost on line 30 that they quoted you. Call the lessor back and find out where the discrepancies occur. Ask again if there are any hidden charges they've neglected to tell you about.

[14] Add lines 29 and 24 (only if you plan to terminate the lease and buy the vehicle ahead of the specified date). Subtract line 16 (it shouldn't apply if you buy the vehicle). Subtract line 28 (if it applies). Subtract line 11 from the total to see how much more it will cost you to lease the vehicle before purchasing it. Compare that with your lowest quote for financing the vehicle with a loan and buying it up front, to see which option is a better deal.

Even those who know enough to negotiate a lower sales price before they disclose the fact that they are willing to lease often assume that the lease contract they sign is based on the price they've negotiated. In reality, many dealers write leases based on the original price, and not the price you've bargained for! Be sure the price you've negotiated is used in computing the capitalized cost on the contract.

Negotiating residual value

The amount the vehicle should be worth by the end of the lease term is called its residual value and is usually based on the vehicle's estimated rate of depreciation. In most cases, the higher the vehicle's residual value and/or your down payment, the lower your monthly payments will be. ("Pay me now or pay me later. . . .")

Insist on negotiating the lowest total cost of the lease before revealing how much you can afford to pay each month. If you don't do this, you'll find that instead of lowering the price of the vehicle to make your monthly payments more affordable, the company will simply raise the estimated residual value, increase the size of your down payment, or lengthen the lease period in order to offer you "lower" monthly payments. These maneuvers will not only leave the higher sales price and all its resultant additional costs intact, but the negative effects of a larger down payment or a longer lease period can result in higher total costs than you were subject to before these "accommodations" were made to lower your monthly payments.

If you want to buy the vehicle at the end of the lease, some contracts require you to pay residual value for it, while others specify fair market value. Although most lessors consult depreciation charts to estimate residual value, you can usually negotiate the estimate before you sign the lease. To avoid confusion, keep this rule in mind:

> *If you plan to purchase a vehicle at lease-end, negotiate the lowest residual value you can.*
>
> *If you don't want to own the vehicle, negotiate the highest possible residual value, because it will lower your monthly payments.*

Other things to keep track of during negotiations

In addition to negotiating the cost of the vehicle and the residual value, you increase your chances of getting a good deal if you make yourself aware of the points discussed in the following sections — and challenge the things that don't make sense to you.

What you're getting

Be very clear about the make, model, and options you want, especially if the vehicle you plan to lease is not on the lot. Ask the pricing sources listed in Chapter 5 for the exact cost of each option you desire. If the dealer tries to charge you the full retail price, try to negotiate a better deal. Remember that you don't have to pay for any options you haven't requested.

Length of the lease period

Although most lease periods run for 24 or 36 months, you may be able to negotiate one that meets your individual needs. Just keep in mind that *the shorter your lease, the higher your monthly payments will be.*

Rate of depreciation

Check the vehicle's estimated rate of depreciation in blue books or through pricing services. The cost of many leases is calculated by subtracting a predetermined residual value from the MSRP (manufacturer's suggested retail price). If you have no plans to buy the vehicle at lease-end, you benefit from a high estimate of its residual value. On the other hand, if you plan to purchase the vehicle, you want to be sure its value at the end of the lease has not been overestimated.

Guaranteed buy-back

To protect yourself further, try for a lease that includes a guaranteed buy-back, which means that if you decide to buy the vehicle at the end of the lease, you pay nothing more than its current fair market value.

Total cost

Be sure the quote for the total cost of the lease includes every last cent you'll have to pay, including registration, taxes, security deposit, down payment, and all the other administrative fees they'd like to collect. Contest any fees or charges that seem unreasonable.

Lease-end service charges

Inquire about lease-end service charges (including the disposition fee, which is what you may be asked to pay to get the car ready to be resold). These fees can amount to hundreds of dollars when it's time to return the car.

Sometimes called a "termination fee," a disposition fee is negotiable and can even be waived completely, so strongly object to paying it on the grounds that getting the merchandise into salable shape is part of every retailer's cost of business and is tax-deductible as an operating expense. You are already subject to penalties if the vehicle you return has suffered more than normal wear and tear, so why should you also pay to have the dealer slick it up in order to make a higher profit on its resale?

Mileage allowance

Most leasing contracts specify a mileage allowance, that is the maximum number of miles — or kilometers — that you can drive the vehicle during the lease term without having to pay excess mileage charges. In the United States, yearly allowances range from 10,000 to 15,000 miles; in Canada, from 20,000 to 24,000 kilometers. The excess mileage charge on many leases is 15 cents a mile, but can reach as high as 30 cents a mile. Even if your lease has a mileage allowance of only 10 cents a mile, you'll still have to pay $100 for every extra 1,000 miles you drive! This is an area where you may be able to negotiate a better deal:

- ✔ **Ask whether the mileage allowance places limits on how many miles you can drive each year, or whether the miles can be spread over the entire lease period.** Obviously, the latter is the better deal.

- ✔ **If you know that you'll have to exceed the specified mileage allowance, ask to have the allowance raised.** If the lessor refuses to raise it, or wants to raise your monthly payments as compensation for the possibility that the vehicle's depreciation may increase because of the extra miles you may drive, try to have the excess mileage charges lowered instead. Failing that, buy extra miles up front. They will cost you less than the penalty you'd have to pay if you exceed the mileage allowance, and they are usually refundable if you don't use them all. For instance, you may have to pay 8 cents a mile up front to add 10,000 additional miles to your lease, but those miles would probably cost you 15 cents each if they exceeded the mileage allowance at the end of the lease. The key is to be sure to investigate this *before* you sign a lease.

Make sure any changes to the mileage allowance or excess mileage charges you've negotiated are written into the lease contract before you sign it.

Have the dealer guarantee the terms of the lease

If the vehicle you want is not on the lot, find out when you can expect delivery and have the dealer guarantee the terms of the lease. If it's going to take a long time, the base value of the vehicle (its price before taxes, fees, and other costs of leasing are tacked onto it) may change before it becomes available, and you certainly don't want any unpleasant surprises.

Have an independent mechanic check a used vehicle

Be sure to have an independent mechanic check a used vehicle before you sign a lease contract. Despite the classy labels, vehicles advertised as "nearly new" or "previously owned" are used vehicles and may have hidden wear or defects that can cost you megabucks in the long run.

Because you'll be responsible for reasonable wear and tear, you don't want to have to pay for something that was "worn and torn" before you took possession of the car. Because brake pads and tires are often rated for only

40,000 miles, ask to have them replaced if they seem too worn to last for the full term and mileage of your lease. This strategy will eliminate arguments over how much wear and tear you put on them, and how worn they were at the beginning of the lease.

Questions to Ask about Leases

Besides doing the research that pertains to both leases and loans (see Chapter 10 for details), be sure to ask prospective lessors about items that are specific to leasing contracts. Use the Lease Comparison Worksheet in this chapter to compare several leases. To be sure the quotes are accurate, always specify the same make, model, year, and options, and ask the following questions:

- **Is the lease closed-ended or open-ended?** See the section called "Leasing Defined" in this chapter for an explanation of the differences between closed- and open-ended leases.

- **What is the mileage allowance, and how much will I have to pay in excess mileage charges if I exceed it?** See the "Mileage allowance" section to find out what a mileage allowance is and how it can unpleasantly affect your wallet at the end of the lease.

- **How is normal wear and tear defined, both on the vehicle itself and specifically on brakes and tires?** See the "Returning the vehicle" section for tips on how to avoid excess wear and tear charges.

- **Does the manufacturer's warranty stay in effect for the time and mileage specified in the lease?** For detailed information about warranties and service contracts, see Chapter 16.

- **Are there restrictions on who does maintenance and repair?**

- **Can I install a bike-, ski-, or roof-rack, or a trailer hitch?**

- **Does the cost of the lease include GAP insurance, or do you expect me to pay extra for it?** GAP coverage pays the difference between the insured value of the vehicle and the costs for early termination of the lease if the vehicle is stolen or totaled in an accident. If the lease includes GAP insurance, you have an opportunity to lower costs by asking the dealer to pay the charges or let you seek the insurance elsewhere at a cheaper rate.

- **Are there disposition fees for readying the vehicle for the next customer? Will any additional charges be imposed when I return the vehicle?** I think disposition fees are totally out of line! See the section called "Lease-end service charges" to find out why.

- **If I decide to purchase the vehicle at the end of the lease, will the buy-out price (what you'd have to pay to buy the vehicle at the end of the lease) be based on residual value (the estimated value at the end** of the lease) or fair market value (the actual value of the vehicle at the end of lease)?

✔ **What happens if the estimated residual value differs from the fair market value?** If the estimated residual value is different from the fair market value, you can refuse to purchase the vehicle for anything more than you'd pay to buy a similar model somewhere else. A dealer who insists you pay a higher price for a vehicle than its current value probably won't find another buyer to buy it for that higher price either, so he may agree to your terms.

✔ **How is the total cost of the lease computed?** Make them take you through this procedure step-by-step until you understand it thoroughly. As an exercise when I was writing this chapter, I used the lease terms in the small print at the bottom of many auto ads to figure out the true total cost of each lease. In most cases, there was no interest rate indicated and no way of accounting for a couple of thousand dollars' worth of discrepancies between the advertised "total cost of lease" and the payments and charges specified in the ad! I hope the new federal leasing reform regulations will change this picture.

Signing a Lease Contract

If, after reading the information in this chapter, you decide to lease a vehicle, take the following precautions before you sign anything:

✔ **Check to be sure the lease includes all the charges, fees, and other disclosures that are now required under the latest regulations of the Federal Consumer Leasing Act:**

- Your name as the lessee.

- Term of the lease, expressed in months or in the maximum amount of time you have in which to pay it off in full.

- The total amount you must pay to take delivery of the vehicle.

- The total monthly payments, including depreciation, rent charge, and any taxes and other fees that are part of these payments.

- How the monthly payments are calculated.

- Other charges in addition to the monthly payments. These can include the security deposit and fees for early termination, excess wear and tear, and excess mileage. Personal property taxes and registration fees are also not included in the monthly payments.

- An itemization of the charges that make up the gross capitalized cost.

- The capitalized cost reduction, which, like the down payment, should be subtracted from the gross capitalized cost.

- Any early termination fee and how it will be calculated if you end the lease ahead of time.

- The definition of excessive wear and tear.

- The mileage limit and excess mileage charges.

- The same trade-in credit for your old vehicle that you'd agreed upon during preliminary negotiations.

- The dollar amount and the independent pricing guide used to determine the vehicle's residual value at the end of the lease.

✔ **Be sure you understand everything before you sign anything.** Check to be sure the implicit lease rate (the figure expressed as a percentage that will enable you to compare the cost of a lease with the APR on a loan) is the one you agreed upon and that additional charges or fees haven't raised the cost above the rate you were quoted.

Because borrowing money for leases is technically different from borrowing money for loans, lessors are no longer allowed to express interest as an APR (annual percentage rate). Instead, because a lease is really a long-term rental contract, the dollar amount of interest is now often called a rent charge. Or you may see a money factor, expressed as a decimal, which is a formula that can enable you to compare the cost of a lease with the APR or interest on a loan if you multiply it by 2400. (For example, multiplying a money factor of .00321 by 2400 would give you an interest rate of 7.7 percent.)

In a recent article on leasing, *Consumer Reports* cited a range of money factors offered by different finance companies on a three-year lease for the same car as .00300 to .00457, a seemingly small difference. However, the interest rate on the lower factor amounts to 7.2 percent, and the higher factor converts to 11 percent. That's a big difference when you apply it to a vehicle that costs several thousand dollars!

✔ **Read the contract slowly and carefully.** If the terms or language is unclear, insist on taking it home to read at your leisure or to show your accountant. If the dealership refuses (a common excuse is "the forms are computer generated in numerical order and can't be printed until you're ready to sign"), ask for a photocopy of a similar contract. If you're not allowed to take even a copy of their contract home with you for review, cancel the deal and leave.

✔ **Make sure no spaces are left blank on the contract.** If you find any, draw a line through them and write N/A (not applicable) in each space. Then have the dealership initial any blanks and changes — and initial each one yourself as well.

✔ **Contest documentation fees.** Who pays you to do the paperwork associated with your job? For that matter, contest all fees and additional charges. What have you got to lose?

✔ **Refuse to pay anything until the contract has been approved by the leasing company.** Otherwise, if the financing involved is not approved, you will end up responsible for finding other financing. If you can't find other financing (or it would cost more than you're willing to pay) and you've put down enough of a down payment to take the vehicle home and drive it, and for some reason you can't return the car — you've added accessories, or damaged it, for example — you're going to be in for a nasty time.

When Your Lease Period Ends

As the time for your last monthly payment approaches, you have to decide whether to return the vehicle, buy it and keep it, or buy it and sell it. The following sections explain each of your options and offer instructions and advice that can make this decision less difficult.

Returning the vehicle

If you've got a hankering for a brand-new set of wheels, you hate the vehicle you've leased, you have good reasons for leasing a newer model, or the vehicle has seriously declined in value, returning it is the best alternative. However, before you take the vehicle back to the dealership, take the following precautions:

- **About six weeks before the lease period ends, bring the vehicle back to the dealership for an inspection.** If the inspection shows that the vehicle needs repairs, this gives you the option of doing the work yourself or seeking out the most reasonable repair facility, rather than paying high penalties for wear and tear.

- **Deal with minor repairs yourself.** Paying an independent shop to eliminate scratches and dents is almost always cheaper than paying the penalties for excess wear and tear. An estimate will tell you if this is true in your case. If you are responsible for replacing worn brakes and tires, get this done at bargain prices before you return the car.

- **Have the vehicle "detailed."** Take it to a specialist who will clean and polish the vehicle meticulously inside and out (rather than just washing and waxing it), until it looks its absolute best. Although this service is never cheap, it's worth the expense because justifying penalties for excess wear and tear on a car that looks almost as good as new is difficult.

- **Make a visual record of the vehicle's condition after you've gotten it into shape.** A video or a good set of photos will be helpful if there's a dispute. Show the absence of body damage by sighting along the sides, hood, and rear so the reflected light reveals smooth, shiny surfaces. Close-ups of the interior will testify that the upholstery, carpeting, and other equipment are in good shape and that there's been no damage to the dashboard or pedals.

Buying a set of inexpensive floor mats when you first take possession of the vehicle is a good idea — they keep the carpets looking new. Seat covers can prevent damage to upholstery, although some people — including me — find them tacky.

Keeping the vehicle

In recent years, as much as 65 percent of the lessees in the United States chose to buy their leased cars. Some benefited by it; others didn't. It usually only pays to buy under the following circumstances:

- ✔ **It would be too costly to return the vehicle.** You've exceeded your mileage allowance or gone so far beyond the limits of normal wear and tear that you'd be better off owning the vehicle than paying high penalties and disposition fees in addition to the cost of leasing or buying another one.

- ✔ **You've fallen madly in love with the vehicle.** This is fine, as long as the vehicle is in good shape, hasn't depreciated too far below the estimated residual value, and the model has an excellent repair record.

Because repairs cost you time and inconvenience as well as money, you may prefer to say a tearful farewell and continue to lease or buy vehicles that have a better chance of staying trouble-free while they're in your possession. A series of costly breakdowns can quickly ruin the most intense love affair and make you wish you'd divorced the old clunker!

Buying the vehicle and selling it

If the car's estimated residual value turns out to be much lower than the current fair market value, why not make money on the resale rather than paying disposition fees so that the dealer can sell it at a profit?

Having a good mechanic inspect a leased vehicle about a month before the lease ends is always a good idea. If, at this inspection, you discover that you'll have to pay for costly repairs when you return the car, you may decide to save money by buying it and selling it in "as is" condition. (You can get into trouble if you advertise a vehicle as being in good condition, and it turns out that you knew it needed work. See Chapter 6 for tips on selling a vehicle yourself.)

You probably won't get the full retail price (fair market value) if you sell the vehicle privately or use it as a trade-in. Also, the time and effort it takes to advertise and sell the car may prove to be more costly than paying the fees to return it. Think this option over carefully.

Part V
Insuring Your Car: How to Cover Your Automotive Assets

The 5th Wave   By Rich Tennant

"Frankly sir, issuing you reasonably priced auto insurance isn't going to be easy given the number of crashes you've been involved in."

In this part . . .

Back in the good old days, when most people could afford to purchase a house, they used to say, "Your car is the second most expensive item you'll ever buy." Today, we pay as much — or more — for a car than we once expected to invest in our residence. Because you'll probably buy more than one vehicle during your lifetime, if you don't own a home, you're likely to spend more money on vehicles than on anything else (unless you collect masterpiece paintings or large diamonds).

So what do you do to protect this major monetary outlay? Buy auto insurance, of course. But does your policy really cover your assets? This part shows you how to check your present auto insurance policy for proper and complete coverage, compare it with other available policies to see if you can do better elsewhere, and move safely through the minefields of the insurance claim process.

Chapter 13

My Premium Is *How* Much? — Shopping for Insurance

In This Chapter

▶ Understanding the things that affect your insurance rates

▶ Comparing insurance companies to find the best one

▶ Interviewing prospective insurers

▶ Knowing what discounts to ask about

▶ Saving money on your premiums

*B*ack in the good old days, when most people could afford to buy a house, they used to say, "Your car is the second most expensive item you'll ever buy." Today, most of us pay as much — or more — for a vehicle than our parents paid for a house. Because you'll probably buy more than one vehicle during your lifetime, if you don't own a home, you'll probably invest more money in vehicles than in anything else (unless you collect old masters or large diamonds).

So what do you need to do to protect this major investment? Buy auto insurance, of course. But does your present policy really cover your assets? Auto insurance is a complicated subject with many things to consider and some dangerous pitfalls along the way. This chapter explores the wide variety of factors and discounts that can affect your premiums, tells you what you need to look for in insurance coverage, and provides the questions you need to ask when interviewing prospective insurers. If you follow the information in this chapter closely, you should find the best available coverage around.

If the idea of plowing through a bunch of dry insurance data boggles your mind, perhaps the "true-life story" that follows will prompt you to buckle down and do your homework. As you follow my trail through the little adventure that was one of my main motivations for writing this book, you'll learn a lot about how to survive the minefields of an insurance claim. So consider this a learning experience.

Learning the Hard Way

One sunny day, I was driving merrily down the freeway, fully covered by auto insurance that included $100,000/$300,000 Liability, $30,000/$60,000 Uninsured/Underinsured Motorist, plus Collision and Comprehensive. I also had a million-dollar Liability umbrella policy in addition to all the above. Surely I was fully covered for whatever mayhem I could commit or anyone else could commit against me, right? Wrong!

As I crested a hill, I saw that cars were changing lanes in random, frantic patterns, like tadpoles zipping out of the way of marauding fish. Traffic suddenly ground to a stop, and I found myself trapped a few feet behind a truck. When I glanced into the rearview mirror, my heart sank. A car was zooming down the hill at full freeway speed, the driver busily engaged in conversation with her passenger. I knew she'd never see me in time. With visions of becoming a sandwich, I frantically tried to get into the next lane and out of her way. Before I could, I was rear-ended with hideous force. The good news was that my long-bed pickup prevented me from wearing her car like a necklace, and the truck ahead of me had moved so I didn't smash into it. The bad news came later.

The other driver emerged from her car and began to apologize. "Oh, I'm so sorry; it was all my fault! I was talking to my brother and had no idea that traffic had stopped. By the time I saw you, I just couldn't brake in time. Please forgive me!" I was feeling somewhat numb, except for the parts of me that were shaking, but I assured her that it could happen to anyone. "You *are* insured, aren't you?" I asked, and held my breath awaiting her reply. She assured me that she was. We exchanged information, and I called the highway patrol and my insurance company to report the accident. When I reached home, I fell into bed, and slept for the rest of the day.

I awoke with a splitting headache and the feeling that if I moved my head, it would topple off my neck. When I got out of bed, the dizziness really hit me, and I could neither walk nor think in a straight line. My chiropractor plopped a collar on my neck and sent me for x-rays. He told me that the nerves that ran from my brain down my neck and spine to various muscles, organs, and nerves had been severely yanked and twisted when the impact of the accident caused my head to slam back and forth on my neck.

"You don't have to hit your head on anything to damage your brain," he told me. "When your head snaps back and forth like that, the impact of your brain hitting the inside of your skull can cause the same kind of trauma and the effects of this kind of injury can be delayed for weeks, months, sometimes even years." He advised me to get a lawyer. "Why do I need a lawyer?" I wanted to know. "I'm insured by a top company, and the other party has admitted her guilt." "It's much more complicated than you think," he warned me. "I've seen a lot of these cases in my time."

Over the next few days, I got worse instead of better. I could hardly hold my head up without my collar, I couldn't think clearly, and my short-term memory had serious blank spots. But, as I'd hoped, my insurance company was sympathetic. They told me that the other driver had admitted her guilt and was indeed insured. Unfortunately, she only carried the minimum liability mandated by California law, which meant I could expect only $15,000 from that source. "But don't worry," they said. "Your Underinsured Motorist coverage will pick up where hers leaves off."

Then reality began to set in. Because my truck was far from new, the blue-book value only amounted to around $3,500. Company policy stipulated that repair estimates be based on original parts from the auto manufacturer, and the estimates came to a little more than $3,500, so they insisted on "totaling" my truck, selling it to a wrecker, and paying me the $3,500 to replace it. I loved my truck, which had only 35,000 miles on it and was in great condition, with a camper shell, a great sound system, and a sunroof. I knew I couldn't buy another one as good for so little money, and I was sure I could have it fixed for under $3,500 with used or aftermarket parts, but that didn't matter to them. Under their terms, it was cheaper to total my truck than fix it.

Then a friend gave me some good advice. Before I turned the truck over to the insurance company, I asked a couple of wreckers to estimate what they'd pay for it. As my pal had predicted, they offered only a few hundred dollars. Armed with these estimates, I bought my truck back from my insurers for $300, had it repaired with used parts and an inexpensive paint job, and was back on the road for under a thousand dollars!

But harder lessons were to come. When a dizzy spell knocked me right off balance, I slammed into a railing so hard I felt my ribs pop. "Now you've really done it," my chiropracter said. "Did you find a lawyer? No? Well, stop procrastinating. You're suffering from post-concussion syndrome and soft-tissue injuries, and you're definitely going to need legal help."

He wasn't the only one who felt that way. A number of friends told me horror stories about trying to be reimbursed after accidents like mine and all of them urged me to find a lawyer. A personal injury attorney agreed to take my case on a contingency basis for a third of any award I received. This seemed like a large sum to pay but, as subsequent events swiftly revealed, it was *my* insurance company he had to fight!

In California, an *anti-stacking* statute specifies that compensation from two different policies "cannot be added together." Although this law was only intended to prevent people from being doubly compensated for the same loss, it allowed my insurer to deduct the amount paid by the other insurance company from the amount due under their own underinsured motorist coverage, *even though the combined awards were not enough to pay for the damage sustained!* Although my injuries, lost wages, and other losses amounted to close to $100,000, my insurance company was able to deduct the $15,000 the other insurance company had reimbursed me from the $30,000 worth of Underinsured Motorist coverage on my policy. Instead of $45,000, at best I could only receive $30,000, leaving me $70,000 in the hole! With a third deducted to pay my lawyer, I stood to lose even more! Unfair? You bet!

To make matters worse, because I had soft-tissue injuries and am self-employed (which means my income fluctuates), my insurance company didn't even want to pay me the $15,000 I had left! Furious, I told my lawyer to sue them. They responded by requesting that we split the cost of mediation. When I angrily refused, they offered to pay for it themselves rather than go to court. "Accept it," my lawyer advised. "If we don't come to an agreement, you can always sue them."

During the next few weeks, I limped around in pain while I rounded up my tax returns for several years and obtained copies of my medical history to show that I'd never suffered from dizzy spells, damaged ribs, or neck or head injuries. I even had a neurologist verify that I was not malingering. When someone suggested I have a whole series of unnecessary tests because "the higher the medical bills you run up, the better your chance of getting a higher award," I vehemently refused. As a consumer spokesperson, that's exactly the sort of thing I'm against. But I must admit I can see where such tactics come from: If people are not fairly compensated by the coverage they've paid for, they may think it's fair to rip off the insurance companies who betrayed them. They don't realize that, ultimately, they are ripping themselves off. Inflated medical bills have driven insurance premiums sky-high. So, everybody loses.

When I thought about dealing with the opposing attorney, I realized that the only approach he was *not* prepared for was friendliness, warmth, and trust. So, instead of visualizing him as a heartless monster, I decided to view him as someone my insurer had hired to prevent unscrupulous people from receiving undeserved awards. Because I deserved the protection I'd paid for, it shouldn't be hard to convince him. Of course, my lawyer thought I was crazy. That's probably why he and the mediator placed me in another room while the negotiations took place.

I read magazines and drank tea for hours, while my lawyer and the mediator presented offers for my approval. I rejected $2,000, $5,000 and $7,000. "I believe I'm entitled to the full $30,000 I paid for, so I certainly won't take less than the $15,000 that stupid law allows." Finally, they came in with $10,000. "You'd better take this. Your insurer will never give you the whole award when they've already paid $2,000 for mediation to avoid doing just that." "No way," I replied. "But before we go to court, could I speak with the opposing attorney?" They went into a huddle, decided it couldn't hurt anything, and ushered me into the deliberation room.

I greeted the opposing attorney with a warm smile and a handshake. He looked startled. Was this the hellcat who had rejected his offers all day? I said I appreciated how swiftly his company had handled my claims in the past, and I knew that before he could give me full compensation he had to be certain that I deserved it. I said I understood that, because I had soft-tissue injuries and my income varied, it might be difficult to determine a fair award, but that I thought I could help him make an accurate estimate. He looked interested.

I settled myself into a chair and explained that, after working my way up in publishing, I'd turned down a promotion to be the publisher of a respected company because I'd finally found a way to "beat the system." The attorney leaned forward. I could hear him thinking, "Ah, she's going to reveal what a cheat she is." My attorney and the mediator looked terrified. "Many years ago," I went on, "I meditated on the nature of work and play and realized that everything one person does for fun, someone else does for money. What's more, since we usually spend eight hours of every twenty-four working, eight sleeping, and eight trying to do everything else, we only get to play if there's any time left over after we finish our chores. But if I could get paid for doing what I'd play at anyway, I'd have the system beat. And 'play for pay' is exactly what I've done ever since.

"I love writing books, and it has supported me well. I love to perform and have made 700 appearances on local and national radio and TV. As a result of this accident, I haven't been able to do what I love best. I'm in pain. My memory has suffered, I can't concentrate, and simple words escape me. Here is a letter from my publisher authorizing a new book with a generous advance; I can't write it. Here are invitations to make personal appearances; I'm in too much pain to go. Here are my tax returns for the past few years; as you can see, I earn a lot of money by 'playing for pay.'" I leaned toward him and looked him in the eyes. "Do you really believe I'd give up doing what I love and being well paid for it just to run up losses that far exceed this small award?" He looked as though I'd hit him with a brick. The mediator and my lawyer, who also looked dazed, ushered me out of the room.

A few minutes later, they were back, grinning like schoolboys. "I can't believe it," crowed the mediator. "I've never had this happen before. He gave you the full award!" He offered me a job working with him and I told him I'd consider it, but only if it seemed like fun.

Factors That Affect Your Rates

When you think of things that affect your insurance rates, no doubt you think of your driving record, and you probably also think of the type of car you drive. According to the Insurance Information Institute (III), you're right: Two of the three most important influences on auto insurance premiums are your driving record and the vehicle you choose to drive. The third is the insurance company you pick. But you may be surprised at all the other factors that can affect your rates. Read on for a real eye-opener.

Your driving record

In a world where people often try to put the blame on someone else, this is one case where you have to deal with the results of your actions. How much you pay for coverage — or whether you qualify for insurance at all — depends largely on your driving record. Most insurers offer discounts for clean records and tack on major penalties for moving violations.

A seriously deteriorated driving record, particularly if you've been cited for driving under the influence, is cause for refusing to renew coverage or dramatically raising rates in most states. Insurance companies have often succeeded, where family and friends have failed, in convincing people whose age and infirmities have seriously affected their driving to get off the road before they do further damage to themselves or others.

 Choose traffic school to avoid having an offense appear on your insurance record. Many municipal courts offer a traffic school option in the hope that you will learn to become a more cautious driver or will dislike spending a day cooped up with a struggling comedian enough to lighten up on the gas pedal. Be warned, however, that although the violation will not be disclosed to your insurance company, it will still appear on your DMV record, and the courts will really sock it to you if you do it again. Traffic school usually is restricted to drivers who haven't attended such a school in the recent past and isn't available in every area.

If your record is so bad that insurers reject you, you may be able to get high-risk, sometimes called "nonstandard risk," insurance, but be prepared to pay dearly for a long, long time.

 To find a company that specializes in high-risk insurance, check with independent agents, who may be able to suggest reputable companies, or call your state insurance department. If your violations or accidents cause even the high-risk specialists to turn you down, you can probably qualify for the "assigned-risk" insurance programs provided by states with mandatory insurance laws. These programs are compelled to accept all applicants. Assigned-risk coverage can be even more expensive than high-risk insurance, but it's better than getting arrested for driving with no insurance at all.

Keep all of this in mind the next time you take to the open road and feel the urge to morph into Speed Racer — or decide to drive after partying a little too long.

The kind of car you drive

The kind of car you drive does not affect how much you pay for Liability and Medical coverage, but it definitely influences Collision and Comprehensive coverage. Check your current vehicle against the factors listed next. You may decide to trade it for a more dependable set of wheels with lower insurance premiums, fewer repairs, and a safer ride. If this is not an option for you right now, file this stuff away until the time comes to buy another car.

"Stealability"

How likely your car is to be stolen can cost you more than the loss of the vehicle. Some vehicles are much more susceptible to theft and vandalism than others, and insurance companies charge higher premiums for insuring these. Most drivers expect to pay more to insure a classic Sunbeam Tiger with flames custom-painted on its flanks or to insure a status-enhancing "Deluxemobile." Few are aware that many less-exceptional cars also require higher premiums because they're so common that their parts bring high prices on the black market. I devote all of Chapter 17 to how you can beat the bad guys at their own games, but my best advice is to buy a less vulnerable vehicle in the first place. If you must have your Dream Car, you'll be comforted to know that insurance rates are discounted for vehicles with antitheft devices. More about that in the section of this chapter called "Check out the discounts."

Safety

Safety is its own reward. Insurance companies base their rates on claim frequency, cost of repairs, and the likelihood of damage to various vehicles. Vehicles with unfavorable collision and physical-injury records usually are responsible for higher liability and medical payments to victims, so insuring them usually costs more. Others are expensive to insure because they tend to suffer major body damage from minor accidents. Recently a lot of publicity has been given to the amount of damage light trucks and SUVs (sport utility vehicles) cause when they're involved in accidents with conventional vehicles, so you may find that trucks and SUVs have higher premiums. But, generally speaking, if you choose a vehicle with a good safety rating, you not only lower your premiums, you lower your chances of being seriously injured in an accident.

Where you live — east, west, home's best . . . or is it?

How you drive and what vehicle you drive are things you can definitely control. Other things are not so easy. Did you know that insurance rates vary widely, not only from state to state but from one neighborhood to the next? I found this out the hard way when I moved from Santa Barbara to Los Angeles. Not only did my auto insurance rates almost double, but I found that if I'd moved into a neighborhood a few blocks south of my new address, I could have saved almost $500 a year on car insurance! When I demanded to know why I should pay higher insurance premiums when my neighborhood was smaller, had only one major street, and had a lower crime rate than the one with lower rates, the answer was that my neighborhood shares the same zip code with a neighborhood just to the north that has a much higher crime rate than mine or the one to the south. The four-digit zip code *suffix* pinpoints my location to a specific *building*, so setting rates based only on the first seven digits seems grossly unfair. If they base rates on zip codes that encompass widely divergent demographics they should use the most specific zip codes possible!

How much weight is assigned to zip codes when determining rates can vary from one company to another. Because many people consider the zip code to be an unfair insurance factor, it is the subject of pending legislation in several states.

Where your car lives

For obvious reasons, vehicles that reside in covered parking spaces or locked garages may command as much as 20 percent lower premiums than those that are parked on the street.

Sources of safety records

Sources of information on a particular vehicle's insurance rating often can be found at your local library. Some are available free from the agencies that produce them.

"Injury, Collision, and Theft Losses By Make and Model" is a pamphlet produced and updated regularly by the Highway Loss Data Institute. It rates four-door and two-door cars, luxury and sports cars, vans, wagons, and utility vehicles from "Substantially Better than Average" to "Substantially Worse than Average" and is available free by calling the National Insurance Consumer Helpline (NICH) at 800-942-4242. You can also order this pamplet through the HLDI Web site at www.carsafety.org or by sending a self-addressed stamped envelope to HLDI, P.O. Box 1420, Arlington, VA 22210-1420. While you're at it, ask them for a free copy of "Nine Ways to Lower Your Auto Insurance Costs," a pamphlet that lists phone numbers for the insurance department in every state.

The Car Book, The Used Car Book, and *The Truck, Van and 4x4 Book,* all by Jack Gillis, classify insurance rates for major models of domestic and foreign cars as "Discount," "Regular," or "Surcharge" and provide auto-theft and occupant-injury data, as well. They are published annually by HarperCollins and are also available from the Center for Auto Safety. To order, write to Center for Auto Safety, 2001 S Street NW, Suite 410, Washington, DC 20009 or go to their Web site at www.autosafety.org.

Sex and the single driver

Everyone's up in arms about sexual harassment, but did you know that insurance companies not only practice sexual discrimination, but age discrimination and marital discrimination as well? Before you run off to picket, a glance at the 1995 statistics in Figure 13-1 may convince you that they have a firm basis for such practices.

Age

Younger drivers are involved in more fatal accidents. If you don't believe this, look at the next-to-last column of the chart in Figure 13-1 and compare the fatal accident rate per 100,000 drivers for drivers from 16 to 19 with the sharply declining rates of more mature drivers. To be fair, however, in a 1990 study done on the basis of miles driven by each age group, the fatal involvement rate per 100 million vehicle miles traveled for drivers aged 75 and over was 11.5, the highest of all age groups. The oldsters may not drive very far, but they certainly have an impact on the road! (When my mother was in her eighties and her driving deteriorated sharply, I convinced her that the money from selling her car, plus the thousands she'd save each year in upkeep and insurance, was more than enough to pay for as many taxis as she'd ever need, with a little left over for an occasional limousine.)

Age of Driver—Total Number and Number in Accidents, 1995

| | | | Drivers in Accidents | | | | | |
| | | | Fatal | | All | | Per No. of Drivers | |
Age Group	Number	%	Number	%	Number	%	Fatal[a]	All[b]
Total	177,432,000	100.0%	50,500	100.0%	17,600,000	100.0%	28	10
Under 16 ...	57,000	(c)	400	0.8	80,000	0.5	(d)	(d)
16	1,488,000	0.8	1,000	1.9	480,000	2.7	67	32
17	2,226,000	1.3	1,200	2.4	580,000	3.3	54	26
18	2,522,000	1.4	1,500	3.0	610,000	3.4	59	24
19	2,760,000	1.6	1,400	2.8	560,000	3.2	51	20
19 and under ..	9,052,000	5.1	5,500	10.9	2,310,000	13.0	61	26
20	2,869,000	1.6	1,600	3.2	540,000	3.1	56	19
21	2,955,000	1.7	1,500	3.0	510,000	2.9	51	17
22	3,166,000	1.8	1,400	2.8	500,000	2.8	44	16
23	3,523,000	2.0	1,400	2.8	500,000	2.8	40	14
24	3,651,000	2.1	1,400	2.8	520,000	3.0	38	14
20-24	16,164,000	9.1	7,300	14.6	2,570,000	14.6	45	16
25-34	39,442,000	22.2	12,300	24.4	4,470,000	25.4	31	11
35-44	39,409,000	22.2	10,000	19.8	3,570,000	20.3	25	9
45-54	29,045,000	16.4	6,000	11.9	2,120,000	12.0	21	7
55-64	19,240,000	10.8	3,600	7.1	1,180,000	6.7	19	6
65-74	15,938,000	9.0	2,900	5.6	840,000	4.8	18	5
75 and over ...	9,142,000	5.2	2,900	5.7	540,000	3.1	32	6

Source: Drivers in accidents based on reports from 16 state traffic authorities. Number of licensed drivers by age are from the Federal Highway Administration.
[a] Drivers in fatal accidents per 100,000 licensed drivers in each age group.
[b] Drivers in all accidents per 100 licensed drivers in each age group.
[c] Less than 0.05.
[d] Rates for drivers under age 16 are substantially overstated due to the high proportion of unlicensed drivers involved.

Figure 13-1: Whether you're a good driver or not, you're at the mercy of the stats in your age group.

©1996 National Safety Council, "Accident Facts"

Gender

Males are deadlier drivers than females. A survey by sex found that fatal accident rates per one billion miles were 27 percent for males and only 17 percent for females. These, and other surveys by the National Safety Council, bear eloquent testimony to the fact that males of any age have worse driving records than females. (Women: You may want to quote this little tidbit the next time you hear any of the males in your life complain about women drivers.)

Marital status

Married people have safer driving records than singles. If you're feeling ambivalent about matrimony, you may be happy to know that lower premiums are one of its rewards — unless you're married to a lousy driver.

One of the advantages to being a single female is that some companies offer special discounts to women between 30 and 65 who are the only drivers in their households. (If you have kids, you're still okay.) On the other hand, if you add up all the factors mentioned previously, you can see why single men pay a lot more for insurance before they turn 25.

The kind of company you keep

Married or single, kids or no kids, the people you live with make a big difference when it comes to premiums. Because insurance covers your *vehicle* (rather than *you*), your company will want to know which other members of your household drive it regularly.

Can I borrow the car keys?

Think twice before you lend your car to anyone. Because you're most likely to allow members of your family or housemates to drive your car, you can see why whom you live with has such an effect on your premium. And what if *they* lend the car to someone in your absence, or one of their friends takes the wheel because they are incapable of driving? Exactly who is covered can vary, but most policies won't cover you if you — or anyone else — lends your car to an uninsured driver or to someone who has had their license suspended or revoked. *To make sure that only responsible drivers have access to your car, specifically exclude all unreliable members of your household from your policy.*

There are other reasons for thinking twice before lending your vehicle to others: In many areas, the authorities can impound a vehicle that is driven by someone who is unlicensed or has had their driver's license suspended or revoked. If your vehicle is impounded for a month, you will have to pay for towing, administrative fees, and thirty days of storage to reclaim it at the end of the impound period. If they prove that you knew the driver was unlicensed, you can suffer misdemeanor criminal charges and fines.

If your spouse has a rotten driving record, or you have a male under 25 years of age in the house, you may be better off specifically excluding them on your policy from driving your car, and insuring them separately. This may not only save you money, but it's also a guilt-proof excuse for refusing to lend them your car. I speak from personal experience. The only way I could insure my classic car was to list myself as its only driver, and this proved to be a godsend. I could shrug and say to everyone who wanted to go joyriding, "I'd love to lend you the car, but my insurance company won't let me." It worked for valet parking, too.

If your child attends an out-of-town school and doesn't drive your car very often, you can save from 10 to 40 percent by listing them that way on your policy. This is usually better than insuring them separately and losing a multi-car discount.

Your job

Your job can also affect your insurance premiums. Underwriters classify policyholders by whether they use their vehicles for business, pleasure, commuting, or farming. From the underwriters' perspective, a person who works at home is less of a risk than one who uses the car to commute every day, and a traveling salesman who uses his car as a mobile freeway office pays more than the farmer's daughter whose vehicle spends most of its time down on the farm.

How much you drive

The longer you're on the road, the greater the chance that you'll get into trouble. That's why insurers offer lower rates on cars that are driven less than the average number of miles per year.

The groups you belong to

Group rates are usually lower than individual ones. Although few employers offer auto insurance along with health insurance packages, some groups have access to coverage with special rates and benefits. Unions, industry associations, and special-interest groups sometimes offer group coverage. If you belong to one of these, check it out:

> ✔ **The American Association of Retired Persons (AARP).** AARP offers auto insurance to its members. Along with generally lower rates, there's a lifetime continuation agreement not to cancel the policy due to age, accident, or violations. The insurer can only cancel for nonpayment of

premiums, material misrepresentation (telling lies), or license suspension or revocation. For information, call 800-932-9922 or write to the AARP at 601 E Street N.W., Washington, D.C. 20045.

The AARP also has an Auto Club that may be the only one you can join *even if you don't drive!* If you're just a passenger in someone else's car, the AARP Auto Club still covers you for towing and other services. Call 800-334-3300 (TTY: 800-235-8737) for more information.

✔ **The United Services Automobile Association (USAA).** The USAA is the insurer of choice for active and former military officers, FBI and Secret Service agents, their dependents, and even their former spouses. A cooperative, nonprofit organization, they offer a wide range of insurance coverage and services. If they make a profit, you get a check at the end of the year. For those who qualify, it's well worth checking out at 800-531-8319.

Finding the Best Insurance Coverage

The best possible insurer will offer the most complete coverage for the lowest rates and respond quickly, sympathetically, and generously when a crisis occurs. Does such a company exist? If this chapter doesn't help you find one, there ain't no such thing! Use the following guidelines to select at least four companies that appear to be good prospects, then compare them, using the Insurance Coverage Comparison Checklist in this chapter.

Check your existing policy

Before you start to look at other companies, be sure the ratings in your current policy are correct. To do so, follow these steps:

1. **Ask your insurer to consider all the factors affecting your rating code and judge whether your rating code describes your status accurately.**

   Your policy carries a "rating code," which determines how much your premium is. (The areas included in the rating code are listed in the preceding section, "Factors That Affect Your Rates.")

2. **Request a list of the discounts you are currently getting and set that list aside to compare with the list of possible discounts in the section called "Interviewing prospective insurers."**

3. **Put your insurer through the interview process described in the "Interviewing prospective insurers" section and then compare their answers with those of other companies to see whether you are getting the best deal.**

If you are considering higher limits or deductibles, ask for quotations, but don't change anything until you have a basis for comparison. Altering your current policy when you may be leaving the company for greener pastures is a waste of time.

> *Don't cancel your old coverage until you're received* written *confirmation of your new insurance.*

Get referrals

The best resource for finding almost any kind of service is a satisfied customer. Whether you're seeking a mechanic, a doctor, or an insurance company, one referral is usually better than a dozen cold calls. Try the following sources:

- **Friends, family, and business contacts.** When you ask these people about their insurance companies, you'll hear both horror stories and praise. If the response is favorable, get the name and phone number of the person's company or agent.

- **The Consumers Union Insurance Price Service (800-807-8050).** This service provides a list of up to 25 of the least expensive policies, custom-tailored to the drivers and vehicles in your household, plus service ratings, their how-to-buy-insurance guide, and money-saving tips. Service is currently limited to Arizona, California, Colorado, Florida, Georgia, Illinois, Louisiana, Nevada, New Jersey, New York, Ohio, Pennsylvania, Texas, Virginia, and Washington, but may be available in your state by the time you read this.

Use the Web

Get on the Information Superhighway and browse "insurance, autos" on electronic databases and the Internet. Locate and read articles from magazines such as *Money, Fortune, Forbes,* and *Business Week* that evaluate specific coverage or companies. Your local library will have some sort of electronic search system. If you've never used it, here's your chance to get familiar with the Internet (Chapter 21 lists lots of great Web sites).

Cruise the Yellow Pages as a last resort, but be especially careful to check out these companies through the rating services listed in the section called "Check the rating services."

Checking Out Prospective Insurers

After you amass a list of insurers (as described in the preceding section), you need to separate the wheat from the chaff, the diamonds from the dross, the good from the garbage. In other words, you need to evaluate them — and you need to pay attention to more than how expensive or cheap their premiums are. To help you get the information you need to make a good decision, the following sections outline the types of questions you should ask and the things you need to examine when choosing an insurer.

See if the company is licensed in your state

To avoid being stuck with a sleazy insurer who may leave you in the lurch, call your state insurance department to be sure each company you're considering is licensed in your state. Although state licensing programs exist, insurance companies don't have to be licensed to sell insurance in a particular state, and unlicensed companies don't need to follow state insurance regulations. They also aren't compelled to participate in state guarantee funds that pay outstanding claims if they go out of business.

You can find the phone number of your state's insurance department under "State Government Offices" in your phone book, or call the National Insurance Consumer Helpline at 800-942-4242 and request a copy of their free pamphlet "Nine Ways to Lower Your Auto Insurance Costs," which lists numbers for the insurance department in every state.

Check insurance regulations in your state or province

Major differences exist between different insurance companies, and how they sell their policies and establish their rates has a direct impact on your pocketbook. No matter where an insurance company is located, it has to abide by laws that change from state to state (or, in Canada, from province to province). If you know the regulations in your area, you have a better chance of getting the best coverage and treatment. In the United States, ask your state insurance department whether insurance policies in your area are competitive, require prior approval, or are noncompetitive. Here are the differences between those designations:

 ✔ **Competitive:** States in which rates are competitive allow insurance companies to set their own rates. In these states, it's most important to shop around before you buy.

✔ **Prior approval:** States in which rates require prior approval allow insurance companies to set their prices subject to the approval of the state insurance commission. As a result, prices in these states don't vary by much, but products and services can.

✔ **Noncompetitive:** States in which rates are noncompetitive mandate the same rates for all insurance companies, but service and other factors may vary.

Check the rating services

You certainly don't want to establish a relationship with an insurer that makes a regular habit of stonewalling its clients' claims, nor do you want your insurance company to go out of business when you have claims pending. To help you weed out the losers, check the financial stability of your prime candidates and their record of claims satisfaction.

Be certain you have the company's exact name. Disreputable insurers sometimes adopt names that are similar to those of established companies.

Several organizations specialize in rating insurance companies, and they're easy to contact:

✔ **Best's Insurance Reports, Property and Casualty.** This is the bible of the industry. You can find a copy of it in your local library. Best's rates companies financially from A+ (Superior), through A and A- (Excellent) and B+ (Very Good), to C- (Fair). It provides the address, phone number, officers, and states in which a company is licensed to do business. It does not rate for service.

✔ **Standard & Poor's Insurance Rating Services (S&P).** This is a subscriber service that rates on the basis of financial ability to pay claims. Ratings range from AAA to D. You can find a copy at your local library, or call 212-208-1527 for a free list of rated insurance companies.

✔ **Duff and Phelps.** Duff and Phelps rates the top property and casualty companies' ability to pay claims. Call its marketing department at 312-263-2610 to inquire about a specific company.

✔ **Moody's Investor Services, Inc.** This service rates about twenty property and casualty companies. Check its reports at the library.

✔ **State insurance departments.** Your state insurance department may offer lists of companies with the least and the most complaints. They may also have information on particular companies with outstandingly good or bad records.

Interview prospective insurers

Call your present company and at least four other likely prospects and grill them. To get the most competitive rates, tell everyone you're comparison-shopping.

Be sure to give each company exactly the same information, and make certain that estimates are for exactly the same coverage and deductibles.

Before you call anyone, copy the Insurance Coverage Comparison Checklist in this chapter. This checklist can help you touch all the bases and compare quotations from different companies easily.

The following questions to ask insurance agents, and the accompanying infomation, will give you all the ammunition you need to nail the best deal.

✔ **Are you a direct writer or an independent agent?**

Some insurance companies sell their policies directly, and others use independent agents. Both types of insurers have advantages and drawbacks.

Direct writers work for insurance companies that sell their policies directly to the consumer. The people you deal with are company employees, not insurance agents.

- **Pro:** Rates from direct writers may be lower because there is no middleperson. Contact with the company is more direct.

- **Con:** If you have an accident, the people you deal with will have divided loyalties, at best. You may be the policyholder, but the company is the boss.

Independent agents represent more than one insurance company. They review the policies offered by several companies and help you decide which one is best for you.

- **Pro:** In the event of an accident, your agent represents you rather than the insurance company, so they should try harder to get you the highest compensation your coverage commands.

- **Con:** Because they work on commission, using an independent agent may result in a higher premium. However, if you tell an independent agent that you have found similar coverage for a lower price, they may locate a company with more competitive rates to get your business.

After considering all the pros and cons I've found that interviewing both direct writers and independent agents and picking the company that offers the best coverage, after all the factors are considered, is the best way to go.

✔ What is your past claims experience with people like me?

For most of us, our past experience affects our present and future relationships. Insurance companies are no different: They take past claims experience into serious consideration when setting rates. One company may have had especially bad luck with young drivers; another may have found that seniors were responsible for a high proportion of claims. Because of this, unless you live in a noncompetitive state, the rates for drivers in your circumstances may differ from company to company. Ask what each company's experience has been and compare rates for the best deal.

✔ Will filing a claim raise my premiums?

Subject to state regulations, each company decides how much and how often it can increase rates and whether to cancel or refuse to renew a policy. Most companies penalize you with a surcharge on your premium for every claim you make that costs the company more than a set amount. How long the penalty stays in effect can be as long as three years. You'll usually only be subject to surcharges on claims where you were at fault, but some companies cancel or fail to renew your coverage if you have more than three claims of *any* kind within a specific period. Be sure to check each company's rules on this.

✔ How soon can I expect payment if I file a claim?

Although most states have legal limits on the time an insurance company can take to review and settle a claim, slow payment continues to be one of the most frequently heard complaints against insurers. Having to pay interest on a loan or lose interest on savings to pay medical and repair bills while your insurance company is happily collecting interest by stalling payment is infuriating. If you don't receive compensation in 30 days, send a certified letter of complaint to the company and a copy to your state insurance department. After they pay the claim, you may want to look for a more considerate insurer.

✔ How and when can you cancel or refuse to renew my coverage?

State regulations usually forbid a company to cancel your policy for anything except nonpayment of premiums, having your license suspended or revoked, committing fraud, or lying on your application. But companies have a lot more leeway when renewal time comes around. Most state laws allow insurers a specific grace period in which to review your policy and decide whether or not to renew it. Ask what that period is and what criteria they use.

To learn what the company must do to cancel or refuse to renew your coverage, as well as how you can appeal this or cancel the policy yourself, take a look at the section called "Termination" in Chapter 14.

✔ How often will my premiums rise?

Ask each company how recently and how frequently they've raised their premiums in the past. Will they guarantee your initial premium for a specific period of time? If the guarantee is only to the next renewal, how often are policies renewed? Yearly? Every six months? What's the use of starting with a low premium if it's constantly on the rise?

If you move from one location to another while your policy is in effect, your insurer can adjust your premium based on the coverage and rates in effect at your new location. If you move to another state, you'll probably be sent a new policy that complies with that state's regulations.

✔ Where does your coverage apply?

Most U.S. policies cover you in the United States, its territories, and Canada. Some extend coverage to within 50 miles south of the Mexican border, but may differentiate between what they'll pay for various areas of coverage. If you plan to travel out of the country, check to see whether the policy contains this coverage and what the exclusions are.

✔ What discounts do you offer?

Most insurance companies offer discounts from 5 percent to as much as 30 percent but, if you don't ask for a specific discount, the agent may not tell you it exists. Be sure to request a complete list of all available discounts from each agent. (See the next section, "Check out the discounts," for more information.)

Compare discounts from different companies in terms of the *total* premium you'll end up paying. Because discounts are deducted from basic premium rates, a company that offers lots of discounts may have such high basic rates that their premiums would still be higher than those of a company with a lower basic rate and fewer discounts.

Check out the discounts

If you already have auto insurance, it may be interesting to see whether you are getting all the discounts you deserve. Call your present insurer *without giving them your name,* and tell them you are shopping for insurance. Check to see which discounts they offer. If you qualify for any that you haven't been getting, call your agent and ask to be reimbursed for everything they owe you from past undiscounted premiums.

The following discounts are offered by many companies:

✔ Accident-free discounts apply on most coverage, providing you have held the policy continuously for a specified number of years (usually three) and you have not had an accident where you were at fault or where claims amounted to more than a specified minimum amount. In some policies, this discount doubles after twice as many accident-free, continuously insured years pass.

✔ **First-accident allowances** guarantee that, if you've had five accident-free years, the rates won't go up after your first chargeable accident.

✔ **Good driver discounts** are offered in many states. Most state laws define a good driver as one who

- Has been a licensed driver for a specified number of years (usually at least three).

- Has had no more than one violation point during that period. (Violation points are determined by the state vehicle code and are assigned for moving violations and accidents where you are at fault.)

- Has not, during the same period, been the at-fault driver in an accident in which anyone was injured or killed.

✔ **Conviction-free discounts** are available if the driving records of all drivers of your vehicle contain no moving-violation convictions during a specified number of years. (Again, the magic number is three.)

✔ **Good student discounts** go to unmarried high school or college students who have less than nine years of driving experience and who maintain a B or better grade-point average.

✔ **Driver training discounts** may lower rates for students who pass driver training courses at school.

✔ **Senior discounts** are usually offered to people who are 50 or over, with no unmarried drivers under 25 in their households. This discount won't apply if you are an inexperienced driver.

✔ **Mature-driver discounts** of from 2.5 to 10 percent of Liability, medical payments, and Collision coverage may apply if the main driver of your vehicle is 50 to 55 years old and has successfully completed an approved "mature driver improvement" course. Here are a few organizations that offer such courses (for other approved courses, consult your auto insurance company):

- *AARP:* "55 Alive/Mature Driving Course." Order by mail from "55 Alive," AARP, 601 E Street, NW, Washington, DC 20045.

- *AAA:* "Safe Driving for Mature Operators." Order through your local AAA Auto Club.

- *The National Safety Council:* "Coaching the Mature Driver." Call 800-544-1030 for details.

- *Amundson & Associates:* "Responsible Driver Course, Home Study Edition." The course is also available in Canada and Mexico. To order, call 800-233-0226 or write to: Responsible Driver Course, P.O. Box 109 H, Whittier, CA 90608.

✔ **Multi-car discounts** result in premium reductions of 15 to 20 percent if the policy covers more than one private passenger vehicle.

✔ **Passive-restraint discounts** on medical payments coverage are available if your car is equipped with factory-installed automatic seat belts. If your car has an air bag system, discounts for vehicles with both driver's- and passenger's-side bags currently are greater than those with driver's-side air bags only. This is another way in which insurance companies gently prod us to make auto safety a major concern.

✔ **Antilock brake discounts** may be available for cars that come equipped with them. For more about antilock brakes (ABS), see Chapter 7.

✔ **Nonsmoker discounts** on Liability, medical benefits, and Collision insurance premiums may be available. Not only are nonsmokers generally healthier, but lighting up can be dangerously distracting (especially if you burn yourself), and blowing cigarette ashes have set more than one passenger compartment on fire. Has anyone ever been sued by passengers who were forced to inhale lethal second-hand smoke?

✔ **Antitheft devices** can lower premiums by 5 to 15 percent — and keep your car from being stolen, too. Discounts apply to electronic devices that sound alarms, lock the hood or steering wheel automatically, disable the ignition, or send tracking signals to law enforcement or tracking organizations. These usually must operate "passively" (automatically) rather than manually, because there's no guarantee you'll use them if you have to set them yourself each time you park the car. For more about these, see Chapter 7.

✔ **Car pool discounts** can lower premiums by 10 to 20 percent. Car pooling also saves fuel and vehicle wear and tear, and gets you to work earlier if there's a car pool lane on your local highway.

✔ **Multi-policy discounts** may be available if you carry home, personal property, umbrella liability, or other insurance with the same insurance company, which also places you in the best possible negotiating position with them.

✔ **Long-term discounts** can lower prices by 5 to 20 percent, if you continue to renew with the same company for a long time.

✔ **Low-mileage discounts** apply if you drive your car less than a stipulated maximum number of miles each year.

Be sure to keep a copy of the Insurance Coverage Comparison Checklist handy when calling for quotations.

Evaluate the agent as well as the company

In case of an accident, your insurance agent or company representative is your first line of defense. For that reason, it may be worth a few extra dollars to pick an independent agent or a company where you can establish a relationship with an individual who will be personally responsible to you, rather than to play Russian roulette with the automated phone system of a cheaper insurer.

Make notes of your impressions of the people you speak with at each company. Are they friendly or impersonal? Do you feel comfortable with them? Do they take time to answer questions in terms you can understand? Do they offer helpful advice? Do you feel empowered to make decisions, or do they insist you leave everything in their hands? Pick an agent you feel you can trust.

Ask to see the actual policy you'll be purchasing

Most prospective insurers will provide a printed summary of the coverage you've specified and the premium you'll be expected to pay, but they don't send you the actual policy until after you've signed the contract and paid your first premium installment. When your policy finally arrives, you may have neither the time nor the inclination to read it closely, and that's why so many of us end up being severely disappointed when we try to collect. We scream that we've been ripped off, but the truth is we've probably neglected to read the "small print." If you haven't taken phone notes and checked the policy beforehand, proving that your agent misrepresented the terms is almost impossible.

Most agents will tell the truth, but not necessarily the whole truth. They may tell you as little as possible about exceptions and limitations. A good way to see whether you're dealing with someone who has both the patience and the skill to help you get the most out of your policy is to ask each of your prime candidates to give you a copy of the policy you're considering and guide you through it, page by page. If an agent claims that company regulations forbid this or refuses to devote the time to do it, look elsewhere.

Saving Money on Premium Payments

After you've found the best company with the most suitable coverage at the lowest price, the way you pay for it can save you additional money. Here are a few options to consider:

✔ **Pay the entire premium in advance.** This will enable you to avoid paying service charges.

✔ **Arrange to have monthly payments automatically withdrawn from your checking account or charged to your credit card.** This is especially good if you lack the ready cash to pay the entire premium at

INSURANCE COVERAGE COMPARISON CHECKLIST

ITEM	PRESENT COVERAGE	FIRST INSURER	SECOND INSURER	THIRD INSURER
NAME OF INSURER:				
PHONE NUMBER:				
CONTACT:				
IND. AGENT OR DIR. WRITER?				
LIABILITY:				
State Minimum: *(i.e. 15/30/5)*	/ /	/ /	/ /	/ /
Desired Coverage: *(i.e. 100/300/10)*	/ /	/ /	/ /	/ /
Bodily Injury				
Property Damage				
Medical Payments				
Personal Injury (PIP)[1]				
UNINSURED/UNDER-INSURED MOTORIST:				
COLLISION:				
Deductible *(i.e.: $250 or $500)*				
COMPREHENSIVE:				
Deductible *(i.e.: $250 or $500)*				
OTHER COVERAGE:				
Car Rental: $ per day				
Max. $				
Max. days				
Travel Expenses				
Umbrella Liability				
DISCOUNTS[2]:				
Accident Free				
First Accident Allowance				
Good Driver				
Conviction Free				
Good Student				
Driver Training				

1. If you live in a no-fault state.

2. Totals above should include discounts.
   (This is just to remind you to ask for them, and so you can compare discounts offered by each insurer.)

INSURANCE COVERAGE COMPARISON CHECKLIST (continued)

ITEM	PRESENT COVERAGE	FIRST INSURER	SECOND INSURER	THIRD INSURER
NAME OF INSURER:				
PHONE NUMBER:				
CONTACT:				
IND. AGENT OR DIR. WRITER?				
DISCOUNTS (*continued*):				
Senior				
Mature Driver				
Mutli-Car				
Multi-Policy				
Passive Restraints:				
Seat belts				
Air bags				
Anti-Lock Brakes				
Non-Smoker				
Anti-Theft Devices				
Car Pool				
Long Term				
Low Mileage				
Premium per <u>Year</u>[3]				
NOTES:				
Penalties				
Payment time limit				
Premium guarantee				
Range: US? Canada? Mexico? International?				
Legal Alternatives: (Mediation/Arbitration)				
Repair Approval?				
Rating[4]				

3. If premiums are semiannual or quarterly, adjust for yearly amount.

4. Obtain rating from your state's insurance department, *Best's*, S & P, or Moody's

once. Because they are guaranteed prompt payment, many insurers impose little or no service charge for doing this, while mailed quarterly or semiannual payments carry more expensive service charges.

As an additional advantage, after you've established an automatic payment plan at your bank or credit card company, you can probably use it to pay a large variety of bills by automatic withdrawals, phone, or computer software. This saves you time, effort, postage, and checks, and enables you to pay your bills when you are out of town.

Check yourself out

While you're checking out insurance ratings, be sure that your own credit and claims ratings are accurate and in good shape. Insurance companies often request credit and claims reports to see if a prospective client is a good risk. Your credit rating can also affect your chances of renting an apartment, getting a mortgage, borrowing money, or getting a job. It pays to call credit companies at least once a year to be sure your record is accurate — and it certainly pays to do whatever is necessary to keep your rating high.

New legislation enables you to receive a free copy of your credit report if you are unemployed and plan to seek employment within 60 days, if you are a recipient of welfare, or if a recent report is inaccurate due to fraud. The companies to contact are as follows:

Equifax (www.equifax.com)
P.O. Box 740241
Atlanta, GA 30374
800-997-2493

Experian (www.experian.com)
P.O. Box 949
Allen, TX 75013
800-397-3742

Trans Union (www.tuc.com)
Consumer Disclosure Center
P.O. Box 390
Springfield, PA 19064
800-888-4213

C.L.U.E. Reports (that's short for Comprehensive Loss Underwriting Exchange) provide a record of every insurance claim you've made in the past five years. C.L.U.E. Auto Reports lists your auto claims, and C.L.U.E. Property Reports provide a similar record of home and property claims. Each of them is available for $8 from the C.L.U.E. National Consumer Service Center (operated by Equifax) by calling 800-456-6004 in the United States. C.L.U.E. reports are also available in Canada at 800-268-5469 and in the United Kingdom as CLUE UK.

When you call, have the following information at hand:

- Your driver's license number.
- Your date of birth.
- Your social security number.
- Your 14-digit claim reference number, if you are calling about a specific claim and your insurance company has provided one.

Chapter 14

Step-by-Step through an Insurance Policy

Several kinds of auto insurance coverage are available. Some are mandatory, others are optional, depending on where you live. Although auto insurance policies differ in style, most of them are based on a standard Personal Auto Policy (PAP), like the one outlined in this chapter. Many states in the U.S. have mandated that insurance policies be "readable," but although some companies have made honest attempts to substitute familiar words for jargon, most policies are still mind-numbingly convoluted. To help you understand what you're getting, I've tried to make the following summary of standard coverage as simple as I can. Believe me, it hasn't been easy!

Get out your present policy and try to follow along, because doing this will help you evaluate your present coverage and decide whether it's worth your while to shop for a better policy.

The last section of this chapter covers no-fault insurance, the subject of a great deal of debate in recent years. Like other controversial topics, no-fault insurance has been both praised and vilified. After a lot of research, I'm convinced that it's the best kind of auto insurance, *if* it's structured properly. Unfortunately, as I write this book, relatively few states have passed no-fault laws. Whether or not you have access to no-fault insurance, understanding what it can provide may encourage you to get out there and fight for it in your state. That's why I suggest you carefully read the section that explains what no-fault insurance is, how it works, and how it can revolutionize automobile insurance.

If you are lucky enough to have no-fault insurance, significant differences will exist in the sections on Liability and Medical Payments between your policy and a standard Personal Auto Policy (PAP) like the one outlined on the following pages. The rest of your policy should deal with the same options no matter what type of insurance you have.

Keeping all your insurance policies in a safe place, like a safe-deposit box, is a good idea, because you'll be able to produce them if disaster strikes.

The Declarations Page

The Declarations page, which you should copy and keep handy for quick reference, provides the basic information about your coverage. It usually contains the following information:

- The name and address of the insurance company and your agent
- Your name and address
- The policy number
- The period of time covered by the policy
- The date the policy became effective
- The year, make, model, body style, and serial number of each vehicle covered
- The types of coverage purchased for each vehicle, the deductible, and where in the policy a description of each type of coverage can be found
- The cost of each type of coverage
- The maximum amounts that can be paid for each claim
- Your total premium
- The service charges that apply if you choose to pay in installments

The Insuring Agreement

The Insuring Agreement is the heart of the policy. It defines key words, specifies who is covered and who isn't, and explains what each type of coverage includes and excludes. Some areas are optional, others are mandatory, and you can choose the maximum amount of compensation in each case. The agreement details every type of red tape you can encounter. Read it very carefully — especially the Limits of Liability and Exclusions clauses — before signing anything.

Liability Coverage

Liability coverage specifies the maximum amount your company pays the victims of an accident when you — or those you allow to drive your car — are at fault. (The rest of the policy covers you and your vehicle, no matter who is at fault.) It also covers legal fees if you are sued.

Liability coverage is divided into Bodily Injury and Property Damage:

> ✔ **Bodily Injury.** This includes medical payments, pain and suffering, loss of income, and other negative effects that result from injuries.
>
> ✔ **Property Damage.** This specifies the maximum amount the insurer pays for damage to victims' vehicles and other property.

Liability insurance is one of the most important sources of protection you can have, and it's mandatory in many states, with minimums ranging from 10/25/5 to 50/100/25. (Here's how you read the numbers: The first number specifies the maximum amount — in thousands of dollars — that the policy will pay each victim involved in an accident; the second number specifies the maximum amount the policy will pay per accident; and the third number specifies the maximum amount the policy will pay for property damage. So liability coverage of 10/25/5 means the insurance company will pay a maximum of $10,000 for bodily injury to each victim, a maximum of $25,000 for bodily injury per accident, and up to $5,000 for property damage per accident.)

Liability minimums

Individual state minimums are often inadequate to cover the high cost of medical treatment, litigation, and auto repair. If you cause a multi-car accident, injure several people, or are sued, even 50/100/25 (up to $50,000 per victim, $100,000 per accident, and $25,000 for property damage) isn't going to go very far. The minimums are generally set for people who can barely afford mandatory auto insurance, and, if they're found liable for an accident, most of them have virtually nothing to lose. Unless you fall into that category, you should buy as much liability insurance as you can afford. In contrast, minimum Liability coverage of $250,000 is mandatory throughout Canada. That's a much more realistic figure, but it can still be inadequate coverage for a major accident.

Although high-end auto liability insurance with $300,000 or $500,000 limits is quite expensive, you'll be happy to know that a cheaper and more comprehensive form of Liability coverage is available. It's covered in the following section.

Umbrella Liability coverage

Umbrella Liability coverage is sold by many insurance companies as a separate supplemental policy. Because it comes into play when you have exhausted any other Liability coverage you may have from auto and home insurance, it's relatively inexpensive. You can buy as much as $1,000,000 of coverage for a couple of hundred dollars a year. Most insurers require that you have at least $100,000/$300,000 in auto or home liability insurance before they'll sell you a policy. But the umbrella then boosts your coverage to much higher limits for hundreds of dollars a year less than higher auto or home liability insurance would cost. Umbrella policies also cover a much wider area of liability than auto or home insurance policies do. If you have property and financial assets to protect, buying umbrella Liability coverage is absolutely the best bargain around.

If you're self-employed, a standard umbrella policy may not cover you for business-related issues. Check carefully to see whether you need special business coverage to protect you.

Supplementary coverage

Supplementary payments for bail bonds, appeal bonds, interest, lost wages, towing, renting cars while yours is being repaired or replaced, and so on are routinely included in most insurance policies, and you may not be told which of these is optional. If you're already covered for any of these items by your auto club or medical or home insurance, have these options removed from your auto policy and your premiums lowered accordingly. (Lost wages protection can cost as much as $100 a year.)

Rental car coverage

Rental car coverage, which pays for a rental car if your vehicle is out of service because of an accident, can be a terrific help, but it may contain many pitfalls:

  ✔ **Coverage may be limited to accidents where you were clearly not at fault.** If the opposing insurance company balks at accepting liability, you may find yourself without rental coverage until the case is settled. If you were at fault, you may receive no rental benefits at all. The best coverage pays for car rentals immediately, no matter who is at fault.

Personal Injury Protection: Why it's good

Personal Injury Protection (PIP) coverage provides for medical payments, wages lost due to injury, and wages of people who are hired to do work the injured person usually does. Payable by each individual's insurance company, it is a feature of no-fault insurance and may also be found on some traditional insurance policies. Federal legislation that requires states without no-fault legislation to make Personal Injury Protection available could be the solution to the current imbalance in medical coverage from one state to another.

In a study by Professor Jeffrey O'Connell — the "Father of No-Fault" who first proposed such compensation back in 1965 — the RAND Institute and the Hudson Institute showed the national adoption of this type of coverage could result in savings of up to $41 *billion* per year in the United States. I hope by the time you read this book, nationwide PIP will have become a reality. If not, you may want to join a consumer group that is actively lobbying to make this coverage available nationally or within your state.

✔ **Daily rates usually do not include sales tax.** Be sure they are at least high enough to pay for the cheapest rental model available in your area. If they aren't, ask for better terms and document your request with recent advertisements or over-the-phone quotes from several car-rental companies in your area.

✔ **Payment periods may be too short.** Payment periods must be long enough to cover you until your car is repaired or you buy another car. Coverage for ten days or two weeks may leave you without wheels too soon. A month is probably the best you can do. Some policies terminate rental car coverage the day the claim is settled. If you've been too injured to car-shop or have had to wait for the settlement check to afford another car, you will still need to rent a car until you can find a new one. Negotiating these terms while you're still shopping for insurance is better than trying to extend them when you're in trouble.

Medical Payments

This part of the policy, often referred to as *med pay,* is like health insurance. It covers the hospital, medical bills, and funeral expenses you, or members of your family who live with you, may incur as drivers, as passengers in your car or someone else's car, and even as pedestrians who are hit while walking in the street, *regardless of who caused the accident.* Med pay coverage also extends to any other passengers in your car at the time of the accident. It usually appears as a maximum per *person.*

Med pay provides compensation for dental work, eyeglasses, hearing aids, and prosthetic devices that are damaged or become necessary as a result of an accident. The limits are usually low in comparison to liability coverage, because it is assumed that you have health insurance to supplement it.

Because neither your medical insurance nor a personal liability umbrella will cover anyone who is not on your policy, be sure that the med-pay portion of your auto insurance is adequate.

Uninsured Motorists/Underinsured Motorists (UM/UIM)

This coverage protects you from other drivers who carry little or no insurance. Because many of these people don't have much in the way of assets, suing them is often futile. As a result, victims who have every right to compensation are left without recourse. UM/UIM coverage is mandatory in some states. The section "Learning the Hard Way," (the story in Chapter 13 of my experience when I encountered an underinsured motorist in an accident) shows you why I consider it as vital as Liability coverage, whether your state mandates it or not. Raising the limits on UM/UIM coverage is not very expensive. Get as much as you can afford.

Physical Damage

Physical damages insurance is divided into two areas: Collision and Comprehensive.

✔ **Collision coverage** applies when your vehicle collides with anything. It doesn't matter whether you hit another vehicle, a fence, a house, a cow, whether you fall off a bridge or roll your car. If your vehicle is damaged, you'll be reimbursed no matter who is at fault or who is driving.

Collision coverage is relatively expensive. If you value your vehicle, this protection is absolutely vital. If your car is financed, the lender or lessor will probably require it. But if you drive an older vehicle that has little or no blue-book value, it may not be worth paying for this type of protection, because your insurer may choose to "total" the car (confiscate it and give you whatever they think it's worth) rather than pay for damages. If your vehicle falls into this category, setting aside the money that you'd normally spend on Collision premiums to pay for repairs or apply toward your next vehicle is a better idea. "Learning the Hard Way" in Chapter 13 tells you how I managed to recover a truck that had been totaled by my insurance company and collect the money for it, as well.

Some insurers also provide "Collision with Uninsured Motor Vehicles" coverage. If you collide with an uninsured vehicle, this coverage either pays the deductible on your Collision coverage or up to a specified amount if you have no Collision coverage.

✔ **Comprehensive coverage** applies to damage caused by something other than collision. Here's the list I found on my present policy: "Breakage of glass, loss caused by missiles, falling objects, fire, theft, larceny, explosion, earthquake, windstorm, hail, water, flood, malicious mischief or vandalism, riot or civil commotion." It also specifies "loss due to hitting or being hit by an animal." Would UFOs be considered "falling objects?"

Neither Collision nor Comprehensive coverage pays for maintenance or mechanical problems due to ordinary wear and tear or defects in the car itself, nor do they cover you for tire damage due to road conditions. Electronic equipment, such as sound systems, radar, and car phones, may not be covered either, but your auto insurance company may be willing to endorse them separately. Before you go for this option, however, check to see whether these items are covered by your household insurance policy.

Physical damage deductibles

These deductibles allow your insurance company to subtract a specified amount before reimbursing you for Collision or Comprehensive damages. For example, if you suffer $2,500 in damages and you have a $500 deductible, your company only pays you $2,000. You can choose the amount of your deductible or opt for no deductible at all. The higher the amount the company is permitted to deduct, the lower the premium you pay.

Because you can lose accident-free discounts and acquire premium surcharges that may cost more than your repairs if you involve your insurance company in minor accidents, paying for low deductibles you'll probably never use is foolish. Ask for rates for deductibles of $250, $500, and $1,000. Then estimate how much you can pay for damages without causing yourself pain, and set your deductible as high as possible.

Limits of liability for physical damage

These limits specify the maximum your insurer pays for Collision and Comprehensive damages. Under the terms of most policies, the company can choose to pay you the "actual cash value" of your vehicle or the cost of repair or replacement, whichever is less. This means they can decide whether to repair your vehicle or total it. How these terms are defined can differ from one policy to the next, and some policies offer better options than others.

Investigating this part of each policy very carefully is important. Question each agent closely, and, if you aren't sure what you're being offered, ask to see the actual policy before you make a decision.

Here is the way these terms are defined in one fairly representative contract:

- **Actual cash value** is "determined by the market value, age, and condition at the time the loss occurred." But who makes that determination? Most agents will tell you that, in the event of an accident, the company will send an investigator to look at the vehicle and estimate its value. If you ask what criteria the estimators use or how they value a stolen vehicle, you're usually told that they rely on books that quote prices for specific makes, models, and years.

- **Specified Limit of Liability** is an option that some companies offer as an alternative to "actual cash value." It allows you to specify an exact valuation for your vehicle at the time the policy is written and guarantees that the company will pay up to that amount for repair or reimbursement. If you have a classic car or one that's unique for one reason or another, consider this option.

To prove that your vehicle is worth the amount you specify, submit appraisals by qualified experts; estimates from repair shops or dealers that specialize in your make and model; classified ads; or listings in car collectors' magazines like *Hemmings Motor News,* whose classified ads are the "bible" for enthusiasts interested in buying or selling their classic vehicles and parts. This publication can be found at most libraries, and it's also on the Web at www.hmn.com. If establishing your vehicle's value seems like a lot of trouble, think how much better it is to do this while your car is in good condition rather than having to go through the same procedure after it's stolen or seriously damaged.

- **The cost of repair and replacement** is usually either based on the cost of repair agreed upon by both you and the insurance company or the lower amount of the following:

  - A competitive bid approved by the insurance company

  - A written estimate based on the prevailing competitive price

A typical policy defines the *prevailing competitive price* as "determined by labor rates, parts prices, and material prices charged by a substantial number of repair facilities in the area, as determined by a survey made *by the insurance company.*" (Emphasis mine.) Some companies provide a list of shops that will make repairs at approved prices and may even "reward" you (actually you have a good chance of being ripped off) for using a facility they've pre-approved. (To find your own repair shop, see Chapter 18.)

Pre-approved repair shops

"Pre-approved" repair facilities can be mutually profitable if the repair facilities chosen by the insurance company are committed to providing the

What it's worth — what to do when you and your insurance company disagree

Most policies give the impression that a valuation is strictly up to the insurance company, but that isn't really true. If your company wants to pay you less than what you think it would take to replace your vehicle with a similar one, you can look up your car's rating in the _Kelley Blue Book_ (from which the generic term "blue-book value" derives), the _NADA (National Automobile Dealers Association) Used Car Guide,_ or the _Red Book_ published by National Market Reports. At least one of these should be available at your local library, bank, or loan agency.

If you feel your vehicle is worth more than blue-book value because it has features that haven't been considered, you can document its worth with recent photographs, service records, and current classified ads for similar vehicles, and have your mechanic or a dealership that specializes in your type of vehicle submit their estimate of its current value. If your company undervalues your vehicle after an accident and the amount involved is high enough, it may be worthwhile to seek legal remedies. You can find out more about those in Chapter 15.

finest work at the lowest price. Unfortunately, to keep costs down, some insurers compel the shops they approve to skimp on repairs and use cheap aftermarket parts instead of OEM (Original Equipment from the Manufacturer). If this is the case, you may find yourself being coerced by your insurer in a variety of ways:

- ✔ If estimates for high-quality repairs from a legitimate shop exceed estimates from low-quality, company-approved shops, you may be forced to pay the difference to get repairs done properly.

- ✔ You may be threatened with higher premiums if you don't use an approved facility.

- ✔ You may be asked to sign a document giving the insurer the right to use any replacement parts they want. (You won't be told that aftermarket replacement parts often don't fit as well or last as long as OEM parts.)

- ✔ You may be told that repairs done by unapproved shops will not be covered by the insurance company's approval or warranty.

- ✔ After being told that "all parts will carry a lifetime guarantee," you may find that there is no record of any such guarantee at all.

- ✔ On the other hand, your company may total your wonderful old vehicle, if the cost of labor and OEM parts exceeds its book value, and refuse to use aftermarket or used parts even though you are willing to accept them. (See "Learning the Hard Way" in Chapter 13 to learn how I foiled my insurance company when it did this to me.)

If this leaves you feeling that the insurance company often holds all the cards, that's exactly the impression they'd like you to have. The truth is, you should have the right to pick your own repair facility, and your insurer should accept it on the basis of only one estimate, if it doesn't seem inordinately high.

It is illegal in many states for an insurer to even suggest — let alone force — you to use a particular shop for repairs. You can avoid these pitfalls by choosing an insurer that allows you to select the repair facility without incurring any penalties. Get that assurance in writing. Then, if your company offers a list of approved shops, checking them out is okay, but don't hesitate to choose another facility that offers original parts and high-quality repairs. To locate such a shop, see Chapter 18.

The other side of the coin — non-preapproved repair shops

Many repair shops submit enormously inflated estimates when they know an insurance company is involved. If these estimates exceed the value of your vehicle, it increases the likelihood of the car being totaled rather than repaired. Ironically, in reaction to allegations that many insurers base their "prevailing competitive prices" on repairs using poorly constructed, nonoriginal parts, some policies attempt to protect the consumer by specifying that only OEM parts can be used. This protection is great if you're repairing a relatively new car. However, if your vehicle is an older model, with a relatively low blue-book value, or a classic for which OEM parts are no longer available, it would be nice to have the option to have it repaired with high-quality used, rebuilt, or nonoriginal parts rather than have it totaled because OEM parts cost more than the car is worth or cannot be obtained. Ideally, I'd like to have the best of both options: a policy that specifies OEM replacements but allows me to waive that requirement to prevent my vehicle from being totaled.

The Settlement of Loss Section

This section of the policy provides more details on how the company can decide to compensate you. It usually spells out their right to decide whether to repair or total your vehicle, return stolen property or confiscate it at an agreed value, and whether deductions will be applied or waived. Although it usually specifies that you cannot make these decisions yourself, you'll be happy to know that you still have some room to maneuver. If you adore your car, and your insurer insists on totaling it, you can try the tactics I used to buy my truck back and have it repaired (see "Learning the Hard Way" in Chapter 13). Just be sure that the purchase estimates you get from wreckers and the estimates you get for repairs are lower than, or at least equal to, the compensation you'll get from the insurance company.

On the other hand, if you hate your car and would rather be compensated for totaling it, you'll probably be happy with the highest estimates you can find. Just be sure that you'll receive enough to replace your vehicle after they subtract your deductible from your old clunker's blue-book value. (Forgot about that, didn't you?)

Out-of-State Coverage

Out-of-State Coverage explains what your company will do if you get into an accident outside the state where your vehicle usually resides, if the area has different rules and regulations. A good policy will agree to meet the minimums required by the local government if they are higher than the maximums on your present coverage.

Other Insurance

The term "Other Insurance" refers to situations where more than one insurance policy is involved. It spells out exactly what share this policy will pay, explains what the "pecking order" is for various kinds of compensation from different sources, and stipulates that you can't receive more than you deserve, no matter how many policies are involved.

Conditions, Duties, and General Provisions

These are additional headings you may find. They differ from one policy to the next, but they all have the same intent — to set definite limits on what you can expect from your policy in a variety of circumstances, including the following:

- ✔ **Bankruptcy:** This explains what happens to coverage in the event that your insurance company goes bankrupt.

- ✔ **Changes of terms:** This stipulates under what conditions terms can be changed and how you will be notified of any changes.

- ✔ **Fraud:** This defines insurance fraud and outlines the actions that the company can take in the event that a fraudulent claim is made.

- ✔ **Recovery of payment:** This explains how you will be paid in the event of a claim.

- ✔ **Change of residence:** This tells you what you need to do if you move.

- ✔ **Termination:** This explains how and under what conditions the policy can be canceled. You can find more details about this in the "Termination" section that follows.

- ✔ **Legal action against the company:** This explains the rules that apply in the event that you want to take legal action against the company. I get into this more closely in the section called "Legal Actions against the Company," later in this chapter.

Most of these are fairly straightforward, but you must check the last two carefully when comparing policies. The following sections take a closer look at them.

Termination

Most state laws regulate how, and under what circumstances, a policy can be canceled. In most cases, no matter who cancels, the notice must be given in writing.

Because most contracts specify that "in writing" just means First Class mail to your last known address or to the address on the Declarations page of your policy, keeping your insurance company up-to-date on your current address is vitally important. If you don't, and you fail to receive notice that your policy was canceled, you may find yourself with no coverage if your vehicle is stolen or an accident occurs.

If you decide to cancel your contract, you should send your notice via Certified mail, Return Receipt Requested, so that you have a record of notification. If you switch your coverage to another insurer, your new insurer usually handles this for you, but I'd notify my company just the same (after the new policy has been approved).

A contract can end for a variety of reasons:

- ✔ **The insurer can terminate your contract while it is still in effect.** State laws usually only allow this if you haven't paid your premiums, if you've committed fraud, if you've lied on your application, or if you, any member of your family, *or anyone you customarily loan your car to* has had their license suspended or revoked. (Another good reason to be very careful about whom you allow to use your car!)

  To give you time to find other coverage, the company must mail you notice of cancellation within a specified number of days before your policy terminates. It must also return any unused portion of your premium. If you feel your insurer has been unfair, the National Insurance Consumer Helpline (800-942-4242) or your state insurance department will have advice on your options for appeal.

✔ **The insurer can refuse to renew your policy when your current coverage expires.** It can also choose to raise your premium at that time. Your agreement should require them to notify you within at least 20 to 30 days before your policy is due to end if they decide not to renew.

✔ **You can cancel your policy at any time and receive the unused portion of your premium, provided that you notify the company in writing before the cancellation date you choose.** You should also call the company, especially if your letter might not reach it by the final date.

Legal Actions against the Company

These clauses set the rules that apply if suits are brought against the company. Although at first glance they only seem to deal with disagreements with other drivers and their insurers about what your company — and possibly you — must pay in damages, they also may apply if you disagree with your own insurer about compensation or cancellation. It definitely pays to read this section carefully when comparing policies, because these clauses stipulate the type of legal action open to you.

Mediation and arbitration are alternatives that may be specified in some contracts. Both remedies call for hiring a third party to help both sides in the dispute settle out of court. Court trials are expensive for everyone concerned (except the lawyers), and an arbitrated case can be settled in three or four months instead of the three years or more it may take to go through the courts, so these remedies are well worth considering. Because the powers of mediators and arbitrators differ, understanding which alternative you are agreeing to before you sign a contract is important. The key is to make sure that if you aren't satisfied with the results of the alternative method, you still retain the right to go to court.

✔ **Mediation** simply allows a mediator to encourage the opposing sides to reach a settlement by bringing them together. A mediator can make suggestions but has no power to make decisions. If no agreement is reached through mediation, the case can go to court.

✔ **Nonbinding arbitration** empowers the arbitrator to make a decision, but both parties must agree to it. If they disagree, they can either continue to negotiate or they can go to court.

✔ **Binding arbitration** sets the arbitrator up as a judge. Both parties agree to accept his or her final decision, whether they like it or not.

✔ **Judicial arbitration** is not a matter of choice for either your insurance company or yourself, but it may be to your advantage to know your rights. In lawsuits worth less than $50,000, the judge may avoid the time and expense of a trial by appointing an arbitrator to try to settle out of court. If you don't agree with the decision of the arbitrator, your attorney can then make a motion for a trial *de novo* (a new trial). Often, rather than face the additional expense of going back to court, your insurance company may respond with a slightly higher offer than the arbitrator proposed, and you can probably negotiate a satisfactory compromise.

In my opinion, mediation and nonbinding arbitration are the best choices. They avoid the expense of court trials (which insurance companies can afford more easily than we can) and still allow us to continue to fight for a fair settlement. (To decide whether or not you should seek legal help, read the section called "Seeking Legal Help: Should You or Shouldn't You" in Chapter 15.)

No-Fault Insurance: Is It As Good As It Sounds?

As you can see, many pitfalls lie on the road to proper compensation through traditional insurance. Wouldn't it be nice if we could cut the need for expensive litigation to a minimum and empower each individual to set his or her own priorities for reimbursement? Along with health care reform, no-fault insurance has been a hot topic for many years.

Basically, *no-fault insurance* calls for your own insurance company to reimburse you for damages, regardless of who was at fault. How much you are entitled to receive is limited by the amount of coverage you choose to buy. You retain the right to sue if damages are particularly drastic or costly. Consumer activists, think tanks, and many insurance companies all seem to agree that no-fault insurance compensates victims more efficiently and offers them the best protection, while lowering costs considerably for everyone involved. Sounds great, doesn't it? Unfortunately, it isn't universally available. Read on, and you'll understand why.

No-fault means less litigation

The biggest obstacle to a no-fault insurance system is that it can only be instituted as the result of legislation. In the United States, in the absence of a federal mandate, each state has to create its own set of no-fault standards and then put it on the ballot for approval. In several states, no-fault has been a reality for years. Elsewhere, proposed no-fault systems have failed to meet with approval or have never been offered. Unless the public comes to understand the issue clearly, we may shilly-shally around for years to come.

To make an educated choice about no-fault insurance, you have to understand the traditional *tort,* or fault-based, system it seeks to replace. Under traditional auto insurance, as the victim, you must prove that the other driver was at fault before the other driver's insurance company will compensate you. This process can lead to costly negotiations by insurance companies to ascertain whose client was guilty, and the rising cost of these negotiations has radically inflated insurance premiums. In California, legal fees consume 20 percent of every premium dollar, and the situation throughout the rest of the country isn't much better.

To make matters worse, receiving the compensation you deserve without the aid of a lawyer is often very difficult. How much you are compensated usually depends on how aggressively your attorney pursues your case, and lawyers working for a percentage of the award are highly motivated to drive awards as high as they can. As a result, insurance premiums have risen drastically. On the other end of the spectrum, those who cannot command legal representation often get little or no compensation.

Under a no-fault system, there should be little need for lawyers. You are paid by your insurance company *no matter who is at fault,* and you get what you've paid for. Consequently, less opportunity exists for overcompensation and fraudulent claims. (According to a RAND study, 35 to 42 percent of all medical costs submitted in support of auto injury claims are excessive.) You're also much less likely to be sued if you injure someone in an accident. With all of this in mind, it doesn't take a genius to see which group is lobbying *against* no-fault insurance.

No-fault means fewer uninsured motorists

The rising cost of coverage has forced many people to drive with little or no insurance because they can't afford the premiums. As a result, in many cases, the guilty driver is underinsured or not insured at all. Compensating policyholders for accidents caused by uninsured motorists drives premiums even higher, so more and more people can't afford insurance. It's a prime example of the snake biting its own tail.

Currently, although you can't register a vehicle without proof of insurance in California, 5.8 million uninsured Californians are driving around, at a cost to policyholders of a *billion* dollars a year. A nationwide study showed that hit-and-run and uninsured drivers were responsible for about 13 percent of all auto injuries.

A good no-fault system would reduce insurance premiums by eliminating the necessity to split awards with lawyers or subsidize uninsured or underinsured motorists. Coverage would be affordable because drivers could choose as much compensation as they could pay for, and uninsured drivers would have to cover their own losses. In this way, no-fault puts responsibility into the hands of each individual. However, if you are the victim of an accident that is too horrendous to be covered by your no-fault policy, no-fault insurance doesn't deny you legal recourse, as explained in the following section.

No-fault protects your right to sue

Perhaps the biggest misconception about no-fault is that it could prohibit you from suing if you've been unfairly treated. Fortunately, this is not so. If you disagree about how much compensation you deserve, require additional compensation for major injuries, or are the victim of negligence or criminal behavior, you do not lose your right to go to court! Although existing and proposed no-fault systems vary from state to state, under most plans you are still able to sue

- ✔ Insurance companies that act in bad faith.
- ✔ Convicted drunk drivers and those guilty of felonious conduct.
- ✔ Automakers, if faulty construction contributes to an accident.
- ✔ If you suffer permanent, disfiguring, or disabling injuries, or require extra assistance to function after an accident.

Traditional systems encourage cheating on medical expenses

Traditional systems compensate victims for medical expenses and for non-economic — or general — damages, such as pain and suffering and loss of work. Because general damages cannot usually be stated in dollars and cents, most evaluations are based on the medical expenses incurred. As a result, there's great incentive to run up the biggest medical bills possible.

As you can see from the information in Figure 14-1, under traditional insurance systems, if your medical bills amount to $700, your award for general damages would be an additional $1,400. But if your doctor charges you $1,100, you get $2,200 for general damages. In view of this, only a saint would insist on keeping medical expenses to a minimum, especially because a large chunk of most awards goes to pay an attorney. What people don't realize is that we all lose by this system in the long run. Inflated awards for excessive claims have been estimated to add $13 to $18 billion to our insurance premiums — an average of $100 to $130 that each of us must pay every year.

Figure 14-1:
Traditional fault-based systems encourage fraudulent claims.

MEDICAL CLAIM = $700		MEDICAL CLAIM = $1,100	
Compensation		Compensation	
Medical costs	General damages	Medical costs	General damages
$700	$1,400	$1,100	$2,200

No-fault thresholds

All no-fault systems contain *thresholds,* or minimum levels of injury that must be sustained before you can collect compensation. Verbal-threshold and dollar-threshold systems are two major types of no-fault insurance in use or under consideration, and the differences in how each evaluates injuries can have a major effect on the number of fraudulent claims. In both cases, the higher the threshold, the lower the cost of the insurance and the shorter the delay in payment.

Dollar-threshold systems

Dollar-threshold systems base compensation on the monetary cost of the injuries, and you don't get general damages unless your medical bills exceed a specified amount. As you can see in Figure 14-2, if the dollar threshold in your state is $1,000, and you only sustain $700 worth of injuries, you could lose as much as $1,400 in general damages. As a result, there is almost as great an incentive to magnify your injuries under this system as there is under traditional insurance.

	MEDICAL CLAIM = $700		MEDICAL CLAIM = $1,100	
	Compensation		Compensation	
	Medical costs	General damages	Medical costs	General damages
Traditional	$700	$1,400	$1,100	$2,200
Dollar no-fault ($1,000 threshold)	$700	—	$1,100	$2,200

Figure 14-2: Dollar-threshold systems can encourage excessive claims.

Verbal-threshold systems

Verbal-threshold systems only allow victims to sue for pain and suffering if their injuries meet specific standards. These range from fractures to disfigurement, severe physical impairment, dismemberment, and death. Fractures, major burns, and other easily perceived injuries are described as hard-tissue injuries. Soft-tissue injuries, such as strains, sprains, and mental/emotional injuries cause pain that can only be described. Soft-tissue injuries are generally disallowed because they are *thought* to be short-term, are usually difficult to prove, and can be relatively inexpensive to treat.

Unfortunately, as I found out the hard way, soft-tissue injuries like the post-concussion syndrome I suffered as the result of an accident, can severely affect memory, impair the ability to work or even think clearly, and cause intermittent pain for two years or more — sometimes permanently. Despite the undeniable fact that soft-tissue injuries are faked in many fraudulent claims, it is becoming increasingly apparent that the incidence and severity of disability from this kind of injury afflicts a great number of honest victims of auto accidents. How soft-tissue injuries are compensated under an existing or proposed no-fault system in your state should be a matter of great concern to you. However, if soft-tissue injuries receive proper medical evaluation as severe impairments, then a verbal threshold no-fault system would encourage people to report their claims honestly (see Figure 14-3).

Figure 14-3:
Verbal-threshold systems encourage honest claims.

	MEDICAL CLAIM = $700		MEDICAL CLAIM = $1,100	
	Compensation		Compensation	
	Medical costs	General damages	Medical costs	General damages
Traditional	$700	$1,400	$1,100	$2,200
Dollar no-fault ($1,000 threshold)	$700	—	$1,100	$2,200
Verbal no-fault	**$700**	—	**$1,100**	—

Take action to promote no-fault insurance

If what you've read about no-fault insurance has convinced you that this kind of reform is necessary, don't just complain about the attorneys and politicos who have blocked it from becoming a reality in most states. Devoting a little time and energy to promoting no-fault may not only pay off in better insurance coverage, it may give you the satisfaction of knowing that, as individuals, we each really do have the power to bring about important change!

Here are some of the things you can do to promote no-fault insurance:

- **Call your state representatives and demand no-fault insurance reform.**
- **Write letters to newspapers.**
- **Call radio talk shows.**
- **Call the White House Hotline (202-456-1111) and send a message to the president that you want universal automotive no-fault insurance.**

You can also use this number to comment on any other national issues that concern you. I find it great for letting off steam and doing my bit to influence executive decisions. What's the use of complaining about how the president handles things if you don't let him know what you think?

Chapter 15

How to Protect Your Insurance Claim When Things Go Wrong

. . . .

In This Chapter

▶ Knowing what to do when you're in an accident

▶ Filing a claim so that you get the best and fastest resolution

▶ Understanding how a claim is processed and what you can do if you disagree with the claims adjuster

▶ Receiving settlement amounts from your (or the other person's) insurance company

▶ Knowing when you need an attorney and when you don't

▶ Getting estimates and finding a reliable body shop

▶ Stopping insurance fraud and protecting yourself from common scams

. . . .

*I*f you're lucky, you'll never have to think twice about the information in this chapter. You'll be able to drive along, avoiding accidents and all the unpleasant stuff that follows — insurance claims, police reports, medical bills for injuries, and everything else. Most of us, though, aren't that fortunate. Even the best, most careful drivers among us become the victims (or cause) of accidents. In fact, so many things conspire against a perfect driving record — bad road conditions, an upsetting day at the office, children fighting in the backseat, and just being in the wrong place at the wrong time — that it's safe to say that you probably *will*, at some point, find yourself on the explaining end of an accident report.

When that happens, make sure you know what to do and when. This chapter gives you all the information you need, both at the scene of an accident and afterward, when dealing with insurance companies — yours and theirs — can be just as fraught with danger as the accident itself. To help you find your way through these minefields, I also provide a way to determine whether or not you need to hire legal help. I wrap up the chapter with a section on insurance fraud — something that can definitely make things go wrong! Fraud is more common that you think, and it has drastically affected insurance rates. Whatever your questions about handling problems with your insurance claim, this chapter has the answers you need to get through unscathed.

What to Do at the Scene of an Accident

The proper procedure for filing a claim begins right at the scene of the accident. Don't wait to be told what to do by your insurance company. Instead, take control of the procedure from the moment the accident occurs. Although both *Auto Repair For Dummies* and *Driving For Dummies: The Glove Compartment Guide* (IDG Books Worldwide, Inc.) both cover in detail what to do in case of an accident, the suggestions that follow can help prevent problems with your insurance claim.

Be prepared

Carry the following items in your vehicle at all times; they can save your hide in an accident:

- **A pad of paper and a pencil** to jot down name, address, license numbers, and insurance information of the other person (or people) involved, names, phone numbers, and license plate numbers of witnesses, and other important details
- **A cheap disposable camera** to take pictures of the accident scene and damage
- **A cellular phone** to call for help

A cellular phone is one of the most effective safety devices around. If you can barely afford the basic monthly rate, just use the phone for emergencies (free cellular phones are often provided as incentives by a variety of companies). Only give the number to a few close friends and family members, and tell them to use it only as a last resort.

If you get in the habit of driving and talking on the phone, you can cause accidents instead of preventing them. The National Highway Traffic Safety Association (NHTSA) reports that driver inattention is a primary or contributing factor in as many as 50 percent of all crashes and cites cellular telephone use as a causal factor.

Get help for the injured

Obviously, the most important thing to do after an accident is to take care of anyone who's injured. Before emergency medical help arrives, you can cover the victims to keep them warm, but *don't try to move them and don't give them anything to drink.* Good Samaritans have found themselves sued by the very people they tried to help. Of course, if someone is in danger of being drowned, burned, or killed by an exploding fuel tank, throw caution to the wind and get them away from the vehicle.

Get witnesses

Immediately look around for people who witnessed the accident and ask them for their names and phone numbers. If you have time, ask them what they saw and make notes in case they forget later on. If they refuse to cooperate, write down their license plate numbers so they can be contacted by your insurance company and subpoenaed if the case goes to court.

Call the police

You should not move your vehicle or leave the scene of an accident until the police have been notified. If people are injured or the flow of traffic has been seriously disrupted, dial 911 on your cellular phone or at a call box or pay phone — if there's one within sight of the accident — or ask someone else to do so. If there's no emergency, do not dial 911, but do notify the local police or highway patrol. When help arrives, take an active part in assuring that you'll have the best possible record of the accident by doing the following:

✔ Write down the names and badge numbers of the police officers and other emergency personnel that arrive at the scene.

✔ Request that both you and the other driver be given breath tests, if you think the other driver has been drinking or using drugs — and you haven't.

✔ Be sure the officer's accident report includes a complete list of the people in the other vehicle and that all spaces for additional names are crossed out.

✔ Ask how you can obtain a copy of the police report — you need it to document your claim.

Carefully document the accident

Documenting the accident is vitally important, no matter who you feel was at fault. Resist the urge to panic or get angry. Even if another driver agrees to forget the incident or to settle it between you, documenting vital information may prove your innocence or save you from exaggerated claims, if he or she later decides to sue.

Get it in writing

Jot down these vital details about each of the vehicles involved in the accident:

✔ **The other vehicles' VINs (vehicle identification numbers) and license plate numbers.** Don't forget to note the state or province. Ask to see vehicle registrations; if a car is registered to someone other than the driver, be sure to get that person's name and address, too.

✔ **The make, model, and year of each vehicle, plus a short description that includes its color and any visible damage.** Note which damage appears unrelated to the accident. (Obviously, if you rear-ended a car, you didn't smash its front headlight!)

✔ **The drivers' names, addresses, phone numbers, driver's license numbers, ages, and any disabilities (such as the need for corrective glasses) that you see on their driver's licenses.** Check to be sure the name and address on each license are current ones. Some people marry or move without having their driver's licenses updated.

✔ **The drivers' auto insurance carriers and policy numbers.** If possible, get the addresses and/or phone numbers of their insurance agents. Some states now require drivers to carry that information in their vehicles, and many insurers provide little cards with these details each time the insurance policy is renewed.

✔ **The names and phone numbers of any passengers in each vehicle, including yours.** Take the time to describe the other passengers: how many there were, their approximate ages, where they were sitting, and any signs of disabilities or injuries — including those that seemed unrelated to the accident.

Get pictures of the scene

Don't allow anyone to move the vehicles until you have photographed the scene accurately. Use your camera, or draw a sketch and ask each driver to initial it to show agreement with what you've drawn. Be sure to record the following details:

✔ **Close-ups of all sides of each vehicle** that show pre-existing damage as well as damage from the accident.

✔ **Long shots of the accident scene** that indicate the location of all vehicles involved.

✔ **Close-ups of any visible injuries to people** (if you can do so without offending them), such as cuts, burns, or abrasions.

Write a brief description of what happened

Within 24 hours, the physical and emotional trauma of even a minor accident can erase details from your mind that can make or break an insurance case. Before you leave the scene, or immediately afterward while the details are still fresh in your mind, jot down the following:

✔ Time of day

✔ Weather conditions

✔ Road surface

✔ Traffic conditions

✔ How fast you were going

✔ What happened

Your notes can be as simple as "Tues. 3/15, 6:45 p.m., dark, rainy, foggy. Asphalt road with potholes. Heavy traffic in both directions. Light turned green as I approached at about 25 mph. Other car entered intersection against the light, without slowing. I couldn't stop in time to avoid collision, and I hit its left rear fender. Other driver emerged from car, appeared unhurt, and apologized for running the light. No passengers in either vehicle. When I asked if he was injured, he said he felt fine. I feel dizzy and have sharp pain in left side of neck."

If you suffer injuries as a passenger or a pedestrian, you are eligible to recover damages from the other drivers' Medical Payments coverage and from their Liability coverage, if fault is established. Although your health insurance company should cover your injuries, they may then go to the other drivers' insurers for reimbursement. If they do, *be sure they recover any deductible you may have had to meet and return it to you.*

Filing a Claim

The way you go about filing a claim can make or break your chances of getting all the benefits of the premiums you've paid. Take all the following steps to give yourself every possible advantage.

Decide where to file the claim

If the other driver is insured and is at fault, you have the option of filing a claim directly against the other driver's insurance company or filing a claim with your own insurer. There are trade-offs involved in each case:

✔ **If you go to your own insurer:** Your insurer will pay you directly from your coverage, so you'll probably get the money more quickly. But it will subtract your deductible from its payment and, if it turns out that you were even partially at fault, it will impose penalties on your future premiums. If the other driver was at fault, your insurer should pay your immediate bills and then ask the other insurance company to reimburse the money your insurer has paid you, *including your deductible.* If you choose this scenario, be sure to remind your agent to return the deductible to you.

✔ **If you go directly to the other driver's insurer:** If the other driver's insurer agrees that he or she was guilty, it will pay you the full amount with no deductible, and your driving record with your own insurer will remain intact with no penalties. But if it finds you even partially at fault, it will go back to your insurer for damages, and you will end up in the soup anyway.

Believe me, the other driver's insurer will try to blame you if it can, so unless you are absolutely certain that you have no responsibility for any aspect of the accident, letting your own insurer carry the ball for you may be the wisest thing to do.

Always notify your insurance company

Even if you don't expect to file a claim or have decided to file directly against the other driver's insurer, be sure to tell your own company, at the earliest possible opportunity, that an accident has occurred. Insurers can only penalize you if you file a claim and are found at fault, so you have nothing to lose by simply notifying them. On the other hand, some insurance companies have time limits for filing claims and, if the other driver suddenly decides to sue you, your company may use late notification as a reason for refusing to handle your claim. At the very least, postponing notification can prevent your insurer from acquiring the firsthand evidence they may need to defend you.

Evaluate whether or not to file a claim by asking your agent the following questions:

✔ **Is this situation covered by my policy?**

✔ **Will my losses exceed my deductible if I file with you?**

✔ **What effect will filing this claim have on my future insurance premiums?**

If you file a claim, make sure that the benefits you'll be paid after your deductible has been met exceed any premium penalties you stand to incur over the next few years for being involved in an accident. If the other driver is clearly at fault, filing a claim against him or her will not negatively affect your coverage. If you are at fault, and there are no injuries and only minor damage, you may save money by paying for the repairs yourself.

✔ **Is there a time limit on how long I can wait before filing a claim?**

✔ **How much time will it take to process my claim? Is there a limit on how long you can take to resolve it?**

✔ **Does my coverage include renting a car? How much per day does it provide? For how long?**

✔ **Do I need to submit repair estimates? If so, how many?**

✔ **Do you have an approved repair facility program?** If there are rewards for selecting an insurer-approved repair facility, it pays to check out the ones nearest you, but get estimates from independent body shops as well. (See the section in this chapter called "Choosing a Reliable Body Shop" and Chapter 18 for help in finding a reputable "car doctor" and making sure the work is done to your satisfaction.)

✔ What other documentation do I need to submit?

✔ Will you follow my claim through to resolution? If not, who will? How can I contact them directly?

Gather all the necessary documentation

Get everything in writing (see the earlier section "Carefully document the accident" to find out what information you need to get at the scene of the accident), keep the originals, and send copies to the insurer. Here's what to do with this information and with all the other reams of paperwork you'll probably amass before your claim is settled:

✔ **Get a large file folder and use it to store *everything*.** This includes all your correspondence, phone notes, police reports, notes you made at the accident, photographs, repair estimates and invoices, car-rental invoices, medical bills, legal bills, and bills for other expenses, such as additional help you've had to hire to do the work you can't handle because of your injuries, records of lost wages, even duplications and postage.

If you decide to hire legal aid, give your lawyer copies of everything, but *always keep the originals in your file.*

✔ **Take notes during phone conversations.** These notes don't have to be terribly detailed; just jot down the date, who called whom, the other person's name and phone number, and each point that's made. Put arrows in the margin pointing to things that need to be followed up. When you speak to the person again, check the arrows to be sure you touch all the bases and add additional notes in a different colored pen. These phone notes will be extremely valuable to an attorney who comes in after the claim is under way. I've gotten into the habit of doing this with every phone call, and I can't tell you how many times I've profited by it when people have changed their estimates or have failed to do what they said they would.

✔ **Send a summary letter every time you meet with your insurers or speak with them on the phone.** Use your notes to be sure it contains everything you talked about and any information you'd like to add. Keep it light and friendly, but address every issue. This letter prevents them from making promises that they fail to keep and shows them that you are keeping a close eye on the progress of your claim. If you decide that you need legal help, this written record alerts your lawyer to whether your insurer has misled you or changed its position on any aspect of your case. Figure 15-1 shows a sample summary letter.

✔ *Don't* **make repairs until your insurer has had time to see your car.** How can they evaluate the damage if you've already had it fixed?

✔ *Don't* **cash checks from other drivers or their insurers without your agent's consent.** If you do, you may invalidate your claim for additional damages.

June 1, 1998

Jack Jones, Customer Representative
Acme Insurance Company
400 Main Street
Anytown, CA 90000

Re: Account #9999999

Dear Mr. Jones,

Thanks so much for taking the time to answer my questions the other day. I was happy to hear that I can file a claim any time within 60 days after the accident and that your company promises to settle the claim within the next six months.

Because the accident was clearly the other driver's fault and I will not incur any penalties for filing my claim, you estimated that the damages I stand to recover will amount to at least $1,000. Consequently, I'll probably file a claim in the near future.

When I get repair estimates from local body shops, I'll also check out TipTop Bodywork, which is recommended by your company. But I'm aware that I can choose any repair facility I like, if their estimate is within prevailing competitive prices in my area.

If any of the above information is incorrect, please let me know. I'd also like to be kept informed of events as they occur, while the claim is in process.

It's nice to know that you will be responsible for my claim, and I look forward to working with you.

Sincerely,

Figure 15-1:
A friendly, but thorough, summary letter can help you avoid broken promises.

How a Claim Is Processed

After you notify the insurer by phone (and letter) that you are filing a claim, an adjuster will probably contact you within the next day or two. If the claim is for a minor fender bender, your agent may handle it over the telephone, but in most cases, you won't get off that easily. To give you the edge in dealing with adjusters, you should have a clear idea of their role in your case.

Claims adjusters wear two hats:

- ✔ **Claims adjusters are responsible for getting you the best settlement possible.** Because their primary job is to be sure that the benefits paid by the company are reasonable and fair, they're on your side, because inflated awards result in higher premiums for everyone. *But always remember that they work for your insurer.*

- ✔ **Claims adjusters are "insurance detectives."** They may personally inspect damaged vehicles, visit the accident scene, take statements from everyone involved, even track down witnesses. Although the police report may say that you're innocent, the bad news is that police reports are not legally conclusive, and you may still be found at least partially guilty for what occurred. If you are, your guilt can seriously affect your compensation.

Adjusters can request access to medical reports and monitor treatment to make sure the injuries that you or anyone else sustains were really caused by the accident. They can also request proof of lost earnings and any other expenses you claim. They will go over the repair estimates, decide whether to repair or total your car, and keep track of what repairs are made.

The following sections offer advice on how you can protect your best interests without alienating the person who can help you — the claims adjuster.

Develop a cordial working relationship

Try to get along with the adjuster. While taking a firm stand to protect your interests is important, it never pays to make an enemy of the person with the key to the cash box. Start out with the assumption that the adjuster is fair, honest, and genuinely desires to help you get the compensation you deserve. From my own experience, this often transforms tigers into pussycats. At the same time, keep tabs on everything that is going on and do not hesitate to disagree if you feel an unfair decision has been made. If you disagree, try to do it in a warm, friendly manner. There's a big difference between saying, "I'm sure that when you have a clearer picture of this, you'll see it my way," and "I knew you'd try to cheat me, you creep!"

You don't have to accept an adjuster's estimate of what it will cost to repair the damage to your vehicle, and no insurer can force you to have work done at a specific shop. If the adjuster wants to choose the place with the lowest bid and you don't feel they're going to do good work, it's quite within your rights to refuse in favor of a more reliable shop whose estimate was reasonable. Consult the section "Choosing a Reliable Body Shop" for help.

Bedtime reading for claims adjusters

A pamphlet distributed by CPU, an insurance underwriters' association, assures us that "Despite what some people believe, adjusters are not rewarded for minimizing claim payments. Rather, they are judged on the number of claims they resolve, the promptness and quality of their reports, their promptness in settling a claim, the number of complaints against them, and their compliance with company rules." With a little luck, your adjuster will have read this pamphlet.

Call your agent if you're not satisfied

If your good intentions fail to get you satisfaction, call your agent — or the adjuster's supervisor, if you're dealing directly with the company — and ask for help. Then present your case in writing, with all pertinent documents attached. If that doesn't get results, send the same package to the manager of your insurer's claims department and to the vice president of customer service or consumer affairs. You can also contact a consumer representative at your state's insurance department. If all else fails, check out the section in this chapter called "Seeking Legal Help: Should You or Shouldn't You?" for information on hiring an attorney, and the "Legal Actions against the Company" section in Chapter 14. Then review the terms of your policy and go for it!

Beware of the "Betterment Game"

If an insurer really wants to get sticky, and you have an older vehicle, the company may invoke a concept called "betterment" and try to reduce your compensation because the new parts used to replace damaged older parts have, hypothetically, raised the value of your vehicle! You can combat this by getting estimates from used-car dealers to show that your vehicle would not fetch a higher price just because some of its parts are new.

Another form of the betterment game is to deduct a prorated share of the cost of replacing parts, like tires, that have to be periodically replaced anyway. My argument would be that, if not for the accident, you'd still be driving happily on your old tires. If they want to go out and find a set of used tires with precisely the same amount of wear as your old ones, they're welcome to do just that. However, if they want to save themselves time and trouble by simply installing new ones, they must pay for them.

Settling a Claim

When you've reached a mutually agreeable settlement, you receive a final check for damages, minus your deductible. If you have a car loan, the check may be made out to both you and the lender, especially if the vehicle has been totaled and the lender deserves reimbursement.

If the car just needs to be repaired, you can save yourself the effort of having to get every check endorsed by the lender if you ask them to notify your insurer that the checks can be made out directly to you.

Sometimes an insurer will pay for repairs or medical treatment before the whole claim is settled. Before cashing these checks, make sure you haven't signed anything that says that your acceptance of the money releases the insurer from further obligation. Lots of people get caught by this one, so stay on your toes!

When you're ready to have your vehicle repaired, you need to choose a competent, reliable body shop. You can find out how to do that in the section called "Choosing a Reliable Body Shop" at the end of this chapter.

If your insurance claim is disputed by your insurance company, or the other person's insurance company is stonewalling a fair settlement, and you don't feel you're getting fair and reasonable compensation for the damage and injury you've suffered, you have the right to take legal action. Unfortunately, these situations are very common, so knowing whether you should get a lawyer is crucial. The section that follows helps you to make a decision that can save — or cost — you a great deal of money.

Seeking Legal Help: Should You or Shouldn't You?

Whether you need a lawyer to represent you depends on a number of factors, not the least of which is who is at fault and whether your insurance company (and the other person's insurance company) can reach a satisfactory settlement. Read the following sections for help in making these decisions, and remember the old Gypsy curse: "May you be involved in a long-term lawsuit, and be certain that you are right!"

Pro bono and contingency

If you do decide that hiring a lawyer is in your best interest, you should seek a lawyer who works *pro bono* on a *contingency basis*.

Personal injury cases are almost always handled *pro bono,* which means the attorney works for a percentage of the settlement. This arrangement should motivate the lawyers you approach to be extremely realistic about whether or not your case is worth pursuing at all. If your attorney wins the case, he or she will usually demand from 33.3 percent — if the case is settled out of court — to more than 40 percent, if litigation is required.

If you lose your case, you have to pay your lawyer's fees and possibly the winner's court costs, too.

Unless you are obviously guilty and need an attorney to cut your losses to a minimum or to defend you from possible imprisonment, the best thing you can do is seek a lawyer who will take your case on a *contingency basis,* which means that your lawyer gets paid only if you win. If several lawyers refuse to work on this basis, it's a sign that your chances of vindication are probably not worth your time and money.

Deciding whether you need an attorney

If you need a determination as to how much your case is worth, an attorney can give you a realistic estimate, provide advice and assistance on persuasive documentation, and represent you if you can't get a fair deal on your own.

Can you settle out of court?

If, in the event of a dispute, your insurance contract calls for mediation or arbitration, either of which calls for a third party to help settle the dispute out of court, is it still necessary to hire a lawyer? Unfortunately, in most cases the answer is "Yes." An attorney can protect your interests in all cases of mediation, but having an attorney present is especially important in the case of either binding arbitration or judicial arbitration, in which the arbiter's decision is final, whether you like it or not. (For more detail on mediation and the types of arbitration, see Chapter 14.)

If the other driver has the same insurance company as you do, consult an attorney if there's any question as to who is at fault, or if you don't feel you're being offered sufficient damages by the insurer.

If the other driver is insured by another company, and there is a question as to who is at fault, you can probably wait until your insurance company has given it its best shot before deciding whether you need legal help. Your insurer will provide and pay for an attorney if its feels you need one. Your insurer's legal staff has every motivation to go to bat for you, because they're the ones who'll have to pay damages (up to the limits of your policy) if you're found guilty. This doesn't mean that you can just lay back and let them carry the ball, however. Make it very clear that you want to be kept informed about their progress, not just the results of the negotiations. If you disagree with how your insurer's lawyers are handling things, or if both insurers find you guilty and the damages amount to more than your coverage, you may want to hire your own attorney to keep your penalties to a minimum. Just remember that you will be responsible for paying his or her fees.

Who's guilty?

If the other driver is clearly guilty, you may or may not need legal assistance. If the driver has sufficient insurance to reimburse you completely and his or her insurance company is willing to pay, your insurance company can probably handle everything. However, if your insurer shows signs of settling for less than you deserve, bring your legal guns into action.

If the other driver is clearly guilty but is uninsured or underinsured, you may or may not need legal help. If your UM/UIM (Uninsured Motorist/ Underinsured Motorist) coverage is sufficient to reimburse you, and your insurer is willing to compensate you fairly, you're in great shape. But if your insurer offers you less than you feel you deserve, try to find an attorney who will take your case on a contingency basis.

A lawyer who must work for a percentage of whatever you are awarded is probably the best person to tell you how much you can reasonably expect to receive. If you will end up with little more — or even less — than the original offer, after legal fees are deducted, you'll probably be told that pursuing the matter is not worthwhile for either you or your attorney.

If you are obviously guilty, your company will certainly be motivated to negotiate damages for you; but having your own legal watchdog on the job as well is probably best. This is especially important if you carry a low amount of liability, and major penalties — or a prison term — are at stake. To prevent costly litigation, your insurer may settle swiftly and leave you holding the bag.

If you're injured

If you are seriously injured and aren't being offered enough to meet your expenses or if you disagree with the medical treatment the insurer will cover, legal representation is vitally important.

If you have *soft-tissue* injuries, such as post-concussion syndrome or damaged muscles, cartilage, or ligaments, rather than broken bones, having legal help on your side is especially important. Although your medical bills, loss of work, and pain and suffering are very real, mustering sufficient empirical proof is difficult. More and more insurers are "stonewalling" on compensation for these hard-to-prove injuries. If they can't see it on an x-ray, they just don't want to believe it.

If it appears that the nature of your injuries will make it difficult to prove how much compensation you deserve, consult a lawyer about what you can reasonably expect. Then, document your injuries and treatment meticulously and let your insurer negotiate the best settlement it can, with your lawyer serving as a watchdog. If it looks as though your insurer isn't pressing hard enough to get you a fair settlement, command your watchdog to attack.

If the prospect of getting involved in a lawsuit gives you the heebie-jeebies, you may want to become an enthusiastic supporter of no-fault insurance, which allows you to pay for as much coverage as you can afford and be compensated for damage, injury, and liability without having to rely on the other people or insurance companies involved in an accident for compensation. You can find the details in Chapter 14, in the section called "No-Fault Insurance: Is It As Good as It Sounds?"

After your claim is processed and your insurance company gives you the "go-ahead" to have your vehicle repaired, you may think you're almost out of the woods. Unfortunately, there are still pitfalls on the road to your car's complete recovery. In order to ensure that the work is done swiftly and properly, you have to find your way past the unscrupulous wolves that may be lying in wait for a bite of your insurance money, and find an honest, competent facility to repair your car.

Choosing a Reliable Body Shop

Just as you want to find the doctor who can best heal your injuries after an accident, it's important to find a shop that will repair your vehicle properly. Chapter 18 provides general information on how to find a good repair facility. Selecting the best body-repair specialist isn't difficult — if you know what to look for and ask the right questions.

Obtain at least three reasonable estimates. Don't submit any estimate to your insurer that is substantially lower than all the others. Chances are the workmanship or the parts would be shoddy. If your first three estimates are spaced widely apart, get more of them until you can identify the shops that charge reasonable prices.

The following sections explain how to pick a reputable — and reasonably priced — shop from the horde of candidates out there.

Ask questions

Be sure to get the answers to the following questions in writing, right on each estimate, so you can make comparisons and get satisfaction if things go wrong:

✔ **Do you employ the latest high-tech equipment?** Body shops can range from back-alley garages with spray booths curtained off from the rest of the area by a plastic tarp, to sophisticated specialists that use lasers, sonar pulses, electric eyes, and computer scanning to measure damage; robots to measure and correct alignment; and advanced filtration, environmentally sealed paint booths, color-matching CD-ROMs, infrared drying lights, and high-temperature finishing processes to perform miracles of cosmetic repair. If your vehicle is badly damaged and you want to restore it to near perfection, ask each shop you call if it has this kind of equipment.

✔ **Do you do all the work in-house or send some of it out?** Most body shops are not equipped to refinish chrome, but an established facility should be able to repair or replace body panels, install new parts, and do the paint work themselves. Why should you have your poor, injured vehicle dragged all over town and then possibly have to pay more so both your shop and an outside specialist can make a profit? You can protect yourself by saying that you'll expect to see the invoices for new parts and any outside labor involved.

✔ **What kind of materials will you use?** Unless you want to keep costs down to avoid having your vehicle totaled, or unless original parts for it are no longer available, ask each shop to confirm that they will use only OEM (original equipment) parts and paint. They should also indicate whether they plan to replace large parts, such as fenders, or just restore them. If the latter is the case, stipulate that they must use sheet metal rather than plastic body-filler to repair major dents and holes. If the estimates for this kind of first-rate work are so high that your insurer threatens to total a vehicle you'd rather keep, go back for lower estimates based on high-quality fillers and used, rebuilt, or aftermarket parts.

✔ **What guarantees and warranties apply to the parts and labor involved?** Some insurance companies guarantee any work they authorize. If yours doesn't, be sure the repair facility will be responsible if problems develop.

Visit the shops

Look around each shop you visit. Is it clean and well organized or a disaster area? Are the paint booths sealed and ventilated? (It takes a very clean environment to do a good paint job.) Also look at the cars that are being repaired. If you see a number of relatively high-priced vehicles, the shop probably has a good reputation.

Check out the shop's work

Ask to see a vehicle that the shop has finished repairing. Find out which areas were damaged and restored and look them over carefully. Do it the way the experts do it:

✔ **Sight along the surface to see if there are ripples, bumps, or depressions.** The body should look "as good as new."

✔ **Check the edges of the hood, rear deck, and doors.** Make sure that they are smoothly aligned with the body.

✔ **Open the doors, the hood, and the trunk.** Are the inside edges neatly painted, or are there oversprayed or unsprayed areas on those surfaces?

✔ **Look at the door handles, chrome, and other fittings.** Were they removed before the car was painted so the paint could extend under them? Or just masked, leaving unpainted spaces around the edges that can develop rust?

✔ **Do the newly painted parts match the parts that weren't repainted?**

The last question is one you should ask yourself: *Would you be satisfied with the work if this vehicle was yours?*

Don't Be Victimized by Insurance Fraud

It's easy to see how fraudulent insurance claims have affected all of us. Premiums have soared due to the drastic rise in the number of fraudulent claims. Compensation paid for exaggerated injuries and staged accidents accounts for a major share of an estimated $20 billion a year in property and casualty insurance fraud. Insurance companies have become paranoid and have tightened their regulations and restrictions until many victims with legitimate injuries have to hire lawyers and part with a large share of their awards in order to receive any compensation at all. Perhaps the worst aspect of insurance fraud is that it can actually place your life in danger. Here are some examples of the kinds of scams that cause great losses to everyone but the perpetrators.

Road kills

You are driving along the highway when disaster strikes without warning. For no apparent reason, the car in front of you stops short, and you cannot stop in time to avoid crashing into it. The driver of the car stumbles out, apparently in pain, and a passenger in that car also seems afflicted. The next thing you know, you are being sued for major damages. Your insurance company pays the bills and then imposes penalties on you that drastically inflate your premiums for at least three years. Even if you come out of the accident physically unscathed, the experience causes you anxiety that may never go away. You are no longer confident on the road, driving becomes a chore instead of a pleasure, and your life is limited in many ways because you no longer feel free to just jump in the car and go. If children, animals, or other passengers are in your car, they may suffer negative effects as well. To add insult to injury, there's a good chance that the entire episode was staged — a cold-blooded case of insurance fraud. If this scenario sounds overly pessimistic, just ask the people who've been through it, such as Bob or Anne in the following stories.

Bob, an elderly friend of mine, was on vacation. One day he drove to a remote lookout with a beautiful view. When he started to leave, the driver — and sole occupant — of the only other vehicle at the site tried to crowd him off the narrow access path. Bob stopped immediately, but the other vehicle kept going until it scraped against his car. Confused and upset, my friend rolled down his window and asked what was going on. The next thing he knew, the other driver — a huge man — forcibly dragged him out of his car, punched him in the nose, and hurled him to the ground, breaking his arm.

When Bob complained to the local authorities, he was amazed to find that the other driver had filed a complaint charging *him* with vehicular and personal assault! By the time the case reached the courts, the other driver was also claiming that two children were in his car, plus the usual elderly aunt, and that they all had been injured. When he turned out to be an off-duty police officer located in that district, guess who narrowly escaped imprisonment, went through months of expensive litigation, and suffered the only real physical injuries in the case?

Anne was in a minor fender bender that resulted in a couple of tiny dings on the other car's rear bumper. The other driver apologized for causing the accident, and they agreed to forget it. She then sued Anne for the full cost of major dental work for her three children. After a frantic series of ads calling for witnesses, two people came forward to testify that the kids had not appeared to be hurt, upset, or in pain, and dental experts testified that the "injuries" to the kids' mouths were nothing more than crooked teeth that could benefit from braces. There must be an easier way to raise money for orthodontia!

If you want to keep from becoming a victim of scams like these, and other forms of highway robbery, you can find a wealth of information in Chapter 17.

Insurance fraud has many faces

The wide variety of fraudulent activity related to insurance bears unsavory testimony to human ingenuity. The most publicized perpetrators are highly organized interstate and international gangs with hundreds of unscrupulous drivers, passengers, false witnesses, crooked doctors, lawyers, mechanics, body shops, and even insurance agents, on their payrolls.

One ring used the same car to report 85 different claims and collected more than three-quarters of a million dollars from several insurers. Even big business gets into the act: A major auto rental firm has been found guilty of billing customers and their insurers millions of dollars in fraudulent auto repairs. But the most numerous perpetrators of insurance fraud are "ordinary people" who don't consider themselves criminals and feel it's fair to make money at the expense of "big, bad, wealthy insurance corporations." The National Insurance Crime Bureau (NICB) estimates that 15 to 20 percent of auto theft claims involve fraud, often with the collusion of the owner. Here's a list of the most common forms of insurance fraud:

- ✔ Listing an adult as the primary driver when the primary driver of a car is actually under 21

- ✔ Withholding information about past accidents, tickets, and claims

- ✔ Including pre-existing damage to the vehicle when submitting a claim

- ✔ Continuing to see a doctor after crash-related injuries have healed

- ✔ Lying about how an accident occurred

- ✔ Not returning to work after injuries are healed in order to get a higher settlement

- ✔ Claiming a higher value for a stolen vehicle than it's actually worth

- ✔ Abandoning a vehicle and reporting it stolen

What you can do to combat insurance fraud

If any of the scams in the preceding section sound familiar, you'll be pleased to know that you don't have to just sit by and let the situation continue. The sections that follow give you specific actions you can take to combat insurance fraud.

Be honest

According to a widespread spiritual belief, whatever you do comes back to you "three times three," which means that if you cheat your insurance company out of $350, sooner or later you stand to lose more than $1,000. When you consider how inflated medical awards alone have raised insurance premiums, you may agree with me that this belief is probably true.

If you've been responsible for any of the fraudulent maneuvers I've listed and didn't feel guilty, the next time your insurance premium is raised, remember that you were partially responsible for it. If you have an accident in the future, be willing to be truthful about the claims you make. If you are injured, don't just sign blank medical forms and go along with whatever your doctor and lawyer may suggest. Check to see that your doctor only charges for services that you required and actually received.

Take action to promote reforms

Simply acknowledging the problem isn't enough. Each of us has the responsibility to take action to remedy the situation. If you've read the section called "No-Fault Insurance: Is It as Good as It Sounds?" in Chapter 14, and you're convinced that we need universal no-fault insurance, are you willing to do your part to make it a reality? If you are, take the time to take the actions to promote reforms that are suggested at the end of that section. If we, the ultimate victims of insurance fraud, don't get involved, how can we expect others to go out of their way to protect us?

Call an insurance fraud hot line

The NICB Hot Line (800-TEL-NICB) is open twenty-four hours a day, seven days a week, worldwide. It provides confidential help for people who feel they have been victims of any type of insurance fraud or simply want to report suspicious activities.

Always protect yourself. Some fake accidents are preludes to carjacking. You can find lots of tips on how to stay safe on the road and during accidents that seem suspicious in Chapter 17.

Part VI
Protecting Your Investment

In this part . . .

What do repair shops, car thieves, and warranties have in common? In each case, the small print (words and fingertips) is worth watching out for because your hearty investment is at stake. In this part, I explain what you can do to find a reliable repair facility, understand and take advantage of your warranties, and protect yourself and your property from carjackers and car thieves.

This part also includes a car rental chapter, a great source for finding out how to save a ton of money (nearly half the regular rental rate) and cover yourself from liabilities when you drive a car that isn't yours.

Chapter 16

Warranties and Service Contracts on New and Used Vehicles

*N*ew and used vehicles come with a variety of warranties and service contracts. Unless you know what your options are, when something goes wrong there's an excellent chance that the coverage you agreed to will leave you unprotected and uncompensated.

Both warranties and service contracts are promises to perform or pay for certain repairs and services, but that's about all they have in common. Warranties are included in the sales price when you buy a vehicle. Service contracts are sold separately at extra cost and can be bought at any time. This chapter helps you negotiate the most comprehensive warranty available and avoid the pitfalls associated with service contracts.

New and used vehicles are not the only products that are covered by warranties and service contracts. The Magnuson-Moss Act (a federal law covering warranties) covers warranties on everything you buy, so keep this chapter in mind whenever you purchase something that's covered by a warranty or service contract.

Types of Warranties

A warranty is a promise to stand behind a product. It can be made by the manufacturer or by a dealer and can cover and exclude any number of things. The following sections take a look at the different types of warranties you may encounter in the United States and Canada. Keep in mind that various systems and parts may be covered by separate full or limited warranties. Because warranty programs vary widely, take the time to compare them closely. You'll find data about specific warranties on new and used cars in the following pages.

Basic warranties

A basic warranty on a new or used vehicle should *always* include the following benefits:

- ✔ It should cover anyone who owns the vehicle during the warranty period, not just the original purchaser.

  Be sure that all warranties can be transferred if you sell your vehicle within the warranty period. Most factory warranties allow you to do this at no additional cost, but second owners are excluded on some leased vehicles.

- ✔ All included services should be free of charge, including removing and reinstalling any system involved.

- ✔ If the dealer is unable to repair the vehicle or part after a reasonable number of attempts, you should be able to choose between a full replacement or a full refund as compensation.

- ✔ You will not be required to perform any duty as a precondition for receiving warranty service, except notifying the dealer that service is needed and having the required maintenance done at the specified times.

- ✔ No limits can be placed on the duration of "implied warranties" (see "Implied warranties" later in this chapter).

Keep in mind that even "bumper-to-bumper" warranties contain exclusions. Some items and circumstances are not covered at all. The following are often excluded from the warranty:

- ✔ Normal wear and tear

- ✔ Normal maintenance costs and damage from improper maintenance, which can void the warranty as well

- ✔ Damage from "acts of God" and improper use by owners or passengers

Additional warranties and special services

Warranties are often broken down into separate coverage for particular items and services. Some items, including tires, sound equipment, and batteries, may be warranted separately by their manufacturers. The first two of the following three warranties should come with your vehicle; the third *may* be included:

- ✔ **Power train and major-component warranties:** These should include at least the engine, transmission, and drive train, and may extend to the steering, suspension, and electrical systems. Power train warranties usually cover longer periods than basic warranties.

- ✔ **Corrosion warranties:** These warranties cover holes in the body due to rust. Some warranties do not cover minor surface or "cosmetic" rust from chipped or damaged paint.

  If you allow a dealer or an independent shop to "rustproof" your new vehicle, you may be in danger of voiding the corrosion warranty.

  Canadian corrosion warranties currently cover from one to three years for surface corrosion and five years or 80,000 kilometers for rust perforation (holes in the body due to rust). Although corrosion warranties are voluntary, Canadian car manufacturers have set these standards and agreed to comply with them.

- ✔ **Roadside assistance programs:** These types of programs may be offered under some warranties. Most of these cover on-the-road help and/or towing for flats, dead batteries, lack of gas, and other common problems. Some programs also lend you a vehicle while yours is in the shop. These programs are sometimes offered to buyers of luxury vehicles at no extra charge, while other warranties offer these programs as optional extras that you can purchase.

Limited warranties

A limited warranty excludes one or more of the benefits found in most basic warranties. It may only cover specific systems instead of the entire vehicle, or it may stipulate that you pay some of the costs of repairs. The Magnuson-Moss Act specifies that dealers must post a Buyers' Guide on all used cars for sale (see the section called "Understanding the Buyers' Guide sticker" for information about Buyers' Guides and the terms that must be spelled out in them when a used car is sold with a limited warranty).

Implied warranties

Implied warranties are kind of invisible. Although they don't appear in the paperwork covering warranties, they protect almost every new or used car bought from a dealer. Laws in every state demand that implied warranties be honored unless the dealer tells you *in writing* that they do not apply. Following are two implied warranties that may come in handy:

- ✔ **A warranty of merchantability** guarantees that a product will do what it's supposed to do, which means that the vehicle you buy should run.

- ✔ **A warranty of fitness** for a particular purpose means that if you tell the dealer you want a vehicle that can pull a trailer, the one he sells you has to be able to do that.

Unless the sales contract stipulates "as is" or "with all faults," implied warranties are in effect *even if problems arise that are not covered by a written warranty or if no warranty was given.* I wonder how much compensation has been lost because consumers didn't know this. The dealers certainly won't tell you!

Although the length of implied warranty coverage varies from one state to the next, it can last for as long as four years. Your local consumer protection office can tell you the time limits in your area. A dealer can limit the time that implied warranties are in effect, but this limitation must appear on your written warranty.

Auto emissions warranties

The federal government requires automakers to pay for all the parts and labor necessary to repair or replace emissions parts and *any* other parts involved when a new or used car or light truck that is under warranty fails an emissions test required by federal, state, or local government standards.

Emission control and emission-related parts are covered for the vehicle's first two years or 22,000 miles. Major emission-related parts such as catalytic converters, electronic emission control units, and onboard emissions diagnostic devices are covered for the first eight years or 80,000 miles. Time and mileage requirements vary for other types of vehicles, and all requirements change over time. Check the owner's manual, warranty booklet, or maintenance schedule for those that apply to your vehicle. You can obtain any of these from the car manufacturer.

Two types of emissions warranties are involved:

✔ **The Performance Warranty** covers the free repair or replacement of any parts that are necessary to make your vehicle pass an emissions test. If you live in an area with an inspection and maintenance program that meets or exceeds federal standards, you are eligible for this protection unless the test failure results from your misuse, tampering, or failure to follow the manufacturer's maintenance instructions in the owner's manual or warranty booklet.

If the manufacturer doesn't respond to your performance warranty claim within 30 days, unless you agree to extend the deadline or the delay is beyond the manufacturer's control, the manufacturer forfeits the right to deny the claim, and you can have the repair performed at any facility you choose, at the manufacturer's expense.

✔ **The Design and Defect Warranty** covers the free repair or replacement of any emission control or emission-related parts that become defective during the same warranty period.

You must take the vehicle to a facility authorized by the vehicle manufacturer to give them the opportunity to diagnose and repair it under these warranties.

It is not necessary to fail an emissions test to qualify for warranty coverage. If you have an emission problem or a defective part, you should have it fixed within the warranty period to avoid having to pay for repairs yourself if your vehicle fails a test after the warranty expires.

It isn't necessary to have scheduled maintenance performed by the dealer. It can be done by anyone who has the knowledge and ability to do it. You may even do it yourself, as long as you follow the manufacturer's instructions in the owner's manual. Keep copies of your receipts for maintenance work. Although proof of maintenance isn't required for warranty coverage, if improper maintenance seems to be the cause of an emissions problem, you'll be able to show that scheduled maintenance was performed. It also pays to keep a log of the parts and labor involved in all repairs, especially if you plan to sell the vehicle some day.

If the dealer or manufacturer refuses to honor an emissions warranty, and you haven't abused the vehicle or failed to maintain it properly, you can appeal their decision by following this procedure:

1. **Get a detailed explanation from the dealership, in writing, of why coverage was denied.**

2. **Ask for the names of the people at the dealership and the manufacturer's regional or zone office involved in the decision.**

3. **Ask whom you should contact at the manufacturer to appeal the denial to an authorized warranty representative.**

4. **Write to that person, requesting coverage and giving the basis for your request.**

5. **If you still fail to get approval, write to the U.S. Environmental Protection Agency at the following address:**

U.S. Environmental Protection Agency
Vehicle Programs & Compliance Division (6405J)
Attention: Warranty Complaints
401 M Street, SW
Washington, DC 20460

Provide the details of the situation, including the basis for your claim and copies of the written denial, your letters to the carmaker, and any receipts for payments involving emission control parts and repairs.

Recalls and secret warranties

Sometimes defects in a particular model become so apparent that the car manufacturer must take responsibility for remedying them. If the defect is life-threatening, the National Highway Traffic Safety Administration (NHTSA) usually forces the manufacturer to recall all the affected vehicles and make repairs at no cost to the owners. If the defect isn't deadly, automakers may publish service bulletins that instruct their dealerships to make free repairs *even if the warranty has expired.*

Because most dealerships aren't exactly thrilled by the prospect of using their time and facilities for free repairs, these offers are known as "secret warranties" — you usually won't hear about them unless your vehicle gives you trouble and you ask to have it repaired at no charge. Manufacturers often label these free repairs "goodwill warranties" or "adjustments," and unscrupulous dealers sometimes charge their customers for work that should have been free.

Finding out about recalls and secret warranties

You can find out whether recalls are in effect for your vehicle by calling the NHTSA hotline at 800-424-9393, Monday through Friday between 8:00 a.m. and 10:00 p.m. EST. You can learn about recalls and secret warranties by sending a letter with your vehicle's year, make, model, and a SASE with fifty-five cents postage to the following address:

Center for Auto Safety
2001 S Street, NW, Suite 410
Washington, DC 20009

You can find more information about the NHTSA hot line and the Center for Auto Safety's additional services in the sidebar on page 41.

Some major car manufacturers have telephone numbers to call to get information about "goodwill" adjustments. Try their company headquarters to find out whether you can at least get copies of their service bulletins for your vehicle.

Reporting problems and defects

Take the time to report defects that you feel deserve recalls or secret warranties to the NHTSA hotline, the Center for Auto Safety, your regional Federal Trade Commission office, state and local consumer hotlines, and politicians.

Disclosure laws to prevent abuse of secret warranties exist in several states. They require carmakers to notify owners if secret warranties (by any name) are issued on their vehicles and to reimburse owners if they've paid for repairs to remedy these defects. Dealers must also tell customers who complain about a defect whether it should be repaired at no charge. To find out whether your state has a disclosure law, contact your state attorney general. If no such law exists, consider lobbying your state representatives until they pass one.

Compare Warranties Carefully!

The Magnuson-Moss Act mandates that warranties must be made available for consumers to read before they make a purchase. This means that dealers and manufacturers can't just make verbal promises; they have to put it in writing. If a salesperson at a dealership makes an oral promise, ask for it to be written into your sales agreement. If the dealer refuses, don't count on it to honor the promise.

After you have the written warranty, be sure to read it carefully *before* you buy. If it doesn't measure up, consider buying another vehicle with better protection.

What to look for

When you're comparing warranties, be sure to look for the following things:

> ✔ **Who is offering the warranty — the manufacturer or the dealer?** If it's the latter, check its reputation with your local Better Business Bureau or consumer protection agency. *Remember:* A warranty is only as good as the company responsible for it.

- ✔ **Who is actually responsible for repairs?** Although it's usually the dealer, it may be the manufacturer of the system or part. How many times have you bought an appliance with a full warranty only to find you had to ship it at your own expense, in the original carton, with the original sales slip, to the manufacturer or an authorized service center located thousands of miles away? I love that "original carton" clause — if we kept all our original cartons, we'd have no room for furniture!

  It is, however, a good idea to always attach your sales slips to your warranties to prove the date of purchase and that you are the original owner.

- ✔ **What happens if the problem isn't repaired to your satisfaction?** Do you get a new part? A new vehicle? Your money back? If you're really unhappy, are there provisions for arbitration, or will you have to go to court?

- ✔ **How long does the warranty last?** Because vehicles break down more frequently as they get older, a longer warranty period can save you thousands of dollars. Warranty coverage on vehicles is usually stated in miles as well as time: "3 years or 36,000 miles, whichever comes first." (This is often expressed as "3/36,000.") If you're buying a new car, get an idea of the terms other automakers are offering. Why buy a car with a three-year warranty if one you like almost as well is covered for five?

  If you buy a "demo" or "floor sample," be sure to find out when the warranty begins and ends. It may begin when you buy the vehicle, or it may have begun when the dealer first put the car into service.

- ✔ **Which parts and problems are covered, and which are excluded?** Are excluded parts, like tires, sound systems, dealer-installed options, and other special equipment covered by separate manufacturer's warranties? Which parts and systems aren't covered at all? This is where reading the fine print really pays off; more people get hurt by exclusions than by any other warranty area.

- ✔ **Does the warranty cover labor as well as parts?** Mechanics deserve to earn a decent living, but hourly rates for labor can be high enough to eclipse the cost of parts. When my microwave died, the labor charge I would have had to pay cost more than buying a new microwave!

- ✔ **Does the warranty cover "consequential damages"?** These are damages caused by defects in the vehicle, including personal injuries and the time and expense it took you to get the damages repaired.

Avoid voiding the warranty

Read your warranty carefully so you don't inadvertently do something to void it. If you have a dealer or an independent mechanic install such options as cruise control or rustproofing, be sure that this won't void your warranty.

Have warranty-required maintenance or inspections done within the specified time or mileage limits. Abuse or misuse may cancel warranty coverage, so don't mistreat your vehicle, and be sure you follow the instructions that come with separately warranted parts.

On the other hand, be aware that your opportunities to void the warranty are probably less extensive than dealers would like you to think. Don't believe a dealer who tells you that you'll void your warranty unless you have the vehicle repaired at that dealership using factory-authorized parts. The Magnuson-Moss Act forbids anyone from demanding that you buy their parts to keep a warranty in force, with two exceptions:

- ✔ **If the dealer provides the parts at no charge.**

- ✔ **If the Federal Trade Commission publishes a statement that a particular factory part is required.** (For more information, call the FTC office in your area or visit their Web site at `www.ftc.gov`.)

Many warranties allow you to patronize another dealer or an independent mechanic without voiding your warranty. If you're unsure, read the fine print or call the manufacturer. If you decide you'd rather have another authorized facility make the repairs, be sure to tell them you intend to patronize them in the future, even though you purchased the vehicle somewhere else.

Warranties on New Vehicles

Today's high costs for mechanical parts and labor have made warranty coverage a vital issue for buyers of new cars. As a result, automakers have become extremely competitive about the original warranties they offer. New vehicles usually carry basic warranties that extend from 3 years or 36,000 miles to 5 years or 50,000 miles or longer, power train warranties for up to 70,000 miles, and as much as 10 years or unlimited mileage for corrosion. (See the earlier section called "Types of Warranties" if you're not sure what basic warranties, corrosion warranties, and so on include.)

Although most warranties still do not cover parts that have to be replaced as part of basic maintenance — such as spark plugs, windshield wiper blades, fuses, and bulbs — today some manufacturers' warranties cover such basic maintenance as lubrication. Owners of luxury vehicles may enjoy "house calls" by dealership mechanics in ritzy vans that handle minor problems right in the driveway! *The Car Book* by Jack Gillis (HarperCollins Publishers, Inc.) publishes an annual comparison of warranties on a variety of popular models, including a list of the best and worst for the current year. *Autopinion,* the CAA's annual car-buying publication, also compares the warranty coverage offered by major automakers.

In addition to the warranties on the vehicle itself, don't forget to look for additional warranties on items that aren't produced by the carmaker. In some cases, the dealer may not be directly responsible for making repairs on those items, but a good dealership should be willing to stand behind anything it sells, until you get satisfaction.

Warranties on Used Vehicles

In the past, although some dealers provided limited warranties on used vehicles, full warranties were out of the question. However, leasing has become a major factor in car ownership; as a result, many two- and three-year-old used cars are turned in after their leases expire. So, many dealerships now offer full warranties on the used vehicles they've brought up to mint condition and limited warranties on older ones.

Negotiating for a better warranty

Here are some tips for getting the best warranty available on a used vehicle:

✔ **Avoid buying any vehicle "as is" or "with all faults."** Some states do not allow used vehicles to be sold "as is," and you should avoid such a deal whether your state allows it or not. If a dealer refuses to consider any warranties, *run!* If he has no faith in your chances of happiness with that vehicle, he probably knows what he's *not* talking about.

✔ **If you can't get a warranty for a year or longer, start negotiations by asking for a limited warranty that covers 100 percent of any defects that show up in 90 days, at no cost to you.** You can fall back from there, if necessary, but don't settle for less than a 30-day, 50/50 deal on parts and labor based on the dealer's actual costs. If the dealer won't accept even half the responsibility for a vehicle for as little as 30 days, why should you have enough faith in it to buy it?

Some dealers have really exotic ideas about what constitutes a 50/50 split. A friend of mine who asked a used-car dealer if they warranted repairs was told, "Sure. We'll be happy to split a $600 extended warranty package with you, fifty-fifty!" Such a deal!

✔ **To discourage unscrupulous dealers from quoting full retail prices instead of their actual costs when splitting the bill for repairs with you, specify that prices be based on your mechanic's estimates if they are lower than those quoted by the dealer.** To discourage dealers from overpricing parts, have your warranty specify that they will provide copies of their suppliers' invoices for parts used in repairs and/or demand the ability to buy parts outside the dealership if you can get them for less than the prices they quote you. There is a difference between a warranty on a used vehicle and the warranties on new parts that have been installed on the vehicle. If recent work was done, ask for the paperwork that protects the new parts against premature malfunctioning.

- ✔ **Beware of "creative guarantees."** One major used car dealer offers "a full refund toward the purchase of any of our other cars if you are not satisfied with the one you've bought." Sounds great until you realize that the dealer may not have another vehicle you'd care to consider.

- ✔ **Ask the dealer or former owner to show you any unexpired warranties that exist.** The original manufacturer's warranties may still be in effect on a late-model vehicle, but some warranties require payment of a fee before they can be transferred to a second owner. If you're unsure whether they can be transferred to you, call the automaker's regional or national headquarters for information. They should all have toll-free numbers.

Understanding the Buyers' Guide sticker

Dealers are required to display a Buyers' Guide sticker on every vehicle, except motorcycles and some recreational vehicles, to inform prospective customers as to whether the vehicle comes with a warranty and what that warranty provides. If you purchase a used car from a dealer, you should receive an original or duplicate copy of the Buyers' Guide for that vehicle, with any changes in warranty coverage you may have negotiated written into its warranty section. The Buyers' Guide overrides any conflicting provisions that may be in the sales contract. The following are terms you'll find in the portions of the Buyers' Guide that are shown in Figure 16-1:

- ✔ **As Is — No Warranty:** This means that you agree to be fully responsible for repairing anything that doesn't work, *even if the dealer tells you that the vehicle needs no repairs*. However, a dealership can be found liable for failing to disclose a defect, *if* you can prove that they knew it existed and didn't tell you. In states that do not allow "as-is" sales, the Buyers' Guide uses the phrase "Implied Warranties Only," but it means the same thing.

- ✔ **Full warranty:** These warranties, covered in the section called "Types of Warranties," earlier in this chapter, are usually only offered on fully-restored, late-model vehicles.

- ✔ **Limited warranty:** These usually split the cost for repairing various parts and systems between the dealer and the buyer. The dealer must list the following limited warranty conditions on the Buyers' Guide for each vehicle it sells:

  - The percentage of repair costs that the dealer will pay for parts and labor.

  - Any deductibles that apply.

  - The time and mileage duration of the warranty for each system.

- The specific parts and systems that are covered by the warranty. (The last page of the Buyers' Guide, shown in Figure 16-2, has a list of major systems where problems may occur. Ask your mechanic to keep them in mind when inspecting the vehicle before you buy it.)

BUYERS GUIDE

IMPORTANT: Spoken promises are difficult to enforce. Ask the dealer to put all promises in writing. Keep this form.

VEHICLE MAKE   MODEL   YEAR   VIN NUMBER

DEALER STOCK NUMBER (Optional)

WARRANTIES FOR THIS VEHICLE:

☐ # AS IS - NO WARRANTY

YOU WILL PAY ALL COSTS FOR ANY REPAIRS. The dealer assumes no responsibility for any repairs regardless of any oral statements about the vehicle.

☐ # WARRANTY

☐ FULL   ☐ **LIMITED WARRANTY.** The dealer will pay _____% of the labor and _____% of the parts for the covered systems that fail during the warranty period. Ask the dealer for a copy of the warranty document for a full explanation of warranty coverage, exclusions, and the dealer's repair obligations. Under state law, "implied warranties" may give you even more rights.

SYSTEMS COVERED: **DURATION:**

_____   _____
_____   _____
_____   _____
_____   _____
_____   _____
_____   _____
_____   _____

☐ **SERVICE CONTRACT.** A service contract is available at an extra charge on this vehicle. Ask for details as to coverage, deductible, price, and exclusions. If you buy a service contract within 90 days of the time of sale, state law "implied warranties" may give you additional rights.

PRE PURCHASE INSPECTION: ASK THE DEALER IF YOU MAY HAVE THIS VEHICLE INSPECTED BY YOUR MECHANIC EITHER ON OR OFF THE LOT.

SEE THE BACK OF THIS FORM for important additional information, including a list of some major defects that may occur in used motor vehicles.

Figure 16-1: The front side of the Buyers' Guide sticker.

Below is a list of some major defects that may occur in used motor vehicles.

Frame & Body
Frame-cracks, corrective welds, or rusted through
Dogtracks—bent or twisted frame

Engine
Oil leakage, excluding normal seepage
Cracked block or head
Belts missing or inoperable
Knocks or misses related to camshaft lifters and push rods
Abnormal exhaust discharge

Transmission & Drive Shaft
Improper fluid level or leakage, excluding normal seepage
Cracked or damaged case which is visible
Abnormal noise or vibration caused by faulty transmission or drive shaft
Improper shifting or functioning in any gear
Manual clutch slips or chatters

Differential
Improper fluid level or leakage excluding normal seepage
Cracked or damaged housing which is visible
Abnormal noise or vibration caused by faulty differential

Cooling System
Leakage including radiator
Improperly functioning water pump

Electrical System
Battery leakage
Improperly functioning alternator, generator, battery, or starter

Fuel System
Visible leakage

Inoperable Accessories
Gauges or warning devices
Air conditioner
Heater & Defroster

Brake System
Failure warning light broken
Pedal not firm under pressure (DOT spec.)
Not enough pedal reserve (DOT spec.)
Does not stop vehicle in straight line (DOT spec.)
Hoses damaged
Drum or rotor too thin (Mfgr. Specs)
Lining or pad thickness less than 1/32 inch
Power unit not operating or leaking
Structural or mechanical parts damaged

Steering System
Too much free play at steering wheel (DOT specs.)
Free play in linkage more than 1/4 inch
Steering gear binds or jams
Front wheels aligned improperly (DOT specs.)
Power unit belts cracked or slipping
Power unit fluid level improper

Suspension System
Ball joint seals damaged
Structural parts bent or damaged
Stabilizer bar disconnected
Spring broken
Shock absorber mounting loose
Rubber bushings damaged or missing
Radius rod damaged or missing
Shock absorber leaking or functioning improperly

Tires
Tread depth less than 2/32 inch
Sizes mismatched
Visible damage

Wheels
Visible cracks, damage or repairs
Mounting bolts loose or missing

Exhaust System
Leakage

DEALER

ADDRESS

SEE FOR COMPLAINTS

IMPORTANT: The information on this form is part of any contract to buy this vehicle. Removal of this label before consumer purchase (except for purpose of test-driving) is a violation of federal law (16 C.F.R. 455).

Figure 16-2:
The back side of the Buyers' Guide sticker.

Last-minute warranty repairs

Having an independent mechanic inspect your vehicle just before the warranty expires is a good idea. Doing so can give you time to have final repairs and adjustments made while the warranty is still in effect. To document the fact that you brought these problems to the dealer's attention before the warranty expired, ask your mechanic for a dated inspection report and be sure to get a copy of the dealer's repair order as well.

If you have a major failure just *after* the warranty on your car expires, you may have some recourse. If you've done your homework ahead of time (maintained the vehicle properly, kept your maintenance records, and so on), you may have a good case. The paperwork you keep can prove you had a problem before the warranty expired. Some major carmakers maintain computerized records of all work done under warranty, filed under each car's VIN. If they have to make a decision about whether or not to extend their warranty to cover problems that occur after the warranty expires, they check to see whether you maintained the car properly and whether you reported other problems before the warranty expired.

If you have reason to believe that major trouble is brewing, you may consider having the engine oil analyzed by an independent testing company to determine whether the engine is aging prematurely. The oil contains traces of metal from any parts that are wearing. By analyzing the different alloys in the metal, the testing lab can tell which parts are wearing and whether they are wearing out faster than they should be, given your particular driving conditions and the number of miles on the car. Such an analysis can also tell you whether antifreeze is present in the oil, which could mean a blown head gasket or a cooling system leak. The news may not be good, but it can be very valuable if you find the proof that qualifies your vehicle for free repairs.

To locate an independent oil testing lab, consult your local yellow pages or call the United Testing Group at 800-394-3669. For a small fee, United Testing will do a single-sample analysis, which includes a basic sample kit in which to package the oil for shipment.

Extended Warranties and Service Contracts

Extended warranties lengthen the period covered by manufacturer's warranties on the whole vehicle or on individual parts and systems. A service contract, on the other hand, is a separate agreement between you and the dealer or service contract company for service on your vehicle. Although both extended warranties and service contracts cost extra, there are important differences:

✔ **If you want to extend your vehicle's warranty, you must purchase the extended warranty from the manufacturer when you purchase the car.** Because most full warranties currently provide coverage for from three to seven years, or 36,000 to 75,000 miles, extended warranties are probably unnecessary except on items that are excluded from the original warranty or only covered for a year or less.

✔ **Although dealers sometimes call it an extended warranty, a service contract is not a warranty at all because you must pay for it and it can be purchased at any time.** (*Remember:* A service contract by any other name is still just a service contract. There are other euphemisms: The "mechanical breakdown insurance" offered by at least one insurance company is basically a service contract in disguise.)

✔ **Extended warranties that are backed by the manufacturer are safer than service contracts provided by dealers.** The reason is because dealers and service contract companies have been known to go bankrupt or simply close up shop and move away, leaving their contract holders without the coverage they paid for.

✔ **Unlike service contracts, the cost of factory-backed extended warranties may be negotiable.** W. James Bragg, author of *In the Driver's Seat: The New Car Buyer's Negotiating Bible* (Random House, Inc.), suggests that you offer to pay only 50 percent and refuse to pay more than two-thirds of the asking price.

Because service contracts can be risky and extended warranties may not be needed, the following sections show you what to watch out for and what questions to ask before you agree to purchase either one.

Watching out for rip-offs

Many dealerships are merely commissioned agents or administrators for independent contractors, some of whom collect large sums for service agreements that they have no intention of honoring, and then disappear quietly into the night. These administrators act as claims adjusters (they authorize payment of claims to the dealers and may even be responsible for making repairs) and they are the ones you may have to deal with in the event of a dispute, so you must check them out very carefully.

On the brighter side, the checks and balances involved in a service contract with the independent administrators can work to your advantage: If the administrator goes out of business, the dealership may still be obligated to satisfy the contract. Conversely, if the dealer folds, the administrator may be required to fulfill the terms of the contract. Whether this is true or not depends on the contract itself and any laws governing service contracts in your state or province.

As you can see, service contracts may be risky. Here are some additional reasons why you could be wasting your money if you buy one:

- ✔ **Most new cars are covered by full warranties for three to five years, so why pay for duplicate coverage?** Compare the extended warranty or the service contract with your basic warranties and keep in mind that any decent new vehicle shouldn't need major systems repaired until the warranty coverage expires. Some unscrupulous dealers will tell you that you must buy a service contract to qualify for financing. Contact the lender personally to see whether this is true.

- ✔ **Before you buy a used car, have an independent mechanic make certain that it doesn't need major repairs.** This presale inspection can substantially lower the risk of something expensive breaking down within the short period of time covered by most service contracts. You're usually better off saving the money you'd pay for the contract and letting it earn interest until the day you need it for repairs.

Deciding whether you need a service contract or extended warranty

Dealers may make service contracts and extended warranties sound like they're a real advantage to you, but to avoid being swayed by the rhetoric, keep this in mind: If the odds weren't against the *buyer (you)* ever profiting from a service contract, nobody would want to sell them.

When should you consider buying an extended warranty or service contract? If your finances are unstable and you're afraid that you may be caught without the cash on hand to pay for repairs, you may consider the contract to be a "forced savings plan" and buy it while you have the money to pay for it. Just be sure the contract period doesn't start until the basic warranties expire. If you have good self-control, another alternative would be to put the money you would have spent on the contract into a separate bank account that's earmarked for such emergencies and let it accumulate interest until you need it.

The following sections can help you decide whether to purchase a service contract or extended warranty and determine exactly what you're getting with one.

Do you need it?

If the warranty that comes with your vehicle covers the same repairs that you would get under the service contract, you don't benefit from having the contract, so why pay for one? If the contract takes effect after the warranty runs out, ask yourself the following questions:

✔ Is the vehicle likely to need repairs during the contract period?

✔ What are the chances that the cost of the repairs will be greater than the cost of the contract?

Your friendly independent mechanic may be helpful here.

Who's responsible?

Find out who will actually be obligated to fulfill the contract, regardless of who sold it to you. It may be the manufacturer, the dealership, or an independent contractor. If the dealer or an independent is responsible, ask the following questions:

✔ **How long have they been in business at the same location? Do they have the financial resources to meet their contractual obligations?** Check your Better Business Bureau or consumer protection agency to see whether complaints have been filed against them.

✔ **Is the contract underwritten by an insurance company?** Dealerships, dealer associations, and some independent administrators buy insurance to cover claims. Ask your state insurance commission about the financial solvency of the insurance underwriter and whether any complaints have been filed against them. Insurance legislation in some states regulates contract fees and requires service contractors to maintain adequate financial reserves.

✔ **What kind of legal recourse do you have?** Find out who arbitrates or settles the claims if you get into a dispute with the contractor.

Are the terms reasonable?

The first thing you need to determine is how much the contract costs. The price is usually based on the make, model, and condition of the vehicle, and the length and coverage of the contract. It can range from hundreds to thousands of dollars. Some of the least expensive service contracts are offered directly by insurance companies. But other factors can impact how much out-of-pocket expense you have and how happy you are with the service you get, so be sure to ask the following questions:

✔ **Are there deductibles?** Some contracts require you to pay a fee every time you take the car in for repairs. Others require you to pay a fee for each separate unrelated repair. Some deductibles are set amounts; others are a percentage of the cost of repairs. A set fee is preferable, because repair bills can go sky-high for major problems.

✔ **Does the contract specify that replacement parts must be new or original equipment?** Or can they be reconditioned or aftermarket parts? Does the authorized repair facility have an ample stock of parts for your vehicle, or will you have to wait until parts are ordered and received?

✔ **How about depreciation?** If a worn part is at fault, some contracts make you pay part of the cost to repair or replace it based on the vehicle's age or mileage.

✔ **Must you lay out the money for repairs and then wait to be reimbursed?** If this is the case, be sure the contract limits the time it takes to reimburse you.

✔ **Can repairs and routine maintenance be performed at the facility of your choice? Only at the dealership who sold you the contract? Or only at locations specified by the contractor?** What if you move out of town or the vehicle breaks down during a trip? Is service limited to a specific geographical area?

Demand the option of choosing an independent mechanic or doing the routine maintenance yourself.

✔ **Does the contract cover towing? Renting a car while yours is in the shop?** Will they pay the total cost of these services? If you need prior authorization, how long will it take to obtain it? Can you get authorization outside normal business hours? On weekends? Is there a toll-free number? Try it to see whether you can easily get through to a real, live human being.

✔ **What maintenance is necessary to keep the contract in effect?** If the contract calls for you to follow all the manufacturer's recommendations, be sure to keep service records and the invoices for periodic tune-ups, lubrication, spark plugs, and filters as proof that you've complied.

✔ **Does the contract extend longer than you plan to keep the vehicle?** If a shorter-term contract isn't available, is the contract transferable if you sell the vehicle to someone else?

✔ **Is there a cancellation and refund policy?** What are the costs if you terminate the contract before it runs out? Will you get a full refund for the unused portion or only partial payment?

What isn't covered?

For all that the service contract claims to cover, there are always things it excludes. Before you sign anything, make sure you know exactly what parts and situations the contract does and doesn't include:

✔ **Does the contract cover routine maintenance?** This is one of the chief reasons why people want these contracts, yet many contracts do not cover this at all.

✔ **Does the contract cover repairs for wear and tear?** A serious loophole can be found here if a contractor decides your problem is due to normal wear and tear and refuses to cover it.

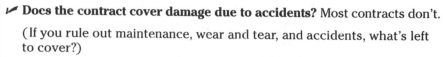

- **Does the contract cover damage due to accidents?** Most contracts don't.

  (If you rule out maintenance, wear and tear, and accidents, what's left to cover?)

- **Does the contract cover *all* parts and systems?** "Bumper-to-bumper" coverage usually doesn't really cover everything it implies. Most contracts exclude routine repairs to such parts as brakes and clutches. For example, an extended-service protection plan from a well-known and respected insurance company promises to cover "virtually everything on your new car from 'bumper-to-bumper' including parts and labor on 'thousands of mechanical components.'" Sounds great, right? Here are their *exclusions* (in the usual small print):

  "Maintenance services recommended in the vehicle maintenance schedule. Other normal maintenance items such as engine tune-up, suspension alignment, wheel balancing, filters, lubricants, engine coolant fluids, belts, hoses, spark/glow plugs and brake pads, linings and shoes. Physical damage, lenses, sealed beams, light bulbs, tires, brake rotors, drums, shock absorbers, exhaust system, friction clutch disc and pressure plate, battery, and rust. Antitheft systems and radio/speaker equipment not installed by manufacturer."

  Check the contract carefully for exclusions and assume that anything that isn't listed specifically as being covered probably isn't. If the contract is limited to "mechanical breakdowns," it probably doesn't cover normal wear and tear.

- **If a part that isn't covered causes damage to a part that is, will the contract cover the repair?** Will it cover the removal and replacement (known as R&R) of a part to diagnose and repair a problem? For example, if they remove the engine and find that the problem is caused by a part that isn't covered by the contract, do you have to pay for the engine R&R?

Protecting yourself when you close the deal

If you still want to buy a service contract, take the following precautions *before* you sign it:

- **Dealerships must provide a copy of the service contract or extended warranty for you to read before you sign, along with a *written* explanation of your right to cancel the contract and get a full or partial refund.** Make sure it specifies in writing when your service contract goes into effect.

- **If the service contract is for a used vehicle, be sure the dealer marks the service contract box on the Buyers' Guide.** They are required to do this by law (the Magnuson-Moss Act) in states that do not have insurance laws regulating service contracts. (For information about the Buyers' Guide, see the section "Understanding the Buyers' Guide sticker" earlier in this chapter.)

✔ **If a dealership sells a service contract within 90 days of the purchase of a vehicle, federal law (Magnuson-Moss again) says that they can't disclaim the implied warranties on any system covered by the contract, even if you bought the vehicle "as is."** As an example, if you buy a service contract that covers the engine, you automatically get implied warranties on the engine that may provide protection not specified in the contract.

✔ **If a dealer sells you a contract that's backed by an independent service contractor, make sure the dealer gives you written confirmation that they've sent your payment to the proper party.** This protects you against finding out that the contract never went into effect when the time for repairs comes around.

Handling Warranty and Service Contract Disputes

If you have problems with obtaining the warranty or service coverage you were promised, be sure to read Chapter 18, which offers a time-tested procedure for getting satisfaction on *all* types of complaints.

Report violations of warranties and related problems to the Federal Trade Commission. Although the FTC cannot represent you directly, it wants to know whether companies are meeting their warranty obligations. Send your written complaints to:

Federal Trade Commission
Correspondence Branch
CRC-240
Washington, DC 20580

Chapter 17

Beating the Bad Guys at Their Own Games

• •

In This Chapter

▶ Debunking common misconceptions about who is at risk

▶ Protecting yourself from dangerous scams

▶ Understanding the available security options

▶ Knowing how to get yourself out of trouble

• •

*U*ntil fairly recently, auto theft usually involved kids joyriding in stolen vehicles. Barring accidents, a car used to be considered a relatively safe place to be; now, professional criminals are hijacking cars (or *carjacking,* as it's commonly called) on the highways and mugging little old ladies in parking lots.

What are your choices? You can pretend nothing's wrong and drive right into trouble, sit at home and worry about being a victim, or seize the initiative and keep the bad guys at bay. Many of us have reservations about packing guns or using pepper spray on strangers, and bodyguards and armored cars are a bit confining (not to mention expensive). After consulting law enforcement and insurance agencies, auto clubs, and security experts, I'm delighted to report that a variety of options exist within financial and ethical parameters that most of us can handle. With common sense, a small investment and good old-fashioned chutzpah, you can keep your car from being stolen and scare molesters away.

Understanding the Game

Recent figures show that, in North America, a car is stolen every 12 seconds. That's over two million auto thefts a year! If you think that's bad, between 1985 and 1994 alone, thefts in the United States grew 61 percent to an annual loss of 200 million dollars. What's more, these grim statistics only cover thefts of vehicles — they don't include "smash-and-grabs" of expensive sound systems, custom wheel covers, air bags, and personal possessions.

If your car is stolen today, there's little more than a fifty-fifty chance you'll get it back within a week; after that, the odds drop dramatically. In 1975, 75 percent of the vehicles that were stolen were used for transportation and recovered intact. Sad to say, most stolen cars are no longer recovered intact. Figure 17-1 shows what's happened since the good ol' days.

To win the game against car thieves, carjackers, and vandals, you've got to understand the game. If you have a clear picture of the games the bad guys play, the strategies to prevent thefts makes better sense. The following sections take a look at some common misperceptions about where — and how — car thieves ply their trade.

Where the games are played

Many people think that because they don't live or work in "high-crime areas," their vehicles are relatively safe. This ranking of places from which vehicles are most likely to be stolen may surprise you. As you can see, private residences make up a huge slice of the pie.

1. Private residences (25 percent!)

2. Malls and shopping centers

3. Apartments and condominium complexes

4. Office buildings

5. Stores

	1970	1996	% Change
Number of Vehciles Stolen	$0.9 million	$1.4 million	+.55%
Total Cost of Vehicle Theft	$3.2 billion (1996 dollars)	$7.5 billion	+134%
Recovery Rates Nationwide	84%	68%	-23%

Figure 17-1: Vehicle theft in the United States: A quarter century comparison.

6. Churches and temples

7. Restaurants and lounges

8. Hotels and motels

9. Hospitals

10. Schools

11. Curbside

12. Airport parking lots

Because our cars are located in at least one of these places 90 percent of the time, they are almost always in danger, unless we take the proper precautions to protect them.

Cars that thieves love to steal

Most of us assume that car thieves are especially fond of brand-new luxury vehicles, but research has shown that this isn't necessarily the case. Many cars actually become more attractive with age — their rate of theft increases from when they are new until they are four to six years old. These are usually mid-priced cars that experience few major design changes over time. Their parts can be used for models built over several years, and some parts may be found on several different models. Unsuspecting owners of these aging beauties tend to underrate them and are less inclined to buy antitheft devices. This increases their allure for thieves because they're so easy to steal. They usually end up in *chop shops* (warehouses or garages where thieves disassemble [chop] the cars into their useable parts).

Where stolen cars end up

In almost all instances, the thieves who steal your car don't end up driving it around; they get rid of it. Stolen cars end up in the following places:

✔ **Chop shops.** These illegal operations dismantle stolen vehicles and sell the parts to sleazy auto repair and body shops. Why should thieves turn a perfectly good car into chop-shop-suey? Because a vehicle's individual components are worth twice as much as the whole car, and they're harder to trace. Because the practice is so widespread, federal law now requires car, light-duty truck, and multipurpose vehicle manufacturers to place VINs on vulnerable parts with high theft rates. The law also demands that repair shops check VINs of used parts against a national database of stolen parts and imposes fines of as much as $25,000 for violations.

✔ **Foreign ports.** Vehicles stolen by professional thieves are often shipped out of the country into foreign ports. Mexico offers an excellent market for stolen vehicles, and states located on the U.S./Mexican border have relatively high theft rates. In 1994 nearly 2,000 stolen cars, worth around $21 million, were returned to the United States by the NICB and a special unit of the California Highway Patrol, which operates in Baja California with the consent of the Mexican government. Authorities think these figures represent only a fraction of the vehicles involved.

Russia has become a prime location for stolen vehicles. The vehicles arrive there in containers marked "household goods" via ships out of Los Angeles, Seattle, and Vancouver, BC. Many four-wheel-drive vehicles end up in South America, and China's growing affluent population is avid for U.S. cars. To give you an idea of how lucrative the stolen car market is in foreign countries: In 1995, a Chevrolet Caprice could sell for more than $130,000 in the Middle East.

✔ **Used car sales.** Clever thieves have many ways of "laundering" stolen cars and selling them to unsuspecting people. Be sure to read the tips on how to identify a stolen vehicle in Chapter 4.

How attractive is my car to thieves?

If you'd like to know whether your vehicle is especially attractive to thieves, call the National Insurance Crime Bureau Hotline (800-TEL-NICB) in the United States and Canada. The NICB is a nonprofit organization funded by more than 1,000 insurance companies to combat crime. It deals with all types of insurance, but focuses principally on property/casualty crimes, which include auto fraud and theft, staged accidents, and faked thefts.

Hundreds of NICB agents investigate car and property thefts and alert law enforcement agencies to patterns of organized theft and fraud. The NICB has developed a computerized database with over 300,000,000 records, which can identify a stolen vehicle in seconds and locate and recover about 50 percent of the vehicles reported stolen. After the World Trade Center bombing, NICB agents tracked half a vehicle identification number found on the twisted frame rail of the bomber's van and discovered that the vehicle was stolen from a rental agency in Jersey City. Within 24 hours, the FBI arrested the person who rented it.

If your vehicle is stolen, be sure to notify the NICB hotline at 800-835-6422. The NICB InfoCenter's computer bulletin board also provides claim-related insurance information. Just use your modem to dial 800-467-3992, download "Crimenet software," and log in as a new user.

Following are other sources of data about frequently stolen cars:

✔ Current lists of "The Most Stolen Cars" in newspapers and popular magazines

✔ *The Car Book,* which you can find at your library, bookstore, or through the Center for Auto Safety (202-328-7700)

✔ The Highway Loss Data Institute report, "Injury, Collision and Theft Losses by Make and Model," available free from the National Insurance Consumer Helpline (800-942-4242)

Games Bad Guys Play

Roughly half of all stolen vehicles are still taken by amateurs, but professionals are rapidly outpacing them with a variety of creative techniques that may involve everything from simple robbery to kidnapping, rape, and even murder. Fortunately, violent incidents are not as numerous as the media would imply and, if enough of us get smart, many of these games should soon cease to be worth the risk.

The simplest and most effective way to keep your car from being stolen is to stay alert and aware of your surroundings instead of driving with your hands on the wheel and your head in the clouds. Statistics show that four out of five vehicles were unlocked when they were stolen, and as many as one out of five had the keys in the ignition.

Your horn is a simple and effective crime deterrent. Don't be afraid to honk — long and loud — if approached by a suspicious person.

With that in mind, the following sections take a look at the most popular car-theft techniques and what you can do about them.

Carjacking

This old game with a jazzy new name involves an attack on a driver who is entering or leaving a vehicle at a gas station, parking lot, fast-food restaurant, or driveway, or who is waiting at a traffic light or stop sign. The thieves rob the driver and then make off with the car — and sometimes the driver as well. Most carjackings occur between 8 p.m. and 11 p.m., half of them on Fridays, Saturdays, and Sundays.

Because drivers and passengers have been killed or injured during carjackings, the Anti-Car Theft Act of 1992 made carjacking a federal offense, punishable by up to life imprisonment. The 1994 Crime Bill increased the penalties and imposed a death sentence if a victim is killed.

Use these strategies to avoid being victimized by carjackers:

- ✔ **Drive carefully and keep an eye out for suspicious vehicles and dangerous situations.** Never, ever tailgate. If the car in front of you repeatedly slows down for no discernible reason and seems to be waiting for you to catch up, slow down to maintain your distance, change lanes, or drive to a safe place. If the driver's behavior appears erratic, jot down the state and license number of the vehicle. If you can't identify the state, note the colors of the license plate. Also note the car's make, model, and color. Describe the suspicious vehicle to local authorities by cellular phone or from the nearest pay phone, if you feel safe stopping at it.

✔ **Choose your routes carefully.** Don't turn down activities that take place in unfamiliar territory, just get there by the safest route possible. If in doubt, consult the AAA (American Automobile Association).

✔ **Don't pick up hitchhikers.** There are safer ways to make friends!

✔ **Drive with the doors locked and the windows raised.** This is where air conditioning really pays off.

✔ **Drive in the center lane.** This is so you can't be forced off the road.

✔ **Keep music low.** Doing so helps you can hear what's going on outside your car.

✔ **At self-service gas stations, turn the ignition off and lock your car doors if you have to walk away from your car to pay the cashier.** Don't use automated self-service stations at night in remote or risky areas.

If you find yourself involved in any road accident, it is usually in your best interest to stop and exchange information. However, because you may be putting yourself in danger — or, in some states, violating the law — by getting out of your car and confronting the other parties involved, taking steps to protect yourself is important.

State laws run the gamut from those that forbid you from leaving the scene of a crash until you exchange information, to those that forbid everyone involved from leaving their vehicles at all. For this reason, you should call your local DMV and find out what the laws are where you do most of your driving. If laws in your state forbid all drivers from leaving their cars at a crash site, then follow your state's authorized procedures or sit tight and wait for the authorities to arrive.

If the circumstances seem suspicious, or the accident takes place in an isolated or disreputable neighborhood, the procedures that follow should enable you to obtain what you need without risking your life. (You can find detailed instructions on what to do to protect your insurance claims at the scene of any automotive accident in Chapter 15.)

✔ **Lock your doors and let the other driver come to you.** Roll your window down a crack and say you don't feel safe in the situation. Conspicuously dial 911 on your cellular phone if you have one.

✔ **If you have no phone, and you can see a call box or pay phone, ask the other driver to summon the police to supervise the proceedings.** Even if there are no injuries, the law should be there in minutes if any of the people involved demand their presence at the scene. If the other driver is willing to wait for them, the situation is probably legitimate.

✔ **If you have no phone and there's none in sight, and both cars are driveable, tell the other driver to follow you to the nearest police station.** If the other car is willing to follow you, they're probably trustworthy. If you don't know where to find a police station, head for a well-lit, well-populated service station, hotel, hospital, or mall where you can drive right up to the entrance and get to a telephone safely or ask a security guard to call the police. If that's impossible, stop at a busy corner and ask someone to direct you to the nearest police station. If you don't feel you can leave your car and enter the station safely, just double-park at the entrance and lean on the horn.

Bump-and-rob

In this new version of "Dodge 'em Cars," a couple of thugs deliberately rear-end another vehicle and attack when its driver stops to deal with the "accident." Because late-model cars with disoriented drivers make the best targets, this racket has threatened the car rental and tourist industries in Florida and other states. Most of the preventive strategies against carjacking apply here as well. If the accident looks suspicious, be sure to follow the same suspicious-accident procedures as outlined in the preceding section. The most important thing to remember is this: *Don't get out of your car until you are in a really safe place.*

According to the National Insurance Crime Bureau, staged auto collisions usually take place in seven easily identifiable steps:

1. The ring leader is typically a corrupt attorney or doctor who hires a *capper* (a street-level collision coordinator).

2. The capper recruits passengers promising financial rewards.

3. All the players script the details of the collision and injuries.

4. The players orchestrate the accident.

5. The capper refers cooperating passengers to an unethical attorney for legal representation.

6. The lawyer directs passengers to a crooked medical provider who inflates the medical billing for often nonexistent injuries.

7. The attorney negotiates a settlement with the insurer for the cooperating victims. Ring members divide the claim payment, and the crooked professionals usually receive the largest share.

The NICB says that in order to protect yourself from becoming a victim of this kind of an accident, you should follow these suggestions:

- ✔ Don't tailgate.

- ✔ Call the police to the scene of the accident for a police report.

- ✔ Carry a disposable camera to photograph damages and passengers of the other car.

Insurance scams

As I mention in the preceding section, crooks have set up elaborate organizations to get rich by staging accidents. Even though your insurance company may compensate you, you not only have to pay your deductible plus premium penalties for having "caused" an accident, but insurance companies have lost so many millions of dollars to these frauds that we're all paying higher premiums to compensate them!

To deal safely with these thieves, follow the suspicious-accident instructions in the "Carjacking" section earlier in this chapter, and all the accident procedures in Chapter 15. And be especially sure to do the following:

> ✔ **Count the number of passengers in the other car and get their names and telephone numbers, if possible.** Use a disposable camera to take pictures. Often, more people will file claims than were actually in the car!

> ✔ **Get a police report, even if the damage is negligible.** This can deter inflated claims for bogus damage later on.

Bad Samaritans

These creeps prey on drivers of disabled vehicles. They approach with seemingly good intentions, lure the driver into lowering the window or stepping out of the car, and then attack. They may also approach you when you're looking for a parking space in a crowded mall and say that your car's brake lights aren't working. They then offer to get in and step on the brake pedal so you can see for yourself. When you get out of the car, the thief tromps on the gas and splits, often not only with the car but with your possessions as well.

If you think you're being approached by a "bad Samaritan," here's what you should do:

> ✔ **If your vehicle is disabled at the side of the road, roll the window down a crack, say "Thank you," and tell them they can help you by notifying the police.** Then follow the rest of the safety procedures mentioned in the section called "Carjacking," earlier in this chapter.

> ✔ **If you are approached at a mall or other public parking area, lock your doors (although they should already be locked!) and say thanks through your closed window.** Don't check your car until you are at a location where you can leave it safely. Or you can ask the mall security guard to help you, for example, check the brake lights. If they prove to be working, report the incident and give a description of the perpetrator to the mall security police.

✔ **Keep your car in good shape.** Top off the fuel tank and check the oil, battery, coolant, hoses, lights, and fan belts before driving in bad weather or in remote or unsafe areas. If you know your vehicle's in good condition, you won't be as unnerved by false alarms.

Car key duplication

Unscrupulous employees of car dealerships have been known to pass on new-car buyers' names, addresses, and ignition key codes to thieves who then have duplicate keys made and steal the cars at their leisure.

Parking lot attendants, hotel valets, car wash and fast-oil-change employees — even mechanics — have been known to play similar tricks on drivers who leave their house keys on their key chains or provide them with their names and addresses by leaving car registrations or personal mail in their cars or on their luggage. You can't do much about dealership scammers except mention this possibility to the police if your new car is stolen soon after you purchase it.

But there are strategies for foiling the rest of the key thieves:

✔ **Keep your car keys on a separate or easily detachable ring.** Take all your other keys with you whenever you turn your car over to someone else, even if it's just for a short time.

✔ **Never put your name and address on a key ring.** Why tell the culprits where to find the goods? If it's vital that lost keys be returned to you, just put "Please return to" and, preferably, your business phone number on the key tag; or use a tag from a service that will return your keys to you if they are dropped into any mailbox.

✔ **Place only your name along with the phone number, city, and state of your *destination* on exterior luggage tags, and use tags with buckled flaps that conceal identification data from curious eyes.** If you're on your way home, just put your phone number on exterior tags and place a card with your full name and address on it, *inside* each of your bags. This will help airlines contact you if your luggage is lost, without revealing that information to not-so-casual observers.

✔ **Carry a copy of your registration on your person — not in your car — and leave the original at home.** Why give thieves proof of ownership as well as your vehicle?

✔ **Never leave personal mail in your parked car.** Same goes for anything with your address.

✔ **If possible, choose a "park and lock" garage or a lot that doesn't require you to leave your keys.**

Smash-and-grab

Smash-and-grab is not a new form of wrestling — it's a game played by thieves who break into parked vehicles and make off with them or their contents. Although every vehicle is vulnerable if someone finds it irresistibly attractive, you can do a lot to encourage thieves to choose somebody else's car instead of yours.

Choose your parking spot carefully

The simple act of choosing a good parking spot can reduce your chances of being victimized:

 ✔ **Park in well-lit, highly visible, well-populated areas where you can get safely to and from the car.** You're better off paying a parking meter than tucking your car into a free, but vulnerable, space in an alley or on a dark or isolated street.

 ✔ **At night, opt for a busy garage with 24-hour attendants or pay for valet parking.** It's the cheapest form of protection around (if you only give them your car keys).

 ✔ **Take the time to sit and wait for a spot near the entrance to a mall; don't park at the back of the lot.** Having your car stolen would cost you more than you'd save by getting to the biggest sale a few minutes faster.

 ✔ **Turn the wheels to the curb or sharply to one side and set the emergency brake to foil thieves with tow trucks they've probably acquired by "unorthodox" methods.** (Ten percent of stolen cars are towed away by thieves.) To make towing even more difficult, park front-wheel drive cars with the transmission in Park and engage the emergency brake. To lock the wheels, leave cars with stick shifts in gear.

The high price of air bags

The HLDI believes that air bag thefts would decrease sharply if carmakers cut replacement costs and provided the NICB with air bag serial numbers. Air-bag grabbers can steal air bags in as little as 45 seconds. Replacement bags are not manufactured in large quantities because relatively few accidents result in air bag deployment, so prices can run from $300 to as much as $1,500. Obviously, unscrupulous repair shops are delighted to pay between $50 and $200 for a "hot" bag and resell it at a huge profit to an unsuspecting customer. To make things worse, a bag that wasn't designed for a specific car may fail to deploy during an accident.

If you must replace an air bag, tell the repair shop that you will want a copy of the invoice they received for buying a new OEM (original equipment) air bag for your vehicle's make and model.

Protect the things inside your car

According to the Highway Loss Data Institute (HLDI), stereos and car phones continue to lead the list of most stolen items because of their high resale value, but as many as 5 percent of all auto insurance claims are for air-bag thefts. Keeping the following in mind may help your car avoid the attention of smash-and-grabbers:

✔ **If you can't live without high-priced stereo equipment in your vehicle, get a system that doesn't draw attention to itself.** Some CD models, for example, are designed to hold several CDs and be installed out of sight (like in the trunk of the car) so that anyone looking into your car would see only the factory installed AM/FM radio. Some stereos are extremely small and are made so you can eject them and take them with you.

✔ **Locking steering wheel covers can help prevent thieves from stealing your driver's-side air bag as well as your car.** See the section "How Much Is Security Worth to You?" later in this chapter for information about this and other security devices for your car.

Salvage switching

This increasingly popular method enables thieves to register a stolen car without alerting the police or the DMV. They buy cheap salvaged vehicles from auto wreckers under phony names and then steal the same model and switch the VIN plate from the wreck to the hot car. They then reregister the stolen car under the same phony name and sell it to an unsuspecting buyer. The new buyer's registration may indicate that the vehicle has been salvaged, but canny thieves solve this problem by reregistering stolen vehicles with bogus VINs in states that do not scrutinize registrations closely or by simply vanishing before the new buyer's registration comes through.

To foil salvage switchers from selling you a stolen car and to prevent your car from being stolen by them, do the following:

✔ **Don't part with more than a small deposit on a used car until you've checked its current registration through the DMV.** If it is listed as "salvaged," your local police will have recourse to two NICB online services that combat this scam:

- *VINassist,* which decodes the Vehicle Identification Number to reveal the original make, model, engine size, and restraint system.

- *EyeQ,* which provides a vehicle's ownership history and appends any salvage record to the VIN.

For further information on how to avoid buying a stolen used car, see Chapter 4.

✔ **Etch your vehicle's VIN on its windshield and rear window, inside the rear bumper, and on the engine and other vital parts.** This strategy is so effective that police in many cities will etch car windows and major parts for you at no cost. You can find your car's VIN on your vehicle registration and on the left corner of the dashboard where you can see it through the windshield.

If you unknowingly buy a stolen vehicle and the police confiscate it, you won't be repaid for your loss!

More Strategies for Foiling Thieves and Carjackers

We've all seen private eyes do their stuff on the screen. Now here's your chance to emulate their cunning tactics. Buckle up your imaginary trenchcoat and really get into these strategies. Even if it turns out to be a false alarm, the chance to play Humphrey Bogart makes it worth the effort.

If you think you're being followed

Check the rearview mirror frequently and observe the vehicles immediately behind you and in the lanes to either side of you. Here's what to do if a vehicle stays suspiciously close to you for too long:

✔ **If you're on city streets, make a couple of right turns around the block.** The idea is not to lose the other vehicle, but to see if it's following you. If it is, drive to the nearest police or fire station, hospital emergency entrance, major valet parking area, or any bright and crowded place. Wait until the other car leaves before getting out or driving on.

✔ **If you're on a highway, get off at the next exit and make a few right turns.** If the other car disappears, head for the next on-ramp. If it doesn't, proceed as described in the preceding paragraph.

✔ **Keep a pad and pencil handy to jot down the license plate number and a general description of the car, its driver, and occupants while your impressions are still fresh.** If the car follows you for a suspiciously long time and then takes off, report the incident to the police or highway patrol. They may be looking for these people.

If someone threatens you with a weapon

The statistics on what happens to people who are kidnapped by carjackers are appalling. It's better to risk injury than torture, rape, or murder. That's why I'm such a big advocate of hidden "panic buttons" (described in the section "How Much Is Security Worth to You?") that can be reached easily from the driver's or passenger's seat to activate a tracking device and silently summon aid. Take a look at a few scenarios and what to do about them:

✔ **If an armed thief demands you open your door when your car is idling at a red light or after an "accident":** Although you may be tempted to comply in the hope that all the thief wants is the car, the police, who play these games more than most, advise you to hightail it out of there! Average human reaction time is between .5 and 1.5 seconds and, believe it or not, in most cases that's enough time to get away. Most cars provide reasonable protection against bullets, so your chances of survival are better if you floor it and drive away than if you allow the creep — and the gun — inside your car.

✔ **If you're accosted outside your car:** Hand over your keys, money, and jewelry immediately. They're worth a lot less than your life.

✔ **If you're in danger of being kidnapped:** Take drastic measures to avoid being forced into the car. Fight back. If you can't run, then kick, scream, create as big a disturbance as you can. Few thieves risk taking time to deal with a victim who is attracting attention.

If your vehicle breaks down on the highway

Even if you don't suspect foul play, you should take measures to insure your safety until help arrives:

✔ **Get your car to the side of the road if possible.** This not only improves the flow of traffic; it keeps your vehicle from being hit. If you can't get the car off the highway, do *not* attempt to cross on foot over several lanes of traffic. You're safer staying in the vehicle.

✔ **Draw attention to yourself.** If you have no cellular phone, place a "Call Police" sun visor or sign in your windshield, wedge a white rag or white piece of paper between your closed window and the door, and turn on emergency flashers to alert passing motorists.

✔ **Don't get out to accept help from strangers.** From the safety of your car, gracefully refuse physical assistance and ask them to phone the police, the highway patrol, or your auto club. Only call 911 if someone is seriously injured or you feel you're in real danger.

- ✔ **Don't walk along the highway alone.** Use a highway call box only if you can park directly in front of it and hop right back into your car.

- ✔ **If someone stops and harasses you,** honk the horn repeatedly and flash the lights to attract attention.

- ✔ **Lobby for freeway service patrols.** Highway police in some areas supply fuel, fix flats, do minor repairs, and even tow you to a safe place. Lobby for this service in your area.

Give yourself the edge

You can also abide by some general rules that will keep you one step ahead of the bad guys:

- ✔ **Don't be a hero.** If you see someone trying to break into your vehicle, do not attempt to stop them. Head for the nearest phone, dial 911, and let the police handle it.

- ✔ **Be alert to those around you when walking to or from your car.** Walk confidently, keys in hand. If someone seems suspicious, walk away and return a little later. If they're still hanging around, call 911.

- ✔ **Place valuables out of sight before you park.** Lock them in the trunk of your car or hide them under the seat before leaving your previous destination, not after you park your car. Who knows who could be watching?

- ✔ **Always look under and into the car before you get in to make sure nobody's hiding inside.** If this makes you feel like a gothic heroine searching under her bed, remember that car thieves have been known to conceal themselves under cars as well as in the back seat area.

How Much Is Security Worth to You?

Unless you slow them down or scare them away, professional thieves can break into your vehicle, hot-wire it, and have it on the road in less than two minutes! Therefore, most security devices are designed to convince would-be thieves that it isn't worth risking the time and effort necessary to steal your car. In 1994 only 24 percent of car owners surveyed had antitheft devices on their cars, and 25 percent of those who did said they didn't always activate the device. If you haven't taken any steps to protect your vehicle, check your excuses against the facts:

Excuse	Fact
"I don't live in a high-crime area."	Maybe not, but you frequent risky places like malls and parking lots. Cars are stolen in the suburbs, too.
"My car is too old."	Used cars are stolen more often than new ones.
"I don't care if my car is stolen."	Fine, but what about possessions in the car that may not be covered by your insurance? And what about your life?
"Antitheft devices are too expensive."	You'll be happy to know that most of them cost less than the insurance deductible you'll pay if your car is stolen, and some will earn discounts that lower your premiums.

How much protection do you need?

There are antitheft contraptions designed to assuage everything from mild concern to major paranoia. The Auto Theft Survey and Guide to Layered Protection, shown in Figure 17-2, was created by the National Insurance Crime Bureau (NICB) as part of their Community Carwatch program. They've graciously allowed me to reproduce it for your use. By answering the questions in the first column and totaling the points assigned to each answer you give, you can see what layer of protection — from the minimum (lock your car doors, take your keys with you, and so on) to the maximum (get a tracking system) your car needs. Even if you don't use this survey to devise a protection plan, it's still a real eye-opener to how much your vehicle is at risk.

Antitheft options

If you've found your layer of protection and want to purchase antitheft devices, or just want to investigate the pros and cons of each type of device, read on:

- ✔ **Factory-installed devices.** Built-in antitheft features can save you more money on a new vehicle than any luxury option, and car manufacturers offer a variety of security features — from basic electronic door locks and alarm systems to such advanced technology as GM's PASS-Key system — as standard or optional equipment.

✔ **Custom-installed devices.** Because everyone knows that you have to do your homework to get ahead in the world, some professional thieves do their best to learn to dismantle the factory-installed devices on the most desirable vehicles. If you choose your own combination of aftermarket alarms and cutoffs and have them custom-installed, you'll make it harder for thieves to figure out how to disable your unique combination of systems.

Figure 17-2:
Use the NICB Auto Theft Survey and Guide to Layered Protection, to see how much protection you need.

AUTO THEFT SURVEY

In order to determine how much protection you might need, you first need to determine how "hot" a target your vehicle is to thieves. Complete this survey, prepared by the National Insurance Crime Bureau, and compare your total points to the layers of protection guide on the next page. Ask your insurance agent which anti-theft devices can result in discounts on your insurance premiums.

LOCATION
What is your city's population?

More than 250,000	8 points	*Although the trend is changing, FBI data indicates city drivers are still more likely to become a vehicle theft victim than suburban motorists.*
250,000 to 100,001	6 points	
100,000 to 50,001	4 points	
50,000 to 10,000	2 points	
Less than 10,000	0 points	

STYLE
What type of vehicle do you drive?

Sports Car	5 Points	*According to the Highway Loss Data Institute, the style of your vehicle is one of the biggest factors in determining a vehicle's theft rate.*
Luxury Car	4 Points	
Utility Vehicle	4 Points	
Sedan	3 Points	
Passenger Van	1 Point	
Station Wagon	0 Points	

AGE
How old is your vehicle?

0-2 Years	1 Point	*Older vehicles are actually stolen more often than newer models. Stolen vehicle parts often become replacement parts for other aging vehicles.*
3-5 Years	1 Point	
6-8 Years	2 Points	
9+ Years	0 Points	

BONUS
Add 1 point to your score if you live near an international border or port.

Vehicles stolen in these communities are sometimes shipped or driven into foreign countries.

POINTS		
	LOCATION	
	STYLE	
	AGE	
	BONUS	
	TOTAL	

A GUIDE TO LAYERED PROTECTION

Professional thieves can steal any vehicle, but make them work for yours. For the best protection, use a "layered approach" to vehicle theft prevention -- the more layers of protection on your vehicle, the more difficult it is to steal.

FIRST LAYER: *Common Sense (0-4 Points)*
An unlocked vehicle with a key in the ignition is an open invitation to any thief, regardless of which anti-theft device you use. The common sense approach to protection is the simplest and most cost-effective way to thwart would-be thieves. You should always secure your vehicle, even if parking for brief periods by:
• Taking your keys from the ignition
• Locking your doors   • Closing all your windows
• Parking in a well-lit area

SECOND LAYER: *Visible or Audible Deterrent (5-10 Points)*
The second layer of protection is a visible or audible device which alerts thieves that your vehicle is protected before they attempt to steal it. Some second layer devices are also effective in protecting your vehicle from burglary and vandalism. Popular second layer devices include:
• Car alarms   • Steering wheel locks
• Steering column collars   • Theft-deterrent decals

THIRD LAYER: *Vehicle Immobilizer (11-15 Points)*
The third layer of protection is a device which prevents thieves from bypassing your ignition and hot wiring the vehicle. Some electronic devices have computer chips in ignition keys. Other manual devices inhibit the flow of electricity or fuel to the engine until a hidden switch or button is activated. A third category passively immobilizes the vehicle by interrupting up to three separate engine systems -- starter, ignition and fuel. Popular third layer devices include:
• Electronic keys   • Starter disablers
• Fuse cut-offs   • Vehicle immobilizers (interrupt
                                   starter, ignition, and fuel systems)

FOURTH LAYER: *Tracking System (16-17 Points)*
The final layer of protection is a tracking system which emits a signal to a police or monitoring station when the vehicle is reported stolen. Tracking systems are very effective in helping authorities recover stolen vehicles.

All theft deterrents fall into two major categories: proactive measures that prevent theft and reactive measures that trace vehicles after they've been stolen. Compare these options and buy whatever you need to feel secure. Prices vary widely, and the most expensive devices are not necessarily the best.

Proactive measures: Preventing theft

First you must decide whether you want active or passive protection. *Active antitheft systems* do not work unless you turn them on or — in the militaristic parlance of the trade — "arm them." This is fine if you live and hang out in a relatively safe area and prefer not to have an alarm that may go off in the middle of the night and annoy the neighbors. Unfortunately, the chances are that just when you neglect to arm your system, the bad guys will come to call. Most insurance companies do not offer discounts for active antitheft devices because they can't trust you to use them all the time. *Passive systems,* on the other hand, are always on the job. For this reason, many insurance companies offer antitheft discounts on cars equipped with these automatic safeguards. The following sections list some of the most popular antitheft devices.

Although many security devices can be bought and installed by amateurs, I suggest that you get professional help. Faulty installation can result in alarms that go off at the slightest provocation — or fail to operate at all — and wiring that can easily be detected and disabled by car thieves. If your system is complex or hypersensitive, be sure that the installers provide fail-safe switches that allow you to disable the system if it fails to operate properly. For instance, I use a remote-control beeper to unlock my car doors. If someone opens the door with a key or other device, the ignition system refuses to start the car. To protect me from my own tendency to forget things, a hidden switch bypasses the ignition cutoff if the beeper is lost or misplaced, or if its battery loses power, and I have to use a key to enter my car.

Alarm systems

Alarm systems can detect motion, sound, breakage, and even changes in air pressure. Options include sirens, flashing lights, horn activators, and any or all of the goodies mentioned in the following paragraphs. Some can even alert you via your pager. Perhaps the biggest drawback of auto alarms is that, because they are so common and go off easily for all the wrong reasons, most people tend to disregard them completely. Anyone who has ever lived right above a large parking garage knows that an alarm can shatter the silence for a quarter of an hour without exciting any human response except a muttered curse and an attempt to burrow under the covers and go back to sleep. To add insult to injury, some authorities ticket owners of cars that are subject to frequent false alarms.

Alarm systems can be active or passive, but you run the risk of forgetting to arm manually operated alarms. Choose one that is sensitive enough to prevent theft but will not go crazy if someone parks close to your car or leans against a fender, or if an animal decides to use a tire as a restroom.

Breaking-glass alerts

Breaking-glass alerts go off if someone tries to enter your car by breaking a window. Unfortunately, some are so sensitive that even tapping the glass sets them off.

Bulletproof armor

You, too, can drive a genuine armored car — if you're willing to pay the price. Lightweight, custom-made, bulletproof armor that doesn't look very different from conventional bodywork goes for $40,000 to $70,000; super-strength side windows are around $3,000 each. If you govern a country or wear jewelry worth millions, this is probably a bargain.

Cellular phone alarm systems

These systems automatically call the police if the vehicle is broken into or in an accident. Some have the ability to provide a complete description of your car, notify the owner, and even send the thief a warning that the police have been notified. These are relatively expensive but very effective, although their signals can be blocked by subterranean garages, buildings, mountains, or tunnels.

GM's OnStar system uses a cellular telephone and a built-in global positioning system (GPS) to contact a 24-hour customer assistance center that automatically locates the vehicle, determines what help is needed, and dispatches assistance. An emergency button signals the center to dispatch police, ambulance, fire, and other emergency services. OnStar also automatically notifies the center whenever an air bag deploys or if the theft-deterrent system is tripped, and tracks the stolen vehicle until it is recovered. It can also tell drivers where they are in unfamiliar territory and provide them with directions to their destination. Other features include returning the driver's seat to a memorized position by sensing which key is used to unlock the doors and unlocking the doors by remote control if the driver is accidentally locked out.

Even the government is getting into the act: NHTSA (the National Highway Traffic Safety Administration) is testing an electronic device that could automatically call 911 for help after an accident. It uses the car's cellular phone to transmit the location of the vehicle to a government satellite, which beams the information to the county sheriff's 911 center computer, which would then display the location of the crash on a map. The device can also transmit information on the severity of a crash and whether the vehicle was hit from the front, rear, side, or rolled over. As if that weren't enough, the car's cellular phone will also automatically establish a channel to the sheriff's department so the occupants can talk to the dispatcher. The system should be available within five years for $200 to $300.

Cellular phones

Cellular phones enable drivers to keep in touch with friends or family while driving late at night or through unsafe neighborhoods, to dial the authorities or your auto club for assistance with breakdowns and accidents, and to report suspicious characters. Some cellular systems not only allow you to dial 911 or the AAA's emergency number free of charge, but their phones feature one-touch access to these numbers.

The FCC (Federal Communications Commission) recently ruled that cellular phone companies must complete emergency 911 calls, even if the caller "roams" and the call originates outside the company's service area. They must also complete calls made by callers who have let their cellular service lapse, or have never subscribed, as long as the phone's "mobile identification number" (usually the same as the cellular phone number) hasn't changed. Even emergency calls from cell phones that lack identification numbers because the phone hasn't been activated yet must also be accepted. The FCC also requires cellular companies to have the ability to tell 911 dispatchers the location of an emergency caller within 125 feet by October 1, 2001.

The use of cellular phones while driving is hazardous: An increasing number of accidents are linked to drivers who were distracted by phone calls. For this reason, and because you must pay for incoming as well as outgoing calls, you should probably only give the number to those closest to you, with instructions to use it only in emergencies. Be sure to anchor all phones safely in your vehicle; in an accident, a loose phone can be a dangerous projectile.

Credit-card keys

Credit-card keys are electronic switches that complete existing circuits and allow the car to start only after a card is inserted into a slot. These are only effective if installed in a manner that discourages thieves from hot-wiring the circuit to bypass it.

Delay devices

Delay devices allow thieves to drive a short distance before disabling the car. These are designed to protect victims of carjackers by giving them time to hand over the vehicle and get away before the thieves realize that they have been duped. One such system provides a toll-free number that alerts a communications center to send a signal that causes the car's horn to beep and headlights to flash. If the thief stops the car and shuts off the ignition, the car won't start again. This system can be augmented to allow you to remotely unlock and start your car, even activate the heater or air conditioner to warm up or cool off the car before you arrive.

Hood locks

Hood locks prevent thieves from stealing batteries and other parts and from disabling under-the-hood antitheft gizmos.

Kill switches

Electronic "kill-switches" can disable a car's starter, battery, or fuel supply to prevent thieves from driving away. They are often part of a package that may also include remote-controlled door locks and alarms.

Locking car covers

Car covers with locks not only protect the vehicle from dust, sunlight, and moisture, but prevent thieves from telling whether your car is worth stealing or has an alarm. Thieves rarely take the time to saw the lock off to remove the cover and find out.

Panic buttons

Hidden panic buttons can be surreptitiously pushed to disable the car or activate a silent alarm or tracking system if someone threatens you or forces his way into your car.

Remote-controlled door locks and alarms

Remote-controlled door locks allow you to enter your car without having to fumble with a key. They may also include "kill switches," which prevent the ignition system from functioning if the doors are opened in any other manner. They can open the trunk, blink the headlights, turn on interior lights, lock the doors after you're inside, and activate an alarm or horn in emergencies. I like one that makes little chirping sounds because my car always seems glad to see me.

Secret switches

Secret switches connect antitheft devices to existing switches in your car. In one version, you have to press the automatic window button before you can start the car.

Smart-key systems

Electronic "smart-key" systems prevent the car from starting unless the correct key is used. Some, like GM's PASS-Key, feature a resistor pellet embedded in the ignition key that is read by electronic sensors in the car. If the code is incorrect, the starter motor and fuel systems are disabled long enough to discourage most thieves. If the electronic unit fails to function or is lost, even the car's own ignition key will be ineffective unless a hidden override is activated. These systems are among the cheapest and most effective theft preventers around. They merit a 10 to 25 percent deduction on some insurance policies.

Steering column shields

Some new vehicles now come with shields that wrap around the steering column to prevent thieves from cutting through it and starting the car without a key. Only certain car models have steering columns that are vulnerable in this way, so be sure you really need this shield before springing for an aftermarket version.

Permanent shields are bulky and make servicing the steering column difficult. Removable versions have to be installed every time you leave the car. Because this is relatively troublesome, you may be tempted to neglect to use the shield just when you need it most.

Steering wheel covers

Steering wheel covers cover the entire steering wheel with a metal "saucer" that locks into place, forcing thieves to saw through the entire contraption rather than simply sawing through or bending the steering wheel. Besides being harder to remove, they also prevent thieves from stealing driver's-side air bags.

Steering wheel locks

Hook-type steering wheel locks, such as The Club, can prevent amateur smash-and-grabs but won't foil professionals who can cut through the steering wheel with bolt cutters, hacksaws, or power saws and slide the device off the wheel in as little as 20 seconds. Enterprising thieves have frozen these locks with liquid nitrogen and shattered them with a hammer or screwed a dent puller into the lock and used a slide hammer to pop them out of their housings; others have managed to drive cars away with the steering wheel lock still in place. Visibility is the chief deterrent. Unless they're out for your specific type of car, many amateur crooks will pass up cars with steering wheel locks in favor of unprotected vehicles.

If you want one of these relatively inexpensive devices, buy one that is sturdy enough to resist hand tools and pinches the wheel in two places instead of only one. Installation with the lock facing the dash may deter some thieves, but makes it harder to get the gadget on and off. You can also buy a device that hooks around your clutch or brake pedal as well as your steering wheel, but after the wheel is cut, the gadget is disabled anyway.

Insurance antitheft discounts are generally not available for this equipment. Claims by some manufacturers that they will pay up to $500 if your car is stolen while using them have been subject to such stiff requirements that actual compensation is relatively rare.

Theft-proof wheels

Expensive aluminum theft-proof wheels come with funny-shaped lug nuts that can't be removed by ordinary wrenches. I'm sure that professional thieves manage to create tools that can remove these, but again, the aim is to discourage casual thievery.

Window stickers and warning lights

Window stickers and warning lights caution thieves that the car is armed against theft. If you can't afford a real system, fake stickers and glue-on dashboard LEDs that blink convincingly have proven to be surprisingly effective deterrents.

Reactive measures: Tracing stolen cars

Electronic car-tracking systems hide a homing device in the vehicle that sends a signal to security agencies or police so they can track the car until they find it. Because about 90 percent of the stolen vehicles equipped with these systems have been recovered, insurance companies are usually willing to offer discounts for their use.

Currently the most popular car-tracking system in the United States, LoJack (781-326-4700), is sold at several thousand car dealerships and satellite offices and is still expanding its markets. When you report your vehicle stolen, police enter a stolen vehicle report into their computer which sends a coded message to the LoJack unit in your car. This activates the unit which sends a reply code indicating the direction to pursue to tracking computers installed in all police cruisers within a 25-mile range of your vehicle's current location. Even though the system doesn't work until after the car is reported stolen, LoJack's arrest rate is five times the national average. This is attributed to the fact that thieves usually park cars only two to seven miles away from where they were stolen to "cool off" for 48 hours before "running for the border." The LoJack signal operates across state lines.

Helping Police Recover Stolen Cars and Property

An average of 86 percent of all stolen vehicles are recovered by the police. Whether the car is relatively undamaged, driveable, or stripped depends largely on your ability to give the police every advantage in their attempts to locate and recover it. The following sections explain what you can do to put the odds in your favor:

- **Report the theft immediately:** The faster the local patrol cars are alerted, the better, so call the police station nearest the crime location. Because car-theft is not their kind of emergency, *don't call 911.*

- **Provide detailed descriptions:** Because most of us do not take these things calmly, a written record comes in handy when reporting a theft. Records should include the license number, color, year, make, and model of each vehicle you own; unique characteristics like window decals, bumper stickers, upholstery, and accessories; as well as noticeable scratches, dents, and decals. Personal possessions should be identified by manufacturer, model, serial number, color, material, monograms, and imperfections.

- **Personalize your vehicle and your possessions:** Etch the VIN on all the places listed in the "Salvage switching" section.

    Drop your business card or return address label between the driver's door and window to help police identify the car even if it reaches a "chop shop." Place another card under the rear seat.

- **If available, participate in an antitheft surveillance program.** In many cities, these programs authorize the police to place a decal on your car saying they can stop your car without probable cause between 1 a.m. and 5 a.m. to identify ownership.

Another piece of advice: No matter which methods in this chapter you choose to employ, don't hesitate to take action to protect yourself from "bad guys." Running scared is a poor alternative to driving confidently. After all, you can even get in trouble waiting for a bus!

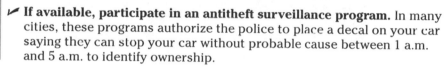

Cover your losses before they occur

The main thing you need to do to cover your losses before they occur, is to review your insurance. Part V covers auto insurance in detail, but here are a few quick tips to get you on the right track:

- **Strike a balance between expensive low deductibles and cheaper high deductibles that may not cover your losses.**

- **Compare policies for the best coverage.** Most insurance companies offer discounts of 5 to 25 percent to drivers who install antitheft devices.

- **Be sure your personal possessions are covered as well as your vehicle.** Auto insurance often doesn't cover loss or damage to personal property left in the vehicle or optional or aftermarket electronic equipment. Homeowner's or renter's insurance may only cover personal possessions stolen from a locked car that was visibly tampered with. Consider covering expensive equipment with a personal articles policy that reimburses you for the full replacement cost, rather than the depreciated value, if it is stolen.

Chapter 18

Finding a Good Repair Facility (And What to Do If You're Ripped Off Anyway)

You've just moved to a new town and your trusted repair shop is too far away to be of any use to you. Or you've bought a new car and your old facility doesn't work on vehicles from that manufacturer. Suddenly you're lost in the marketplace without the faintest idea of where to go for servicing or where to turn for help in an emergency. The Yellow Pages are full of ads, and the streets are full of service stations, but how can you tell which shop is reliable and which is just waiting to take advantage of you or ruin your splendid set of wheels? Relax, dear friend, you have come to the right place for advice.

Mechanic is no longer a catchall word for anyone who works on your car. Now that most vehicles feature elaborate electronic systems, the proper word is *technician*. To keep from boring you with endless repetition, I use both terms (*repairperson* seems a bit awkward). But you should use *technician* when you're speaking to professionals and want to make a good impression.

Choosing the Type of Facility You Need

For obvious reasons, you should find a good shop *before* your vehicle needs service or repairs rather than waiting for an emergency and rushing about in a state of panic. When you find a shop you like, take your vehicle in for a simple maintenance or repair job to test the quality of their service so you'll know if you can trust them if major surgery is ever required. Several kinds of facilities are available, and each has its drawbacks and advantages. The following sections can help you decide which type is best for you.

Dealerships

New car buyers frequently use the dealership's service department, at least until the warranty period is over. The truth is, you can have most warranty work done by any licensed technician as long as all the service requirements listed in the owner's manual are fulfilled. There are some exceptions, so check all the warranties before going elsewhere.

Dealership service departments may offer the following advantages:

- ✔ **They often provide extra service to ensure goodwill.** They can often make more of a profit on service during the life of a vehicle than they made on the original sale. And, of course, they want you to stay with them when it's time to buy another car.

- ✔ **They usually have a variety of specialists right on the premises.** This means that you can have brake, air-conditioning, or transmission work done at the same facility. Their technicians are factory-trained to work on your vehicle's make and model.

- ✔ **They stock a wide variety of OEM (original) parts made specifically for your vehicle.** In most cases, these parts prove more durable and trouble-free than aftermarket parts, and if you're restoring a classic car you absolutely don't want to use anything but original equipment or else you will reduce your car's value.

- ✔ **If you have a complaint, you will be dealing with an established company that is financially able to reimburse you and is insured to cover any major lawsuits that may result.**

However, dealership service departments have disadvantages to consider:

- ✔ **A dealership is usually more expensive.** Having work done at a dealership generally costs more than having it done at an independent shop, which has lower overhead to support.

- ✔ **The sales and service departments of a dealership are generally run separately.** What this means is you may find that the service staff doesn't really care that much about whether the dealership will sell you another vehicle. Instead, their attitude may be, "We have more work than we can handle so if you're not happy here, you can go somewhere else."

✔ **You may not receive the personalized service you'd get from an independent shop.** At a dealership you generally talk to a service writer who then assigns your vehicle to whichever technician is available when its number comes up. Of course, if you build a good relationship with the service writer, he or she may honor your request for a specific technician, or at least see that your car doesn't get handed to a different person every time it comes in for repairs.

National chains and department stores

You can choose to have repair and maintenance work done at mass merchandisers with automotive service departments. Of course, like anything else, having service done in one of these shops also offers pros and cons:

✔ **They are generally less expensive than dealerships and usually stock a wide variety of parts, many of which are made to their specifications and carry their brand name.** How these parts compare to the original equipment supplied by the car manufacturer will vary in price and quality.

✔ **They usually provide good guarantees on parts and labor.** If you have a complaint, they're generally motivated toward keeping your goodwill.

✔ **They maintain branches all over the country that honor each other's warranties and guarantees.** This can be very beneficial if you travel a lot.

Car manufacturer's service centers

Because 70 percent of consumers forsake the more expensive dealerships and take their vehicles to independent repair shops after their warranties have expired, American carmakers have begun to open freestanding service centers. The carmakers hope these service centers will be viewed as having the best advantages of both dealerships and independent shops. Chrysler and Ford have pioneered this effort, and other manufacturers are watching closely to see whether to follow suit.

The first of six prototype Chrysler Neighborhood Service Centers opened in February 1998. It features a children's playroom, computer docking bays, and a catwalk from which customers are encouraged to talk to the technicians who are working on their cars. Ford's Auto Care centers are based on similar concepts.

Although these shops are owned by licensed Ford and Chrysler dealers and carry their respective Motorcraft and Mopar auto parts, they are expected to operate independently and have been placed close to residential neighborhoods and shopping malls. If one of these has opened in your area, you may want to check it out. If the price is right, access to manufacturer-trained technicians and original equipment may make these centers an attractive alternative to traditional repair facilities.

✔ **They are good training grounds for inexperienced technicians who are just out of school and working at their first professional jobs.** This can cut two ways: If your car falls into incompetent hands, it may turn out to be a guinea pig as well as a gas hog; or your car may be lucky enough to be tended to by bright, enthusiastic mechanics with all the latest techniques still fresh in their minds.

✔ **They usually employ service writers.** The work may tend to be impersonal, with a different technician working on your vehicle each time.

✔ **Some of these service departments pay their technicians a commission on the parts they sell.** This may result in your being told that your vehicle requires work it doesn't really need, or you may be sold new parts when it would have been cheaper to repair the old ones.

Independent shops

An independent shop can be the best — or the worst — alternative for the following reasons:

✔ **Honest, reliable, and experienced independents often provide personal service based on high standards of excellence.** You will usually be able to communicate directly with the owner, manager, or a technician who knows you and knows your vehicle.

✔ **Most independents rely on referrals for new customers.** For this reason, they care a great deal about maintaining a good reputation.

✔ **Many independent shops offer lower prices than those charged by dealerships.** Others, especially those that service only expensive luxury cars or sports cars, may offer the finest workmanship at relatively exorbitant rates. A cherished few provide fine workmanship at low prices — these are probably saints disguised in greasy coveralls!

✔ **Expertise, the availability of specialized tools, and the variety of special parts on hand may vary from one shop to another, so checking carefully to be sure you've found a good one is especially important.** A reliable independent will know where to find the proper talent, borrow the tools, and buy the high-quality parts at the best price. An unreliable shop will patch things together with crummy aftermarket parts and hope for the best.

Specialists

Specialized chains deal with a particular area of automotive repair. An independent specialist shop can either specialize in specific repairs, such as chrome-refinishing, brake work, or glass replacement; or only work on specific makes or types of vehicles, such as vans or classic cars.

A reliable independent specialist can provide the experience, specialized tools, and an extensive inventory that may be unavailable at a shop that handles everything in general and nothing in particular. If you know that the trouble with your car resides in a specific area (such as a leaking radiator, holes in the muffler, or transmission problems), you may want to look for a well-established independent that specializes in that particular system.

National specialized chains that sell and install cheapo parts such as brakes, transmissions, and mufflers are often more interested in selling new parts than in repairing old ones. Their "lifetime guarantees" that keep you coming back to pay for the labor to replace their "free" but short-lived merchandise are probably more profitable than providing high-quality, durable parts that need little further attention. Be sure to check the reputation of a specialized chain in consumer publications before heading to them for repairs.

Which type of facility you choose may vary with the type of repair your vehicle needs. Generally speaking, major tire chains usually have the lowest prices on new tires. When it comes to repairs, a reliable, competent, and experienced independent will probably give you the best value for your money.

Finding a Reliable Shop

Unless you live in a small town or rural area, there are usually so many auto repair establishments to choose from that finding a good one can feel like searching for a needle in a haystack. Here's what you can do to identify an honest, competent facility that will provide good service over a long period of time.

Look for signs of approval and achievement

Several organizations test, rate, and certify automotive facilities and individual technicians. If you're unsure about a particular shop, you can feel pretty secure if you see that a shop or technician has achieved recognition in one of the following ways.

AAA- and CAA-approved auto-repair facilities

The American Automobile Association (AAA) and the Canadian Automobile Association (CAA) have similar Approved Auto Repair Programs. They frequently visit and evaluate auto repair facilities and approve those that meet their high standards for good work at a fair price and a willingness to resolve problems when things go wrong. Any customer complaints that have been made about the shop to the local Auto Club office are taken into account. Because these programs operate on a cost-recovery basis, repair facilities have no way to "buy" approval. Participation in these programs does not impose price limitations on approved shops; they cover the full spectrum from low-cost to high-priced establishments. The two organizations have a reciprocal agreement that allows members of one club to enjoy the same services and benefits when using the facilities approved by the other.

To qualify for approval, facilities must provide customers on request with written estimates of all costs and offer a minimum warranty on parts and labor of at least 180 days or 6,000 miles, whichever comes first.

When negotiations between a repair facility and a member are getting nowhere, both the AAA and the CAA are willing to arbitrate disputes between their members and their approved shops. There are two exceptions to this, however:

✔ They will not go to bat for you just because you found that you could have had the work done for less money somewhere else.

✔ They will not decide whether a specific job is covered by a manufacturer's warranty.

Members with unresolved complaints about service they've received by an approved shop can simply contact the Approved Auto Repair Service Program at their local Auto Club office to get investigative proceedings under way.

Contact your local or regional Auto Club office to find out if there is an Approved Auto Repair Service Program in your area, or look for the AAA or CAA logo on display at repair shops. For a list of all Approved Repair Facilities in your area, contact your local club or the Auto Club's national headquarters at one of the following addresses or phone numbers:

Approved Auto Repair Program
Automotive Engineering and
Road Division
American Automobile Association
1000 AAA Drive
Heathrow, FL 32746
(407-444-7761)

Approved Auto Repair Service Program
Canadian National Office
Canadian Automobile Association
1145 Hunt Club Road, Suite 200
Ottawa, Ontario K1V 0Y3
(613-247-0117)

ASE-certified technicians

The National Institute for Automotive Service Excellence (ASE) is an independent, nonprofit organization that has certified more than 440,000 automotive technicians through a series of voluntary tests in a variety of automobile repair specializations, including brakes, transmissions, engine repair, and so on. ASE certifies the individual, not the shop, so look for a blue-and-white ASE shoulder insignia on a technician's uniform or obtain a list of certified technicians in your home state by writing to the ASE at 13505 Dulles Technology Drive, Suite 2, Herndon, Virginia 20171-3421.

Authorized Diesel Specialists (ADS)

Owners of diesel vehicles that are out of warranty who are looking for a reliable diesel mechanic can look in their local yellow pages under "Automobile Repairing and Service" for a shop that displays the ADS logo. ADS-authorized shops must send their technicians to factory schools to keep abreast of new parts, techniques, and systems. The shops must also meet high standards for cleanliness and must stock sufficient tools and parts to deal efficiently with most diesel repair and maintenance jobs.

Independent Garage Owners Association (IGO) members

Although the IGO has nothing to do with qualifying individual technicians, it does have a code of ethics that garage owners have pledged to live up to if they want to stay in the organization. An IGO shield or sign indicates that the owner of an independent shop is a member of this association.

Service and achievement awards

Take a look at the framed certificates hanging in the shop's office. Reliable facilities often receive service awards for participating in community and civic organizations. They may also earn awards for customer-service excellence. While you're at it, look for grateful letters from satisfied clients and certificates awarded to individual technicians who have completed factory training programs that qualify them to operate specialized electronic equipment or to work on your make or type of vehicle.

Better Business Bureau members

A Better Business Bureau membership certificate is a good sign that the shop is serious about its reputation. Call your local BBB office to see whether the shop has been the subject of numerous consumer complaints.

Referrals

I've always felt that the best way to find a good repair facility is the same way that you find a good doctor, lawyer, or plumber — through referrals. Ask people who drive vehicles from the same manufacturer as yours where they get their repairs done. Then check out the establishments, starting with the ones that are most conveniently located. As a fringe benefit, you'll also learn which repair shops to avoid, because most of the people you ask will also have horror stories to tell.

Personally evaluate the facility

A quick way to do a preliminary check is to call a shop and ask for its basic prices on easy jobs like tune-ups, flushing the cooling system, or changing the oil and the oil filter. While you're at it, ask what its hourly rate for labor is and whether it uses original parts for replacements. A telephone interview can give you a good idea of whether the shop's prices are competitive; it will also give you a feeling of its overall vibes. If the person you speak to is surly and uncommunicative over the phone, chances are you're going to run into trouble when you have to deal with the shop in an emergency. Follow up a positive phone interview with an unannounced visit to check on the following things:

- **Is the place clean and well-organized, or filthy and cluttered?** This is a good indication of general attitude. Automotive repair calls for patience and precision. If the shop is sloppy and disorganized, chances are the work will be, too.

- **Does it have modern electronic diagnostic and testing equipment?** These devices save time by accurately and automatically pinpointing trouble areas and checking adjustments and tolerances. Quick, accurate diagnostics save you money when it comes to paying labor charges. Of course, this equipment is only as good as the person using it. Ask if anyone at the shop frequently attends factory schools and the seminars run by diagnostic equipment manufacturers to learn how to use the more sophisticated analyzers and keep up-to-date on new systems. You should also scan the wall in the office for certificates that verify that a technician has completed such courses.

- **What kind of vehicles are they working on?** Take a look at the vehicles on the hoists and in the parking lot. Are there expensive models among them or just a bunch of junk heaps? Are the vehicles on the lot covered with dust? If so, your car could join the group as it waits weeks or months for parts or attention. Do you see any vehicles of your make and model? If not, do they have experience with it, or do they specialize in vehicles from other manufacturers?

- **Are the technicians qualified?** Ask to see proof of the technician's qualifications and the scope of repairs covered by such qualifications.

- **Does the shop have an up-to-date service manual for your vehicle?** I usually buy one for my car's year, make, and model and offer to lend it to the shop when repairs are needed. After all, they can't stock one for every car in the world. I also leaf through the section in the manual that deals with the system in question, to get an idea of how much work and which parts are involved so I can communicate intelligently, and so I have a basis for questioning any parts or labor charges that seem out of line.

- **Does the shop have the necessary tools and expertise to do the work your vehicle requires?** Ask if any part of the job will have to be sent out to a specialist. If so, will your shop mark up the cost of the specialist's work, or simply charge you what the specialist charged them? If they have to bring your vehicle to the specialist and then pick it up again, they probably are going to want something for their time. Unless the specialist's role is a minor one, you may save money by dealing with the specialist directly. A good general repair facility should direct you to a specialist, if that is the only work required.

Investigate how they charge for repairs

How does the shop structure the price you pay for repairs? This not only has a great impact on your wallet, but on the quality of the work performed, as well. The following review of the advantages and disadvantages of various pricing systems is based on an article by automotive expert, David (Dre) Solomon, editor/publisher of *Nutz & Boltz,* an automotive newsletter.

✔ **By the clock:** Any type of automotive repair facility may determine the cost of a job by multiplying a fixed hourly labor rate by the time it took to complete the work.

- *Advantages:* This system is simple and easy to understand and encourages technicians to take the time to do their best work.

- *Disadvantages:* It also makes it difficult to accurately estimate what the job will cost because unexpected technical problems can seriously raise the price.

✔ **Pre-established price lists:** Specialists and major chains, such as brake, muffler, and transmission shops, often set fixed prices for specific jobs. Sometimes several basic services are combined into one package.

- *Advantages:* Prices are easy to understand and are usually competitive. You don't pay more if the job goes slowly.

- *Disadvantages:* There are none, unless the only service you need can only be done as part of a package.

✔ **Flat rates:** Most shops base their prices on a *Flat Rate Manual,* which lists every job that can be done, as well as the amount of time it should take to accomplish the job on a specific vehicle.

- *Advantages:* Estimates are accurate because they aren't affected if a job takes longer than normal.

- *Disadvantages:* You may be charged for the amount of time listed in the manual, no matter how little time the work actually took. Few shops will keep a technician who can't "beat the book" by a substantial amount of time, which means that mechanics may skimp and cut corners to complete repairs as quickly as possible.

✔ **Variable flat rates:** Some dealerships price jobs not only by the *Flat Rate Manual,* but also by the level of skill necessary to do the work properly.

- *Advantages:* Maintenance jobs are usually priced at a lower rate than more sophisticated repairs. You aren't penalized if the job takes longer than expected.

- *Disadvantages:* You may have to pay for expensive repairs when the problem could have been corrected in a quicker and cheaper fashion. For instance, some automatic transmission problems are caused by insufficient transmission fluid, but some shops will rebuild or replace the entire transmission instead of simply adding enough fluid to bring the level up to the full line on the dipstick.

✔ **Flat rates and parts commissions:** At many chains or department stores, the mechanic shares in the profits on the sale of parts.

- *Advantages:* You aren't penalized if the job takes longer than expected.

- *Disadvantages:* In addition to the disadvantages of flat rates, you may have to pay for replacing a part that could have been cheaply and easily repaired or for parts you never needed in the first place.

Ask other questions

Before you decide on a facility, ask the following questions:

✔ **What forms of payment do they accept?** Will they take credit cards? Checks? Only cash? Paying by credit card not only is convenient, but if there's a dispute, it gives you the ability to withhold payment until your credit card company investigates the situation.

✔ **What guarantees do they provide on their repairs?** These can vary from none to anywhere from a month to a year. If a shop doesn't expect its work to hold up for at least three months, I'd go elsewhere.

✔ **Will they allow you to call a few customers for references?** You'd want references before you hired an employee, wouldn't you? A vehicle worth thousands of your hard-earned dollars certainly deserves the same assurances.

Taking Precautions When Major Repairs Are Needed

As I've said before, a big repair job is like major surgery. Not only do you want to have the best possible surgeon, but you also want to be sure the surgery is necessary and that it will be done under the best possible terms.

Guidelines for your protection

Whenever you bring your car in for maintenance or repair, it's wise to follow these guidelines:

✔ **If you are dealing with a new mechanic or are faced with major repairs, get at least one second opinion and an estimate of costs from another repair shop.** If there's a big discrepancy, additional estimates and opinions are in order. If one shop is much lower in price than the others, this is not necessarily the best place to go. Be sure that the work will be of the same quality before you go for the cheapest job.

✔ **Ask for a written estimate.** Many states require one anyway and require the shop to call you if they find that it will cost more than originally estimated. Beware of general statements; try to get as detailed an estimate of what is involved as possible.

✔ **Ask that all the parts they replace be returned to you, whether the laws in your state require that they do so or not.** That way you can be sure that you got what you paid for.

✔ **Ask for credit for the core charge on any rebuildable part that is going to be replaced with a new part.** If you are buying a rebuilt part as a replacement, the core charge should be deducted from the price of the part you buy in exchange for trading in your old part, which will then be rebuilt and sold to someone else.

✔ **Be sure that the invoice for the job includes a written guarantee on parts and labor, and find out if any of the parts they have installed come with their own warranties.** This is especially important if it is a big job that involves expensive parts. It always pays to know just where the responsibility lies in the event of a dispute or a malfunctioning part.

Familiarize yourself with the invoice

Standard invoices, like the one in the sample in Figure 18-1, include several separate areas. Each area serves a particular purpose. In order to help you decipher the sample, the number of each item in the section which follows corresponds to the number on the invoice where it is located.

① **Itemizing the work:** This area should list each job that needed to be done. Be sure to check this item-by-item to see that everything was taken care of.

② **Labor charges:** These are given in terms of fractions of an hour. If a job seems to have taken an excessively long time, ask to check the *Flat Rate Manual,* which is a listing of every job that can be done on a car, with the amount of time it should take to accomplish it. If the hours seem right, multiply them by the shop's hourly rate to make sure they've done the math right. Then check to be sure the "labor" total is the same as that shown in the "totals" column of the invoice ⑤.

Most shops charge you for the amount of time listed in the manual, no matter how little time it actually took them to do it, and few shops will keep a technician who can't "beat the book" by a substantial amount of time (see the section called "Investigate how they charge for repairs" for details).

③ **Parts used:** Each part should be listed, with its price. Make sure they have added correctly and that the "parts" total is the same as that shown in the "totals" column.

④ **Subcontracted repairs:** This area should show all the work that was sent out of the shop to be done by a specialist. The total costs should be repeated in the "totals" column.

⑤ **The "totals" column:** All charges are listed here. You pay the final figure.

Every invoice should also have a space for ⑥ **a written estimate** and for ⑦ **a number where you can be reached if necessary.** You will be asked for ⑧ **your signature** on the estimate.

Be sure to read the small print above the signature before you sign. The fine print should *only* cover your approval of the estimate and the fact that you're willing to allow them to drive the car in order to diagnose, repair, and test it.

The reverse side of the invoice often contains information on the shop's warranty and on the *mechanic's lien,* which allows mechanics in some states to sell your car if you refuse to pay for services. For this reason, it is important that you pay your bill and then seek restitution, if a dispute occurs. For more information on complaint procedures, see the section "Getting Satisfaction When You're Not Happy with the Job" later in this chapter.

Getting the Most for Your Money

Finding a repair facility that is reliable, honest, efficient, and relatively inexpensive isn't enough. You deserve more. Every shop has its most favored customers and will go out of its way to make them happy. If you've been lucky enough to discover an outstanding repair facility, the ball is now in your court when it comes to establishing a good and lasting relationship.

Even though most small businesses are struggling to stay alive these days, a good auto repair shop is an exception. Every outstanding one I've encountered has more business than the time to deal with it. When I moved to a new city and needed someone I could trust to do major work or emergency surgery on Honeybun, my precious little classic car, I literally had to beg the man who came most highly recommended to take me on as a customer because he hadn't accepted new business in over five years. It took a referral from an outstanding car restorer, plus my credentials as an automotive writer and classic-car freak, plus the fact that I had restored Honeybun myself, plus all my charm and my assurances that I would never bother him with "mickeymouse" maintenance work before he agreed to be there for me if something came up that I couldn't handle myself. We eventually became very good friends, in no small part because I faithfully followed the guidelines outlined in the following list:

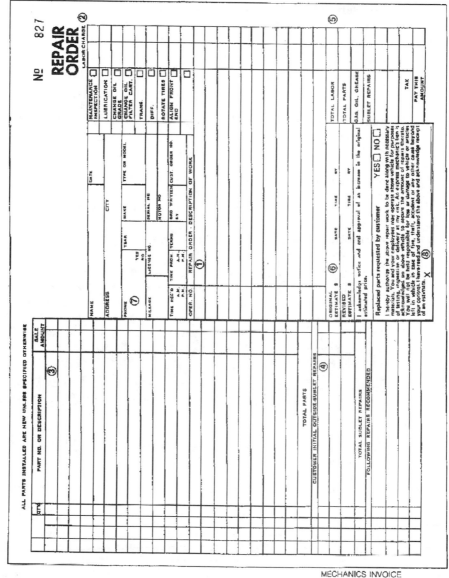

Figure 18-1:
A standard
invoice
for auto
repairs. The
numbers
correspond
to the items
listed in the
preceding
text.

MECHANICS INVOICE

✔ **Call for an appointment.** Don't just show up and expect them to drop everything and take care of you.

✔ **Get your car into the shop early** (at least by 8:30 or 9:00 a.m.) if you hope to get it out the same day. If you're on your way to work, allow sufficient time to give the technician or service writer a full account of what you want done or what you have found to be wrong with the car. Sometimes a test-drive helps demonstrate the problem, so be sure you have the time to go on one if they seem favorably inclined to the idea.

✔ **Bring along a written list of the things you want serviced or repaired.** Include a phone number where you can be reached if questions occur or if the work is going to cost more than was originally estimated.

✔ **Bring a written list of symptoms** for the technicians who will diagnose the problem and do the work. Important symptoms include the following:

- Warning lights and abnormal gauge readings

- Changes in acceleration, gas mileage, handling, steering, and fluid levels

- Drips, leaks, odors, vibrations, and smoke signals

- Unevenly or prematurely worn belts, tires, hoses, and so on

Be specific. If possible, provide the following information about each symptom:

✔ **What exactly is happening.** ("The car stalls." "It pulls to the right." "It runs roughly." "It seems to be losing power." "It's overheating.")

✔ **When it happens.** Is the trouble persistent or intermittent? Does it happen only when the engine is cold or after it warms up? Does it only happen under certain weather conditions? Is it associated with a particular action like shifting, accelerating, or braking? How long has it been going on? ("The car hesitates when I drive up a hill." "It won't start when it rains." "It smokes when I change gears." "It pulls to the left when I brake." "This started after the last oil change.")

✔ **Where the trouble seems to be located.** ("I smell gas when I open the trunk." "There's a vibration under the front seat." "There's a squeak under the right front fender.")

If you can provide information like this to help a technician diagnose the trouble more easily, you can reduce the charges for diagnosing the problem. All too often the time spent on electronic analysis and test-drives costs more than the work needed to make a simple adjustment or repair.

When providing information, keep this important rule in mind:

> *Report the symptoms, but do not diagnose the problem yourself!*

If you tell a shop that your vehicle needs a specific job done, that is the work they will do — and you will have to pay for it *whether or not it solves the problem*. If you want to know if the trouble is due to a malfunction in a specific part, that's fine. But be sure you ask a question instead of making a statement. The final diagnosis must be up to the repair shop so that it can be held responsible if the work it performs doesn't solve the problem.

Keep a maintenance and repair log

Keep a log of the maintenance and repair that's been done on your vehicle. If the shop hasn't done all the previous work, bring a photocopy of it for their files. *Auto Repair For Dummies* (IDG Books Worldwide, Inc.) provides blank forms you can photocopy and use to keep track of maintenance as well as parts numbers and specifications for each of your vehicles.

Be patient and courteous

Being patient and courteous can go a long way.

- ✔ **Don't press to get the job done fast unless you're really in a bind.** Making a diagnosis, getting the proper parts, doing the work, and testing the results properly takes time. Nobody likes to work under pressure. A great way to get the pressure off everybody is to see whether the shop has a "loaner" you can borrow while your vehicle is being repaired.

- ✔ **Call to be sure the car is ready before you come to pick it up.** If it isn't, try to be understanding, unless the shop is chronically slow about getting work done on time. If it's a matter of unavailable parts that must be ordered, the shop can do very little about it. If they're overbooked with work, be polite but firm about your need to get your vehicle back quickly.

- ✔ **Show your appreciation for a job well done.** Thank the technician who did the job. Call the owner or manager and praise the technician's work, or send a grateful letter they can display. If you find out that your mechanic likes a particular brand of beer, bring along a six-pack in a paper sack when you come to pick your car up at the end of a busy day. If you're lucky, you may get invited to share it. I've received some of my most valuable tutoring strolling around a garage after working hours, brew in hand, while an automotive guru expounded on the secrets of the art.

When your car is ready

When the time comes to pick up your car, keep the following things in mind:

- ✔ **Ask what was wrong and what they did to repair the problem.** Add the information to your repair log for future reference.

- ✔ **Come prepared to spend a little time test-driving to be sure the job's been done to your satisfaction.** You're better off returning immediately with your complaints than showing up several days later when any number of things may have happened to mess things up.

Getting Satisfaction When You're Not Happy with the Job

Even if you've followed all of my advice on how to avoid getting ripped off, there's still a chance that you may get into a dispute over a transaction. I believe that if you immediately attack, on the assumption that the people you go to for compensation are going to do their best to weasel out of their responsibilities, you will put them on the defensive and make things much harder for yourself. On the other hand, if you approach them with the assumption that you will be treated fairly and honestly, you have a much better chance of getting what you want. The next section shows how to make this theory work for you.

Use this time-tested complaints technique

An excellent human-potential trainer taught me the following complaints procedure many years ago, and I'm delighted to pass it on to you. Don't just use it for automotive complaints; it's effective in any situation — in person or over the phone. Begin by memorizing this vital rule:

> *The best way to get what you want is to maintain a friendly attitude in all disputes — and refuse to be swayed from your purpose.*

Believe me, this combination of friendliness, sympathy, and inflexibility really pays off. I have seen people really go out of their way to come up with extremely creative solutions after they realize that I expect them to genuinely want to help me, that I appreciate the difficulties they may have in doing so, *and that I'm not going to give up until I get some satisfaction.* Try it. What can you lose? You can always bring the big guns out as a last resort. Here are the steps to success:

✔ **Before you contact anyone, take the time to decide exactly what you want them to do.** Presenting a concrete plan for remedial action is much more powerful than waiting passively for someone else to decide what they're willing to do for you.

✔ **Time your campaign carefully.** Don't call just before lunchtime or at the end of the working day, because someone who's hungry or eager to get home to his kids isn't going to want to spend a lot of time trying to help you. I like to call 24-hour customer service numbers in the middle of the night. It must get pretty tedious for the staff to just sit there waiting for the phone to ring. How grateful they'll be when you provide a little entertainment!

This trick also works wonderfully with airlines reservation people. I get them all excited about the trip I'm planning, they tell me all about their own great adventures, and they end up turning heaven and earth to get me the fastest, least stressful flights at the lowest possible cost.

✔ **Approach each person you contact with the assumption that she sincerely wants to do everything in her power to settle the issue fairly.** After all, what used to be the Complaints Department is now usually called Customer Service. Why would a company create such a department if they don't want to serve your needs? (I don't want any smart answers, just keep reading!)

✔ **Open with a little friendly conversation.** Establishing a relationship as human beings is important. When you encounter people who go into robot mode, it's even *more* important to greet them warmly and get through to their essential humanity. ("Hi! How're you doing today? I'll bet you're glad it's Friday!") If possible, get on a first-name basis. Most people who handle complaints have been trained to deal with aggression, suspicion, and anger, but very few have defenses against friendliness, trust, and compassion. When they encounter it, all the battle tactics they've learned become useless.

✔ **No matter how many people you encounter in this process, when you've got them warmed up, state your problem — along with what you'd like them to do about it.** Tell your story as though you were telling it to sympathetic friends — simply and clearly, without blaming the person you're talking with. Keep it as short as possible and don't cloud the issue with unnecessary details, which will only confuse or bore them.

✔ **Be prepared to back yourself up with as much documentation as possible.** You should always keep a file with guarantees, warranties, invoices, and a record of all the maintenance and repairs that have been done on your vehicle. You don't have to mention that you've got all this stuff; just save it as your second line of defense. If you're ever asked to document your case, *never part with your originals; just send copies.* Why place your strategic weapons in the hands of a company that has everything to gain by "losing" them?

✔ **Listen patiently to the responses you get.** Don't interrupt; listen to the litany of woes and excuses until they run down. If you're given a hard-luck story to explain someone's negligence or inability to give you satisfaction, be sympathetic. ("Gee, I can image how hard it must be to deal with something like this, so what can you do to help me?") Caring about people's problems will encourage them to care about yours.

✔ **Whenever the ball's in your court, reiterate your complaint and ask the person to find a way to rectify the situation.** Be reasonable. If he can't do exactly what you've suggested, be willing to negotiate and consider other alternatives, *just as long as the problem is taken care of.*

✔ **Encourage the other person to see the problem through your eyes.** ("Lois, put yourself in my place. How would you feel if you spent a week fighting your way on and off a crowded bus during rush hour only to pick up your car and find that it still isn't working properly? And when you drive all the way back to the garage, they tell you it won't be ready for another 10 days!")

✔ **If the person you speak with doesn't have the authority to help you, ask who can.** ("What a pity. I can see that your hands are tied, and I must have this problem resolved. So whom should I contact to get it taken care of?")

✔ **If you're told it's "company policy" not to provide a remedy for your situation, stay cheerful — refuse to accept it.** Kid them out of it. ("Oh, come on, there's got to be someone who can take this load off your shoulders. Whom do you go to for advice? I'm sure your company wants to deal fairly with its customers, so who has the power to 'temper justice with mercy'?") At this point, you'll probably be directed to a supervisor.

✔ **Repeat the process with the person you're referred to — and keep repeating it until you get satisfaction.** As the next section explains, there's a whole hierarchy of people you can contact if you're willing to hang in there and put in the time and effort. One of them will eventually help you.

If you find you're losing your cool, take a break, have a snack, play a little music or computer solitaire, and then go on to the next person. Treat it as a game rather than a frustrating situation. If you're pressed for time, stop the process completely and then pick it up again when you aren't too stressed to enjoy it. The impatience you feel is not only in inverse proportion to how confident you are that you'll win, but also is directly related to how much you fear the consequences if you lose. Ask yourself what the worst thing is that can happen if you don't get what you want. We're not dealing with the end of the world here. After this technique has worked a couple of times, you'll begin to enjoy the challenge.

Climbing the ladder

It is always good policy to take a complaint first to the person you dealt with and then work your way up to people at higher levels of power. Going over someone's head rarely pays off, unless that person has proven to be unsympathetic or unable to help you. If the lower echelons fail to be of help, however, it pays to contact the highest authority you can. Even if the Big Boss sends your complaint back down the ladder, the fact that it came from the Executive Suite prompts the underlings to deal with the chance that the boss will follow up to see how well your complaint has been handled.

Here are the steps to climb when working your way up the auto repair complaint ladder.

1. The technician who did the repairs.

2. The manager of the shop, or the service manager if it's a dealership or a large chain.

3. The owner of the shop, dealership, or franchise.

4. The factory representative at the car manufacturer's nearest regional office, if you've had no satisfaction from a repair facility. Write to them and tell them what happened and what you want done to resolve the issue. Be sure to include the following information:

   - Name and address of the establishment.

   - Names and titles of the people you've already dealt with.

   - Make, year, and model of your vehicle and its Vehicle Identification Number (VIN). You can find the VIN on your registration or on the left-hand corner of the dashboard, where it can be seen from outside the vehicle.

   - Copies (not originals) of any documentation you think is required, such as invoices, warranties, and previous correspondence.

5. The car manufacturer's president or CEO. Some people suggest going to the Public Relations or Customer Service Department first, but since chief executives and PR departments often send complaints back to the regional office for action, I'd rather have the CEO or president's initials on the letter when it shows up again at regional headquarters.

If you still "can't get no satisfaction"

Write to your local Better Business Bureau and your state's Consumer Protection Agency. They may suggest taking the matter to a mediation service, or they may apply some pressure of their own. Some states have special departments dedicated solely to handling auto repair disputes. You can also do the following:

- **If the shop has AAA, CAA, ASE, IGO, or ADS accreditation:** Write to those organizations with the full specifics of your complaint.

- **If your problem is with a dealership:** Write to the National Automobile Dealers Association (NADA) at 8400 West Park Drive, McLean, VA 22101, to see if your state has this service. These people have no clout with independents, however.

- **You can take any repair facility or dealership to small claims court:** In many states, new laws have raised the maximum of small claims settlements to levels that will cover all but the most expensive auto repair disputes. The fees involved are generally negligible, and you don't need a lawyer. In my experience, small claims procedures are usually swift, fair, and designed to allow the little guy to pursue a case without the need for legal or technical expertise or great amounts of time and money. If all else fails, don't hesitate to avail yourself of this alternative. Many establishments would much prefer to settle a dispute personally rather than lose valuable time in court and have the fact that they have been sued by dissatisfied customers be known to the general public and the Better Business Bureau.

✔ **If it's an option for you, pursue arbitration:** For example, the Canadian Motor Vehicle Arbitration Plan (CAMVAP) offers binding arbitration as a "fair, fast, friendly, final, and free alternative to court proceedings" to Canadians who have followed an auto manufacturer's dispute resolution process and have given the dealer and the manufacturer a reasonable number of opportunities to resolve their problems concerning warranties or alleged manufacturing defects. The largest arbitration plan in Canada, CAMVAP is fully funded by vehicle manufacturers and is designed to ensure that an independent and neutral arbitrator will make a decision that is fair to both the consumer and the manufacturer. This decision cannot be contested by either party. CAMVAP may also help the consumer and manufacturer settle their differences without the need for arbitration. CAMVAP is available to residents of Canadian provinces and territories, other than Quebec, who purchased their vehicles from an authorized Canadian dealer. Vehicles must be employed primarily for personal and family use and be from the current or previous four model years. For more information, contact CAMVAP at 800-207-0685 and ask for a copy of its brochure, which provides all the steps involved in its proceedings.

✔ **If you're really riled, complain to your local Federal Trade Commission office or write to their U.S. national headquarters at the following address:**

> Federal Trade Commission
> Bureau of Consumer Protection
> Pennsylvania Ave. at 6th Street NW
> Washington, DC 20580

✔ **To register complaints about defects or to obtain data about recalls, fuel, tires, child seats, seat belts, or other safety-related issues,** call the Auto Safety Hotline at 800-424-9393.

✔ **Consult** *The Consumer's Resource Handbook.* It's is another excellent guide to obtaining satisfaction. Write for a copy at Dept. 579L, Pueblo, CO 31009.

✔ **Contact** *The Consumer Federation of America.* This is a federation of 240 nonprofit organizations that represents the consumer interest through advocacy and education. You can reach them at 202-387-6121, or write to CFA, Complaint Resolution, 1424 16th Street NW, Washington, DC 20036.

No matter which line of recourse you decide to follow, find out if your state still honors the "mechanic's lien," which allows mechanics to sell your car if you refuse to pay for services. If it does, you want to avoid having your vehicle towed away and sold to pay a bill that amounts to just a fraction of the car's value: *Pay the disputed bill first, and then get 'em!* As mentioned earlier, if you pay by credit card, you may be able to have the credit card company withhold payment until the matter is investigated.

Chapter 19

Renting a Car

· ·

In This Chapter

▶ Understanding the criteria for renting cars

▶ Getting around a poor driving record when you want to rent a car

▶ Getting adequate insurance coverage for a rental car

▶ Protecting yourself from rental car rip-offs

▶ Knowing where to go to resolve problems and handle complaints

▶ Staying out of danger from rental car thieves

▶ Renting a car for international travel

· ·

*W*hen an accident or other need for repairs leaves you without a car, or a business trip or vacation takes you far from home, finding another vehicle is often necessary. But how do you choose a rental car? Do you succumb to the sales pitches in millions of dollars' worth of media ads? Do you pick the agencies that provide your favorite makes and models? Do you assume that the coupons provided by airlines and organizations offer the best rates available? Do you believe that all rental companies are alike, and go for the agency with the cheapest rates? Or do you just let your travel agent make arrangements for you?

All these methods have something in common: You're very likely to pay more than you need to, and you run the risk of getting into serious trouble! This chapter shows you how to find the best set of wheels (reasonable) money can rent and protect yourself from being ripped off if problems occur.

Determining whether You're Qualified to Rent a Car

The first question to consider is: Can you rent a car at all? Most companies require a valid driver's license, proof that you're over 25 years of age, and a credit card. Except for the first item, none of these is written in stone, but overcoming the obstacles to renting a car without them takes time, planning, and effort.

Is your driver's license acceptable?

A valid driver's license must be:

- ✔ **Unencumbered.** If your license has been suspended, revoked, or has expired, and you use it to rent a car, you risk fines, imprisonment, and cancellation of any coverage against loss, damage, or liability.

- ✔ **Accepted in every country where you plan to drive the car.** The United States and Canada usually accept each other's licenses, but other countries may not. Check with the AAA (American Automobile Association) and the CAA (Canadian Automobile Association) to see whether you need a special International Driver's License to rent a car in any country you plan to visit. If you do, these consumer-oriented auto clubs can supply one for you.

- ✔ **Able to pass a DMV driving record check.** Most major rental agencies can check your driving record with one fast phone call, and they're doing it as a matter of routine in many states. You find out more about this record check in the section called "Renting a Car If Your Driving Record Is Poor."

Are you under 25?

If you are less than 25 years old and want to rent a car, try the following:

- ✔ **Use a corporate credit card for business rentals.** Although all major rental companies have a 25-year age limit, some of them rent to people who are younger if they use a corporate credit card to rent for business purposes.

  Don't try using a corporate card to rent a car for pleasure unless you get signed permission from your employer. If you get into trouble, the rental insurance provided by the corporate card could be invalidated.

- ✔ **Try the little guys.** Get out the Yellow Pages and call the smaller rental agencies. Some set their age limit at 20, and a very few rent to people who are 18 or over.

- ✔ **Expect to pay for the privilege.** Companies that rent to younger drivers often impose a daily underage surcharge to cover the additional risk.

What if you don't have a credit card?

Thrillers usually depict people in fascist countries as having to meet constant demands to produce their identity papers before they can undertake the simplest transactions. Sad to say, driver's licenses and credit cards seem to have taken the place of identity papers throughout the "free world."

I honestly don't know how people who don't drive or can't qualify for a credit card manage to get through the day. The good news is it is possible to rent a car without a credit card; the bad news is that you may need a month or more to set it up. You can do this in several ways:

✏ **Contact the rental company and tell them you want to pay cash.** Most states have laws that set a 30-day limit for credit qualification, so this cannot be a last-minute procedure. The credit qualification check tells the rental agency whether you have the assets to cover the cost of the rental and sufficient coverage to replace or repair it, if necessary.

A few companies will rent a car for cash without a lengthy credit qualification, but they may require a return airline ticket, a verifiable home phone number in your name, proof of employment, and/or a hefty cash deposit in addition to payment of all the rental charges in advance. Some impose nonrefundable processing fees of as much as $50.

Alamo currently pre-approves a rental at no charge in as little as 24 hours if you have a return airline ticket to your home city. If this policy is still in effect when you need it, take advantage of it — it's a very good deal.

✏ **You can use someone else's credit card if they are present at the counter.** Just have them rent the car and name you as a designated driver. The only problem with this tactic is that the credit card holder must assume primary responsibility for the car, and companies often charge a fee for each additional driver.

If you have a credit card but don't want to use it to pay for the car, that's no problem. Just produce your card at the rental desk when you pick up the car so they can run a blank credit slip and attach it to your record. When you return the car, pay the bill with cash and be sure they tear up all copies of the blank charge slip before you leave. If they insist on keeping it, cross through the "total" box and write "paid by cash" right on the face of the slip and on the rental invoice as well. It doesn't hurt to have the counter clerk initial it. This may sound paranoid, but you don't want to risk leaving blank credit card slips around after you've paid for the car. It's the same as giving someone a blank check. And people have been billed twice — in error? Obviously, you can't pay cash at automatic return facilities, so remember to allow enough time to return the car and pay for it in person.

Renting a Car If Your Driving Record Is Poor

Even though you have a confirmed reservation, you may find yourself turned down at the rental counter if you fail to pass a driving record check. Most car rental companies have taken advantage of the increasing computerization of DMV records and, as of 1997, every state's DMV is required to provide driving

Umm . . . could I have a copy of that, please?

Most rental companies use T.M.L. Information Services; others use Dateq Information Network to check the driving records of potential renters. If you'd like to see the report that may be sent to any auto insurance and car rental companies that inquire about you, call T.M.L.'s Travelcheck program at 800-388-9099. They will charge their fee to your credit card ($9.95 plus tax — there's a discount for AAA members) and send you a printout by fax or mail. Dateq does not provide this information to individuals, but that could change in the future. There are also many Web sites for checking driving records.

record information to rental agencies that request it. It's as easy as checking a credit card, and you really can't blame them for taking this precaution. They won't check your record until you actually get to the counter, because they must pay these credit companies a fee for each inquiry, and there are too many no-shows to make advance checks worthwhile.

Definitions of a good driving record may vary from one rental company to another. Most agencies consider three or more moving violations or traffic accidents in the past two or three years to be cause for rejection. Some even count parking tickets! Rental companies have been known to refuse cars to drivers with DUIs on their record within the past six years and to reject drivers for leaving the scene of an accident, driving without insurance, and even for being injured as passengers in car accidents! Some of the smaller companies don't check records at all. Other companies only check if you're renting one of their top-end models or for a long period of time.

If you're unsure whether you're a candidate for rejection, your local DMV can check your driving record for you. If your record isn't good, be sure to ask about the rental company's rejection criteria *before* you reserve a car.

Beware of getting a traffic ticket while driving a rented car. People used to be pretty cavalier about tickets they received in other states, but the party's over — you now must pay for your traffic violations, preferably before you leave town. In this wonderful world of data networks, you can be arrested as a scofflaw in your home state if the rental company gives the local police your name, address, and driver's license number.

Choosing the Right Company — and the Right Car

Each of the major rental companies features vehicles from specific manufacturers. The reason for this is that most major companies are owned by auto makers; for example, Ford owns Hertz. Although I've never cared enough to do it, you may find an advantage to renting the same model you own, because you can hop right in and drive away without having to go through the usual search for interior and exterior light switches, windshield wipers, and that little gizmo that lets you get your keys out of the ignition at the end of the ride. On the other hand, driving something different is fun. If it matters to you, call around to find out where you can rent your favorite make and model.

Most companies won't guarantee that you'll get the exact model you choose. They prefer to reserve size categories rather than specific cars. For more on this, see the sidebar called "The magic key to renting the vehicle you want."

Consider your priorities

The company you select should offer the best possible deal based on your needs. When choosing a vehicle, take the following into consideration:

- ✔ The kind and number of passengers you'll be driving around
- ✔ Where and how far you plan to go
- ✔ The type and condition of the roads you'll be driving on
- ✔ How much luggage and other stuff you'll be carrying
- ✔ If it matters, what kind of impression you want to make

In addition to the preceding, you may want to keep in mind the following suggestions. They could make your trip safer, more convenient, and more economical:

- ✔ **If some of your passengers are disabled or elderly, you'll probably want a four-door model so they can get in and out easily.**

- ✔ **If you're traveling with children, you may want to be sure that the car includes air bags, childproof door and window locks, child-safety seats, and other safety features.**

- ✔ **If you're carrying baggage, keep your possessions as hidden from view as possible.** Tourists in rented cars are frequently the victims of car thieves. Why give the show away by displaying a car full of luggage? Avoid low-cost hatchbacks that provide little concealment and choose a vehicle with enough enclosed trunk space to hold all your goodies.

- ✔ **If you don't plan to drive very far, you may get a better deal if you choose a car with a hundred or more "free miles" per day rather than one with unlimited mileage.** Getting maps from the AAA (a good idea anyway when exploring new territory) and estimating the distances between the airport and the various places you plan to visit may pay off. Be sure to leave a comfortable margin for getting lost and for unexpected side trips. If you go over the maximum, those extra miles can be expensive.

✔ **If you're really going to hit the highway, unlimited mileage programs are best.** Just be sure that there are no hidden geographical or time restrictions. For long trips, upgrading to a larger, more comfortable model with cruise control, a decent AM/FM/cassette or CD player, and plenty of concealed storage space also pays off.

✔ **If you're heading for sunny climes, a sunroof is *not* a good idea.** Opening a sunroof allows your air conditioning to evaporate. And having the sun beat down on your head or bake the interior of the car while it's parked is not anyone's idea of a good time. If you want lots of sun and fresh air, spend a little more and rent a convertible. Otherwise, stick with a standard model and be sure the air conditioner works before you drive away.

✔ **If you'll be driving in a high-crime or deserted area, a cell phone may be your best option.** Many car-rental agencies now offer phones as optional equipment. They don't want to fall victim to crooks any more than you do. However, be sure to ask whether the area you intend to visit can be accessed by the cellular company, or if it falls outside of the roaming area.

✔ **If you're carrying special gear, you can rent ski, bike, or roof racks.** Be sure you reserve them well in advance; not only will you give yourself a better chance of obtaining these specialty items, but you won't have to wait around while they install them.

✔ **If you're only going one way, consider delivering a car.** If you return a rental car to a different location from the one at which you received it, you almost always have to pay a drop-off fee, and these can really be killers. If you're planning to drive cross-country from one city to another and you don't have rigid time limits, you may do better to check the classified ads for people who would like their cars delivered to your destination, or check the Yellow Pages under "Automobile Transporters" for a "drive-away" car delivery company and offer your services. To qualify, you must have a good driving record, and you may be asked to fork over a couple of hundred dollars as a deposit.

Delivering a vehicle can get you there for nothing except tolls and fuel. You may even get a few extra days of the car's use for business or pleasure if you arrive at the destination before your delivery date. Have the car cleaned, inside and out, and the tank filled with fuel before you hand it over at the destination. It's considered good manners.

Reserve your car well in advance

The availability of various makes and models varies with the season, the city, and whatever major conference or exposition is currently in town. If you want the best chance to reserve the car you want and actually find it waiting for you when you get there, reserve as far in advance as possible.

Options for the disabled

In most cases, a driver for a visually-impaired or disabled customer can be listed as the authorized driver with no surcharge.

If they're given enough notice, many car rental agencies provide specially-equipped cars for people with disabilities. These include cars with left- or right-hand brake and accelerator controls and other special services for the physically impaired. If you request a vehicle with special controls, you must produce a valid handicapped driver's license that says that you are familiar with such controls. Because requirements for a handicapped driver's license vary from state to state, if your license lacks this distinction you may want to check with your local DMV to be sure it qualifies you for whatever controls you need. When you reserve your car, ask for a display card that allows you to park in zones reserved for disabled drivers.

Most major renters have nationwide 800 numbers. Consult the Yellow Pages, a computerized reservations system such as SABRE. Or try Web sites such as Guide to Airport Car Rentals (www.bnm.com) or Car Rental Direct (www.car-rental-direct.com). If you're too busy doing brain surgery to make your own calls, ask your travel agent to find the best rates and reserve a car for you, but don't expect them to research things thoroughly — the booking just isn't worth that much time to the agent. On the other hand, a travel agent may get you a package deal for plane tickets and car rental at a lower price than they would cost separately.

Before you — or anyone else — calls to reserve a car, be sure you have the following information at hand:

- ✔ Your credit card number and expiration date.
- ✔ The date and time you want to pick up the car and a reasonable estimate of how long you plan to keep it.
- ✔ The airline and flight number, if you're picking up the car at an airport; the hotel and arrival time if you're picking it up at your hotel.
- ✔ If possible, a phone number where they can reach you.
- ✔ The make and model of the vehicle you'd prefer.

Some people make a practice of always reserving the rental agency's cheapest model in the hope that all of these popular low-priced cars are rented by the time they arrive. When this happens, the rental company has to upgrade you to the next largest model they have available at the low price of the car you reserved. If this ploy doesn't work, and you find yourself stuck with little more than two seats and an engine installed in an eggshell, I suppose you can always change your mind and pay for an upgrade to something less claustrophobic.

The magic key to renting the car you want

Automated reservation systems have established a general classification code called the Expanded Vehicle Matrix, which uses a series of four-letter groupings to identify cars. Because many of us have begun to rent our own cars through on-line systems such as SABRE, I include it here for your convenience. It's also a useful way to check that your reservation is for exactly the model you specified. You simply choose one letter from each column.

Expanded Vehicle Matrix Codes

Class	Type	Transmission	Air Conditioning
M = Mini	C = Car	A = Automatic	R = A/C
E = Economy	W = Wagon	M = Manual	N = No A/C
C = Compact	V = Van		
S = Standard	L = Limousine		
I = Intermediate	S = Sports		
F = Full Size	T = Convertible		
P = Premium	R = Rec. Vehicle		
L = Luxury	F = 4-Wheel Drive		
X = Special	X = Special		

Be aware that some auto and credit card insurance policies will not cover any vehicles except cars and may not cover cars in the P, L, and X classes. If you go for these, be sure to accept all the protection waivers the rental company has to offer. (I get into these waivers in detail in the section called "Protecting Yourself against Accidents and Theft.") Each waiver adds to the daily cost of the car, but if you're determined to rent one of these high-priced beauties, you probably won't care.

When you call, be sure to jot down the name of the person you talk with. Knowing the name comes in handy if the information they give you doesn't jibe with the situation you encounter when you're ready to pick up the car.

Questions to ask when making reservations

Go over these questions and find the ones that are relevant to your needs and circumstances. Then photocopy the Rental Company Comparison checklist in this chapter and use it to compare quotes from several rental companies.

RENTAL COMPANY COMPARISON CHECKLIST

Company:	#1	#2	#3
Phone:			
Name of Contact:			
Make/Model/Year or Size			
Rates: Daily (From__ / __ To__ / __)	$	$	$
Weekend (From__ / __To__ / __)	$	$	$
Weekly	$	$	$
Hourly (is there a minimum?)	$	$	$
Frequent Flyer miles (airline?)			
Discounts			
Blackout dates			
Late charge (grace period?)	$	$	$
Fuel refill charge ($ per gallon?)	$	$	$
Fuel-tank special ($ per gallon?)	$	$	$
State/City surcharges	$	$	$
Airport access fees	$	$	$
Drop-off fee	$	$	$
Additional driver fee	$	$	$
CDW/LDW waivers	$	$	$
SLI (liability insurance)	$	$	$
PAI (personal accident insurance)	$	$	$
PEP (personal effects protection)	$	$	$
Other Charges	$	$	$
Taxes	$	$	$
TOTAL COST	$	$	$
Rates guaranteed?			
Refundable deposit?			
Airport/Shuttle/Cab?			
Quick Check-out/Return?			

What are your best rates by the day, weekend, or week?

If you're planning to rent for five days or more, reserving for the week is often better because weekly rates are rarely more than five times the daily rate. The only hitch here is that if you return the car before the week is out, they may void the weekly rate and charge you by the day. If you'll be using the car over a weekend, check out the weekend specials described in the section "How does your rental contract define 'day' and 'weekend'?"

What discounts are available, and when do they apply?

Always request the lowest possible rate and ask whether they are running any special discount programs. Then ask about any other discounts for which you may qualify. If a company offers frequent flyer miles, be sure they're for an airline you use regularly. Many major agencies offer frequent-flyer miles and discounts for those using certain airlines, credit or phone cards, and hotel chains, as well as special rates for seniors, members of the AAA, CAA, AARP, large corporations, and some business and professional organizations. These programs are quite costly for car rental companies, who usually have to guarantee them for at least a year. As a result, they try to fix a rate that compensates them for charging less during high-rate seasons. For this reason, current special discount programs are often better buys than organizational discounts. Some of the best specials feature larger cars for the same cost as economy models.

When calling about a specific discount program, be aware of the following:

- ✔ You may be asked to supply the rate code on the ad or discount card.
- ✔ Some special programs are unavailable on "blackout dates." Be sure to ask whether they will be available during the period you have in mind.
- ✔ You may lose a special discount by returning the car early or late.
- ✔ Some rental companies offer standard rates that are cheaper than the discounts offered by other companies.

How does your rental contract define "day" and "weekend"?

This concept varies widely from one rental company to another. Some define a day as a calendar day; others base their calculations on the actual time the car was rented. Here's an example of the vast difference this can make in a week:

Actual time from 9 a.m. Monday to 9 a.m. Friday = 4 days

By the calendar day from 9 a.m. Monday to 9 a.m. Friday = 5 days

On a brighter note, at some companies a "weekend" can extend from noon Thursday to noon Monday. If you schedule meetings for Thursday afternoons, Fridays, and Monday mornings, you can take advantage of these "weekend specials" and enjoy the car for half a week for 33 to 50 percent less than the daily rates.

Do you have an hourly rental rate?

If you just need a car for a few hours, you'll be happy to know that some car rental companies are offering ultra short-term rentals for as little as 99 cents per hour with no time minimums. If this proves to be a profitable way of increasing revenues from cars that may otherwise sit idle, this option may be universal by the time you read this book.

Will you guarantee my rental at today's prices if your rates go up before I arrive?

Some companies guarantee rates for as long as a year from the time you make your reservation. A few even offer discounts of 15 to 20 percent for doing this, but they impose a cancellation fee if you change your mind. Be aware that rental companies automatically raise the rates when their computer shows that a certain number of cars have been reserved at a location. For that reason, reserve early and lock in the rate.

If the car I reserve is not available when I arrive, will you guarantee me a free upgrade to the next available model?

Most rental agencies will do this or will pay for a cab to your destination and send the car along later. But what if you've reserved a special vehicle such as a minivan or 4-wheel drive, and they don't have another that meets your requirements? In most cases, the company will offer you a credit toward another rental as compensation. Typical credits currently run from $25 to $50 but can go higher for specialty vehicles. Hertz guarantees that if you've reserved a special vehicle, or one in peak season, and have paid for it in advance with a credit card, they will give you a $100 credit toward another rental if they cannot provide the vehicle you've chosen when you arrive. The downside is that they charge a cancellation fee if you cancel the reservation less than 24 hours in advance.

What are your charges for late drop-offs? Is there a grace period?

Companies vary widely here. One may charge by the hour, and another may stick you for an extra day. Most provide at least a small grace period for late returns, but you're better off allowing an extra half hour for getting lost in unknown territory or for encountering unexpected road work or traffic jams.

If I choose to leave the car at a different location, do drop-off charges apply? How much will this cost?

Leaving a rental car at a location other than the one where you received it almost always racks up exorbitant drop-off fees. An alternative is to deliver a car. See the "Consider your priorities" section for details.

Beware of hidden costs

In addition to the ones I mention earlier in this chapter, a number of other fees and charges may be imposed on you. You may have to pay some of them, but there are ways to escape others. Forewarned is, after all, forearmed. To find out where the hidden costs are and to avoid them if you can, ask the following questions:

- ✔ **Do you have counters and car lots at the airport, or will I have to take your shuttle?** If you're going to be pressed for time, choosing a company with airport facilities may be worth a higher daily rate. Then you won't have to wait impatiently for transportation between the airport and the rental agency.

- ✔ **Are your rates cheaper if I pick up the car at the airport? At your location in town? At my hotel?**

- ✔ **If the car can only be picked up and dropped off at my hotel or at a local agency, who pays for the cabs from and back to the airport?**

- ✔ **Does the car come with a full tank of gas? If not, must I return it at the level at which I received it or with a full tank?** Check the fuel gauge to be sure your agreement accurately shows how much gas is in the tank before you start out, and note the tank level on the contract when you return it. Fuel policies vary not only from one company to another, but also from one location to another within a company.

Do you have a "fuel deal"? Some rental agencies offer the option of paying for a full tank of gas in advance. This is great if you want to avoid having to hunt like mad for a gas station when you're running late returning the car. The catch is that, although the fuel will cost you less than the rental company would charge if you brought the car back with less fuel than when you started, most companies still charge more than the going price at local stations, and they won't refund your money if you don't use the entire tank.

On a recent week-long trip, I refused this offer and found that I'd only used a quarter of a tank when I refueled the car before returning it! If you will only drive a few short hops from your hotel a couple of times a day, chances are you won't need to replace a full tank either. Judge for yourself how much this "convenience" is worth.

A January 1998 survey by *USA Today* showed that National was the only rental company that consistently charged less than the lowest price available at local gas stations. Alamo charged more than the highest going rate in every city surveyed. The other major renters either charged more or a little bit less than the highest prices around.

- ✔ **Do you feature quick checkout and automatic return procedures?** These can be a mixed blessing. I'll get into why in the section called "Avoiding Rental Rip-offs for Damage You Didn't Cause."

✔ **Are there geographical restrictions in the area I plan to visit?** Restrictions generally apply to crossing borders, state lines, unpaved roads, wilderness areas, and the like. Knowing about these in advance is best, because if you violate them, they can void your contract, special discounts, or your insurance coverage.

✔ **Do you supply maps?** If not, bring one with you if you're going to be in unfamiliar territory. The AAA provides detailed road maps of states, major cities, and foreign countries at no cost to its members.

✔ **Do you offer frequent-flyer miles?** Be sure they're for airlines you use regularly.

✔ **If the car becomes disabled, will you deliver a replacement?** Most rental companies will pay for towing and mechanical repairs unless you've violated the contract by driving the vehicle off-road or elsewhere. If you're stuck in a remote area, you may have to pay the bills yourself and be reimbursed later on. If this is the case, be sure to save all the receipts. (But you knew that, didn't you?)

✔ **What waivers and special protective coverage do you offer?** Many of us refuse collision and theft waivers in the belief that our auto insurance or credit card car rental insurance provides sufficient protection. As you may be horrified to discover, this may not be the case. See the later section, "Protecting Yourself against Accidents and Theft" for details.

Be Aware of Surcharges

When you arrive at the rental desk, you may be hit with a number of surcharges in addition to the rental fee. To help you avoid unpleasant budget-busting surprises, the following list takes a close look at what you may encounter:

✔ **State and city car rental surcharges and taxes.** Like bed taxes, many local governments have strange ways of greeting the visitors they spend millions in advertising to attract. Although many of us think we should be paid to drive in these congested areas, more than 50 major cities impose surcharges and special taxes on car rentals, and these surcharges can go as high as 24 percent. Costs in Tulsa, Las Vegas, Reno, Phoenix, Denver, New Orleans, Chicago, and Seattle led the list in a 1997 survey by the Consumer Reports Travel Letter. Fuel is taxed in some places and not in others. Some cities impose sales tax on the total bill, including fees. Others simply tax basic rental charges. Sometimes taxes on cars rented at airports are higher than those for rentals at other locations. It may be wise to pick up the vehicle at an office outside the airport. The next item tells you how to do this without incurring more fees aimed at visitors to the city.

✔ **Airport access fees.** Also referred to as *airport service charges* or taxes, these usually only apply if you pick up the car at the airport or leave the airport by rental company shuttle to pick up your car. Costs can run from as little as 25¢ to as much as 10 percent of the final rental bill. You can avoid paying this by using a taxi or private auto to get to the rental facility or choosing a rental company whose lot is a short walk from the airport. If you do this, ask the rental agent at the counter to give you an exemption certificate certifying that you did not exit the airport using their shuttle service. Another method is to rent the car from an agency located at or near your hotel and use the hotel shuttle to and from the airport.

✔ **"No-show" and cancellation fees.** Some companies impose a fee if you fail to pick the car up or cancel your reservation fewer than 24 hours ahead. These fees usually apply only to specialty vehicles like 4-wheel drives, minivans, luxury cars, and convertibles, but rental companies may extend them to ordinary rentals.

✔ **Refundable deposits and credit card holds.** Some companies may impose a deposit when you pick up the car; others may place a hold on your credit card that freezes your credit, often for thousands of dollars. They'll defend this by saying that it doesn't really cost you anything because they're putting it on your credit card and will cancel the charges when you return the car. What they may not tell you is that this drastically lowers the available credit on your card — and therefore your travel budget — sometimes by as much as $2,500. This practice is fairly standard on international rentals, and it's a great reason for traveling with more than one credit card. Use one card for these deposits and the blank slips hotels run when you check in, and another card for day-to-day expenses. American Express cards have no credit limit and are especially useful for these contingencies.

Protecting Yourself against Accidents and Theft

Your flight has arrived late, and suddenly that comfortable margin you provided for renting a car and driving to your meeting has evaporated. You dash up to the rental counter only to be met with at least a page of small print and a bunch of options to accept or reject. *Across-the-board acceptance of all the protective options can double the costs per day for renting the car!* Refuse, and you can be liable for repairing or replacing the vehicle and end up paying thousands more in damages if you cause an accident. It's a heck of a time to have to make such major decisions.

The really expensive luxury car

Dora and John were only visiting San Francisco for a couple of days, and they decided to treat themselves to a luxury car at a rental agency. Because they had low-deductible auto insurance, they had no qualms about rejecting the agency's collision damage waiver (CDW).

When Dora began to back the car out of its stall, she found that when she looked into the rearview mirror, she couldn't see through the rear side windows. The next thing she knew, she'd run the right rear fender into a post. What a wonderful way to start a vacation! John was unruffled, because he knew their insurance would cover the damage. Sure enough, when they called from the rental desk, their insurer said the repair bills were covered, minus their deductible. Relieved, they hired another vehicle and resumed their trip.

The bad news didn't hit until a few weeks later when a bill for nearly $500 arrived from the rental company. Furious, John called the company and demanded an explanation. "It's true that your insurance covered repairing the car," he was told. "But it didn't cover our loss of its use while the car was in the shop and we couldn't rent it out. It took well over a week to install and paint a new fender and get the car back on the road. Our policy is to charge you the amount the car normally rents for, times the number of days it is out of service, times the average amount of time it is usually rented during such a period."

John, an accountant, protested that the loss of the use of the car was a risk that the rental agency should assume as a normal business expense. Nobody paid him when he lost business because his computer system crashed or an important associate became ill. If this was a recurring problem, he felt that the rental company should insure themselves against it or charge it off to equipment maintenance or depreciation.

This story does not have a happy ending. Under the terms of his rental contract, John had to pay the full amount. The CDW offered by the rental company would have covered loss of use, but his own insurance didn't. The only bright side is that he was lucky his insurance covered renting a luxury car. Many policies don't.

Collision damage and loss waivers (CDW/LDW)

It's common knowledge that car rental agencies often instruct their employees to pressure customers to purchase a collision damage waiver (CDW) and other forms of protection whether they need it or not. How do you thread your way between the perils of inadequate coverage and paying for protection you don't need?

Ask yourself *before* you leave home whether you are equipped to handle the responsibility of having a rental car stolen or involved in an accident. Take a close look at the coverage provided by your existing auto, home, and liability umbrella insurance and any rental car insurance provided by your credit cards. If you do this ahead of time and find you aren't fully covered for the circumstances under which you usually rent cars, you'll be able to decide whether you want to add additional "non-owned vehicle" options to your auto insurance, opt for a Gold or Corporate credit card that features rental coverage, or accept the CDW and additional insurance supplements at the rental desk.

The following sections guide you through the maze of options and conditions offered by car rental companies and give you an idea of what your alternatives are.

A *collision damage waiver (CDW)* is *not* insurance. It is an agreement by the rental company to waive reimbursement for any damage to the car while it is in your possession. (This seems to be an important distinction to them, but I haven't found a good reason to bore you with the details.) Every car rental agreement offers CDW at an additional cost that currently runs as high as $16 *per day*. CDW is illegal in some states. In New York and Illinois, it's included in the basic rental rate.

CDW only protects you if you *damage* the vehicle, but rental cars are prime targets for theft and carjacking, too. You certainly don't want to have to pay thousands of dollars to replace an expensive car (or even a cheap one), if it's stolen.

Some rental companies offer waivers that include reimbursement for loss as well as collision. This kind of protection is called a *loss/damage waiver* (LDW). I doubt it covers forgetting where you left the car at the shopping mall, but it definitely protects you against car thieves. In any case, for purposes of brevity I call both collision and loss waivers "CDW."

Always remember to inquire whether the company you plan to rent from will waive loss as well as damage.

What happens if you refuse CDW?

Many people refuse CDW because they believe that their own auto insurance, liability umbrella, home insurance, or credit card car rental insurance is sufficient to handle any problems that may arise. But is it? As John and Dora discovered (see the sidebar "The really expensive luxury car"), if you refuse CDW, the rental agency needs no permission to charge you for any expenses your insurance doesn't cover.

Unless the rental company limits liability, if you initial the CDW refusal box on the rental contract, you are assuming full responsibility for anything that happens to the car while your contract is in effect. If you plan to waive CDW, be sure to bring your auto insurance card with you.

Is it "primary" or "secondary" protection?

CDWs can vary in another important way: Some rental companies provide "primary" protection, which means they waive all remuneration for vehicle damage and/or loss. Others just provide "secondary" protection that only pays for the deductibles and expenses that your other insurance doesn't cover. Therefore, if you are tempted to accept CDW to avoid the possibility of involving your auto insurer in an accident that could result in raised premiums and surcharges, keep in mind that secondary waivers are not of any use to you. The rental company tattles to your insurer to keep its own responsibility to a minimum.

If you want to keep your auto insurer out of the picture, be sure to select a rental company that provides *primary* CDW protection. Failing that, be sure to charge your rental on a credit card that provides primary protection. But in either case, you may still need additional coverage.

When must you refuse CDW?

If you intend to rely on your auto or credit card insurance, you usually must refuse CDW for those options to take effect.

Keep in mind, though, that collision and comprehensive auto insurance may not cover your rental. You must check to be sure that your auto policy covers rentals and that you carry enough "C&C" to cover the car you plan to rent. If you own an older car, your collision and comprehensive coverage may not be adequate to protect a brand-new rental vehicle, especially if it's a more expensive model.

If you have more than one car, and only one of them is covered for collision and comprehensive, be sure the policy number you give the rental company is the one for the car with C&C coverage.

Protection against loss of life and limb

If you accept CDW or rely on credit card insurance, you must be aware that this insurance usually protects only the car. It does not cover your injuries, loss of personal articles, or liability for damage or injury to other people or their vehicles and property. The following takes a look at your options for safeguarding yourself against these additional contingencies.

Health and life insurance

Health and life insurance cover your injury or death. If you don't carry this kind of protection because you don't feel you need it — or can't afford it — in most circumstances renting a car without it probably won't make much difference to you. However, if your health insurance coverage doesn't extend outside your home country, or if you are traveling in an area that you feel increases your risk, you'll be happy to know that temporary protection, called travelers insurance, is available. It's described in the following section.

Travelers insurance

Travelers insurance can be obtained, often at surprisingly low rates, just for the specific period you'll be away. It usually covers medical expenses, flying you back home for medical treatment (or shipping your body home if you really buy the farm), and the theft or loss of personal articles. Your travel agent should be able to provide the names of several sources.

The only drawback is that, even though most health insurance policies won't cover you outside the country for more than a month, I've been unable to find a health insurance company that is willing to suspend my policy while I'm covered by travel insurance. As a result, when I go abroad for several months, I have to pay for both my health and travel policies or cancel my health insurance, lose any deductible I've satisfied, and then go through the hassle of getting a new policy when I return. If anyone knows of a health insurer that is willing to either cover me or suspend its coverage when I'm traveling abroad for extended periods, I'd love to hear about it.

Personal accident insurance

Personal accident insurance (PAI) is an option offered by rental companies that covers your death or medical expenses if you are injured while driving their car. It may be offered as a separate option or as part of an "extended insurance package."

Liability for injury and damage to others

Although a lost or damaged rental car or personal injuries could cost you plenty, this can be small potatoes compared to the enormous amounts you'd lose if you are found liable for the damage, injuries, or even deaths involved in an accident you've caused. Many of us are blissfully unaware that most major rental companies have now established rules making the customer liable in the event of an accident. As a result, most CDWs do not include "third party" liability protection. And why should they? The rental companies have no motivation to save your hide if you get into trouble; they just want to be sure their vehicle can be repaired or replaced.

Even in states with laws specifying that, as the owner of the "at-fault vehicle," the car rental company is responsible for third-party damage and injuries, the rental firms still have the right to go back to the driver for as much compensation as they can get. And even the states that require car rental companies to include liability protection in their basic rental fees usually only ask for the minimum required by state law. A few companies, such as Hertz, include this protection in every contract whether it's required or not. Others offer optional liability coverage. The bottom line is that, once again, you are ultimately responsible for the results of your actions — including failing to protect yourself!

The following sections take a look at the various sources of liability coverage available to you.

Liability insurance

Auto liability insurance may not cover you properly for rented cars. It has been estimated that at least 60 percent of car renters are protected by their own auto insurance, but many only carry state minimum liability — which is often insufficient to cover major accidents — and little or no collision and comprehensive coverage. One can only assume that the remaining 40 percent either have auto insurance that doesn't cover rentals or have no insurance at all. The last group are not necessarily scofflaws — they may have little need to own a vehicle and only rent cars for vacations and business trips.

TRUE STORY

Please, don't do me any more favors!

Like many others, I have always waived CDW and SLI protection because I carry high-limit auto insurance. Judging by my premiums, I should even be covered if I run a Rolls Royce off a cliff. With the wonderful simultaneity that often accompanies writing a book, as I was working on this chapter, I received a little pamphlet from my insurer informing me that they'd changed their coverage for "non-owned cars." Knowing that changes in coverage are like "new and improved" breakfast cereals, I braced myself for the bad news. Sure enough, they'd decided to exclude rental cars used for business because "the cost of business use of rental cars should be paid for by the business which benefits from that use." This almost made sense until I realized that I am self-employed, and so the business responsible is . . . me!

Under the heading "More days of coverage for other non-owned cars," the pamphlet went on to inform me that instead of covering rentals of 21 consecutive days, with a 45-day per year maximum, they now would only cover 21

days *per year* for every car I had insured. Well, my driveway no longer is stuffed with vehicles belonging to kids, my spouse, and "others residing on the premises." In short, I only own one car. How can cutting my coverage by over 50 percent be construed as "more days of coverage"? Beats me. They also informed me that they didn't cover "loss of use."

Then came the "good news": If I want my coverage to include business rentals and other goodies, all I have to do is ante up about $100 more a year for a couple of extra options. Such a deal! When I interviewed other insurers about their rental car coverage, I found that most of them simply include rental cars under their ordinary liability and C&C, without exclusions. I'm now seriously considering switching to a company with a more "neighborly" policy toward single entrepreneurs. You may want to stop right now and check your auto insurance policy to see how well it covers rented cars. If you have trouble deciphering it, Chapter 14 can help.

Supplementary liability insurance

Supplementary liability insurance (SLI or LIS) is offered by many rental companies in amounts of up to one million dollars. This protection varies from one company to another and can take the form of primary or secondary coverage. If you are already covered for rental car liability by an auto insurance or a liability umbrella policy (I get to that in a minute), then secondary coverage will pick up where your other insurance leaves off. But if you don't want to involve your auto insurance company, choose a car rental company that offers *primary* SLI coverage. Be aware that SLI may not cover any other authorized drivers on the rental agreement or your family members or people who reside in your household.

Homeowner's and renter's liability

Homeowner's and renter's liability coverage usually doesn't extend beyond your property lines. It may come in handy if you lose personal articles, but as a source of rental car liability protection, it's useless.

Liability umbrella policies

Liability umbrella policies come in handy. They can supply as much as a million dollars' worth of broad liability coverage at a relatively low cost. You can read all about them in Chapter 14. Once again, be sure that coverage extends to any mayhem you may cause with a rented car, anywhere in the world.

Protection for your possessions

In the two preceding sections, I cover physical damage and loss for the car, ourselves, and others. But what about all that lovely gear we usually tote around? *CDWs don't cover loss of, or damage to, personal effects.* Consequently, you may want to find another way to protect luggage, clothing, jewelry, cameras, computers, and other precious stuff.

- ✔ **Personal effects protection (PEP)** is for articles that are damaged or stolen while in the car is offered by some car rental companies, but it usually isn't extensive enough to cover really expensive items and may even exclude cameras and jewelry. Check your homeowner's or renter's insurance coverage before you agree to pay for this option.

- ✔ **Homeowner's or renter's insurance** usually protects your possessions both within and outside your residence, but it may contain dollar limits that are too low to cover expensive gear, and your policy may contain vital exclusions.

If you find your present property coverage inadequate, personal articles policies and "floaters" are available from your home insurer to cover theft or damage to items that are too expensive to be protected under standard home insurance limits.

> ✔ **Personal articles policies** cover jewelry, cameras, computers, and other expensive paraphernalia on an item-by-item basis. Rates are quoted per $100 of value. These policies are usually in force for the same period as your homeowner's or renter's coverage.
>
> ✔ **Floaters** are policies you buy to insure specific items just for the time they'll be out in the cold, cruel world. These have become harder to obtain.

If you opt for either a personal articles policy or a floater policy, don't wait for the last minute. The insurer may require documentation of value in the form of sales slips or current appraisals before issuing coverage. Once that documentation is part of their records, however, you can usually set up and cancel these policies within 24 hours. Be sure you'll be protected against damage and loss as well as theft in the countries and conditions you plan to encounter.

Credit card car-rental insurance

Why, you may ask, should I bother with all the exclusions and pitfalls inherent in relying on auto, home, and umbrella insurance protection, when I can insure a rental car at no cost just by using my credit card to pay for it? Good question. Unfortunately, the chances are that your credit card provides only incomplete coverage, if it covers you at all. I spent weeks interviewing the major credit card companies and found serious loopholes in the protection they provide.

Not every credit card provides car rental insurance, and in most cases, it's only secondary coverage, unless you have no auto insurance of your own. At present, Diners Club provides primary coverage. American Express provides secondary rental loss and damage coverage on their no-frills, standard green cards as well as on Optima, Gold, Platinum, and Corporate cards. Although some banks may provide extra insurance services, most Visas and MasterCards only offer coverage to Gold, Platinum, and Corporate cardholders. Gold-card insurance is usually secondary, Platinum coverage varies, and Corporate cards usually provide primary coverage as long as you can prove you were using the car for business purposes. Right now, Discover Card offers no rental insurance at all.

Most credit cards do not cover liability or personal articles. Like rental agency CDWs, many cards do not cover liability or personal property. If you have an accident or lose personal articles, you are as vulnerable as you would be with only CDW protection.

Gold Visas and MasterCards usually limit coverage to as little as two consecutive weeks, with no renewals. American Express currently insures cars for 30 days. If you plan to rent for longer periods, you may have to return the car when the credit card's insurance period runs out and then rent another car. Some credit cards allow you to rent the next car with their card; others won't, and you'll have to use a different credit card to insure the next car. *Note:* Credit card car-rental insurance often doesn't cover special vehicles such as 4-wheel drive sport models, large vans, campers, trucks, and antique and luxury cars.

If you decide to use credit card car rental insurance, be sure to refuse the rental company's CDW by initialing the refusal box. If you don't, your credit card's coverage will be disallowed. This is also true of some auto insurance companies.

While you still have time to make some educated choices, read those little pamphlets that came with your credit cards and see just what they have to offer. If you're still not clear, call their customer service 800 number and grill them.

Non-owner's auto insurance

Contrary to popular belief, life is possible without owning wheels. I grew up in New York City where it was faster and easier to take the subway than to find a place to park (assuming you survived the drive to get there). I didn't own a car until I was well into adulthood and only did so because I'd moved to California, where the car has replaced the horse, with little in the way of other options. My assumption is that if you are reading this book, you probably own a car, but you may have friends or relatives who don't. If that's the case, be kind and let them know that they have another option for protection when they rent a car. It's called non-owner's auto insurance, and coverage currently ranges from $100,000 to $300,000 for between $250 and $300 per year.

Finding the best deal on rental car protection

After reviewing your insurance policies and credit cards, you may have found that your protection has serious holes. What are you going to do about it? By all means, find out just how much adequate liability, personal article, and non-owned vehicle coverage will add to the cost of your current insurance policies and, with those figures in mind, take the time to call the customer service 800 numbers for several car rental agencies and ask them the following questions:

- ✔ **Does your CDW provide primary or secondary coverage?** What does it cost per day? Any exclusions?

- ✔ **Do you cover theft (LDW) as well as collision?** What does it cost? Any exclusions?

✔ **Do you offer a PEP option to cover my personal effects for damage and loss if the car is in an accident, broken into, or stolen?** What does it cost? Are there exclusions?

✔ **Does your contract cover third-party liability and medical expenses if I cause an accident?** If not, do you offer supplementary liability insurance (SLI)? What does it cost? How much will it cover?

✔ **Will you reimburse me if I'm injured as a result of damage or mechanical failure of the car?** If not, do you offer personal accident insurance (PAI)? How much does that cost?

When you have these answers, estimate how many days a year you usually rent cars and decide whether it pays to

✔ Patronize the rental company that offers the fullest range of protection at the lowest cost and buy these options each time you rent a car.

✔ Invest in more extensive auto insurance protection for rental cars.

✔ Get an umbrella liability policy.

✔ Buy personal articles insurance or floaters to cover expensive gear.

✔ Opt for a more expensive gold or corporate credit card.

✔ Buy non-owner's auto insurance if you don't own a car.

Remember, it will probably take more than one of these options to cover yourself completely, but the cost in time and money to determine the best combination will more than pay for itself if you ever get into an accident with a rental car.

Filing a Claim

If you have an accident or your rental car is stolen, you will have to file a claim. Although the rules vary with the type of protection you've chosen and the company that provides it, these guidelines should help in any situation:

✔ **Report the claim as soon as you possibly can.** Each company has a deadline for reporting claims. Most range from 20 to 30 days after the incident. If you wait longer than that, you run the risk of having your claim disqualified. To avoid problems, read the literature or contract provided with the protection you choose and carry the address of the claims department with you if you're going far from home.

✔ **Be sure you have the required documentation.** After you report the claim, you will usually be sent an official claim form to fill out and a list of documentation they require. Here are some of the things you'll probably be asked to supply:

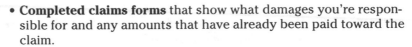

- **Completed claims forms** that show what damages you're responsible for and any amounts that have already been paid toward the claim.

- **A copy of the repair estimate or itemized repair bill** showing what, if anything, has already been paid, and by whom.

- **The company and policy number of any auto or liability insurance you have that may cover all or part of the accident.** Carrying a copy of the Declarations page with you when you go abroad is a good idea, because it provides a summary of your coverage. See Chapter 14 for information on the Declarations page.

- **A copy of your auto rental contract** showing whether you refused or accepted their CDW protection.

- **A copy of the credit card charge slip used to pay for the rental,** if you're relying on credit card insurance.

- **A copy of the police report or accident report.**

- **Photographs of the damaged vehicle.** An inexpensive disposable camera comes in handy here. Even if they don't ask for it, photographic evidence can prevent the rental company from billing you for unnecessary repairs.

✔ **If the rental company bills you for loss of use, request a copy of their utilization log to determine whether you've been billed correctly.** Most companies figure loss of use the same way John's did (see the sidebar "The really expensive luxury car"). Here's the formula:

(Days out of service) × (rental fee per day) × (% normal utilization — usually 80 to 90 percent)

After the rental, insurance, or credit card company has reimbursed you, they may try to collect their damages from other parties involved in the accident. Most agreements specify that you assist them in this by transferring your "rights and remedies" to them so they can file suits, by being willing to sign documents and by responding to any "reasonable" requests they may make.

Avoiding Rental Rip-Offs for Damage You Didn't Cause

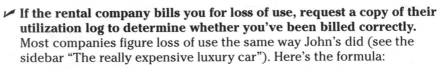

Brand-new cars are hard to find at rental agencies, so the chances are good that the car you'll be assigned will have experienced the not-so-tender ministrations of a variety of other drivers. This may not be a bad thing — the only rental car I ever drove that had fewer than a thousand miles on the speedometer left me betrayed and abandoned on a remote road when the entire exhaust system fell off without warning!

But I digress. The point here is that you must make the rental agent aware of all the little dents, dings, and other love taps the car has received from your predecessors before you leave the lot, or you stand the chance of being blamed — and charged — for them.

Check the car out when you receive it

In the good old days, rental agents walked you out to the car and personally introduced you to it. They not only verified the car's condition, they showed you where the windshield wipers and turn signals were and where that miserable secret button was that allows you to get the key out of the ignition when you park. Today, you're usually given a batch of paperwork and a key and then dropped off at your vehicle by a van that takes off as soon as you've gotten your luggage onto the pavement. There are even quick checkout procedures that involve no humans at all: You put your credit card into a slot, punch a couple of buttons on a touch-screen monitor, and the papers and key emerge from appropriate orifices. Hopefully, there's a human being around whom you can notify if the car is in less-than-perfect shape.

The burden of verifying the condition of a rental car is now firmly up to you. Even if you're in a hurry, take the time to check the car out properly *before you leave the lot.* To be sure you've touched all the bases, photocopy the Rental Checklist in this chapter and bring it with you when you rent a vehicle. Put the name of the agent who assists you right on the list and on the rental agreement, as well. If you're dropped off at your vehicle in the middle of a dark parking lot, drive to the most well-lit area in the lot and inspect the vehicle closely.

Don't leave the lot until you're sure the car is in good shape. Taking it for a spin around the block to check the ride, handling, and brakes before you take to the highway isn't a bad idea. If you find any problems, head straight back to the rental counter and either demand another vehicle or have the agent record the damage right on your sales slip, sign, and date it. The guard who examined my papers at the exit from the lot did that for me recently.

Return the car in person

Most of us are rushing to make a plane when it's time to return a rental car, and automatic-return facilities certainly have their advantages. Unfortunately, they may involve dropping the vehicle off at an unstaffed location and having the rental charged to your credit card without the chance to verify the condition of the car or the total cost. Many people have dropped a vehicle off in perfect condition only to find horrendous charges on their credit card bills for damages they had nothing to do with. If at all possible, try to return the car during business hours and allow time to go over it with a real live person.

RENTAL CHECKLIST

Name of Agent:		Phone:		
Location:				
Rental Invoice#:		Date/Time Out:	Back:	
ITEM			**Out**	**In**
Dents, dings, scratches and missing exterior trim? Location/Description?				
Interior: Tears, burns, and stains in the upholstery, carpeting headers, or door panels? Location/Description:				
Missing dashboard knobs? Door handles? Window cranks?				
Is there an owner's manual in the glove compartment? Consider it a miracle.				
Adjust the seats and mirrors to suit yourself.				
Start the car. Check the oil, fuel, and other gauges.				
Fuel Level: Out: E_____1/4_____1/2_____3/4_____F_____ In: E_____1/4_____1/2_____3/4_____F_____				
An ABS warning light on the dash will tell you if the car is equipped with anti-lock brakes and whether the system is working.				
Locate and test the horn and the emergency brake.				
If the car is equipped with them, locate and test remote trunk and fuel-tank latches, power windows and door locks.				
Try *all* the lights. Not just the headlights but the parking lights, tail lights, brights, and turn signals as well. If you're not alone, have your companion check the brake lights while you operate the pedal.				
Try the windshield wipers. Is there windshield-washer fluid in the tank?				
If it's winter, is there a windshield scraper? If not, ask for one.				
Test the air conditioner, heater, defroster, and radio.				
Tires properly inflated? Sufficient tread? Any hubcaps missing?				
Is the spare tire in good shape? Properly inflated?				
Is there a jack? Does it have a handle? Do you know how to use it?				

Because car rental firms have the right to assess a car and charge you for any damage they find, there is usually no way to prove your innocence after you've returned the car and signed it in. To add insult to injury, because you probably no longer will even be in the same city by the time the bill arrives, you'll never know whether or not the damage really exists!

If you must use an automatic drop-off that requires you to turn in all copies of your rental agreement, be sure to make a copy for yourself beforehand and note the final mileage on it when you return the vehicle. Don't pay their charges on your credit card bill until you receive the rental company's invoice and are sure the figures are correct. If you feel you were over-charged, call your credit card company and dispute the charge.

If the return facility is on an unstaffed lot, take the time to drive into a nearby service station and ask the manager to go over the vehicle with you and witness that it's in good shape. Because you're probably going to want to fill the gas tank before you return the car to avoid being charged cham-pagne prices for fuel by the rental company, you won't even have to go out of your way to do this. A short signed and dated note from the station manager, right on the rental contract or on the checklist, can be an ace in the hole if you're wrongly accused. Be sure to get the name, address, and phone number of the gas station so you can reach the manager, if necessary.

Refuel the car yourself

When you refuel the car before returning it, don't buy more fuel than you need to reach the required level. Fuel gauges respond slowly to change, so shut off the engine but leave the ignition key turned to "On" so you can read the fuel gauge. When you get within a quarter of a tank of the required level, stop pumping fuel. The gauge will continue to climb, perhaps as far as necessary. If not, just pump short bursts with pauses to read the gauge, until you've pumped just the amount you need.

If you must return the car with a full tank, put the pump nozzle as far into the filler neck as you can. Pump as fast as you can until the pump nozzle clicks off. Although the gas gauge will read "full," you may save as much as two or three gallons of fuel because of the pressure in the tank. If you think this is unfair, be aware that the rental company may have used the same technique to fill the tank in the first place.

Review the Rental Checklist

When you return the car, don't forget to check it against the Rental Checklist again. If you find anything amiss, have the counter assistant copy your checklist and attach it to your agreement. Get that person's name, too.

Check your bill carefully before you pay it

Take the time to go over the final invoice before you leave the counter. If you find a discrepancy later on, it can be difficult to resolve. Be sure the prices they've charged reflect any discounts you deserve. Get the name of the person who assists you in case discrepancies come to light later on.

Be sure the final fuel level on the contract agrees with the fuel gauge in the car. It takes time for the gauge to reach its real level when the car is started. If it reads low, have the agent wait a few seconds for the gauge to read accurately.

Complaint Procedures

If all the precautions I've suggested in this chapter fail to prevent you from being ripped off or maltreated by a car rental agency, you have recourse from the company and other sources. If you've experienced any of the following, the first place to go for recourse is to the rental company itself. Car renting is a very competitive industry, and most companies go a long way to keep customers satisfied.

A quick guide to protecting yourself from rental car thieves

Although Chapter 17 covers carjacking in more detail, here are a few additional things to remember when you're renting a car in a strange city:

✔ **Don't leave the counter until you thoroughly understand how to get where you're going.** Ask the counter representative for detailed, *written* directions to your destination, including the number and direction of all the freeway entrances and exits you'll use.

✔ **Request a map and be sure you can read it.** If you get lost, don't just pull over and study your map or directions — it's a dead giveaway that you are a stranger in town. Instead, drive to a nearby, well-lit, public place such as a service station or restaurant, and get your information more discreetly.

Some car renters now supply vehicles with electronic, satellite-driven screens that not only feature maps with step-by-step directions, but also with voices that tell you what your next move should be. These wondrous devices also supply the location of the nearest gas station, telephone, hotel, restaurant, police station, hospital, and other facilities, and tell you how far you still have to go and the estimated time it will take to get there. As I write, these have just become available on a few expensive vehicles and in limited locations on a test basis (the local city must have a satellite system that can provide this service). Eventually, they should be standard equipment on all cars.

✔ **Take the shuttle to your hotel and rent a car there.** If you are going to be arriving or departing after dark in a risky area, using the hotel shuttle to get to and from the airport and renting a car from an agency near your hotel may be a safer option.

✔ Were you greeted at the counter with the news that the car you reserved isn't available and you have to rent a larger model at a higher price?

✔ Did you have to purchase protection you didn't need?

✔ Have you found charges for car washing, cleanup, or other weird stuff on your bill?

✔ Were you penalized for undisclosed restrictions on "unlimited mileage" deals?

✔ Are the rates on the bill the rates that you agreed upon?

✔ Did you get little or no response or assistance from the company when a vehicle broke down and left you stranded?

✔ Have you been overcharged for repairs or replacements after an accident?

✔ Are you dissatisfied by any other aspect of your rental?

To get satisfaction with the least amount of hassle, take as many of the following steps as you need:

✔ **Complain to the person at the counter when you rent or return the car.** Customer service reps at several companies have told me that they often authorize counter personnel to reimburse complaints for $50 or less right on the spot.

✔ **Call the company's 800 customer service number and tell your story.** If necessary, be prepared to back up your statement with *copies* of your agreement and final bills or invoices, repair bills, photos of the damage, and whatever else seems relevant. The company will check the problem out, review computer input, talk to the agent who handled the transaction, and make a decision. In most cases, they will do whatever they can to make you happy because they know that if you feel you can trust their company to satisfy complaints, you'll probably continue to choose them over a competitor that may not be as fair.

✔ **Use the city, county, and state government listings in your local telephone directory to contact any or all of the following agencies:**

  • The consumer division of the state attorney general's office

  • Your state or city department of consumer affairs

  • Local and national consumer action lines or consumer protection agencies

  • Your local Better Business Bureau (many car rental agencies are local franchises)

  • **Contact ombudsmen (people who investigate claims on behalf of the public).** They are featured on television, in newspapers, and in some travel publications.

International Rentals

Many experts believe that car rentals in foreign countries cost less if you negotiate them at home. They recommend renting from a major company with branches overseas or asking your travel agent to do it for you. After traveling abroad a good deal, I've found that this is often not the case. It really depends on which countries you are visiting and the availability of cars when you arrive. I've often negotiated much lower prices with local people in foreign countries for cars, hotels, and tourism packages than those quoted by U.S. travel agents. Generally speaking, if you are visiting a country with very low prices, you're probably better off waiting until you get there unless you are visiting at peak season, require a special vehicle, or plan to rent in a small or remote location where you run the risk of finding that no cars are available.

If you want to hedge your bets, reserve a car before you leave home and, if you find much better rates when you arrive, simply cancel or return the car and rent another at bargain prices. Just be sure beforehand that no cancellation or early return fees will be involved.

Things to know when you rent a car abroad

Whether you reserve your car before you leave or rent one while you're abroad, there are significant differences between domestic and international car rentals. To avoid unpleasant surprises, keep these facts in mind:

- ✔ **Most auto insurance policies will not cover you outside the United States and Canada.**

- ✔ **Most secondary credit card car rental insurance becomes primary insurance abroad.** This means it covers you completely whether you have auto insurance or not.

- ✔ **Many countries insist on CDW protection, and others require theft protection (LDW) as well.** Be sure these waivers are included in all price quotes.

- ✔ **Some foreign rental companies place a hold of as much as $5,000 to $14,000 on your credit card to protect themselves if you total the vehicle.** Unless you have an American Express card with no credit limit, this can effectively render your card useless as a source of funds for your trip. The way to beat this is to use one credit card to rent cars and another card for the rest of your expenses.

✔ **Some foreign countries require you to buy local insurance when you rent a car.** New Zealand, Mexico, and Italy are prime examples. Call consulates or tourist boards, or ask your travel agent to check whether this is the case in the countries you plan to visit.

✔ **Many countries impose a "value added tax" (VAT), which can be quite high.** For example, in France the tax is currently 18.6 percent; in Italy, 19 percent. Be sure any price quotes you get include the VAT.

✔ **Some countries restrict their own citizens from driving after they reach a certain age.** Probably for this reason, although no major rental agencies impose maximum age restrictions in the United States and Canada (except for Budget, whose age limitations vary in different parts of Canada), some have upper age limits in foreign countries.

If you are over 65, be sure to ask the reservations clerk about age restrictions on car rentals in the countries you plan to visit. If they apply to you, see whether you can pay a surcharge to avoid them. If this isn't possible, consider hiring a driver or traveling with someone under the age limit who can do the driving for you.

✔ **The least expensive foreign cars usually have manual transmissions.** If you think that these are unique forms of exotica, you may want to learn to drive one before you leave home, because automatic models can cost as much as $90 a week extra.

✔ **If you are unaccustomed to shifting manually,** don't try to learn in a country where they drive on the left side of the road. Driving on the "wrong" side is confusing enough without trying to shift with your left hand and manage a clutch pedal, too!

✔ **Some foreign cars are extremely small.** When making reservations, be sure to mention how many people and how much luggage your rented vehicle must accommodate. If you've ever tried to see a country while stuffed into the back seat of a tiny car, you'll know why spending a bit more for a roomier vehicle definitely pays off in the long run.

✔ **Ask for written confirmation, including the price in local currency, when you reserve a car.**

✔ **Traffic tickets and fines can be unbelievably expensive in some localities.** Be sure you understand the speed limits and the rules of the road, and remember that there's a big difference between miles and kilometers per hour!

✔ **Try to pick up and return the car during business hours.** The rental agency may be closed at night or on weekends.

✔ **Be doubly sure that your final bill is correct before you leave the agency.** It would be hard to try to contest the bill after you're back home.

Where to rent cars for international travel

Here are the names and international travel programs for several companies that offer car rentals in foreign countries:

- **Avis Worldwide** (800-331-1084) handles reservations throughout the world. Its "Know Before You Go" (800-297-4447) is a 24-hour service that answers questions about driving in Great Britain, France, Germany, or Italy. Its "On Call" program provides 24-hour toll free numbers for support services in Great Britain, France, Germany, and Italy, including message-retrieval and locating English-speaking doctors, cash machines, and other amenities. You can reach them at www.avis.com.

- **Hertz Worldwide** (U.S.: 800-654-3001; Canada-English: 800-263-0600; Canada-French: 800-263-0678) has agencies in 140 countries. Hertz has a program that allows you to rent a vehicle in one of 16 countries and return it in another for a relatively small fee. It also has a "Le Swap" program that allows you to leave your left-hand-drive car in England, take the train through the Chunnel (Channel Tunnel), and pick up a right-hand-drive car on the French side in Calais, or vice versa, with no drop-off fee when you return the second car. Check out their Web site at www.hertz.com.

- **National Europcar** (800-227-3876) is a National affiliate that offers a guaranteed rate called "Advansaver." Find out more at their Web site at www.europcar.com.

- **Auto Europe** (800-223-5555) is a booking agency that uses Avis, Europcar, and independent operators in 26 European countries. Reach them by mail at P.O. Box 7006, Portland, ME 04112, or find them on the Web at www.autoeurope.com.

- **Kemwel** (800-678-0678) is a U.S. booking agency whose "Super Saver" program draws on various rental companies in 25 European countries. Its address is 106 Calvert Street, Harrison, NY 10528, and the Web address is www.kemwel.com.

- **AutoNet International** (888-880-8999) advertises low air and hotel rates as well as major-brand cars at budget prices. Take a look at their services by pointing your Web browser to www.autonet-intl.com.

Part VII
The Part of Tens

In this part . . .

Negotiating for the best car deal can feel like a jog on paper-thin ice. If you're interested in a few clues about how to slide through the process without falling for a foolish compromise, set foot on this part's ten (and then some) car-buying tips. This part contains fun and interesting information that takes only a couple of minutes to read. Surely you can spare that much time while you're waiting for the tow truck.

Chapter 20

Ten Things Not to Do During Negotiations

. . . .

In This Chapter

▶ Avoiding common negotiating mistakes

▶ Figuring out how to negotiate your way into a good deal

. . . .

*I*f you're like the rest of the world, you hate the thought of haggling with a dealer over the price of a car. But don't be intimidated by the car-buying process. You can come out on top by avoiding some common pitfalls along the way. In this chapter I explain those pitfalls and tell you how to steer clear of them. Winning the negotiating game requires a few tools — and you'll find them here.

Don't Go to a Dealership Unprepared

Car dealers are great at spotting unprepared customers. In fact, most people who enter a dealership haven't done their homework. So the best way to surprise the people trying to sell you a vehicle is by blindsiding them with your knowledge. Look at it this way: A car is one of the biggest purchases most people make — second only to a house. So doing a little research before you go in to buy makes sense.

Before you even set foot on a car lot, you should know several things:

- ✔ How much the dealer paid for the car you want
- ✔ How much your trade-in is worth
- ✔ Exactly which features and options you want
- ✔ How much you're willing to pay

If you're not sure where to begin looking for this kind of information, check out Chapters 4 and 5 for information on used cars. If your heart is set on a new vehicle, Chapters 7, 8, and 9 will get you on the road to success. And Chapter 21 provides more than ten great Web sites geared specifically toward helping you get the best deal possible when you buy a new or used vehicle. While you're at it, don't forget your public library — a great source for car magazines filled with details on the latest models, as well as pricing information.

Don't Limit Yourself to Only One Dealer

You may have already decided which car you want. And a dealership that sells that car may be just down the road. But when you're buying a car, shopping around definitely pays off. Dealerships, and the people who work there, vary greatly. What one dealership can offer you may be significantly different from the deal offered by another.

Be sure to tell the salesperson when you walk in the door that you're seriously shopping for a car and that you intend to visit several dealerships in search of the best deal. Ask each dealership for its best price, and tell the salespeople that, as much as you'd like to buy your car from them, you will definitely go with the lowest bidder. Dealers may be more likely to give you the lowest price they can if they know they're bidding against their competition. If you've been to other dealerships, refuse to divulge what you've been offered elsewhere. Why give salespeople the opportunity to just lower the price a few dollars below the lowest bid, when you might get a *much* lower offer if you leave them in the dark? However, if a dealership is only a few dollars away from your best offer, and you like and trust them more that the competition, it may be a good idea to divulge the better price and ask them to meet it. If they can't, you may still feel that their service will be worth a few extra dollars.

Don't Blurt Out Exactly What You Want As Soon As You Walk in the Door

You should definitely have at least an idea of which vehicles you'd like to consider. But if you walk into a dealership proclaiming your love for a specific model, you give the salesperson an advantage. If he knows that you've always wanted that little red convertible, he also knows that he can quote you a higher price and you'll be less likely to walk away. Hold back your enthusiasm until you've signed your name and made the deal. Then feel free to tell the dealer you've been dreaming about this car since you were 16!

Don't Give the Dealer a Price Range

Even though you know when you walk in the door how much you're willing to pay, you shouldn't tell the dealer that price. If you give the dealer a price range, you can bet that she won't try to sell you a car in the low end of your range. She'll aim high — and you'll have a harder time negotiating her down. If she asks you for your price range, say, "I'm interested in *that* car. What's the best price you can give me?" Forcing her to name a price ensures that she's not quoting you figures based on what you've told her you're willing to spend.

When you go to a dealership, don't wear your expensive clothing or jewelry. Salespeople assess you from the minute you arrive, and if they think you have money, they'll quote higher prices. Wear your diamond earrings or Rolex watch when you come back to pick the vehicle up. And smile as you drive off the lot!

Don't Shop or Negotiate When You're in a Hurry

Allow yourself plenty of time — a few days even — to spend shopping. If you're in a hurry, you're less likely to check out each vehicle for problems or read the fine print on a sales contract. And if you're in a rush to buy, you may not have the patience it takes to demand the options you want and stick with the price you want to pay. In other words, you may end up going along with the price the dealer quotes just because you don't have the time to negotiate.

Don't Negotiate a Price Based on the Window Sticker

The sticker price gives the dealer a huge profit. And while any dealer would love to sell you a car for the price listed on the sticker, most dealers expect you to negotiate lower. So know how much the dealer paid for the car. Then take two percent off that figure, and start negotiating from there. The dealer may tell you that he needs to make a profit and you're being unfair. But remember that dealers often get a *holdback* — money from the manufacturer to advertise and market that car — and the holdback can be considered part of the dealer's profit. Starting negotiations with a really low price is much better than starting high. You can always work your way up if the dealer refuses to budge, but you'll never be able to work your way down. (The *Automotive News* and other publications carry listings of buyer discounts and dealer incentives offered by manufacturers. See Chapter 5 for more sources.)

Don't Think of the Price in Terms of Monthly Payments

If you tell the dealer how much you want to pay every month, she can make just about any car fit that monthly payment. But you may end up having to cough up a bigger down payment or pay much more in interest over the long haul. Always negotiate for the *total* cost of the car. Refuse to even talk about whether you're interested in leasing or financing until after you've settled on a sales price.

If you do end up leasing or getting a loan, be sure the contract is based on the price you've negotiated. Unscrupulous dealers have been known to base these contracts on the sticker price, and unsuspecting customers have signed on the dotted line.

Don't Forget to Check Out the Vehicle

Remember: A car is probably one of the most expensive items you'll ever buy, so you need to be sure you know exactly what you're getting. If you're buying a used car, having the vehicle inspected by an independent mechanic is critical. But don't forget to look a new car over, too. No matter how well you negotiate, your time and energy could all be wasted if you get the vehicle home and then start noticing problems. Chapters 4, 7, and 8 provide all the information you need on test-driving a new or used vehicle, checking it for defects, and making sure it has all the features you want. Take the checklists in each chapter with you to be sure you haven't missed anything.

Don't Fall Victim to Sales Tactics

Dealers have all kinds of tricks up their sleeves — after all, that's their job. (They don't call them "dealers" for nothing!) But *your* job, as a knowledgeable customer, is to know how to defend yourself against those sales tactics. Just as you prepare answers for commonly asked questions when you go for a job interview, you should prepare your responses to the sales pitches you'll receive from car dealers.

The main things you need to remember are these:

- Always bargain up from the factory invoice price, not down from the sticker price.
- Be firm about the price you want to pay, and question everything you see.

- ✔ If they tell you they can't sell you the car for the price you think is fair, walk out the door.

- ✔ If they try to make you feel guilty for not giving them enough of a profit, remember the holdbacks they get from the manufacturer.

- ✔ And if they ask you too many questions, take control of the situation and start asking the questions yourself.

You hold control of the situation because you're the one with the money — and you don't have to give them any of it.

Don't Tell the Dealer You Have a Trade-In Until the Last Minute

Refuse to talk about a trade-in until you've negotiated the price of your new vehicle. If the dealer knows you have a trade-in, he'll figure in the cost of the trade-in when he quotes you a price for the new car.

Park your car down the street and walk to the car lot. This way the dealer doesn't make any assumptions about a trade-in — and you get a better deal.

After you've arrived on a final price for your new vehicle — and have gotten that price in writing — mention that you have a car you'd like to trade in. If the dealer seems annoyed that you didn't mention it earlier, don't let that bother you. His annoyance is just a sign that you've gotten the upper hand in your negotiations — which is exactly what you want.

Chapter 21

Ten Great Automotive Web Sites

*T*he Internet is a fantastic resource for finding information on cars and other vehicles. Thousands of Web sites are devoted to the topic, and I've culled through many of them to bring you a list of my top ten picks. These Web sites provide you with information on buying a new or used car, as well as maintaining the car you own. They also provide up-to-date information on the industry — including racing events, career opportunities, and automotive news. If you have access to a computer, any car-related information you could possibly want can be found on the Web. The following sites are great places to start.

Edmund's Automobile Buyers' Guides

Long considered one of the top resources for buyers of new and used cars, Edmund's started providing its services on the Internet in 1994. This site provides prices and reviews of new and used cars, vans, pickups, and sport utility vehicles (SUVs). You can find information here on incentives and rebates, road tests, and automotive news, as well as get advice on buying a new or used car. You can even participate in discussions with other car owners to find out everything you want to know about a particular vehicle. If you're even considering buying a car, this site should be the first stop you make. Just point your browser to the following address:

```
www.edmunds.com
```

Kelley Blue Book

Similar to Edmund's, the Kelley Blue Book site provides pricing information on new and used cars. One highlight of this site is the links it provides to the Web sites of car manufacturers — everything from Jeep to Jaguar, Saturn to Saab.

Distinct differences in the suggested prices provided by Edmund's and the Kelley Blue Book are frequent, so you should definitely look to more than one source when doing your research. Check out the Kelley Blue Book at the following address:

```
www.kbb.com
```

All Things Automotive

All Things Automotive is currently the best resource on the Web for finding general automotive information. It provides links to over 3,000 Web sites in the following categories: classics, classifieds, clubs, dealers, enthusiasts, finance and insurance, interactive, manufacturers, miscellaneous, motorcycles, NetZines, organizations and government, parts and services, sales, and sports. No matter what your automotive interests are, you can find the resources you need at the following address:

```
www.autodirectory.com
```

Consumer Reports Online

Consumer Reports Online provides great free advice on buying a new car and checking out a used car, as well as useful information on warranties and insurance. For a fee of $2.95 per month, you can subscribe to the site and get complete access to the Consumer Reports ratings of new and used cars and trucks, and find help in choosing the car that's right for you. (You'll also have access to the entire Consumer Reports Web site, which has information on lots of other subjects, ranging from appliances and electronics to health and food.) Car buyers have trusted Consumer Reports for years, and with good reason: It accepts no advertisements or product samples from manufacturers, so the information it provides is unbiased and is meant to serve the consumer (that's you!). You may find the information you receive well worth the subscription rate. Point your browser to the following address:

```
www.consumerreports.com
```

Microsoft CarPoint

Microsoft's resource for finding information on cars is called CarPoint, and it's definitely one you should check out. In addition to providing helpful articles, such as one that gives tips on shopping for tires or another that lists the winners of recent NHTSA crash tests, this Web site includes classifieds for used cars in your area. With CarPoint's New-Car Buying Service, you choose the vehicle you want and enter your zip code. Within 48 hours, a dealership in CarPoint's network of dealers contacts you with the best price the dealership can offer. You're under no obligation to buy, you can walk away at any time, and best of all, the service is free! Check it out at the following address:

```
carpoint.msn.com
```

eAuto: Everything Automotive

This Web site provides information on car buying, as well as classifieds and news updates on automotive issues. You can check out its reviews of other car-related Web sites and chat with automotive enthusiasts about issues that interest you. eAuto provides links to other Web sites in different categories, including automakers, dealers, auto parts, wheels/tires, accessories, motor sports, and leftover parts. This site also offers a service with Progressive Insurance that gives you insurance quotes from several different companies in an effort to find the lowest rates. Check out eAuto at the following address:

```
www.eauto.com
```

Autoweb.com

Covers all things automotive, including buying and selling cars, financing and insurance, car reviews, and recent research. This site features an easy-to-use format and offers online forums for all sorts of car issues. You'll find free tips from Pep Boys, information about recalls, and up-to-date service bulletins. You can also get a good look at the new cars of the season in their showroom with prices, mpg, and specs. Includes a link to their Canadian Web site as well. They can be found at the following address:

```
www.autoweb.com
```

Consumers Car Club

Unlike most automotive Internet sites, Car Club gives you several ways to car shop. It has a national dealer referral network offering preset, no-hassle prices on most makes and models. Car Club also offers you the option of paying a small fee to have them do the shopping, price negotiation, and paperwork for you. Or, they will obtain several firm price quotes for you from local dealers. You can even order a vehicle custom-built to your specifications from several major manufacturers.

Car Club also offers a Used Car Buyers Protection Program that takes the risk out of buying a used vehicle. You can obtain pricing and title history reports on most vehicles built since 1981, an on-site inspection of the vehicle by a professional mechanic, and an extended mechanical warranty if the vehicle passes the inspection. This site has won top ratings from *PC World* and *Yahoo! Internet Life* magazines, both for overall customer service and for delivering significant savings to car buyers.

```
www.carclub.com
```

Auto-By-Tel

Auto-By-Tel offers pricing of new and used cars, information on the latest car models to hit the market, and the lowdown on loans and leases. You can find the average loan rates for your state or for the nation as a whole, as well as look at the trends in loan rates over the past three months. Auto-By-Tel says that over a million people have used its services to receive free, no-obligation quotes. Over 2,700 dealerships are accredited by Auto-By-Tel nationwide. If you're in the market for a vehicle, this is one site you definitely shouldn't miss. Check it out at the following address:

```
www.autobytel.com
```

AutoVantage

This site provides you with free pricing information on new and used cars, as well as classifieds listing used cars for sale. AutoVantage is part of a larger Web site called netMarket. If you choose to become a netMarket member, you can also get discounts on car maintenance at a service center in your area; discounts on car rentals at Avis, Hertz, National, Budget, and Alamo; and maps and directions for your next big road trip. To decide whether the cost of membership (currently $1.00 for the first 3 months and $69.95 to continue for a full year) is worth it, check out this site at the following address:

```
www.autovantage.com
```

Index

• B •

(continued)

• *M* •

WWW.DUMMIES.COM

Discover Dummies™ Online!

The *Dummies* Web Site is your fun and friendly online resource for the latest information about ...*For Dummies*® books on all your favorite topics. From cars to computers, wine to Windows, and investing to the Internet, we've got a shelf full of ...*For Dummies* books waiting for you!

Ten Fun and Useful Things You Can Do at www.dummies.com

1. Register this book and win!
2. Find and buy the ...*For Dummies* books you want online.
3. Get ten great *Dummies Tips*™ every week.
4. Chat with your favorite ...*For Dummies* authors.
5. Subscribe free to *The Dummies Dispatch*™ newsletter.
6. Enter our sweepstakes and win cool stuff.
7. Send a free cartoon postcard to a friend.
8. Download free software.
9. Sample a book before you buy.
10. Talk to us. Make comments, ask questions, and get answers!

Jump online to these ten fun and useful things at **http://www.dummies.com/10useful**

SURF THE NET

WWW.DUMMIES.COM

For other technology titles from IDG Books Worldwide, go to **www.idgbooks.com**

Not online yet? It's easy to get started with *The Internet For Dummies*® 5th Edition, or *Dummies 101*®: *The Internet For Windows*® *98*, available at local retailers everywhere.

IDG BOOKS WORLDWIDE

Find other ...*For Dummies* books on these topics:
Business • Careers • Databases • Food & Beverages • Games • Gardening • Graphics • Hardware
Health & Fitness • Internet and the World Wide Web • Networking • Office Suites
Operating Systems • Personal Finance • Pets • Programming • Recreation • Sports
Spreadsheets • Teacher Resources • Test Prep • Word Processing

The IDG Books Worldwide logo is a registered trademark under exclusive license to IDG Books Worldwide, Inc., from International Data Group, Inc. Dummies Tips, the ...For Dummies logo, The Dummies Dispatch, and Dummies are trademarks, and Dummies Man, ...For Dummies, For Dummies, and Dummies 101 are registered trademarks of IDG Books Worldwide, Inc. All other trademarks are the property of their respective owners.

IDG BOOKS WORLDWIDE BOOK REGISTRATION

Register This Book and Win!

We want to hear from you!

Visit **http://my2cents.dummies.com** to register this book and tell us how you liked it!

- ✔ Get entered in our monthly prize giveaway.

- ✔ Give us feedback about this book — tell us what you like best, what you like least, or maybe what you'd like to ask the author and us to change!

- ✔ Let us know any other *...For Dummies*® topics that interest you.

Your feedback helps us determine what books to publish, tells us what coverage to add as we revise our books, and lets us know whether we're meeting your needs as a *...For Dummies* reader. You're our most valuable resource, and what you have to say is important to us!

Not on the Web yet? It's easy to get started with *Dummies 101*®: *The Internet For Windows*® *98* or *The Internet For Dummies*®, 5th Edition, at local retailers everywhere.

Or let us know what you think by sending us a letter at the following address:

...For Dummies Book Registration
Dummies Press
7260 Shadeland Station, Suite 100
Indianapolis, IN 46256-3917
Fax 317-596-5498

™
···FOR
DUMMIES

**BESTSELLING
BOOK SERIES**